WORDSWORTH AND COLERIDGE

The Radical Years

NICHOLAS ROE

CLARENDON PRESS · OXFORD
1988

Oxford University Press, Walton Street, Oxford OX2 6DP
Oxford New York Toronto
Delhi Bombay Calcutta Madras Karachi
Petaling Jaya Singapore Hong Kong Tokyo
Nairobi Dar es Salaam Cape Town
Melbourne Auckland
and associated companies in
Beirut Berlin Ibadan Nicosia

Oxford is a trade mark of Oxford University Press

Published in the United States
by Oxford University Press, New York

British Library Cataloguing in Publication Data
Roe, Nicholas
Wordsworth and Coleridge: the radical years
—(Oxford English monographs).
1. Coleridge, Samuel Taylor—Criticism and
interpretation. 2. Wordsworth, William, 1770–1850
—Criticism and interpretation
I. Title
821'.7'09 PR4484
ISBN 0–19–812868–1
Library of Congress Cataloging in Publication Data
Roe, Nicholas
Wordsworth and Coleridge
(Oxford English monographs)
Bibliography: p. Includes index
1. Wordsworth, William, 1770–1850—Political and
social views. 2. Coleridge, Samuel Taylor, 1772–1834—
Political and social views. 3. Radicalism in literature.
4. Radicalism—Great Britain—History. 5. France—
History—Revolution, 1789–1799—Literature and the Revolution. 6. Great
Britain—Politics and government—
1789–1820. 7. London Corresponding Society. 8. Great
Britain—Intellectual life—18th century. 9. Authors,
English—19th century—Biography. 10. Radicals—Great
Britain—Biography. I. Title. II. Series.
PR5892.R27R6 1987 821'.7'09 87-15381
ISBN 0–19–812868–1

Set by Rowland Phototypesetting Ltd.
Printed in Great Britain by
Biddles Ltd., Guildford and King's Lynn

To *the memory of*
JOHN THELWALL
Citizen, Poet, Prophet
1764–1834

'And please what's Hulks?' said I.

'That's the way with this boy!' exclaimed my sister, pointing me out with her needle and thread, and shaking her head at me. 'Answer him one question, and he'll ask you a dozen directly. Hulks are prison-ships, right 'cross th' meshes.' We always used that name for marshes in our country.

'I wonder who's put into prison-ships, and why they're put there?' said I, in a general way, and with quiet desperation.

It was too much for Mrs Joe, who immediately rose. 'I tell you what, young fellow,' said she, 'I didn't bring you up by hand to badger people's lives out. People are put in the Hulks because they murder, and because they rob, and forge, and do all sorts of bad; and they always begin by asking questions.'

(Charles Dickens, *Great Expectations*, ch. 2)

Preface

On Tuesday, 30 September 1794 the following advertisement appeared on the front page of the *Morning Chronicle*:

Those Families whose Husbands and Fathers are now in Confinement under a Charge of HIGH TREASON, and whose Trials will come on in a few Days intreat the IMMEDIATE PECUNIARY ASSISTANCE of the REAL Friends to Liberty.

The husbands and fathers charged with treason were the leaders of the London Corresponding Society and the Society for Constitutional Information. They had been arrested the previous May and held in the Tower and Newgate over the summer. Not surprisingly their dependants were in need of support after four months, hence the subscription organized by the Corresponding Society's 'Committee of Correspondence'.

The 'REAL Friends to Liberty' responded generously. On 19 November the committee announced that £314 19s. 3d. had been collected, and published a list of subscribers. Among them were the Countess Dowager of Stanhope, £20; Charles James Fox, £10; Thomas Walker of Manchester, 3 guineas; and Francis Place, breeches-maker, 5s. But one contribution in particular leaps out of the list: 'Citizen Wordsworth 1s.—0d.' This donation was received by John Smith, a bookseller who lived in Portsmouth Street, Lincoln's Inn Fields. Smith was also a leader of the 29th Division of the Corresponding Society, and a member of the committee that had organized the subscription. But who was 'Citizen Wordsworth' and was he in fact William Wordsworth?

As it turns out, no. 'Citizen Wordsworth' was Henry Wordsworth of Jewin Street, London, and a member of bookseller Smith's 29th Division. But the intriguing possibility that William Wordsworth might be found among the massed friends of liberty in the Corresponding Society was my starting-point for the more extensive study of Wordsworth's and Coleridge's radical years in this book. I have taken the years between 1789 and the poets' departure for Germany in September 1798 as my period, but have also looked back at religious dissent in Cambridge since

1770 to provide a context for Coleridge's politics, and forwards by way of incorporating *The Prelude, The Friend, Biographia Literaria*, and other later writings. The Introduction presents some of the difficulties in Wordsworth's and Coleridge's retrospective accounts of their own radicalism, and is in effect a manifesto for the historical and biographical research that is the foundation of the whole study. Such an approach has perhaps lost favour in recent years to more fashionable 'theoretical' criticisms, and I hope that my book will go some way towards balancing this tendency in a topic which has, with one or two exceptions, been somewhat neglected in recent studies of both poets.

The book is structured in a broadly chronological sequence. Chapters 1 and 2 comprise Wordsworth's visits to France in 1790 and 1792, and his intervening months in London during spring 1791. Chapter 3 is a retrospective survey of radical dissent at Cambridge in the decades prior to 1789, focusing upon William Frend and George Dyer as models for Coleridge's political career from 1794 on. Taking bearings from these different backgrounds, Chapter 4 treats both poets' opposition to war after February 1793, and argues that contemporary literature of protest liberated Wordsworth's imaginative encounters with social victims and outcasts in 'Salisbury Plain', *The Borderers*, 'The Ruined Cottage', and some of his poems in *Lyrical Ballads*. Chapter 5 reconsiders Wordsworth's and Coleridge's connections with the democratic reform movement, and to John Thelwall and William Godwin in particular. As with 'Citizen Wordsworth', I cannot claim to have found conclusive evidence that either poet was involved as a paid-up member of the Corresponding Society, but at various times in 1794 and 1795 both poets were so much in company with the Society's leaders and spokesmen that the matter of formal membership becomes a quibble. Furthermore, their near-coincidence in these circles is an important precedent for the poets' eventual meeting at Bristol in August or September 1795. Chapter 6 suggests that in 1794–5 Robespierre was a monitory but not necessarily unattractive figure for Wordsworth, Coleridge, and Thelwall, and argues that the poets' self-recognition in the Jacobin leader throws light on Wordsworth's crisis of confidence in *Political Justice* and Coleridge's ministry of 'living help' during their early friendship. My final chapter uses the Spy Nozy incident to establish the political status of the poets' residence at Nether Stowey and Alfoxden in 1797–8. Their experience of defeat is presented alongside that of other contemporaries who figure throughout the book, by way of complicating the reductive paradigm in which radical commitment is succeeded by 'withdrawal' or 'apostasy'. In all chapters I have tried to show how the radical years are integral to each poet's later creative life; to substantiate this, a short Epilogue gives a close reading of 'Fears in Solitude' and 'Tintern Abbey'.

Inevitably, there are some areas of this territory that one would have liked to treat in more detail. Thomas Carlyle's tantalizing anecdote that Wordsworth saw Gorsas guillotined at Paris in October 1793 seems to me to ring true; I may be mistaken in this, but have not been able to substantiate or rule it out. An early draft chapter on Southey has been omitted, and he deserves more thorough consideration than has been possible in this study.

My work has involved many debts of gratitude and it is a pleasure to acknowledge them here. I am grateful to the staff of the following institutions: Bath Public Reference Library; the Bibliothèque Municipale, Blois; The Bodleian Library; Bristol City Library and Bristol University Library; The British Library; Cambridge University Library; Dove Cottage Library, Grasmere; Dundee Public Reference Library; the libraries of Emmanuel College, Cambridge, and Nuffield College, Oxford; the Public Record Offices at Chancery Lane and Kew; St Andrews University Library; Tullie House Library, Carlisle; Queen's University Library, Belfast. I would like to thank the following for permission to quote from manuscripts: Lord Abinger, for the Abinger–Shelley Papers; Viscount Knebworth, for the Lovelace–Byron Papers; the Librarian of Bristol University Library for the Pinney Papers; the Trustees of Dove Cottage for Basil Montagu's 'Narrative of the birth and upbringing of his son'. My research has been materially helped by grants from the President and Fellows of Trinity College, Oxford; from Queen's University, Belfast; and from the University of St Andrews.

Like many others I have benefited from Richard and Sylvia Wordsworth's genial hospitality at the Wordsworth Summer Conference and Winter School in Grasmere. Part of Chapter 5 was delivered to the Summer Conference in 1982, and subsequently published as 'Citizen Wordsworth' in the *Wordsworth Circle*; earlier versions of Chapters 1 and 7 have also appeared in the *Wordsworth Circle*, and I am grateful to the editor, Marilyn Gaull, for permission to reproduce this material here. Chapter 6 was presented as a lecture at the Wordsworth Summer Conference in 1984, and published as an essay in *Coleridge's Imagination: Essays in Memory of Peter Laver* the following year. Passages in the present study that refer to George Dyer have been drawn from a lecture on 'Radical George' given at a meeting of the Charles Lamb Society in April 1984, later published in the *Charles Lamb Bulletin* and reproduced by kind permission of the editor, Mary Wedd.

Many friends and colleagues have offered support and advice during the ups and downs of writing this book. I would particularly like to thank Michael Alexander, Michael Allen, Tony Brinkley, Dennis Burden, John Cronin, Ashley Goodall, Julia Green, Ken Johnston, Pete Laver, Molly Lefebure, Terry McCormick, Lucy Newlyn, Neil Rhodes, Simon Taylor, Sally Woodhead, Robert Woof. Kim Scott Walwyn has seen the book through the press with patient kindness, and I have been fortunate in Mary Taylor's skilful preparation of the typescript.

I am much indebted to specific volumes in the Cornell Wordsworth Series and the Bollingen *Collected Coleridge*; Mary Thale's *Selections from the Papers of the London Corresponding Society, 1792–1799* has been an invaluable reference. Five scholars in particular have inspired my own efforts: David Erdman, Stephen Gill, Albert Goodwin, E. P. Thompson, and, especially, Jonathan Wordsworth, who has guided and encouraged for many years. Needless to say, anything wild or wayward in what follows is my responsibility.

N.H.R.

St Andrews

Contents

List of illustrations

Abbreviations

Account	William Frend, *An Account of the Proceedings in the University of Cambridge against William Frend, M.A.* (Cambridge, 1793).
A-S Dep.	Abinger-Shelley papers, in the Bodleian Library.
B L	S. T. Coleridge, *Biographia Literaria*, ed. J. Engell and W. Jackson Bate, CC vii (2 vols; Princeton, 1983).
Bod.	Bodleian Library, Oxford.
B U L	Bristol University Library.
Butler	William Wordsworth, '*The Ruined Cottage*' and '*The Pedlar*', ed. J. Butler (Cornell Wordsworth Series; Ithaca, N Y, 1979).
B V	Jonathan Wordsworth, *The Borders of Vision* (Oxford, 1982).
B W S	Jonathan Wordsworth (ed.), *Bicentenary Wordsworth Studies* (Ithaca and London, 1970).
C C	*Collected Coleridge* (Bollingen Series 75; Princeton, N J, 1969–).
C L	*The Collected Letters of Samuel Taylor Coleridge*, ed. E. L. Griggs (6 vols; Oxford, 1956–71).
C P W	*The Complete Poetical Works of Samuel Taylor Coleridge*, ed. E. H. Coleridge (2 vols; Oxford, 1912).
C U L	Cambridge University Library.
Curry	*New Letters of Robert Southey*, ed. K. Curry (2 vols; New York and London, 1965).
D C	Dove Cottage.
E T	S. T. Coleridge, *Essays on his Times*, ed. D. V. Erdman, C C iii (3 vols; Princeton, N J, 1978).
E Y	*The Letters of William and Dorothy Wordsworth*, ed. E. de Selincourt, 2nd edn, *The Early Years, 1787 –1805*, rev. C. L. Shaver (Oxford, 1967).
Friend	S. T. Coleridge, *The Friend*, ed. B. Rooke, C C iv (2 vols; Princeton, N J, 1969).
G D	William Godwin's M S Diary, in the Abinger-Shelley Deposit at the Bodleian Library.
Gill	William Wordsworth, *The Salisbury Plain Poems*, ed. S. Gill (Cornell Wordsworth Series; Ithaca, N Y, 1975).
Goodwin	A. Goodwin, *The Friends of Liberty: The English Democratic Reform Movement in the Age of the French Revolution* (London, 1979).
Gunning	Henry Gunning, *Reminiscences of the University,*

	Town and County of Cambridge, from the Year 1780 (2 vols, London, 1854).
HO	Home Office files at the Public Record Office, London.
Howe	*The Complete Works of William Hazlitt*, ed. P. P. Howe (21 vols; London, 1930–4).
L-B Dep.	Lovelace-Byron papers, in the Bodleian Library.
LD	James Losh's MS Diary, at Tullie House Library, Carlisle.
Lects. 1795	S. T. Coleridge, *Lectures 1795 on Politics and Religion*, ed. L. Patton and P. Mann, CC i (Princeton, NJ, 1971).
Lefebvre, i, ii	G. Lefebvre, *The French Revolution*, i. *From its Origins to 1793*, trans. E. M. Evanson (London and New York, 1962); ii. *From 1793 to 1799*, trans. J. S. Hall and J. Friguglietti (London and New York, 1964).
Marrs	*The Letters of Charles and Mary Anne Lamb*, ed. E. W. Marrs, Jr. (3 vols; Ithaca, NY, 1975–8).
MH	Jonathan Wordsworth, *The Music of Humanity* (London, 1969).
Moniteur	*Réimpression de l'Ancien Moniteur depuis la Réunion des États-Généraux jusqu'au Consulat (Mai 1789– Novembre 1799)* (31 vols; Paris, 1840–7).
Moorman	M. Moorman, *William Wordsworth, A Biography: The Early Years, 1770–1803* (Oxford, 1957).
MWC	E. P. Thompson, *The Making of the English Working Class* (Harmondsworth, 1968).
N&Q	*Notes & Queries.*
Osborn	William Wordsworth, *The Borderers*, ed. R. Osborn (Cornell Wordsworth Series; Ithaca, NY, 1982).
P.	William Wordsworth, *The Prelude* (1805); see note on texts.
P&U	William Frend, *Peace and Union, Recommended to the Associated Bodies of Republicans and Anti-Republicans* (St Ives, 1793).
Parl. Hist.	*Cobbett's Parliamentary History of England. From the Norman Conquest, in 1066, to the Year, 1803* (36 vols; London, 1806–20).
PJ	William Godwin, *Political Justice* (2 vols; London, 1793).
PMLA	*Publications of the Modern Language Association of America.*
Pr. W.	*The Prose Works of William Wordsworth*, ed. W. J. B. Owen and J. W. Smyser (3 vols; Oxford, 1974).

P V	MS minutes of *Les Amis de la Constitution* at Blois, Procès Verbaux des Sociétés Populaires, Bibliothèque Muncipale de Blois, France.
P W	*The Poetical Works of William Wordsworth*, ed. E. de Selincourt and H. Darbishire (5 vols; Oxford, 1940–9).
R.	Edmund Burke, *Reflections on the Revolution in France, and on the Proceedings in Certain Societies in London Relative to that Event*, ed. C. C. O'Brien (Harmondsworth, 1968).
Reed	M. L. Reed, *Wordsworth: The Chronology of the Early Years, 1770–1799* (Cambridge, Mass., 1967).
R M, i, ii	Thomas Paine, *The Rights of Man, Part One and Part Two*, ed. H. Collins (Harmondsworth, 1969).
Sequel	William Frend, *A Sequel to the Account of the Proceedings in the University of Cambridge* (London, 1795).
State Trials	*Cobbett's Complete Collection of State Trials . . . from the Earliest Period to the Present Time* (33 vols; London, 1809–28).
Thale	*Selections from the Papers of the London Corresponding Society, 1792–1799*, ed. M. Thale (Cambridge, 1983).
T L S	*Times Literary Supplement*.
Tribune	John Thelwall, *The Tribune* (3 vols; London, 1795–6).
T S	Treasury Solicitor files at the Public Record Office, London.
T W C	*The Wordsworth Circle*.
Watchman	S. T. Coleridge, *The Watchman*, ed. L. Patton, *CC* ii (Princeton, NJ, 1970).

A note on texts

All references to *The Prelude* will be to William Wordsworth, *The Prelude, 1799, 1805, 1850*, ed. J. Wordsworth, M. H. Abrams, and S. Gill (New York, 1979). Quotations will be from the 1805 text unless designated *1799* or *1850*. I have occasionally cited an additional abbreviation, *P.*, to identify quotations from the 1805 *Prelude* where this may not be evident from the context.

Unless indicated otherwise, quotations from Wordsworth's poetry will be from *The Poetical Works of William Wordsworth*, ed. E. de Selincourt and H. Darbishire (5 vols; Oxford, 1940–9), and quotations from Coleridge's poetry will be from *Poems*, ed. J. Beer (London, 1973). Poems by Wordsworth and Coleridge published in *Lyrical Ballads* will be quoted from the text in *Lyrical Ballads, 1798 and 1800*, ed. R. L. Brett and A. R. Jones (London, 1963).

Quotations from Chaucer's poetry are from *The Complete Works of Geoffrey Chaucer*, ed. F. N. Robinson (2nd edn.; Oxford, 1974); quotations from Milton are from *Paradise Lost*, ed. A. Fowler (London, 1968) and *Complete Shorter Poems*, ed. J. Carey (London, 1968); quotations from Shakespeare are from *Complete Works*, ed. P. Alexander (London and Glasgow, 1951); quotations from Spenser are from *Poetical Works*, ed. J. C. Smith and E. de Selincourt (Oxford, 1970).

Throughout this book square brackets are editorial.

Introduction

Voices from the Common Grave of Liberty

TWELVE years after the fall of the Bastille, William Godwin recollected the response to that event in Britain. 'Where was the ingenuous heart which did not beat with exultation', he enquired, 'at seeing a great and cultivated people shake off the chains of one of the most oppressive political systems in the world, the most replenished with abuses, the least mollified and relieved by any infusion of liberty? Thus far we were all of us disinterested and generous.'[1] Coleridge disagreed. In the margin of his own copy of Godwin's pamphlet *Thoughts Occasioned by the Perusal of Dr Parr's Spital Sermon*, Coleridge wrote beside this passage:

Had this been the fact, which the whole History of the French Revolution in its' first workings disproves a posteriori, it would have been *a priori* impossible that such a revolution could have taken place. No! it was the discord & contradictory ferment of old abuses & recent indulgences or connivances—the heat & light of Freedom let in on a half-cleared, rank soil, made twilight by the black fierce Reek, which this Dawn did itself draw up.—Still, however, taking the sentence dramatically, i.e. as the then notion of good men in general, it is well—and just.[2]

While conceding that Godwin's immaculate revolution was true to 'the then notion of good men in general' in 1789, Coleridge emphasized that with hindsight it was not 'the fact'. When seen 'a posteriori' it appeared flawed from the outset, an abortive and 'contradictory ferment' that had deceived a generation of liberals and radicals throughout Europe and America. However, Coleridge's early poem 'The Destruction of the Bastille' reveals that he too had shared Godwin's 'disinterested' exultation,

> I see, I see! glad Liberty succeed
> With every patriot virtue in her train!
>
> (ll. 23–4)

[1] William Godwin, *Thoughts Occasioned by the Perusal of Dr. Parr's Spital Sermon* (London, 1801), pp. 2–3, reproduced in William Godwin, *Uncollected Writings, 1785–1822* (Gainesville, Florida, 1968) [cited hereafter as Godwin, *Thoughts*, and Godwin, *Uncollected Writings*].

[2] Coleridge's manuscript marginalia appear in Godwin, *Uncollected Writings*, pp. 285–7.

—and although they appear to differ in their later ideas of revolution, Godwin's pamphlet and Coleridge's note had a common purpose. Each was concerned to justify his former support for the French Revolution in the aftermath of its failure.

Godwin's immediate motive had been to rebuff recent criticism of *Political Justice* by invoking the generous spirit with which it had originally been written: 'My book, as was announced by me in the preface, was the child of the French revolution,' he claimed.[3] William Hazlitt remembered that when *Political Justice* first appeared in February 1793 it was treated as 'the oracles of thought', its author 'talked of . . . looked up to . . . sought after' (Howe, xi. 16). Eight years later the popularity of Godwin's book had diminished, and he was at pains to explain why. 'If the temper and tone in which this publication has been treated have undergone a change,' Godwin wrote in his pamphlet, 'it has been only that I was destined to suffer a part, in the great revolution which has operated in nations, parties, political creeds, and the views and interests of ambitious men. I have fallen (if I have fallen) in one common grave with the cause and love of liberty . . .'.[4] Godwin's 'great revolution' in public opinion was conditioned by the demise of revolutionary idealism and subsequent imperial expansion of France, and by repressive hostility to political and social reform in Britain during the 1790s and throughout the Napoleonic wars. In *The Prelude* Wordsworth dates his own experience of betrayal precisely to February 1793, and the outbreak of war between France and Britain:

> Not in my single self alone I found,
> But in the minds of all ingenuous youth,
> Change and subversion from this hour.

> (x. 231–3)

That drawn-out and disenchanting process of 'change and subversion' is Wordsworth's subject in *The Prelude*, Books Ten and Eleven, where it appears as the immediate context for his emergence as poet and friend of Coleridge. For Coleridge, on the other hand, the 'hour' of final disappointment did not come until February 1798 when France attacked Switzerland and threatened to invade Britain. That moment of disillusion is recorded in two poems, 'France, an Ode' and 'Fears in Solitude'; it stands at

[3] Godwin, *Thoughts*, p. 2.   [4] Godwin, *Thoughts*, p. 2.

the threshold to Coleridge's declining creativity in the years following, and is bound up with opium dependence in the larger anguish of his family life and relation to Wordsworth and Sara Hutchinson. For Wordsworth as writer of *The Prelude* revolutionary disappointment was compensated in his power and calling as a poet; for Coleridge it issued as breakdown and creative paralysis. These differing experiences inevitably coloured the ways in which each looked back upon his earlier radical self.

'[J]uvenile errors are my theme', Wordsworth announces a little over half-way through *The Prelude*, Book Ten (x. 637). In *Newspapers Thirty-Five Years Ago* Charles Lamb similarly recalled his first 'boyish heats' of political awareness 'kindled by the French Revolution, when if we were misled, we erred in the company of some, who are accounted very good men now'.[5] But of course it only appeared that those good men had 'erred' in retrospect; there was no sense of being 'misled' at the time. Coleridge's note in Godwin's pamphlet registered this double perspective by allowing the generous welcome for revolution in 1789 but also pointing out that, 'a posteriori', another view might be possible. Elsewhere, Coleridge was less candid about his own politics during the revolutionary decade. In his letter to Sir George and Lady Beaumont of 1 October 1803, for instance, Coleridge announced that during the 1790s he had been

utterly unconnected with any party or club or society—(& this praise I must take to myself, that I disclaimed all these Societies, these Imperia in Imperio, these Ascarides in the Bowels of the State, subsisting on the weakness & diseasedness, & having for their final Object the Death of that State, whose Life had been their Birth & growth, & continued to be their sole nourishment—. All such Societies, under whatever name, I abhorred as wicked Conspiracies—and to this principle I adhered immoveably, simply because it was a principle . . . (*C L* ii. 1001)

Not so: Coleridge never adhered 'immoveably' to a principle 'simply because it was a principle'. The grotesque and laboured disgust with which Coleridge emphasizes his distance from the popular reform movement betrays his own uneasiness at vindicating a position no one would have thought to challenge in 1803; rather than confirming his independence from such

---

[5] *The Works of Charles and Mary Lamb*, ed. E. V. Lucas (7 vols; London and New York, 1903–5), ii. 225.

'wicked Conspiracies', his letter to the Beaumonts is a memorial of personal complicity. Coleridge was ill, unhappy, and sleepless when writing it; granted, but he was also misrepresenting his former self to his 'dear Friends'. He repeated his claim to have been 'utterly unconnected' with other reformists in his essay 'Enthusiasm for an Ideal World' in *The Friend*. 'I was a sharer in the general vortex,' he concedes there, 'though my little world described the path of its revolution in an orbit of its own' (*Friend*, i. 223). A little later in this essay Coleridge says that, while he rescued himself from 'the pitfalls of sedition, . . . there were thousands as young and as innocent as myself who, not like me, sheltered in the tranquil nook or inland cove of a particular fancy, were driven along with the general current!' (*Friend*, i. 224).

By representing his then beliefs as 'a particular fancy' of his 'innocent' youth, Coleridge blurred and sentimentalized that period of his life. In 1817 he used an identical strategy to defend Southey's authorship of the recently pirated *Wat Tyler*, arguing in the *Courier* for Southey's 'lofty, imaginative, and *innocent* spirit' in writing the play while still 'a very young man' (*E T* ii. 459).[6] By so doing Coleridge contrived to hide the past, but at a cost. He was deliberately betraying ideals and opinions once fundamental to his own identity and career, the disappointment of which had inevitably proved damaging and disabling. If Coleridge had indeed been 'sheltered' from the mainstream of British radicalism in the 1790s, there was no need for his later elaborate justifications of that position (why all the pother, if he had *not* been involved?). But this had never been the case. It was Coleridge's self-implication in that cause and its ultimate defeat which provided the motive for his subsequent evasiveness and falsification.

Coleridge's letter to George Dyer in February 1795 indicates that he was very much 'connected with a party' at Bristol, and by no means sheltered from the 'general current' of radical politics. 'The Democrats are . . . sturdy in the support of me,' he says, 'but their number is comparatively small,' and then goes on to tell Dyer about the 'scarcely restrained' threats of attack at his lectures (*C L* i. 152). If one allows a little exaggeration for Dyer's benefit, it is nevertheless clear that Coleridge was a popular figure among the Bristol opposition; equally, his political concerns were

---

[6] 'Mr. Southey', *Courier* (18 Mar. 1817).

not confined to a merely local 'orbit' as he later pretended in *The Friend*. In December 1795 one of his 'chief objects' announced in the Prospectus to the *Watchman* was explicitly 'to co-operate . . . with the PATRIOTIC SOCIETIES' in opposing Pitt's and Grenville's Two Acts, and in pressing for 'a Right of Suffrage general and frequent' (*Watchman*, p. 5). At this moment 'PATRIOTIC SOCIETIES' meant the London Corresponding Society and its provincial associates in the campaign for parliamentary reform—precisely those societies he later told the Beaumonts he had 'abhorred as wicked Conspiracies'—and, to underline the extent of his co-operation and commitment, he set out on 9 January 1796 on an extensive tour through the Midlands canvassing subscriptions for his journal.

Fourteen years after Coleridge's 1803 letter to the Beaumonts, reformists were once again active following the end of the Napoleonic wars. Coleridge's concern to distance himself from this revival was one encouragement to the misconstrutions in Chapter ten of *Biographia Literaria* where, for example, he claimed that his opinions had been 'opposite . . . to those of jacobinism or even of democracy' (*BL* i. 184). John Thelwall's memory did not coincide with this version of the past. In the margin of his own copy of *Biographia*, Thelwall replied:

that Mr C. was indeed far from Democracy, because he was far beyond it, I well remember—for he was a downright zealous leveller & indeed in one of the worst senses of the word he was a Jacobin, a man of blood—Does he forget the letters he wrote to me (& which I believe I yet have) acknowledging the justice of my castigation of him for the violence, and sanguinary tendency of some of his doctrines . . .[7]

The point at issue here is not whether Coleridge's opinions had been democratic, levelling, 'Jacobin', or 'sanguinary', although I shall return to these matters later on. Thelwall's note is most salutary for identifying the reality of Coleridge's letters, lectures, and poems during the radical years that his later accounts in *Biographia* and elsewhere contrive to suppress or forget.

Wordsworth did not deliberately misrepresent his former revolutionary sympathies to the same extent. Although he had visited France at least twice between 1790 and 1793, his personal

---

[7] B. Pollin and R. Burke, 'John Thelwall's Marginalia in a Copy of Coleridge's *Biographia Literaria*', *Bulletin of the New York Public Library*, lxxiv (1970), 81.

active commitment to a political life was never so extensive or as consistent as Coleridge's, nor was it integrated with religious belief as with Coleridge's unitarianism. Moreover, Wordsworth's successive experiences of hope and disappointment between 1792 and 1796 had a seminal relation to his imaginative life, in his poetry of achieved belief and lasting vulnerability in 'Tintern Abbey' and, later on, in *The Prelude*. Wordsworth did not share his friend's sense of personal failing as a motive for disguising his revolutionary self; rather the reverse, for in Books Six, Nine, and Ten of *The Prelude* he explores that self by way of assuming it within the history of his own mind. In that Wordsworth conceived *The Prelude* as preparatory to *The Recluse*, the philosophic poem ordained by Coleridge as a propitiation for revolutionary failure (*C L* i. 527), his treatment of his own radical years would prove a worthless foundation for the greater work if not ideally honest. 'Thus, O friend', he says to Coleridge towards the end of Book Ten,

> Through times of honour, and through times of shame,
> Have I descended, tracing faithfully
> The workings of a youthful mind, beneath
> The breath of great events—its hopes no less
> Than universal, and its boundless love—
> A story destined for thy ear . . .
>
> > > (x. 940–6)

When Wordsworth writes about his Godwinian self with a genial irony in Book Ten, therefore, one suspects that this oblique tone may have a specific point beyond acknowledging the drawbacks of *Political Justice* viewed with eleven years' hindsight in 1804. Looking back to the time when he had been much influenced by Godwin's ideas, he says that

> This was the time when, all things tending fast
> To depravation, the philosophy
> That promised to abstract the hopes of man
> Out of his feelings, to be fixed thenceforth
> For ever in a purer element,
> Found ready welcome. Tempting region that
> For zeal to enter and refresh herself,
> Where passions had the privilege to work,
> And never hear the sound of their own names—. . .
>
> > > (x. 805–13)

The privileged working of 'passions' among devotees of Godwin's philosophy is a sly jibe at *Political Justice*, which had denied emotion for the 'purer element' of reason. The more subversive thrust of Wordsworth's irony is its covert eroticism, in the 'tempting region' of abstract thought with which Godwin had seduced his disciples much as Acrasia lured her lovers to the 'horrible enchantment' of her 'Bowre of Blis' in *The Faerie Queene*. The attractions of Godwin's rationalism had proved similarly deceptive and deadly; this had long been apparent to Wordsworth when he wrote these lines in 1804, and the passage confirms Godwin's own sense of the changed 'temper and tone' in public estimation of *Political Justice*.

Wordsworth's account of Godwin in Book Ten is of course infected by his memory of the intellectual confusion to which *Political Justice* had led him, and which coincided with his first meetings with Coleridge between 1795 and 1797. Coleridge himself had been alive to the shortcomings of Godwin's philosophy as 'turned aside | From Nature' (*P*. x. 885–6) since 1794, and he would have appreciated Wordsworth's portrait of his Godwinian self as a memorial to their earliest acquaintance at Bristol and Racedown. But in 1794 *Political Justice* had certainly not appeared to Wordsworth as it is recalled in Book Ten; the passage actually obscures the quality of Wordsworth's 'ready welcome' for Godwin's thought at that time, and the reality of Wordsworth's Godwinian self disappears. Nothing is said in *The Prelude* about Wordsworth's personal friendship with Godwin as it is, notably, with reference to William Taylor, Michel Beaupuy, Coleridge, and Dorothy. Godwin himself is not mentioned by name, unlike the revolutionaries Carra, Gorsas, Louvet, and Robespierre, and the political implications of Wordsworth's presence among Godwin's circle in London are left in silence. In retrospect perhaps these appeared ephemeral factors in his own development, an intellectual dead end. Contemporary evidence in Wordsworth's writing between 1794 and 1796 suggests otherwise; that Godwin was actually the immediate ancestor of Coleridge as Wordsworth's philosophic mentor and guide, and that this period of his life was a crucial precedent to his emergence as a poet. Its oblique treatment in *The Prelude*, Book Ten, can only be rectified by returning to those former times and reconstructing, so far as is possible, what actually happened. E. P.

Thompson once said that there has been 'insufficiently close attention to [Wordsworth's and Coleridge's] actual lived historical experience' in the early 1790s.[8] Given the various strategies with which both poets recollect this period in later writings, his comment deserves to be taken seriously, although recent critics, with one or two exceptions, have failed to take the hint. It is only by plotting Wordsworth's and Coleridge's immediate responses to events, and their contemporary relation to other good men and women, that their true radical selves emerge most clearly.

Delineating our present oppositionists

> To delineate with a free hand the different Classes of our present Oppositionists to 'Things as they are,'—may be a delicate, but it is a necessary Task . . .
>
> *(Lects. 1795*, pp. 7–8)

In his *Moral and Political Lecture* Coleridge differentiates four categories among the 'present Oppositionists'. The first he describes as 'indolent' and inconsistent, depending 'with weathercock uncertainty on the winds of Rumor, that blow from France' (*Lects. 1795*, p. 8). His 'second class' are 'wild' and potentially violent, while the 'third class among the friends of Freedom' appear 'steadily' but selfishly interested, 'with narrow and self-centering views' (*Lects. 1795*, pp. 9, 11). It was with the fourth category of oppositionists, 'that small but glorious band, whom we may truly distinguish by the name of thinking and disinterested Patriots', that Coleridge identified himself, along with four others: Joseph Gerrald, Maurice Margarot, Thomas Muir, and Thomas Fysshe Palmer (*Lects. 1795*, pp. 12, 14).

All of these men welcomed the French Revolution in 1789, and agreed on the need for parliamentary reform and liberty of conscience in Britain. Nevertheless, Coleridge's 'small but glorious band' also represented three subsections of contemporary opposition. Gerrald and Margarot were leaders of the popular reform movement in the London Corresponding Society, and both were delegates to the first British Convention at Edinburgh where they were arrested on 5 December 1793 (Goodwin, p.

---

[8] E. P. Thompson, 'Disenchantment or Default? A Lay Sermon' in C. C. O'Brien and W. D. Vanech (eds), *Power and Consciousness* (London and New York, 1969), p. 150 [cited hereafter as 'Disenchantment or Default?'].

303). Thomas Muir was a lawyer and founder of the relatively moderate whig Friends of the People in Edinburgh. Thomas Fysshe Palmer was a Cambridge graduate and unitarian minister at Dundee where he also belonged to the Friends of the People, thereby representing the political radicalism of religious dissent. All four of Coleridge's patriots were tried for sedition between August 1793 and March 1794. They were found guilty and transported to Botany Bay; Margarot was the only one of the four who lived to return to Britain.

In Southey's poem 'To the Exiled Patriots', Gerrald, Margarot, Muir, and Palmer are hailed as

> Martyrs of Freedom—ye who firmly good
> Stept forth the champions in her glorious cause,
> Ye who against Corruption nobly stood
> For Justice, Liberty, and equal Laws.
>
> (*Lects. 1795*, p. 16)

—and for Coleridge too they were men of vision, perseverance, and patience, qualities that he later associated with his 'elect' in 'Religious Musings'. Coleridge's own position in 1795 was close to Thomas Fysshe Palmer in that both were Cambridge men, unitarians, reformists. But, while he shared Palmer's academic and religious background, Coleridge's political lecturing was more akin to John Thelwall's activities in London as a leader of the London Corresponding Society, and their opinions frequently and strikingly coincided between 1794 and 1797. Differentiating opposition in the 1790s remains a 'delicate task'. Superficially distinct groupings of radicals and reformists tended to overlap. The Friends of the People, the Society for Constitutional Information, and the London Corresponding Society all shared common interests and aims, and members concerted their efforts for reform in petitions, subscriptions, dinners, meetings, and so on. Godwin's circle of friends, to which Wordsworth belonged in 1795, also included the leaders of the London Corresponding Society and others actively involved in metropolitan opposition. Among them can be found John Thelwall, political lecturer; John Binns, plumber's labourer; William Frend, unitarian; Felix Vaughan and James Losh, radical barristers; Thomas Holcroft, atheist member of the Constitutional Society, acquitted of treason in December 1794. Not only does this suggest that

Wordsworth was moving close to—and very probably within
—the popular reform movement while in London during 1795, it
should give pause to those who still cherish the image of Godwin
holding himself discretely aloof from active political affairs.[9]

It is essential to unravel the complexities of Wordsworth's and
Coleridge's radical years, not simply to identify where they
agreed or disagreed, but because in a longer perspective those
similarities and differences were to form the basis of their creative
interaction in later years. The problem can be focused in their
crucial early meetings at Bristol and Racedown in 1795 and 1797.
The poets' first acquaintance at Bristol in August and September
1795 was apparently encouraged by sympathetic political
opinions, subsequently reflected in Coleridge's admiration of
'Salisbury Plain' and Wordsworth's reciprocal esteem for
'Religious Musings' (*C L* i. 215–16).[10] Each had opposed the war
since 1793, and they would have agreed on the urgent need for
reform. Looking back to the period of their first meetings in *The
Prelude*, though, Wordsworth reminds Coleridge of a significant
difference between them: 'Ah, then it was', he says,

> That thou, most precious friend, about this time
> First known to me, didst lend a living help
> To regulate my soul.

> (x. 904–7)

Wordsworth's chronology is vague—'about this time'—because
his concern here was to emphasize his need for the intellectual and
philosophic guidance Coleridge was able to offer him over a
period of years. *The Prelude* does not recall the coincidence of
two like minds, but the dynamic potential released through
disparity. While their political opinions were superficially identical and with their shared literary ambitions would have warmed
each to each, it was the philosophic divergences within otherwise
compatible politics that proved decisive in their emergent creative
relationship. In *The Prelude*, Book Ten, Coleridge and Dorothy
are presented as redeeming figures who sustained Wordsworth in
the moral 'despair' to which Godwinian rationalism had brought
him. When Wordsworth remembered that time, he did so in the
knowledge that Coleridge's power to 'lend a living help' was

---

[9] See Chapter 5 below for a full discussion of this.
[10] In R. Woof, 'Wordsworth and Coleridge: Some Early Matters', *B W S*, 82–3.

related to his earlier rejection of *Political Justice* at a time when Wordsworth himself had been a worshipper at 'the oracles of thought'.

Coleridge's earliest recorded reference to Godwin occurs in his letter to Southey of 11 September 1794: 'Godwin *thinks* himself *inclined* to *Atheism*—acknowledges there are arguments *for* deity, he cannot answer—but not so many, as *against* his Existence—He is writing a book about it. I set him at Defiance—tho' if he convinces me, I will acknowledge it in a letter in the newspapers—' (*CL* i. 102). In mid-1794 Wordsworth did not share Coleridge's desire to set Godwin 'at Defiance'. Three months before Coleridge's letter to Southey, Wordsworth had told William Mathews that 'every enlightened friend of mankind' had a duty to 'diffuse by every method a knowledge of those rules of political justice', and elaborated plans for their journal the *Philanthropist* in terms that demonstrate his familiarity with Godwin's book (*EY*, p. 124). Just over a year before they met, therefore, Wordsworth was drawing encouragement from *Political Justice* while Coleridge was in conflict with its author. The major issue on which Wordsworth and Coleridge would have differed was the question of Godwin's atheism. For Wordsworth it was not an obstacle; as Britain appeared to be following France towards a violent repression in 1793–4, *Political Justice* offered a philosophic justification for progress that eliminated recourse to revolutionary action. But for Coleridge Godwin's system threatened a moral and spiritual breakdown, in that it neglected the reconciling love of God which was vital to Coleridge's idea of human society. While Wordsworth and Coleridge would have agreed on any number of day-to-day issues in contemporary opposition, Coleridge's radicalism was inseparable from religious principles Wordsworth did not hold. This set their different bearings towards Godwin, and is perhaps well enough known. But the wider implications of their respective attitudes to Godwin have been misunderstood.

In the Introduction to their excellent edition of Coleridge's *Lectures 1795 on Politics and Religion*, Lewis Patton and Peter Mann allege that Coleridge's defiance of Godwin 'affected his attitude to the whole radical movement', and that it is 'the key to much of his social and religious thinking in 1795' (*Lects. 1795*, lxvii). They elaborate this argument in some detail:

Coleridge's complex and critical feelings about Godwin, Paine, Holcroft, Thelwall, and other radical figures, the majority of whom were 'infidels' of some sort, made it additionally difficult for him to sustain a strong and consistent attitude during the 1790's, when events in France, combined with repression and reaction at home, made political agitation difficult, dangerous, and dispiriting. In addition, his distrust of the political methods of the Corresponding Societies . . . necessarily isolated him to some extent from the most important active forces for reform . . . (*Lects. 1795*, pp. lxxvii–lxxviii)

The precise extent of Coleridge's 'necessary isolation' is not defined, nor are his 'complex and critical feelings' about other leading political and intellectual radicals explained. Nevertheless, Patton and Mann acknowledge that their account is substantially what Coleridge wished the Beaumonts to believe in 1803, when he told them he had been 'insulated' from other reformists. It is unfortunate that the editors' final words on Coleridge's position in 1795 reiterate his later version of this year without question: 'By reason of his Christian, moral, and philosophical principles, which he attempted to clarify and justify in his lectures, Coleridge found himself in a state of 'insulation' (to use his own expressive word) from the democratic movement and its ideas' (*Lects. 1795*, p. lxxix). This would have delighted the author of *The Friend*, but it seriously misrepresents Coleridge as an active political figure in Cambridge, London, Bristol, and the Midlands between 1792 and 1796. Yes, his religion did mean that his attitude to Godwin, Holcroft, and other radical leaders was complex and sometimes critical, but the corollary is not that he should have been 'necessarily isolated'. To differ with Godwin was not to reject the ideas and aspirations of other friends of liberty, as the Prospectus to the *Watchman* demonstrates. Nor is it the only 'key' to Coleridge's social and religious thinking, his relation to other radicals and to Wordsworth in particular. This must be sought in the 'Christian, moral, and philosophical principles' that influenced his response to Godwin in the first place and which, contrary to Patton's and Mann's argument, enabled Coleridge to maintain a remarkable stability in opposition through years when Wordsworth experienced

> sorrow, disappointment, vexing thoughts,
> Confusion of the judgement, zeal decayed—
> And lastly, utter loss of hope itself
> And things to hope for.
> (*P.* xi. 4–7)

Wordsworth's radicalism was the product of his own experiences in France and was responsive to the changing course of the
Revolution thereafter. As peaceful progress was succeeded by
terrorism and war in 1793, he turned to *Political Justice* to sustain
his 'solicitude for man', eventually to discover that Godwin's
philosophy was inadequate to the practicalities of social change,
and to his own experience of human nature. With that realization, Coleridge's critique of Godwin became relevant and access-
ible to Wordsworth as the 'regulating' and inspiring influence
recollected in *The Prelude*, Book Ten. Coleridge was not forced to
shift his political and philosophic allegiances to the same extent
and there were, I think, two principal reasons for this. The first
was Coleridge's consistent effort to reconcile 'all the affairs of
man as a process' within God's providence; the second reason
was that the religious principles on which he based his idea of
political progress belonged in a tradition of radical dissent that
was encouraged by the French Revolution, but not inextricably dependent upon its course from day to day. As late as January 1798,
when other friends of liberty had been exiled, emigrated, gone
underground, or withdrawn from politics, Coleridge was still
preaching against war and the political and religious establishment
to the unitarian congregation at Shrewsbury (Howe, xvii. 108).

In this perspective Coleridge was not 'isolated' or 'insulated' at
all. He relished the thought of himself as successor to such
eminent dissenters as Richard Price, Joseph Priestley, Thomas
Fysshe Palmer, and, most importantly, William Frend. Each of
these men had welcomed the French Revolution in 1789 as the
advent of political and religious liberty elsewhere in Europe; all of
them had delivered political sermons and lectures, and published
controversial pamphlets too. Not one of them was 'isolated' from
the general current of radical affairs by his faith; on the contrary,
their dissent urged them to the forefront of controversy in calling
for the removal of Test Acts and an extension of the suffrage.
Price's exultant welcome for revolution—'Tremble all ye op-
pressors of the world! Take warning all ye supporters of slavish
governments, and slavish hierarchies!'—alarmed Burke into
composing his *Reflections* as a counter to 'this spiritual doctor
of politics' (*R.*, p. 97).[11] Priestley's unitarianism offered no

---

[11] Richard Price, *A Discourse on the Love of Our Country* (2nd edn; London,
1789), p. 50 [cited hereafter as Price, *Discourse*].

'insulation' from the church-and-king mob at Birmingham in 1791; his radical dissent was precisely the reason for the attack on his home and laboratory. Two years later William Frend's 'Christian, moral, and philosophical principles' afforded no defence before the university court at Cambridge in May 1793, nor did Fysshe Palmer's dissent serve to mitigate his seven years' exile at Botany Bay in September of that year. When Joseph Gerrald protested to Braxfield that Christ himself had been a reformist, the judge chuckled in reply, 'Muckle he made o' that; *he* was hanget' (*M W C*, pp. 139–40). There is no reason to suppose that Coleridge's religious or philosophic thinking made him any less exposed than Priestley, Frend, and Fysshe Palmer, or that his opposition was in any way separate from the wider democratic reform movement as he later tried to claim. The anonymous *T L S* reviewer (E. P. Thompson?) of Patton's and Mann's volume puts the matter succinctly: 'the curve of Coleridge's commitment, in 1795–6, took him very close indeed to the popular societies—or towards their more intellectual component . . . and such a trajectory, if it had not been arrested by the retirement at Stowey, would almost certainly have led him to prison.'[12]

On Sunday, 21 December 1794 Coleridge met Godwin for the first time at Thomas Holcroft's house. Godwin noted in his diary 'talk of self love & God', which suggests that Coleridge fulfilled his promise to challenge Godwin's atheism. A little over two months later, on 27 February 1795, Wordsworth also met Godwin over tea at William Frend's house—but as disciple rather than critic and in company with some of the most prominent radicals in London. By this time Coleridge had already written and delivered three political lectures at Bristol. His meeting with Godwin and his wish to counter Godwin's intellectual influence among other reformists served to accelerate his emergence as an active political figure, drawing him into contemporary controversy rather than pushing him off into an orbit of his own. The near coincidence of Wordsworth's and Coleridge's first meetings with Godwin reveal both of them in much the same company, at the epicentre of British radical life. Each had found his way to the author of *Political Justice* by a different path, but both had started in the same place: Cambridge University.

[12] See 'Bliss was it in that Dawn: The Matter of Coleridge's Revolutionary Youth', *T L S* (6 Aug. 1971), 929–32.

1

'Europe was Rejoiced'

Responses to Revolution, 1789–1791

Bastille and *Fédération*

In 1789 Cambridge University welcomed the French Revolution. Henry Gunning remembered that 'a great number of members of the Senate [were] friendly to the French Revolution; and soon after the destruction of the Bastile there was a proposal for a dinner to celebrate that event . . .' (Gunning, i. 290–1). There were dinners in London too. On 4 November 1789 the London Revolution Society met to commemorate the Glorious Revolution of 1688. After hearing Richard Price hail the 'eventful period' of the French Revolution at the Old Jewry, the Society retired to dine at the London Tavern. Afterwards, they unanimously approved Price's motion that an address be sent to the National Assembly congratulating the French 'on the Revolution in that country, and on the prospect it gives to the two first kingdoms in the world, of a common participation in the blessings of civil and religious liberty'.[1] William Godwin joined the company for dinner, and noted who else was present: 'Nov.5.W. Dine with the Revolutionists: see Price, Kippis, Rees, Towers, Lindsey, Disney, Belcham, Forsaith, Morgans, Listers, S. Rogers & B. Wits. Present, earl Stanhope, Beaufoy, H. Tooke & count Zenobio. see B. Hollis, Jennings, Lofft & Robinson' (GD ii).[2]

The majority of these men were unitarian dissenters, and although they met to celebrate the Glorious Revolution they also looked forward to further changes in Britain. The 'prospect' they anticipated was the removal of the exclusive Test Acts, and a 'common participation' in the civil and religious liberties enjoyed by the French after the Revolution. Back in Cambridge William

---

[1] Price, *Discourse*, Appendix, p. 13.

[2] Godwin's diary suggests that the dinner took place on the day after Price's sermon, but is probably mistaken. In 1790 he once again attended the Revolution Society's anniversary dinner, noting this in his diary for 5 Nov. but then deleting and correcting to 4 Nov. Goodwin, p. 106, has both sermon and dinner on 4 Nov. 1789.

Frend, the unitarian fellow at Jesus College, was also 'rejoicing' at
events in France and for the same reasons. Four years later he
looked back to this moment, 'when the whole nation was of one
mind, and this university thought it a duty to impress the sentiment on our young men, by giving them as a proper subject for
their talents, the taking of the bastile' (*Account*, p. 92). On 4
November 1790 one of those young men, John Tweddell, responded to the mood of nation and university in a prize-winning
speech delivered at Trinity College chapel. 'The mention of the
French is at this time peculiarly connected with the subject of
national revolutions,' Tweddell declared, then went on to enquire
'who . . . that should view this race of recent freemen achieving
such deeds of glory, would not even wander, were it necessary,
from his immediate way, and stay a while to refresh his spirit with
such a banquet, ere arrived at the conclusion of his journey?
Liberty has begun her progress, and hope tells us, that she has
only begun.'[3]

Another young man, who may have been among Tweddell's
audience, had recently made just such a detour from his immediate journey. A few days before Tweddell's speech Wordsworth
had returned to Cambridge from his walking tour with Robert
Jones to the Alps. En route, they had spent 'near a month' in
France, and had joined delegates from the *Fête de la Fédération* at
Paris in celebrating the first anniversary of the Revolution. 'All
hearts were open', Wordsworth recalled in *The Prelude*, Book
Six,

> every tongue was loud
> With amity and glee. We bore a name
> Honoured in France, the name of Englishmen,
> And hospitably did they give us hail
> As their forerunners in a glorious course . . .

> (vi. 408–12)

Wordsworth was most likely acquainted with Tweddell at
Cambridge, and in November 1790 they doubtless joined in
hoping that the Revolution would be achieved peacefully and

---

[3] John Tweddell, 'A Speech on the Character and Memory of King William the
Third', *The Remains of John Tweddell*, ed. Robert Tweddell (London, 1815), 109
[cited hereafter as Tweddell, *Remains*].

constitutionally, like its 'glorious forerunner' of 1688. Three days before Tweddell's speech, though, Burke had published his *Reflections on the Revolution in France* as a reply to Price's 'very extraordinary miscellaneous sermon' of November 1789. As is well known, Burke condemned the Revolution Society's address to the National Assembly as a 'manifest design of connecting the affairs of France with those of England' (*R.*, p. 91). For Burke there could be no comparison between the Glorious Revolution, which was a matter of constitutional succession embodied in the Declaration of Right, and the Revolution in France which was 'systematically subversive': 'Laws overturned; tribunals subverted; industry without vigour; commerce expiring; the revenue unpaid, yet the people impoverished; a church pillaged, and a state not relieved; civil and military anarchy made the constitution of the kingdom . . .' (*R.*, p. 126). In Burke's opinion the consequence of such breakdown was inevitable: 'There must be blood', he claimed, 'because the evil is radical and intrinsic' (*R.*, p. 339). In fact, nothing that had so far happened in France gave grounds for his prophecy that the Revolution would be overtaken by violence. The *Reflections* was, nevertheless, a decisive influence in dividing British opinion on the Revolution. By ridiculing Price and the Revolution Society, Burke polarized attitudes to parliamentary reform and, inevitably, to religious dissent as well. The nation was no longer of 'one mind' concerning France after 1790, and this division was subsequently confirmed by two developments in France and Britain. In 1792 events in France apparently started to deteriorate with the September Massacres and the declaration of the republic. At the same time the wide circulation of Paine's reply to Burke, *The Rights of Man*, caused serious concern to the British government. This gave way to alarm when Paine's ideas were adopted and promoted by the London Corresponding Society as part of its campaign for parliamentary reform.

The mood of Cambridge after 1790 reflected growing anti-French opinion elsewhere in the country. This change provides a significant demarcation between the period leading up to Wordsworth's departure from St John's in January 1791, and Coleridge's arrival at Jesus on 16 October of that year. Henry Gunning was exaggerating a little when he recollected that 'the bloody and ferocious proceedings of the National Convention had so disgusted those who originally rejoiced at the French Revolution, that there was but one feeling in the University, of disgust and abhorrence, at the conduct of those who at that time tyrannized over France' (Gunning, i. 291), but it is clear that the university became less indulgent to those who retained their former sympathy for the Revolution. Wordsworth's Cambridge had joined with liberals and dissenters throughout the country in welcoming the Revolution, whereas Coleridge's Cambridge was divided by the argument as to what the Revolution had achieved, and whether it represented an ideal of social and political change. Coleridge joined in the debate, and many years later his undergraduate friend C. V. le Grice remembered how during 1792–3 'Pamphlets swarmed from the press', and that 'Coleridge had read them all; and in the evening, with our negus, we had them *viva voce* gloriously'.[4] But the excitement of debate swiftly hardened into outright confrontation. Paine was judged guilty of sedition—albeit in his absence—on 18 December 1792, days after Wordsworth returned from his second visit to France. Five months later William Frend was tried before the Vice-Chancellor's court at Cambridge following the publication of his pamphlet *Peace and Union* in February 1793. Gunning remembered that, despite his unitarianism, 'the great object in prosecuting Frend was of a political rather than of a religious character' (Gunning, i. 303). In his speech to the court Frend vindicated his support for the Revolution in 1789, and mentioned his uneasy feelings about the more recent violence at Paris. 'I did rejoice at the success of the french revolution', he said, 'and is there an englishman, who did not exult on this occasion? . . . but does it follow, that I was pleased with the scenes which succeeded, that I now look with joy and not with horror on the dreadful outrages to which that country has been exposed? The massacres and bloodshed, disgracing so noble a cause, have pained every lover of freedom . . .' (*Account*, p. 92).

But Frend's reasonable defence was to no avail, and the court banished him from Cambridge. He moved to London during September 1793, where he became a leading member of the Corresponding Society in 1794–5, and was well known among London dissenters and the intellectual friends of William Godwin

---

[4] 'College Reminiscences of Mr. Coleridge', *Gentleman's Magazine*, NS ii (Dec. 1834), 606.

and Thomas Holcroft. Although he had been forced to leave Cambridge, Frend's migration to dissenting and radical circles in London was a route already taken by a number of Cambridge men during the latter decades of the eighteenth century. Among them were John Jebb and Theophilus Lindsey, who founded the Essex Street unitarian chapel in 1774, and Gilbert Wakefield who left Jesus in 1779 for a post in Warrington Academy where Priestley had formerly taught. Wakefield later became a tutor at Hackney dissenting college, for which Frend was also invited to teach mathematics. Frend's friend George Dyer of Emmanuel was an important dissenting figure at Cambridge until 1792, after which he too was involved in London politics. He first met Coleridge in August 1794, introduced him to Wakefield, and became Coleridge's most important political contact in London during 1795.

Coleridge's career after leaving Jesus College in June 1794 largely conforms to this pattern in which Cambridge University, religious dissent, and radical politics are linked together. Perhaps more than any other person, William Frend represented an immediate model for Coleridge's emergent political identity while at Jesus. He stood out as an individual persecuted for his opinions, providing a figure with whom Coleridge and other sympathetic undergraduates could identify. While resident at Cambridge he gave Coleridge access to the past in the tradition of dissent and reform in university and town prior to 1789, and also to the contemporary radicalism of dissent that had gained momentum with the French Revolution. After 1793 he represented a link from Jesus College to the metropolitan radical groups in which Cambridge graduates such as George Dyer, Felix Vaughan, James Losh, John Tweddell, and Wordsworth were also moving during 1794 and 1795. Unlike Coleridge, however, Wordsworth's political bearings had not been determined by his years at Cambridge to quite the same extent.

At the beginning of *The Prelude*, Book Six, Wordsworth recalls his return to Cambridge in October 1788, but adds that he 'need not linger o'er the ensuing time', and that the following two winters 'may be passed | Without a separate notice' (vi. 19, 25–6). During this period his idea of the French Revolution seems to have taken no distinct political or emotional form. He presumably joined contemporaries such as Tweddell, Losh, and William

Mathews in welcoming the events of 1789, though perhaps
without enquiring more precisely into their political, social, and
human significance. In *The Prelude* Wordsworth says he had
'looked upon' events in France

> As from a distance—heard, and saw, and felt,
> Was touched but with no intimate concern
>
> (vi. 695–6)

—but if he was 'distanced' he was not wholly uninformed. In
1790 he witnessed the first anniversary of the Revolution for
himself. Immediately after his return to Cambridge Burke's
Reflections was published, and the first replies subsequently
appeared on the bookstalls in spring 1791 whilst Wordsworth
was living in London and well placed to follow the developing
debate about the Revolution and reform in Britain. His tour in
France and residence in London emerge as two formative
moments when Wordsworth was 'touched' by contemporary
politics, while not yet drawn into personal commitment to the
Revolution as a cause. Both moments fostered Wordsworth's
expectations on his second visit to France in December 1791,
from which he would return as a republican, and influenced his
relation to the British democratic reform movement in succeeding
years. As such, each deserves consideration in some detail.

On the evening of 13 July 1790 Wordsworth and Robert
Jones stepped ashore at Calais. It was a moment Wordsworth
remembered for the rest of his life:

> a time when Europe was rejoiced,
> France standing on the top of golden hours,
> And human nature seeming born again.
> Bound . . . to the Alps, it was our lot
> To land at Calais on the very eve
> Of that great federal day; and there we saw,
> In a mean city and among a few,
> How bright a face is worn when joy of one
> Is joy of tens of millions.
>
> (vi. 352–60)

The 'great federal day' to which he awoke the next morning was a
nationwide celebration in which the whole of France seemed to
join in rejoicing at the achievements of the previous year. As
Wordsworth and Jones left Calais on 14 July to walk through

villages decorated with 'triumphal arcs | And window-garlands', Helen Maria Williams joined the citizens of Paris at the massive *Fête* in the Champs de Mars. 'It was the triumph of human kind', she wrote in her *Letters from France*,

it was man asserting the noblest privileges of his nature; and it required but the common feelings of humanity to become in that moment a citizen of the world. For myself, I acknowledge that my heart caught with enthusiasm the general sympathy; my eyes were filled with tears; and I shall never forget the sensations of that day, 'while memory holds her seat in my bosom'.[5]

Not everyone was united in 'general sympathy' for the Revolution, and the *Fédération* did not in fact correspond to the political reality of 1790. Nevertheless, the celebrations at Paris and elsewhere provided a powerful symbol of national unity and revolutionary idealism which Wordsworth was to recollect fourteen years later as a time when 'human nature [seemed] born again'. His memory coincides with Helen Williams's idea of the Revolution as the common cause of humanity; 'the sensations of that day' were as unforgettable for Wordsworth as they were for her, and provide the key to his first encounter with the Revolution as a human event rather than a political abstraction. 'I must remind you', he wrote to Dorothy in September, 'that we crossed [France] at the time when the whole nation was mad with joy, in consequence of the revolution. It was a most interesting period to be in France, and we had many delightful scenes where the interest of the picture was owing solely to this cause' (*E Y*, p. 36).

This sounds as if he responded to the 'delightful scenes' merely as a tourist with an eye for the picturesque. But his experience in France was more ambiguous and enduring than his letter to Dorothy suggests. In some respects it coincided with that of Felix Vaughan, who had recently graduated at Jesus, Cambridge, and who also witnessed the *Fédération* at Paris. In a letter to William Frend, 19 July 1790, he described the *Fête* and discussed the attitude of the French to the English. '[I]n every principal town throughout France', he told Frend,

this same ceremony of federation was performed at the same hour & I hope with the same success.—You may judge by these circumstances of

---

[5] Helen Maria Williams, *Letters Written in France, in the Summer 1790* (London, 1790), 14.

the feelings & sentiments prevailing here, (which I think much finer than all the spectacles in the world) & how little credit is to be given to those vile libels in the London newspapers, & especially in the morning Herald on the subject of French politics. I assure you they do an Englishman no service here, for otherwise the French speak of us with great respect, & wish much for an alliance with England & peace with all the world. —Every man seems to wear a face of content, & the king seems to be the idol of his people. I think they are an example for mankind in general & I trust such a one as will not remain without imitation.[6]

Vaughan's letter confirms Wordsworth's memory of joyful faces, and the hamlets and towns 'Gaudy with reliques of that festival' through which he walked after leaving Calais. It also substantiates Wordsworth's account of his meeting with the *fédérés* —provincial delegates returning from the *Fête* at Paris—with whom he and Jones sailed south down the Rhone:

> We bore a name
> Honoured in France, the name of Englishmen,
> And hospitably did they give us hail
> As their forerunners in a glorious course . . .
>
> (P. vi. 409–12)

Wordsworth apparently believed with the delegates that the Glorious Revolution was a genuine forerunner of the French Revolution, but Felix Vaughan was less complacent. While he welcomed French hopes for 'an alliance with England & peace with all the world', Vaughan also anticipated that French liberties would 'not remain without imitation' in Britain. He was, of course, thinking of Frend's exclusion from political rights as a unitarian dissenter. Like Richard Price in November 1789, Vaughan joined Frend in looking for 'a common participation in the blessings of civil and religious liberty' currently enjoyed in France. While Wordsworth was happy to enjoy French hospitality, Vaughan was interested in following the French example, and their contrasting responses on visiting France help to clarify Wordsworth's position at this time.

As an undergraduate Wordsworth apparently did not respond to the substantial dissenting presence at Cambridge, nor did his idea of the Revolution share the millenarian optimism of Richard Price, Joseph Priestley, and other members of the Revolution

---

[6] CUL Add. MSS 7886/263. Felix Vaughan to William Frend, Paris, 19 July 1790.

Society. This is not to pretend that Wordsworth was unaware of the dissenters' political disadvantages; it does, however, indicate his lack of interest in the controversy in 1790 much as another contemporary liberal issue, the emancipation of slaves, 'had ne'er | Fastened on [his] affections' (P. x. 218–19). His recollection of the *Fédération* in *The Prelude*, Book Six, implies that, while he welcomed events in France, he retained a belief that England was still the true home of liberty, 'First ever of the first and freest of the free' as Coleridge put it in the last line of 'The Destruction of the Bastille'. Towards the end of 1790, though, he would have been encouraged to take stock of his political allegiance rather more precisely. Burke's *Reflections* forced the issue of France, making the Revolution and its political repercussions elsewhere in Europe the major subject of political debate. Wordsworth's radical identity started to form from this moment, during his months in London between January and May 1791. This was also the period of his first significant encounter with dissenting and reformist opinion.

The Nicholson connection

In the 'Fenwick Note' to *The Excursion* Wordsworth recalled his 'frequent residences in London at the beginning of the French Revolution', and his visits to the dissenting meeting-house at the Old Jewry where Richard Price had addressed the Revolution Society in November 1789. Just over a year later Wordsworth came to hear 'a Mr Fawcett': 'It happened to me several times to be one of his congregation,' he told Isabella Fenwick, 'through my connection with Mr. Nicholson of Cateaton Street, Strand, who at a time, when I had not many acquaintances in London, used often to invite me to dine with him on Sundays; and I took that opportunity (Mr. N. being a Dissenter) of going to hear Fawcett, who was an able and eloquent man.' (*PW* v. 374–5).[7] Samuel Nicholson was a unitarian, and Wordsworth's 'connection' with him was his cousin Elizabeth Threlkeld, who patronized Nicholson's wholesale haberdashery in Cateaton Street, and her father

---

[7] Cateaton Street was in Holborn, not off the Strand. Wordsworth possibly confused Nicholson's house wth William Mathews's father's bookshop at 18 Strand (*EY*, p. 111), or William Frend's house in Buckingham Street, which ran from the Strand to the Thames embankment.

Samuel who had been unitarian minister at Penrith and Halifax
(*E Y*, pp. 2n., 16n.). Wordsworth and Nicholson probably first
met in spring 1791, 'a time when [Wordsworth] had not many
acquaintances in London', and their Sunday visits to the Old
Jewry would have been to hear Joseph Fawcett's lectures delivered on Sunday evenings during the winter. 'The house was
amazingly crowded with the most genteel people', another visitor
to the Old Jewry recollected, 'and though we were forced to stand
still in the aisle, [we] were much pressed.'[8]

William Godwin counted Fawcett—with Coleridge—among
his 'principal oral instructors'. Both were Calvinists when they
met at Ware in June 1778, and Fawcett impressed Godwin as 'the
first man [he] had ever known of great originality of thinking: . . .
He was a declared enemy of the private & domestic affections; &
his opinions on this head, well adapted to the austerity &
perfection which Calvinism recommends, had undoubtedly great
influence on mine.'[9] Fawcett's influence upon Godwin's attitude
to 'private and domestic affections' was to appear in the rational
philosophy of *Political Justice*, but by 1791 the two men had
diverged on religious matters. Godwin had been an atheist since
1788, whereas Fawcett's lectures offered a rational argument for
divine providence: 'Reason . . . informs the thoughtful, and
revelation assures the believing, that the Dispenser of adversity is
the author only of good.'[10] Fawcett's comfortable words fore-
shadow Coleridge's position in 1795–6, 'Rest awhile | Children
of wretchedness!', but his 'austere Calvinism' lacks Coleridge's
compassionate commitment to social amelioration. 'Not a single
needless sigh ascends from the human bosom. Not one unnecessary tear flows down the face of man', Fawcett told his 'genteel'
congregation: 'Habitude has a power, not only of softening the
hardest pillow; lifting the lowliest cot; refining the coarsest bread;
converting inconvenience to ease; and making the weather's
inclemencies mild; it is able to dull the point of circumstance that
pierce to the soul of happiness.'[11] Fawcett and Godwin shared a

---

[8] 'Anecdotes of Mr. Robert Bloomfield', *Dodsley's Annual Register for the Year
1800* (London, 1801), 'Characters', pp. 319–20.
[9] A–S Dep. b. 228/9.
[10] Joseph Fawcett, 'On the Comparative Sum of Happiness and Misery in Human
Life', *Sermons* (2 vols; London, 1795), i. 66.
[11] Fawcett, *Sermons*, i. 67, 87.

belief in the power of benevolent reason, but Fawcett's Christianity wanted the motive to progress and improvement that informed the necessarian dynamics of *Political Justice*. In this respect his position is close to that of Richard Watson in his *Sermon to the Stewards of the Westminster Dispensary*, which prompted Wordsworth to write his *Letter to the Bishop of Llandaff* in 1793. Two years earlier, though, his response to Fawcett was less volatile: he was apparently most impressed by Fawcett's 'eloquence', much as he recalled being 'rapt' by Burke's 'eloquent tongue' in speeches to the House of Commons (*1850*, vii. 517).

When Wordsworth recollected Fawcett in his conversations with Isabella Fenwick he said that it was Fawcett's poem 'The Art of War', published in 1795, which 'made [him] think more about [Fawcett] than [he] should otherwise have done' (*PW* v. 375). He nevertheless also identified Fawcett as his 'chief' model for the Solitary in *The Excursion*, the 'lonesome and lost' victim of revolutionary failure and what Wordsworth retrospectively termed 'the wild and lax opinions' associated with that period (*PW* v. 375). He may well have had Hazlitt's *Life of Thomas Holcroft* in mind, where Fawcett is mentioned as 'one of the most enthusiastic admirers of the French Revolution', although 'the disappointment of the hopes he had cherished of the freedom and happiness of mankind, preyed upon his mind, and hastened his death' (Howe, iii. 171n.). Hazlitt claimed to have known Fawcett since 'early youth' and presumably had first-hand knowledge of his later life and death on 24 February 1804. However, Fawcett actually seems to have sustained his hopes for France longer than most contemporaries, and Hazlitt's idea of him as a man destroyed by the course of the Revolution is somewhat at odds with what is known of his life.[12] But his account of Fawcett's demise does bear a curious resemblance to Wordsworth's own observations in a letter to Hazlitt of 5 March 1804, where he says he 'was sorry to see from the Papers that [Hazlitt's] Friend poor Fawcett was dead; not so much that he was dead but to think of the manner in which he had sent himself off before his time' (*EY*, p. 447).

Wordsworth's concern for Hazlitt's friend in March 1804

[12] See M. Ray Adams, 'Joseph Fawcett and Wordsworth's Solitary', *PMLA* xlviii (June 1933), 508–28.

coincided with renewed work on *The Prelude* prompted by Coleridge's forthcoming voyage to Malta. 'I am now writing a Poem on my own earlier life', he told De Quincey on 6 March, 'and have just finished that part in which I speak of my residence at the University' (*E Y*, p. 454). He mentions the 'tributary' relation of this poem to the 'larger work' projected in *The Recluse*, and adds that he has 'also arranged the plan of a narrative Poem' which appears to be Wordsworth's earliest reference to *The Excursion*. Having completed work on his 'residence at the University' by 6 March, Wordsworth was almost certainly contemplating an account of his journey through France to the Alps in 1790, which would eventually form *The Prelude*, Book Six. He may also have realized, though perhaps less distinctly, that the poem on his 'earlier life' would have to be further extended to treat his subsequent experiences in London and France during 1791 and 1792.

Early in 1804 Wordsworth's creativity, his plans for *The Recluse* and 'a narrative Poem', were closely bound up with his fears for Coleridge's health and life after his departure from Dove Cottage on 14 January. 'I am very anxious to have your notes for the Recluse', he wrote to Coleridge on 6 March; 'I cannot say how much importance I attach to this, if it should please God that I survive you, I should reproach myself for ever in writing the work if I had neglected to procure this help' (*E Y*, p. 452). Again, at the end of the month, he repeated the same request with redoubled urgency: 'I would gladly have given 3 fourths of my possessions for your letter on The Recluse', Wordsworth wrote on 29 March; 'I cannot say what a load it would be to me, should I survive you and you die without this memorial left behind' (*E Y*, p. 464). Coleridge was seriously ill and Wordsworth's unease was justified, but it is also possible that at some level he identified the recent death of 'poor Fawcett' as an adumbration of his friend's imminent demise. If that was so, then Wordsworth's memory of Fawcett later in life as one who 'had not strength of character to withstand the effects of the French Revolution' appears as an oblique admission that the failure of revolution, and not opium-related illness, had been a root cause of Coleridge's broken health and paralysed creativity on leaving England for Malta.

In Fawcett Wordsworth could acknowledge Coleridge as his own damaged counterpart, an identification that in March 1804 he could not perhaps admit directly but which is implicit in his contemporary idea of *The Recluse* as a 'memorial' for Coleridge. That recognition would also provide an immediate motive for extending work on *The Prelude* to include an exploration of his revolutionary self, the compensating history of one who had turned political disappointment to creative gain—and a further preparation for composition of *The Recluse*. It also implies that the Solitary in *The Excursion*, who 'from the pulpit' had 'zealously maintained | The Cause of Christ and civil liberty' (ii. 220–1), may be modelled as much upon Coleridge as Fawcett. The whole tripartite structure of *Prelude, Excursion,* and *Recluse,* present perhaps as a shadowy conception in the letter to De Quincey of 6 March 1804, emerges as an elaborate ministration to Coleridge's post-revolutionary anguish.

Fawcett died at a crucial moment in Wordsworth's life as a poet. In doing so he provided a liberating external focus for Wordsworth's distress at Coleridge's plight and his sorrowful recognition of the widening disparity between them. The period to which Fawcett would have drawn Wordsworth's memory as the full measure of that difference, and a seminal moment in his political and creative life, would have been Wordsworth's 'residences in London at the beginning of the French Revolution'. Back in spring 1791, though, it was Samuel Nicholson and not Joseph Fawcett who had the more immediate impact.

Nicholson's significance to Wordsworth in 1791 lay less in his religious beliefs than in his attitude to the Revolution, to parliamentary reform, and to the pamphlet war initiated by the *Reflections* the previous November. Given his unitarianism, it would have been unusual for Nicholson not to have been connected with reformists in London. He was almost certainly acquainted with the liberal publisher and unitarian Joseph Johnson, which might account for Johnson's publication of 'An Evening Walk' and 'Descriptive Sketches' in 1793. Nicholson's house in Cateaton Street was close to Johnson's bookshop in St Paul's Churchyard; they might have met at the Old Jewry or the Essex Street chapel; and a third, more definite link between Nicholson and Johnson can be established through their political activities.

Johnson's stature and influence as a publisher was very considerable. His name would have been familiar to Wordsworth as

Cowper's publisher, but Johnson's bookshop was also a well-known meeting-place for London radicals throughout the 1790s. It was here, for instance, that Godwin met Paine and Mary Wollstonecraft over dinner on 13 November 1791; the talk was of 'monarchy, Tooke, Johnson, Voltaire, pursuits and religion' (GD iv). Johnson was also connected with the Society for Constitutional Information, and it was through this dissenting and reformist society that he could have met Samuel Nicholson, who was also a member.

In May 1794 the government seized all papers and minutes belonging to the SCI to substantiate its charge of high treason against six leading members: John Horne Tooke, John Augustus Bonney, Stewart Kyd, Jeremiah Joyce, Thomas Wardle, and Thomas Holcroft. The loss of these records contributed to the Society's demise later in the year, but also ensured the preservation of its papers. Among them is a list of members whose subscriptions were in arrears in 1793, and there appears

Josh. Johnson St Paul's Churchyard 1yr 1—1—

—with the member who was to apply to him for payment: John Horne Tooke. Elsewhere in the Treasury Solicitor's files is a notebook which records subscriptions received during 1785–7. Alongside John Jebb, the radical lawyer John Frost, and John Horne Tooke, is

Mr Saml. Nicholson Cateaton Street 1yr. 13 Novr 1785—1—1—

—and a few pages later is a second entry,

Saml. Nicholson Esqr. 1yr Novr 86. 1.1

The official ledger of the SCI also confirms Nicholson's membership. Although this evidence suggests Nicholson's membership might have been earlier than Johnson's, an undated list headed 'Penny Post' contains both names as well as 'Mr J. Fawcett—Camomile St'. All three apparently coincided as members or associates of the SCI sometime in the 1780s, and this places Samuel Nicholson at the centre of the movement for parliamentary reform in the years just before the French Revolution.[13]

---

[13] For SCI subscription arrears in 1793, see TS 11 952 3496 (2); for the SCI subscription notebook 1785–7 and the 'Penny Post' list, see TS 11 960 3506 (1). For a brief reference to Joseph Johnson and the SCI, see G. P. Tyson, *Joseph Johnson: A Liberal Publisher* (Iowa, 1979), 156 [cited hereafter as Tyson].

The S C I was founded by Major John Cartwright in April 1780, and the Society's first *Address to the Public* announced its intention to press for a reform in 'the Commons' House of Parliament':

It is the aim of this Society . . . to revive in the minds of their fellow-citizens, THE COMMONALTY AT LARGE, a knowledge of their lost Rights; so that, knowing the value of their Inheritance, and the absolute necessity of exercising their Election Rights as *extensively* and as *constantly* as our sacred Constitution and its great Founders intended, they may restore Freedom and Independency to that branch of the legislature which originates from, represents, and is answerable to THEMSELVES.[14]

The 'great Founders' of the English constitution were the Saxons, but the yoke of 'arbitrary kings' since the Norman Conquest had destroyed its former charters and liberties. The 'lost Rights' to which the S C I referred were annual elections to parliament, and an extension of the franchise to provide full male suffrage and political rights for dissenters: 'the *poor* Man has an *equal* Right, but *more* Need, to have a Representative in Parliament than the rich one.'[15] By distributing its pamphlets free of charge, the S C I intended to spread political information 'throughout the realm . . . and even to introduce it into the humble dwelling of the cottager'.[16] But, although the S C I hoped to educate 'the cottager', its expensive subscription of one guinea a year meant that the poor could not afford to join. The more democratic reform movement emerged in 1792 with the founding of the London Corresponding Society, which drew its membership from all ranks of citizens and charged fees of 1*d.* a week or 1*s.* 1*d.* a quarter. The majority of subscribers to the S C I were middle-class dissenters, many of whom were also members of the Revolution Society. At a dinner in 'the Shakespear Tavern' on 8 December 1784, for example, Nicholson was present with John Jebb and Thomas Brand Hollis, and other important members were John Towill Rutt, Andrew Kippis, Capel Lofft, Richard Price, and Robert Robinson—all unitarians except Robinson who at

[14] *An Address to the Public from the Society for Constitutional Information* (London, 1780), 2.
[15] *A Second Address to the Public from the Society for Constitutional Information* (London, 1780), 16.
[16] *An Address*, p. 2.

this time was a Baptist.[17] There was a significant link with Cambridge University among members of the SCI too. In 1780 Lofft and Robinson collaborated in founding the Cambridge Constitutional Society, which was to act as a forum for dissenting and reformist opinion in town and university. During the following decade the society helped foster the liberal environment which had a formative influence upon the radicalism of Frend and Dyer, and, through them, upon Coleridge as well.[18]

The limited membership of the SCI in London contributed to its varied fortunes in the 1780s, and numbers declined in the years immediately before the French Revolution as a result of the repeated failure of their petitions for removal of the Test Acts. However, in 1789 the fall of the Bastille and hopes for the political regeneration of France and Britain revived the SCI's activities, and brought a fresh influx of members. On 16 December the society met at the London Tavern and passed a series of resolutions in favour of 'the most strenuous efforts for procuring a Parliamentary Reform', before following the example of the Revolution Society in toasting 'the destruction of the Bastille . . . and the exertion of the rights of national representation'.[19]

As a member of the SCI Nicholson would have supported a reform of representation in the House of Commons and an extension of the suffrage. As a unitarian, he would have looked more specifically for repeal of the Test Acts. He also appears to have been interested in penal reform, for inside the SCI ledger book is a 'list of those Gentlemen who have had Mr. Lofft's Book "Thoughts on the Construction and Polity of Prisons"'. The book was actually written by John Jebb, with an introduction by Capel Lofft, and Nicholson appears in the list of interested gentlemen who borrowed the book.[20] Like other members of the Constitutional Society, Nicholson would have welcomed the Revolution in 1789, possibly attending the London Tavern meeting of 16 December. Given his liberal and reformist politics he would certainly have been provoked by Burke's *Reflections*, and particularly so by Burke's contemptuous reference to the SCI as a 'poor charitable club' and sarcastic mockery of its publications

[17] TS 11 961 3507, Minutes of the SCI, vol. i.
[18] For the Cambridge Constitutional Society, see Chapter 3 below.
[19] See Goodwin, pp. 114–16, for this revival of the SCI.
[20] TS 11 961 3507.

and programme of political education (*R.*, p. 87). If he read the *Reflections* soon after publication in November 1790, he most likely also acquired some of the many contributions to the ensuing pamphlet war.

The most widely read reply to Burke was Paine's *Rights of Man*, the first part of which appeared on 16 March 1791 while Wordsworth was in London. Although Johnson had originally undertaken publication, only a dozen copies appeared under his imprint before it was transferred to J. S. Jordan—probably because Johnson thought Paine too outspoken.[21] Burke had lamented the 'fresh ruins of France, which shock our feelings wherever we can turn our eyes', but Paine welcomed 'an age of Revolutions, in which everything may be looked for' (*R.*, p. 126; *R M* i. 168). Besides countering Burke's attack on the Revolution, Paine reprinted the *Declaration of the Rights of Man and of Citizens* made by the National Assembly in August 1789, and applied its democratic principles in his criticism of the British political system. For Burke constitutional right was established by tradition, and Paine replied appropriately by denying that 'a parliament, or any description of men, or any generation of men, in any country [are] possessed of the right or the power of binding and controlling posterity to the "*end of time*," or of commanding for ever how the world shall be governed, or who shall govern it . . .' (*R M* i. 63). In 1780 the Constitutional Society had appealed to the 'great Saxon founders' of the constitution to justify contemporary reform. But for Paine Britain had no constitution at all. He took his precedent from 'the time when man came from the hand of his Maker' by way of proving man's natural equality; nature, for Paine, was the foundation of all civil and political rights. It followed that unequal representation in parliament was unconstitutional because unnatural, like the arbitrary government of France before 1789: 'The continual use of the word *Constitution* in the English Parliament, shows there is none; and that the whole is merely a form of Government without a Constitution, and constituting itself with what powers it pleases' (*R M* i. 153).

Paine's ideas encouraged Thomas Hardy to found the London Corresponding Society in January 1792, and were adopted by the

---

[21] Tyson, pp. 123–4.

society to substantiate its claims for parliamentary reform. 'The right to reform is in the nation in its original character', was Paine's message, 'and the constitutional method would be by a general convention elected for the purpose' (R M i. 95). The Corresponding Society's first *Address* embodied the new militancy in Painite radicalism in declaring that 'THE NATION IS UNREPRESENTED ... THE PRESENT SYSTEM IS TOTALLY UNCONSTITUTIONAL—if by the word CONSTITUTION any thing is meant.'[22] However, it was the French connection in Paine's ideas, and the Corresponding Society's admiration for French achievements, which caused the government particular concern. In 1792–3 the democratic reform movement gathered momentum just as the French Revolution adopted republicanism and entered its period of violence. Although the Corresponding Society never openly advocated republicanism, as Paine did, the government consistently but mistakenly confounded its reformist ambitions with revolutionary plots. This misrepresentation encouraged the repressive backlash of 1793–4, the treason trials, and culminated in Pitt's and Grenville's two 'gagging acts' of December 1795 which effectively silenced the reform movement.

The publication of the first part of *The Rights of Man* was therefore a crucial moment in the development of the democratic reform movement in the 1790s. It was immediately influential in presenting the French Revolution as an ideal model of social and political change, 'a renovation of the natural order of things, a system of principles as universal as truth and the existence of man, and combining moral with political happiness and national prosperity' (R M i. 166). Wordsworth was not only in London when *The Rights of Man* first appeared on the bookstalls, he was moving in circles likely to be receptive to Paine's ideas. In 1787 Paine had been elected an honorary member of the SCI, and on 23 March 1791—a week after publication of *The Rights of Man*—the society voted Paine its congratulations and set about promoting the pamphlet.[23] Nicholson would certainly have been among the first to acquire a copy, in view of the SCI's patronage and the notoriety that *The Rights of Man* quickly acquired. Wordsworth's happy experiences in France in 1790 would have

[22] *The London Corresponding Society's Addresses and Regulations* (London, 1792), 1.
[23] Goodwin, p. 176.

inclined him against Burke in favour of the pamphlets that contradicted his *Reflections*. In Nicholson's house he could expect to find the latest publications from Joseph Johnson as well as the major political pamphlets, among them the *Reflections* and *The Rights of Man*.

A Letter to the Bishop of Llandaff reveals that Wordsworth had read both Burke and Paine, and Book Nine of *The Prelude* recalls that before his second visit to France he 'had read, and eagerly | Sometimes, the master pamphlets of the day' (ix. 96–7).[24] The obvious moment for him to have done so was spring 1791, when the *Reflections* was fresh and controversial and the various replies rapidly appearing. Wordsworth's *Letter* draws upon his own experience in France in 1792 to defend the Revolution and the new republic, but it also reveals his knowledge of and sympathy for the aims of the reform movement in Britain. 'If there is a single man in Great Britain, who has no suffrage in the election of a representative,' Wordsworth says, 'the will of the society of which he is a member is not generally expressed; he is a helot in that society' (*Pr. W.* i. 46). This differs markedly from his attitude in 1790, and reflects a keener awareness that a substantial section of the population were without political rights or representation in parliament. There can be little doubt that Samuel Nicholson drew Wordsworth's attention to the political disabilities of dissenters and to the reformist efforts of the SCI during the 1780s. This in turn would have encouraged his support in the *Letter* for 'the general call for a parliamentary reform' co-ordinated by the more radical Corresponding Societies founded during his year in France (*Pr. W.* i. 48).

Besides exercising a formative influence upon Wordsworth's politics in the early 1790s, his 'connection' with Nicholson has an extended significance in his later development as a poet. In May and June 1794 Wordsworth suggested to William Mathews that their projected journal the *Philanthropist* should 'inculcate principles of government and forms of social order', and that it should 'forcibly illustrate the tendency of particular doctrines of government' (*EY*, pp. 119, 125). The *Philanthropist* had a topical relevance to crisis in 1794, as will be seen later on, but Wordsworth's specific proposals recall the plans for political

---

[24] See *Pr. W.* i. 50–66 for the editors' detailed notes on Wordsworth's debt to Paine in his *Letter*.

education initiated by the Constitutional Society in 1780 and sustained by the Corresponding Society after 1792. In 1796 Coleridge's *Watchman* was similarly and explicitly intended to 'co-operate . . . with the PATRIOTIC SOCIETIES, for obtaining a Right of Suffrage, general and frequent' (*Watchman*, p. 5).

Just over two years afterwards, during 1798–9, the missionary purpose of the reform societies, the *Philanthropist*, and the *Watchman* resurfaced in Wordsworth's and Coleridge's scheme of *The Recluse* as a poem of 'considerable utility' (*E Y*, p. 214) that 'would do great good' in the aftermath of revolutionary failure (*CL* i. 527). Much has been written about the extent to which Wordsworth's earliest ideas of *The Recluse* were dependent upon his conversion to Coleridge's philosophy in the months after their meeting at Racedown in 1797. But the poem also has a source in Wordsworth's successive radical identities during the years of revolution, and finds its fullest significance in the integration of this background with the more immediate influence of Coleridge's thought. That will be a recurring concern in subsequent pages. For the moment, though, a germ of Wordsworth's idea of *The Recluse* in March 1798 can be found in his reading of pamphlets—especially *The Rights of Man*—exactly seven years earlier in spring 1791.

'I have written 1300 lines of a poem in which I contrive to convey most of the knowledge of which I am possessed', Wordsworth told James Webbe Tobin on 6 March 1798: 'My object is to give pictures of Nature, Man, and Society' (*E Y*, p. 212). Five days afterwards he told James Losh that the poem was to be entitled '*The Recluse or views of Nature, Man, and Society*' (*E Y*, p. 214). At this moment the '1300 lines' of *The Recluse* would have comprised 'The Ruined Cottage' and 'The Pedlar', perhaps also 'The Discharged Soldier', 'Old Cumberland Beggar', and 'A Night Piece'. 'Nature, Man, and Society' offers only a bare outline of Wordsworth's concerns in these poems, without suggesting any unifying philosophic intention. It does, however, recall very precisely Paine's formulation of democracy seven years earlier in *The Rights of Man*. Man's 'natural rights', Paine had argued, 'are the foundation of all his civil rights' (*R M* i. 90), and his pamphlet demonstrated the practical regeneration of nature, man, and society through revolutionary change comparable to that in America and France.

In spring 1798 Tobin and Losh would most likely have recognized Wordsworth's invocation of Painite democracy in his plans for *The Recluse*. But the erosion of the revolutionary idealism that sustained *The Rights of Man* would have left them uncertain as to how Wordsworth's 'pictures' and '*views*' of 'Nature, Man, and Society' were related, and in what their 'considerable utility' was supposed to consist. Neither of Wordsworth's letters offers an explanation, but at this time both Wordsworth and Coleridge would have identified the poem's 'utility' as translating the hopes of former years in the sustaining philosophy of One Life. For Coleridge in 'Religious Musings' the One Life offered a sublime assurance that

'tis God
Diffused through all, that doth make all one whole.
(ll. 139–40)

—whereas Wordsworth's letters to Tobin and Losh suggest that for him the particular attraction of Coleridge's philosophy was its reconciliation of 'Nature, Man, and Society' as 'Parts and proportions of one wond'rous whole' (l. 137). The One Life offered a vision of universal participation, a transcendent justification of Paine's 'system of principles as universal as truth and the existence of man'. It simultaneously permitted the internalization of those principles as functions of individual thought and feeling.

Wordsworth explores this inward translation of regenerative possibility in his description of 'The Pedlar', which was composed at the same period as his earliest announcements of *The Recluse* in February and March 1798. 'In his steady course', Wordsworth writes,

No piteous revolutions had he felt
No wild varieties of joy or grief
Unoccupied by sorrow of its own
His heart lay open and by nature tuned
And constant disposition of his thoughts
To sympathy with man he was alive
To all that was enjoyed where'er he went
And all that was endured . . .
(Butler, p. 361)

For the Pedlar 'revolution' has become synonymous with distress, the confusion of 'joy' in 'grief'. But the genial and restorative power with which Paine had associated revolution has been preserved, to appear now in the relation of the Pedlar's heart and mind to 'Nature' and his consequent 'sympathy with man'. Paradoxically, however, the philosophy that gave Wordsworth this creative access to inner life, and which seemed to offer an immaculate regeneration of 'Nature, Man, and Society', was radically unsuited to the systematic exposition proposed for *The Recluse*. Wordsworth's and Coleridge's scheme for a philosophic poem was disabled by the philosophy which, in its earliest conception, it was supposed to present. As a result, Wordsworth's proposed '*views of Nature, Man, and Society*' in his letters of March 1798 appear as the external shell of a system, the vital principle of which has been assumed by the individual mind. That assumption was encouraged by Coleridge's immediate influence upon Wordsworth during 1797–8, but it was also conditioned by more distant events at the start of the decade, specifically in Wordsworth's response to the idea of revolution in 'the master pamphlets of the day'. However, his reading of those pamphlets had an ambiguous effect upon his attitude to the Revolution when he returned to France for his second visit in December 1791.

'Through Paris lay my readiest path', Wordsworth recalls at the beginning of *The Prelude*, Book Nine,

> and there
> I sojourned a few days, and visited
> In haste each spot of old and recent fame—
> The latter chiefly

(ix. 40–3)

—but the sights and activities he witnessed appeared incomprehensible despite his effort to understand. 'I stared and listened with a stranger's ears', he recalled. Neither the euphoria of the 'great federal day' in 1790, his talks with Nicholson, nor his reading of Burke and Paine supplied the key to the Revolution Wordsworth now experienced at first hand. The 'master pamphlets' presented the Revolution as 'a renovation of the natural order of things', or its ruinous opposite; for Burke the razing of the Bastille had been 'a thing in itself of no consequence whatever', but for Paine its 'downfall . . . included the idea of the downfall of Despotism'. Such ideas nevertheless failed to touch the deeper human significance of what had happened in France, which was why the pamphlets seemed at best a 'half-insight', the revolutionary capital an unintelligible cipher, the Bastille an inarticulate symbol. The reformer John Horne Tooke had a chunk of rubble from the old fortress 'deposited in a conspicuous place in his study',[25] and Wordsworth also conscientiously

> gathered up a stone,
> And pocketed the relick in the guise
> Of an enthusiast
>
> (ix. 65–7)

—but was aware that his own gesture of enthusiasm lacked substance. '[I]n honest truth', he continues,

> I looked for something which I could not find,
> Affecting more emotion than I felt.
>
> (ix. 67, 70–1)

While he failed to discover 'something' adequate to the Bastille's symbolic status, Wordsworth's memory also suggests the fragility of his emotional identification with the cause up to now. '[A]ll things were to me | Loose and disjointed', he says, 'and the affections left | Without a vital interest' (ix. 106–8). His experiences in the following months were to supply that 'vital interest', confirming the Revolution as a living cause rather than matter for the political debate with which he had familiarized himself during 1791.

[25] A. Stephens, *Memoirs of John Horne Tooke* (2 vols; London, 1813), ii. 112.

2

'Pretty Hot in It'

Wordsworth and France, 1791–1792

Revolutionary selves

Oh, sweet it is in academic groves—. . .
To ruminate, with interchange of talk,
On rational liberty and hope in man,
Justice and peace. But far more sweet such toil
(Toil, say I, for it leads to thoughts abstruse)
If Nature then be standing on the brink
Of some great trial, and we hear the voice
Of one devoted, one whom circumstance
Hath called upon to embody his deep sense
In action, give it outwardly a shape,
And that of benediction to the world.

(ix. 397, 401–410)

Half-way through *The Prelude*, Book Nine, Wordsworth reminds Coleridge of their different circumstances twelve years earlier. In 1792 Coleridge was drinking negus in his rooms at Jesus College, and discussing political pamphlets with other undergraduates. At the same time Wordsworth was witnessing the French Revolution at first hand, meeting individuals actively participating in 'that great change' as well as some 'bent upon undoing what was done' (ix. 137). For Coleridge the Revolution was an ideal cause only; he never crossed the channel to see it for himself. But to Wordsworth in 1792 France offered an opportunity for personal action and involvement, and an experience that was to reverberate through his poetry of later years.

Wordsworth arrived in France late in November 1791, and returned to England a little over twelve months later in December 1792. That year was marked by a change in the character and direction of the Revolution: from non-violent constitutional reform to the bloodshed of the September Massacres; from peaceful co-existence to war with Austria and later with Britain after February 1793; from a limited constitutional monarchy established in September 1791 to the declaration of the republic and subsequent execution of Louis. Despite his reading of 'the master pamphlets', Wordsworth found himself, as he recalled, 'unprepared | With needful knowledge' and unable to understand the machinery of revolutionary government (ix. 92–108). He emerged from his year in France as the author of *A Letter to the Bishop of Llandaff*, a republican. Wordsworth's political radicalism was bound up with his personal experience of revolution and responsive to its changing course. The immediate challenge of France, however, was the possibility of realizing his self-commitment as action, and in retrospect it appears as a crux between alternative revolutionary identities, and the self who became poet of *The Prelude* and *The Recluse*.

In *The Prelude*, Book Ten, Wordsworth says that to counter the increasing violence of the Revolution late in 1792 he would

> willingly have taken up
> A service at this time for cause so great,
> However dangerous

> (x. 134–6)

—and despite all obstacles 'made a common cause | With some who perished, haply perished too' (x. 194–5). The 'service' he seems to recall here would have involved his collaboration and downfall with the Gironde in their power struggle with the Jacobins early in 1793. It is a possibility that has usually, and too easily, been dismissed as wishful thinking on Wordsworth's part. The evidence of imagination in *The Borderers, The Prelude*, and *The Excursion* insists upon Wordsworth's awareness of his active revolutionary self and, more significantly, of that self as potentially violent and extreme as Robespierre and his Committee of Public Safety. One can discount the reassuring image of William as a martyr of revolutionary moderation from the outset; a number of later poems are not intelligible unless one admits the more sinister conjecture that Wordsworth's 'devoted service' might have led to his making 'a common cause' with Robespierre in prosecuting the Terror to save the Revolution in France.[1]

Some such recognition on Wordsworth's part is implicit in Book Three of *The Excursion*, where the Solitary recalls:

[1] For Wordsworth as collaborator in John Oswald's scheme to effect a British revolution by force, see D. Erdman, 'The Man who was not Napoleon', *TWC* xii (Winter 1981), 92–6 [cited hereafter as Erdman, 'not Napoleon'].

                      The tranquil shores
        Of Britain circumscribed me; else, perhaps
        I might have been entangled among deeds,
        Which, now, as infamous, I should abhor . . .

                                    (iii. 812–5)

Surviving contemporary evidence suggests that in 1793–4 Wordsworth had indeed been 'circumscribed' by the coast of Britain. But if that was in fact the case, the Solitary's idea of the Terror as confusion of benign purpose in abhorrent deeds serves as a projection of what 'might have been' had Wordsworth not quitted Paris for London in December 1792. The moment to which one should look occurs right at the start of the Terror, in Thomas Carlyle's reminiscence that Wordsworth had witnessed the execution of Jean-Antoine Gorsas at Paris on 8 October 1793:

He had been in France in the earlier or secondary stage of the Revolution; had witnessed the struggle of *Girondins* and *Mountain*, in particular the execution of Gorsas, 'the first *Deputy* sent to the Scaffold;' and testified strongly to the ominous feeling which that event produced in everybody, and of which he himself still seemed to retain something: 'Where will it *end*, when you have set an example in *this* kind?'[2]

In *The Prelude*, Book Nine, Gorsas is mentioned, along with his fellow revolutionary journalist Carra, as 'names, forgotten now'—like Milton's 'bad angels' in *Paradise Lost*, 'blotted out and razed | By their rebellion, from the books of life' (i. 362–3). Milton is alluding to the third chapter of Revelations here, and ironically so, for he goes on to list the 'new names' subsequently acquired by the fallen angels on earth. Similarly, the disappearance of Gorsas was not so complete as Wordsworth's own allusion to *Paradise Lost* might suggest at a first glance. His name lived on in *The Prelude*, and also in the seventh volume of Wordsworth's own set of *The Works of Edmund Burke*, which is preserved at Dove Cottage Library. On p. 305 Gorsas's name appears, marked with a cross and pencilled note in Wordsworth's hand: 'I knew this man. W.W.'[3] Since Gorsas's activities as a

---

[2] *Reminiscences by Thomas Carlyle*, ed. C. E. Norton (2 vols; London, 1887), ii. 303.
[3] Wordsworth's edition of Burke was *The Works of the Right Honourable Edmund Burke: A New Edition* (16 vols; London, 1803–27). I am grateful to Peter Swaab for pointing out Wordsworth's marginal note.

journalist and deputy to the National Assembly kept him at Paris, Wordsworth must have met him while passing through the city late in 1791 or , more likely I think, on his return there in autumn 1792. But Carlyle's account of a further encounter in October 1793 remains unsubstantiated as historical fact, despite his emphasis that Wordsworth had witnessed the death of Gorsas 'in particular'. Given that lack, perhaps Carlyle's recollection should be taken as an imaginative truth, in which case Wordsworth's shadowy presence at the scaffold was not only as appalled spectator but simultaneously as victim and as executioner too.

As such, the moment focuses Wordsworth's ideas of an active role in events as a complex psychic drama, issuing in his own ineluctable responsibility for the Terror: that he might have written or spoken out against political violence (Wordsworth–Gorsas, journalist and delegate), but that he might equally well have been 'entangled' in furthering those deeds he sought to prevent (Wordsworth as executioner, or Wordsworth—Robespierre). With hindsight, the deadly opposition of these two revolutionary selves confirmed his thoughts of a 'common cause' with France as ultimately self-destructive; but the ineffectual demise of the one, and murderous prosperity of the other, devolved equally upon Wordsworth as passive looker-on: the poet-yet-to-be. Wordsworth's return to London in December 1792, 'Compelled by nothing less than absolute want | Of funds' was a double bind, not an acquittal. The price of publishing 'An Evening Walk' and 'Descriptive Sketches' the following year was the betrayal of France, and Wordsworth's later vocation as a poet involved the burden of expiating that culpability in poetry 'of lasting inspiration'. The poet of *The Recluse* consequently inherited the 'service' of Wordsworth's third revolutionary self of 1792—a patriot soldier and comrade of his friend Michel Beaupuy; his calling, to articulate

> *the voice*
> Of one devoted, one whom circumstance
> Hath called upon to embody his deep sense
> In action, give it outwardly a shape,
> And that of benediction to the world.

> (ix. 406–10; my italics)

As an old man, Wordsworth remembered that he had once (as he said) 'studied military history with great interest, and the strategy of war; and he always fancied that he had talents for command; and he at one time thought of a military life'[4]—so that a Wordsworth 'of other mold— | A patriot' like Beaupuy is by no means implausible given these youthful ambitions. The question remains as to how close Wordsworth came to realizing these revolutionary selves during 1792, and the relation of Wordsworth–Gorsas, Wordsworth–Robespierre, and Wordsworth–Beaupuy to the 'devoted voice' of the poet he eventually became.

'Through Paris lay my readiest path', November–December 1791

Wordsworth's return to France in December 1791 was prompted, he says in *The Prelude*, 'chiefly by a personal wish | To speak the language more familiarly' (ix. 36–7). By crossing the channel, too, he escaped family pressures to take up an uncongenial career in the church (*E Y*, pp. 57–9). But he was doubtless also curious to see the Revolution once again, like James Losh, Felix Vaughan, Tom Wedgwood, James Watt (son of the engineer), and John Tweddell's brother Francis—all of whom visited France between 1790 and 1792, some of them coinciding with Wordsworth. He left London on Tuesday, 22 November, and while delayed at Brighton called on Charlotte Smith who gave him introductory letters to friends at Paris, among them Helen Maria Williams (*E Y*, p. 69). He sailed on Sunday, 27 November and arrived at Paris on the evening of Wednesday, 30 November.

Like any foreign visitor Wordsworth changed his money and set out to see the sights, visiting 'In haste each spot of old and recent fame— | The latter chiefly' (ix. 42–3). He saw 'the field of Mars', site of the *Fête* witnessed by Helen Williams and Felix Vaughan back in July 1790; the 'suburbs of St. Anthony' which surrounded the ruins of the Bastille; Montmartre, the Pantheon, and presumably also Notre-Dame (ix. 43–6). But, unlike France in 1790 where 'joy of one' had seemed to be 'joy of tens of millions', all things in Paris in December 1791 appeared 'loose and disjointed'. Wordsworth recalled that he had

[4] *The Prose Works of William Wordsworth*, ed. A. B. Grosart (3 vols; London, 1876), iii. 451–2.

> stared and listened with a stranger's ears,
> To hawkers and haranguers, hubbub wild,
> And hissing factionists with ardent eyes,
> In knots, or pairs, or single, ant-like swarms
> Of builders and subverters, every face
> That hope or apprehension could put on—
> Joy, anger, and vexation, in the midst
> Of gaiety and dissolute idleness.
>
> (ix. 55–62)

As a stranger Wordsworth was confused, but then so was the whole of Paris in December 1791: the city was divided against itself, suspicious of counter-revolutionary plots that were rumoured to be organized by aristocratic *émigrés*. In June 1791 the royal family had tried to escape from Paris; in July anti-monarchists were massacred at the Champs de Mars, and in August the Brunswick Manifesto threatened Prussian aggression. Wordsworth's memory in Book Nine is of popular unease, the government assailed and paralysed by faction and intrigue:

> In both her clamorous halls,
> The National Synod and the Jacobins,
> I saw the revolutionary power
> Toss like a ship at anchor, rocked by storms . . .
>
> (ix. 46–9)

On 19 December Wordsworth told Richard that he had been 'at the national assembly', and had been 'introduced by a member'—quite possibly Brissot, leader of the Gironde and a likely acquaintance of Charlotte Smith (*EY*, p. 71).[5] At this time the Legislative Assembly, and Brissot personally, were preoccupied with events in the Caribbean colony of St Domingo, where slaves had risen against the white planters. Earlier in 1791 the Constituent Assembly had granted equal rights for blacks in the French colonies, but white reaction in St Domingo led to rebellion and civil war. Brissot, who had founded a society of *Amis des noirs* in the 1780s, spoke out against the violence on 1 and 3 December and proposed 'a new colonial assembly' for St Domingo in which there would be no colour discrimination.[6]

[5] See also J. R. MacGillivray, 'Wordsworth and J. P. Brissot', *TLS* (29 Jan. 1931).

[6] For St Domingo, see Lefebvre, i. 172–3. On *Les Amis des noirs*, see J. M. Thompson, *Leaders of the French Revolution* (Oxford, 1962), 72, and for Brissot's speeches and proceedings at the Legislative Assembly, 1–5 Dec. 1791, *Moniteur*, x. 515–52.

Wordsworth's response on his first visit to the 'clamorous' hall of revolutionary government is not easy to judge. He was already confused by Paris, and colonial affairs might have seemed remote and irrelevant. Nevertheless, it was most likely this moment that Wordsworth recalled when he heard of the imprisonment of Toussaint L'Ouverture in 1802, for resisting Napoleon's reintroduction of slavery in St Domingo. In his memorial sonnet Toussaint appears not as heroic rebel but as victim of imperial tyranny, 'the most unhappy man of men', an emblem of the many reverses of intervening years.

Wordsworth stayed only four full days in Paris, and on Monday, 5 December, travelled south to Orléans. Three years before his death, in November 1847, he recalled that he moved away from Paris at this time, 'with a view of being out of the way of [his] own countrymen' and to make himself speak French (*Pr. W.* iii. 374). During 1792 a sizeable contingent of English, Irish, and Scottish radicals were resident at Paris. Their activities were noted by the British ambassador Earl Gower and by the spy George Monro, both of whom despatched reports to London. Wordsworth's initial contact with these expatriots may once again have been through Charlotte Smith, who was well known to them: among their toasts at the patriotic dinner on 18 November 1792 was the '"lady defenders of the Revolution, particularly Mrs. Charlotte Smith, Miss Williams and Mrs. Barbauld"' (Goodwin, p. 249).

De Quincey mentions that Wordsworth encountered the itinerant Scottish radical 'Walking' Stewart in Paris and had been impressed by his conversation, but he gives no date for this meeting.[7] Late in his life Wordsworth told J. P. Muirhead that he 'went over to Paris . . . at the time of the revolution in 1792 or 1793, and so was *pretty hot in it*; but [he] found Mr. J. Watt there before [him], and *quite* as warm in the same cause'—which suggests that this meeting, if it happened at all, was in mid-1792 when Wordsworth had 'warmed' to the cause rather than earlier.[8] In any case, James Watt, Junior, was not in Paris in

[7] *The Collected Works of Thomas De Quincey*, ed. D. Masson (14 vols; Edinburgh, 1889–90), iii. 106.

[8] J. P. Muirhead, *The Life of James Watt* (London, 1858), 493–4. See also J. P. Muirhead, 'A Day with Wordsworth', *Blackwood's Magazine*, ccxxi (June 1927), 728–43.

December 1791, nor was he there when Wordsworth returned in October 1792. He arrived with the Manchester radical Thomas Cooper in April 1792, on a business trip. On 13 April both were introduced to the Jacobin Club by Robespierre, where they presented a fraternal address from the Manchester Constitutional Society. Two days later they joined a patriotic procession in the Champs de Mars, Watt carrying a British flag and Cooper a bust of Algernon Sydney. Watt stayed at Paris over the summer, and on 14 August was one of the signatories to an 'address of several Englishmen to the National Assembly', congratulating the French 'on having crushed all the plots of their internal enemies' on the *journée* of 10 August, and subscribing 1,315 *livres* to the widows and orphans of 'those brave citizens who sacrificed their lives'. After witnessing the September Massacres, Watt left for Italy: Wordsworth may therefore have met him on an unrecorded visit to Paris in mid-1792, or perhaps Watt travelled down to Blois. Alternatively, Wordsworth's memory should be understood, '[he] found Mr. J. Watt [had been] there before [him]'—but that they did not coincide. Whether they met, or Wordsworth only heard of or read about Watt's connection with the Jacobins, both were apparently moving in similar circles. Watt's acquaintances in Paris included his father's scientific friends, among them the chemist Lavoisier, and also the leading revolutionaries: Robespierre, Danton, Pétion, Jean Roland, Paine, maybe Brissot too. Between April and September 1792 Watt believed that such connections made him 'more safe than any Englishman in Paris', although the September Massacres encouraged him to leave the country as swiftly as he could.[9]

In December 1791 Wordsworth encountered at least one member of the assembly, as well as meeting some of his 'own countrymen' in passing. These contacts were to be more influential when he returned to Paris as a republican late in 1792, while the National Convention was debating the king's fate and receiving news of imminent revolution in Britain almost every day. For the moment he left to take up his 'more permanent residence' at Orléans.

[9] For Watt and Cooper at Paris, April 1792, see Goodwin, pp. 202–3. A more detailed account of Watt in France is E. Robinson, 'An English Jacobin: James Watt, Junior, 1769–1848', *The Cambridge Historical Journal*, xi (1953–5), 349–55 [cited hereafter as Robinson, *CHJ*]. For Watt and the address to the National Assembly, see J. G. Alger, *Paris in 1789–1794* (London, 1902), 324–5 [cited hereafter as Alger], and *Moniteur*, xiii. 423.

Wordsworth in the salons: Orléans, winter 1791–1792

When Wordsworth left Paris for Orléans and Blois, he was following Felix Vaughan's footsteps exactly one year earlier. Vaughan told William Frend on 6 December 1790 that he had 'staid but one day' at Orléans,

> by reason of a wretched inn, that afforded nothing, which an Englishman could eat; and in the caffés there were no 'journeaux', nor did the people although it was market day talk about anything but common occurrences. The cathedral there is the only thing worth seeing their cotton manufactory being kept secret.[10]

Wordsworth took more happily to the city, telling Richard on 19 December 1791 that he had 'every prospect of liking this place extremely well' (E Y, p. 70). Charlotte Smith's letter of introduction to Helen Williams, who had recently lived in Orléans, proved useless. Like Felix Vaughan she found the city 'confined, illiberal, and disagreeable', and had left for Paris earlier in December. Wordsworth was consoled 'by introducing [himself] to a Mr Foxlow an Englishman' who owned the cotton factory to which Vaughan referred, and anticipated joining 'the best society this place affords' (E Y, p. 69).

Had Wordsworth encountered Helen Williams at Orléans he would presumably also have met local patriots with whom she was acquainted. By introducing himself to Foxlow, he entered the fashionable salons of Orléans where talk of the Revolution was taboo:

> a short time
> I loitered, and frequented night by night
> Routs, card-tables, the formal haunts of men
> Whom in the city privilege of birth
> Sequestered from the rest, societies
> Where, through punctilios of elegance
> And deeper causes, all discourse, alike
> Of good and evil, in the time, was shunned
> With studious care.
>
> (P. ix. 114–22)

This society satisfied Wordsworth for a while, as it would not have done Felix Vaughan, and their differing attitudes to Orléans once again serve to establish Wordsworth's position in December

---

[10] CUL Add. MSS 7886/264.

1791. In 1790 Vaughan had looked for newspapers and significant talk, and was irritated not to find either. Wordsworth appears comparatively open-minded, happy to mix with aristocrats and royalists but also concerned to use this experience to clarify his own idea of the Revolution. 'I find almost all the people of any opulen [ce are] aristocrates and all the others democrates', he told Richard; 'I had imagined that there were some people of wealth and circumstance favorers of the revolution, but here there is not one to be found' (*E Y*, p. 70). That simple realization, mentioned only in passing, separates the naïve response of former years from Wordsworth's nascent republicanism of 1792.

The federal ceremonies witnessed by Wordsworth and Jones in 1790 had shown the nation apparently united, but at Orléans Wordsworth discovered that the Revolution continued to involve class conflict. In the first part of *The Rights of Man* Paine had claimed that 'The French constitution says, *There shall be no titles*; and of consequence, all that class of equivocal generation, which in some countries is called "*aristocracy*", and in others "*nobility*", is done away, and the *peer* is exalted into MAN' (*R M* i. 102), but the salons of Orléans proved him wrong. Wordsworth found the 'class of equivocal generation' neither converted to the Revolution nor 'done away'; the aristocracy maintained its elegant life-style, while nursing a silent grudge against the revolutionary 'democrates'. Among Wordsworth's aristocratic company at Orléans was a group of royalist cavalry officers with whom he lodged (*E Y*, p. 69), and who formed the 'chief | Of [his] associates' at this time (*P.* ix. 129–30). Their hostility to the Revolution was undisguised:

> all
> Were men well-born, at least laid claim to such
> Distinction, as the chivalry of France.
> In age and temper differing, they had yet
> One spirit ruling in them all—alike
> (Save one only, hereafter to be named)
> Were bent upon undoing what was done.[11]

(ix. 131–7)

[11] The 'one only' is Beaupuy, who was not among the officers Wordsworth met at Orléans. His regiment was garrisoned at Blois, and was loyal to the Revolution. Book Nine does not distinguish Orléans and Blois, and refers only to a 'city on the borders of the Loire' (ix. 39). By placing Beaupuy among royalists, however, Wordsworth distinguishes him as one 'of other mold | A patriot'.

Orléans showed Wordsworth that the Revolution had split French society, that these divisions extended throughout the nation and excited the popular unrest he had already seen in Paris. The Jacobin society in Orléans was active and corresponded with the club at Paris, but its influence was countered by the loyalty of other citizens to Louis and by the determination of the municipal authorities to uphold the constitution of September 1791. The city merchants in particular had been disenchanted by Brissot's support for the blacks of St Domingo. During 1792 these antipathies were aggravated by economic problems: a poor harvest the previous summer resulted in high prices for flour and bread, and this was compounded by inflation which depreciated the *assignat* by 50 per cent against the pound between July 1791 and March 1792. All of these pressures built up during the year and led to riots at Orléans in September, when Wordsworth was once again residing in the city and working on 'Descriptive Sketches'.[12]

From the moment Wordsworth realized that 'all the people of any opulen [ce are] aristocrates and all the others democrates', his commitment to the Revolution as a democratic and republican cause was only a matter of time. In Book Nine of *The Prelude* he explains to Coleridge that his schooldays and Cambridge years had predisposed him to 'the government of equal rights', that he was already a republican before he set foot in France (ix. 218–49). More certainly, Wordsworth's developing interest in the Revolution over the previous two years was accelerated by his experiences at Paris and Orléans. The argument between Burke and Paine in the 'master pamphlets' now took on a 'vital interest' as a cause in which living people were involved, with whom he could identify emotionally. The 'formal haunts' of Orléans initiated this change; the citizens of Blois were to confirm it.

---

[12] Background material on revolutionary Orléans in this chapter comes from two studies: G. Lefebvre, *Études orléanaises* (2 vols; Paris, 1962–3) [cited hereafter as *EO*], and Eugene Bimbenet, *Histoire de la Ville d'Orléans* (5 vols, Orléans, 1884–8) [cited hereafter as Bimbenet]. For class conflict, municipal government, and merchants at Orléans, see *EO* ii. 59, and Bimbenet, v. 1153–5; for bread shortages and riots, see *EO* ii. 64 and Bimbenet, v. 1211–21. See Lefebvre, i. 231 for inflation.

Wordsworth among the Jacobins: Blois, February–September 1792

From [Orleans] I passed through a beautiful vine country to Blois . . . As it is my practice to talk with every body, I asked the girl of the inn what she thought of what had taken place in the last twelvemonth, and was much pleased with her answer viz. that although she and her father lost money by the few travellers who came amongst them since that time, they both knew that all would go well by and by. Upon asking her what she thought of the queen, she exclaimed Ah! c'est une villaine gueuse que celle-la.[13]

So Felix Vaughan reported his favourable impressions of Blois to William Frend on 6 December 1790. He was pleased by the 'striking' site of the city on the banks of the Loire, by the old château, and equally so by the inn girl's belief in revolutionary achievements and contempt for Marie-Antoinette. A little over a year later Wordsworth was similarly impressed, and his republicanism can be dated most precisely to his months at Blois during spring and summer of 1792.

On 19 May 1792 Wordsworth wrote to William Mathews from Blois, mentioning that since his arrival 'day after day and week after week' had passed 'with inconceivable rapidity' (*E Y*, p. 76). While at Orléans he had met Annette Vallon; they had fallen in love, and when she returned home to Blois sometime between January and March Wordsworth presumably went too. Annette's company explains the swift but pleasant passage of time, and the buoyant mood of Wordsworth's letter to Mathews; the exact date of his arrival at Blois, however, is uncertain. It may have been as early as 3 February, for on that day a member of the revolutionary club at Blois, *Les Amis de la Constitution*, 'requested permission to nominate two Englishmen for membership, and enquired whether they were bound to take the oath as foreign visitors. The matter was discussed, and it was decided that membership should not be granted but that the two might nevertheless attend at meetings' (*P V*, p. 115). One of those Englishmen was very likely Wordsworth.[14] There had been 'few travellers' at Blois since the

---

[13] CUL Add. MSS 7886/264.
[14] Reed, p. 130n., notes that one Edmund Dayrell, an Englishman living near Blois, has been suggested as the second person introduced on 3 Feb.

Revolution, as Vaughan told Frend, but Wordsworth was certainly in the city early in 1792. The confirming evidence for Wordsworth's presence among *Les Amis* appears in a number of passages in his *Letter to the Bishop of Llandaff*, and in the striking similarities between events recorded in the society's minutes and Wordsworth's memories in *The Prelude*, Book Nine. It was at these meetings, too, that Wordsworth probably met Michel Beaupuy.[15]

Les Amis de la Constitution at Blois first met on 23 March 1791 in the church of St Laumer, thereafter the focus of revolutionary activity in the city. Local citizens formed the core of the society, and soldiers from Beaupuy's 32nd (Bassigny) regiment garrisoned at Blois also took an active part in meetings. One function of the society was to encourage patriotic feeling with pageants and parades. On 13 November 1791, for instance, the citizens decided to honour the Constitutional Bishop of Blois, Henri Grégoire, by electing him president of the society. He was fetched from his palace by an elaborate procession 'in the presence of des *Dames Citoyennes*, our brothers in the Bassigny regiment and their noble and patriotic officers, as well as a number of the National Guard. The most attractive features of this procession were the crowned busts of the great Mirabeau, and of the philosopher Jean Jacques [Rousseau]' (*PV*, p. 85; my italics). These festivities were complemented by philanthropic projects that were markedly in contrast to the selfish formal society of Wordsworth's associates at Orléans. On 13 February 1792 *Les Amis* voted to amalgamate all private book collections in a single public library, for which Grégoire offered a room; on 14 May they debated where best to plant the tree of liberty (*PV*, pp. 119, 138). These emotive, democratic proceedings of *Les*

---

[15] G. M. Harper wrote about Wordsworth and *Les Amis* in 'Wordsworth at Blois', *John Morley and Other Essays* (Princeton and London, 1920), 111–24. In this pioneering study Harper rightly emphasized the significance of *Les Amis* to Wordsworth, and the likelihood that he met Beaupuy at the Society. But his eagerness to discover Beaupuy's name apparently coloured his transcription of the minutes; on 29 Jan. 1792 he records a 'name not plainly legible, but very much like Beaupuy'. This 'name' is actually 'Baigny', probably an abbreviation of 'Bassigny', Beaupuy's regiment. Harper was mistaken, too, in claiming that the politics of *Les Amis* were 'on the whole' moderate. By aligning with the Gironde in 1792, the Society followed the most progressive political group then in power; during this year the Society also anticipated the republic by voting for abolition of the monarchy, as will be seen later on in this chapter.

Amis provide the background to Wordsworth's emergent republicanism, although his political bearings were set more precisely by the immediate influence of two individuals: Michel Beaupuy and Bishop Grégoire. It was from them that Wordsworth derived the militant republicanism of his *Letter to the Bishop of Llandaff* and the prophetic authority of his poetry that is first heard in the concluding lines of 'Descriptive Sketches'.

During Wordsworth's months at Blois, the revolutionary society was increasingly preoccupied by events of national importance, especially the war with Austria and, later on, the fate of the royal family. News from Paris reached Blois quickly and, as Wordsworth recalls in *The Prelude*, Book Nine, heated discussion followed readings of the 'public news' (ix. 156–8). On 19 May 1792 he told William Mathews that he was isolated in 'a petty provincial town', but in the same letter he shows himself well aware of 'the general concerns' of the country:

The horrors excited by the relation of the events consequent upon the commencement of hostilities, is general. Not but that there are men who felt a gloomy satisfaction from a measure which seemed to put the patriot army out of a possibility of success. An ignominious flight, the massacre of their general, a dance performed with savage joy round his burning body, the murder of six prisoners, are events which would have arrested the attention, of the reader of the annals of Morocco, or of the most barbarous of savages. The approaching summer will undoubtedly decide the fate of france. (*EY*, pp. 77–8)

The Legislative Assembly had voted for war with Austria one month earlier on 20 April and, as Wordsworth's letter indicates, events had promptly turned against France. The army was ill-prepared, inexperienced, poorly disciplined, and its intention to strike a swift blow against the Austrians on the northern frontier led to disaster. Two columns of soldiers under the command of Duke Biron and General Théobold Dillon turned and retreated at first sight of the enemy on 29 April. Dillon returned to Lille, and was murdered there by his own soldiers.[16] News of these developments reached Paris in two days, and the 'ignominious flight' was

---

[16] See Lefebvre, i. 228–9, for this disaster. Wordsworth's dismay was shared by Helen Williams: 'the murder of Dillon and the prisoners was a stain which nothing could efface—Its unhappy effects were not confined to Paris; it was a blow given to the cause of liberty in every country' (*Letters from France* (2nd edn; London, 1796), 39).

reported in the *Moniteur* on 2 May—a little over two weeks before Wordsworth wrote his own account for Mathews:

This barbaric mutiny is a dreadful violation of the rights of man. It will encourage a wretched opinion of France throughout Europe just when we stand at the threshold of war, and especially so among those who might otherwise have been well disposed towards us. It will demoralise our officers, and lead to the complete breakdown of military discipline. What an opportunity for the aristocrats to slander patriot citizens and the army! They won't trouble to hide their smiles at this turn of events! (*Moniteur*, xii. 272)

Wordsworth's letter to Mathews echoes this gloomy summary of defeat and mutiny, but remains confident that the Revolution will endure present opposition:

It is almost evident the patriot army, however numerous, will be unable [to] withstand the superior discipline of their enemies. But suppose that the German army is at the gates of Paris, what will be the consequence? It will be impossible to make any material alteration in the constitution, impossible to reinstate the clergy in its antient guilty splendor, impossible to give an existence to the *noblesse* similar to that it before enjoyed, impossible to add much to the authority of the King: Yet there are in France some [millions?]—I speak without exaggeration—who expect that this will take place. (*E Y*, p. 78)

This passage shows Wordsworth as emergent patriot, with the salons of Orléans already well behind him. In December 1791 he had been surprised to discover opposition to the Revolution; five months later he reveals a knowledge of recent revolutionary history, and predicts the long-term consequences of French defeat in terms that suggest the direction in which his political sympathies were developing. Like the *Moniteur*, he sees the inexperience and indiscipline of the patriot army as a serious weakness. While he now recognizes the forces of reaction that threaten the country, however, he emphasizes the impossibility of a counterrevolution. Paine had already pointed out in *The Rights of Man* that 'There does not exist in the compass of language, an arrangement of words to express so much as the means of effecting a counter-revolution' (*R M* i. 141), but Wordsworth's awareness now strikes deeper than rhetoric, being rooted in his own experiences at Blois and his response to the war in particular.

The opening months of war in Europe demonstrated the Revolution at work as a popular movement. In January 1792 *Les*

Amis debated the relative merits of Brissot's policy of war as a crusade against counter-revolution, and Robespierre's opposing view that war would encourage the very reaction which the Girondists sought to crush. On 15 January the citizens of Blois listened to a reading of Brissot's speech 'on the necessity of war', and showed their support with loud applause (*P V*, p. 104). Thereafter, meetings were given over to discussion of and practical preparations for the conflict. On 2 March they demanded a list of citizens who had not volunteered for 'la garde nationnal'; on 14 March soldiers of the Bassigny regiment were invited to 'assist at meetings' (*P V*, pp. 124, 127). Volunteers paraded before the society, revolutionary hymns were sung, and patriotic speeches 'sur le danger de la patrie' drew enthusiastic applause and encouraged more recruits to come forward. The noisy, emotional scenes at these meetings are vividly recorded in the minutes for 5 August:

A woman from the charitable society placed two confiscated crowns upon the desk. She then made her way to the tribune where she gave the following speech, a second reading of which was voted.

'Courageous young soldiers, selfless defenders of *la patrie*, you look as if you are competing with each other for the glory of being first to arrive at the frontier! Your patriotism compels tyrants to tremble, and confounds traitors! Courage brave volunteers! . . . Go and beat down the tyrants, teach them that they are Caesars and you are Brutuses! You will return victorious!'

'All of France will honour you! Old men, women, children, all of whose hopes rest upon your weapons, your valour and loyalty. Think of the joy with which we will greet you, parade these civic crowns before you, and hail you as defenders of liberty!'

'Brave, beloved soldiers of France, you fight for an oppressed nation! That alone will give you all strength to subdue tyranny, and you will come back as conquerors!' (*P V*, p. 159; my italics)

In *The Prelude*, Book Nine, Wordsworth recalls that proceedings such as these, witnessed 'day by day', had convinced him that the Revolution was 'a cause | Good' (ix. 289–90). The roads at that time 'Were crowded with the bravest youth of France', he writes,

> And all the promptest of her spirits, linked
> In gallant soldiership, and posting on
> To meet the war upon her frontier-bounds.
> Yet at this very moment do tears start

> Into mine eyes—I do not say I weep,
> I wept not then, but tears have dimmed my sight—
> In memory of the farewells of that time,
> Domestic severings, female fortitude
> At dearest separation, patriot love
> And self-devotion, and terrestrial hope
> Encouraged with a martyr's confidence.
>
> (ix. 269–80)

These 'promptest spirits' are the revolutionary counters to the embittered and defeated royalists with whom Wordsworth had formerly 'consorted', their 'patriot love | And self-devotion' contrasting with the self-consuming jealousy of those others 'quite mastered by the times'. Book Nine presents Wordsworth's identification with 'the bravest youth of France' as a first moment of emotional commitment to their cause:

> Even files of strangers merely, seen but once
> And for a moment, men from far, with sound
> Of music, martial tunes, and banners spread,
> Entering the city, here and there a face
> Or person singled out among the rest
> Yet still a stranger, and beloved as such—
> Even by these passing spectacles my heart
> Was oftentimes uplifted . . .
>
> (ix. 281–8)

Such stirring sights settled Wordsworth's allegiance to the Revolution as a democratic cause, and hardened his attitude to its opponents as 'lost, abandoned, selfish, proud', perversely aligned against 'equity and truth' (ix. 291–3). The ranks of volunteers had given the Revolution a human manifestation, but in a peculiarly significant form: the 'martial tunes, and banners spread' of an army prepared for war. Book Nine of *The Prelude* is the fullest celebration of military heroism and power in Wordsworth's poetry, although this aspect of the poem and of his experience at Blois has passed almost unnoticed. The 'farewells of that time' were not merely 'passing spectacles' but a permanent bond of feeling with the past, a memorial of Wordsworth's own parting from Annette,

> Domestic severings, female fortitude
> At dearest separation
>
> (ix. 277–8)

—and a reminder of his own devoted thoughts of a service comparable to that of his friend Beaupuy. Before he too left for the 'frontier-bounds' in July 1792, Beaupuy gave Wordsworth's military patriotism a distinct political identity: republicanism.

Philosophic warriors, and a hunger-bitten girl

Michel-Arnaud Bacharetie de Beaupuy was born in 1755, and was therefore 37 when Wordsworth met him in 1792. His family belonged among the aristocracy of Périgord, he had enjoyed a privileged childhood, and had been educated in the liberal tradition of the French enlightenment: the family apparently possessed 'an immense library' dominated by the *Encyclopédie*. Following the example of four elder brothers, Beaupuy entered the army in 1771, transferring two years later to the 32nd Bassigny regiment. Promotion was slow and when garrisoned at Blois in 1791 he had only reached the rank of captain. After this his bravery and revolutionary zeal—and the vacancies left by emigrating officers—contributed to his swift rise to Général in January 1795.[17]

Following Beaupuy's death on 18 October 1796 his obituary in the *Moniteur* recalled him as the personification of 'l'esprit religieux de la Révolution'. He had been involved in revolutionary politics since 1789, when he represented the *Sénéchausée du Périgord* in delivering their *cahier des doléances* to the Electoral Assembly. The document he read to the Assembly criticized the greed and corruption of the royal court, but did not call for abolition of the monarchy:

'First of all we wish to emphasise that the enormous deficit caused by ministerial greed and profligacy can only lead to the ruin of France, and it will not be in our interest to prevent that. Let this be a salutary reminder! Kings must learn that the willing hearts of their subjects supply sounder resources than the plots and conspiracies of ministers.'[18]

Complaints of this nature were common in the *cahiers* of 1789, but so too were protestations of loyalty to Louis. Beaupuy's

---

[17] See Georges Bussière and Émile Legouis, *Le Général Michel Beaupuy* (Paris and Périgueux, 1891), 1–16, for Beaupuy's family background (cited hereafter as *Beaupuy*]. For his army career, *Dictionnaire de Biographie Francaise* (13 vols publ.; Paris, 1929–75).

[18] *Beaupuy*, p. 18. For Beaupuy's obituary, see *Moniteur*, xxix. 168, and *Beaupuy*, p. 173.

education and participation in the early stages of the Revolution align him with other first-generation revolutionary leaders concerned for peaceful constitutional reform. His obituary in the Moniteur described him as '"le Nestor et l'Achille de notre armée"', an elder father of the Revolution who presumably would have welcomed the limited monarchy established by the Constitution of September 1791. Eighteen months later, though, Beaupuy's journal reveals him as an outspoken republican.[19]

Between 1789 and 1793 Beaupuy's political opinions developed with the changing course of the Revolution. Wordsworth must have met him shortly after, say, February 1792, and they had parted by 27 July when Beaupuy's regiment left for the Rhine frontier. Their friendship therefore flourished at the period when the Revolution was becoming more overtly hostile to the monarchy. Tom Wedgwood was in Paris briefly during July, and wrote to his father that he was lodging 'in the same house with young Watt', whom he described as 'a furious democrat—detests the King and Fayette'. Wedgwood mentions the uneasy, suspicious mood of the city and his friend's idea of its likely outcome: 'Watt says that a new revolution must inevitably take place, and that it will in all probability be fatal to the King, Fayette, and some hundred others. The 14th of this month will probably be eventful. He means to join the French army in case of any civil rupture.'[20] Watt never fulfilled his intention to join the patriot army, but Wedgwood's letter makes Wordsworth's similar thoughts of service seem much less extraordinary, particularly when considered in the light of events at Blois.

There, Les Amis were becoming markedly critical of the King. On 25 June the Legislative Assembly heard a petition from Les Amis recommending '"Il est temps que vous le déclariez déchu d'un trône"' (Moniteur, xii. 762); on 2 August a citizen addressed Les Amis 'on the dangers threatening the country' and 'demanded the removal of the King' (P V, p. 158). The increasingly military and republican character of the Revolution in 1792 was embodied for Wordsworth in Michel Beaupuy. This is the key to understanding his influence upon Wordsworth as a mediator of

---

[19] Beaupuy's journal dates from the period after his departure from Blois, and is reproduced in Beaupuy, pp. 55–87.

[20] R. B. Litchfield, Tom Wedgwood: The First Photographer (London, 1903), 25–6.

the contemporary revolution in 1792, and which in turn gives substance to Wordsworth's aspiration to model himself after Beaupuy as

> one whom circumstance
> Hath called upon to embody his deep sense
> In action . . .

(P. ix. 407–9)

The portrait of Beaupuy in *The Prelude*, Book Nine is for the most part a literary idealization. 'A meeker man | Than this lived never', Wordsworth writes,

> Meek, though enthusiastic to the height
> Of highest expectation. Injuries
> Made *him* more gracious, and his nature then
> Did breathe its sweetness out most sensibly . . .

(ix. 298–303)

Wordsworth has Chaucer's Knight in mind, as he is described in the 'General Prologue' to *The Canterbury Tales*:

> And though that he were worthy, he was wys,
> And of his port as meeke as is a mayde.
> He nevere yet no vileynye ne sayde
> In al his lyf unto no maner wight.
> He was a verray, parfit gentil knyght.

(ll. 68–72)

As Beaupuy's disciple in Book Nine, Wordsworth also finds his own appropriate counterpart in the Knight's squire,

> A lovyere and a lusty bacheler . . .
> Of twenty yeer of age he was, I gesse.

(ll. 80–2)

Chaucer presented his Knight as a paragon of 'chivalrie', and Wordsworth recalls Beaupuy as a model patriot among royalists, 'thence rejected by the rest' (ix. 296). Beaupuy's actual circumstances had been more comfortable, and 'Nos frères du 32 régiment' appear frequently in the minutes of *Les Amis* as participating members of the society. Nevertheless, the parallels between Beaupuy and Chaucer's Knight can be taken a little further. The Knight, Chaucer says, 'foughten for oure feith at Tramyssene', and Beaupuy was similarly bound to the poor

> As by some tie invisible, oaths professed
> To a religious order

(ix. 312–13)

—finally leaving Blois to sacrifice his life in battle for that cause: 'He perished fighting', as Wordsworth has it in Book Nine, 'For liberty, against deluded men' (ix. 431–3).[21]

In *The Prelude*, Book Ten, Wordsworth says that he might have followed Beaupuy in making 'a common cause | With some who perished' (x. 194–5), and his recollection of their discussions in Book Nine identifies their possible joint endeavour in a revolutionary crusade, a 'philosophic war | Led by philosophers' (ix. 423–4). 'Oft in solitude | With him did I discourse', Wordsworth recalls,

> about the end
> Of civil government, and its wisest forms,
> Of ancient prejudice and chartered rights,
> Allegiance, faith, and laws by time matured,
> Custom and habit, novelty and change,
> Of self-respect, and virtue in the few
> For patrimonial honour set apart,
> And ignorance in the labouring multitude.

(ix. 328–36)

This is all very generalized, and rather closer to the controversy between Burke and Paine—'Custom and habit, novelty and change'—than to the issues confronting France in 1792. As with Wordsworth's reading of the 'master pamphlets of the day', his discussions of political theory with Beaupuy lacked the 'vital interest' which would engage his emotions. Their encounter with a 'hunger-bitten girl', however, was an instance when Beaupuy's political creed meshed with Wordsworth's personal response to suffering and realized their objectives as 'philosophic warriors' with the force of sudden revelation. 'And when we chanced', Wordsworth writes in Book Nine,

---

[21] Wordsworth believed that Beaupuy died in the Vendée during 1793, although he actually survived another three years and was killed at Emmendingen in Oct. 1796. I offered a source for Wordsworth's mistake in a misleading report in the *Moniteur* (27 Dec. 1793). See my note 'Wordsworth's Account of Beaupuy's Death', *N&Q* (Sept. 1985), 337.

One day to meet a hunger-bitten girl
Who crept along fitting her languid self
Unto a heifer's motion—by a cord
Tied to her arm, and picking thus from the lane
Its sustenance, while the girl with her two hands
Was busy knitting in a heartless mood
Of solitude—and at the sight my friend
In agitation said, ' 'Tis against that
Which we are fighting', I with him believed
Devoutly that a spirit was abroad
Which would not be withstood, that poverty,
At least like this, would in a little time
Be found no more . . .

(ix. 511–24)

Such sights must have been common in and around Blois during 1792. The high price of flour and grain in the area actually led to riots at the nearby village of St Dyé in March, and Beaupuy's regiment was called out to quell the unrest by force.[22] On a superficial level this passage suggests that Beaupuy used local poverty to objectify his political aims, which no doubt he did, and that Wordsworth responded to his humanitarian compassion. The moment is complicated, though, for being written in an imaginative idiom such that it almost becomes a spot of time. Their 'chance' meeting with the girl recalls Wordsworth's unforeseen encounter with the discharged soldier at 'a sudden turning of the road'. Her hopeless subordination to the animal, 'waiting, as it were, body and soul devoted to the poor beast', is established in the syntactic turn by which the heifer displaces the girl as subject of the poetry.[23] This 'brings home the cruelty of the situation' as Jonathan Wordsworth says, but her passive suffering has an inward register in her abstracted state of mind,

busy knitting in a heartless mood
Of solitude

[22] 'In March 1792 the inhabitants of the villages of d'Onzain, Saint-Dyé and Muides hijacked a consignment of grain; the ensuing punishment of the villagers at St. Dyé, by the Bassigny regiment, resulted in bloodshed.' See *Mémoires de la Societé des Sciences et des Lettres De la Ville de Blois, 1834–5* (Blois, 1836), 268.

[23] For a comparable encounter with a woman and cow, see Dorothy Wordsworth's 'Recollections of a Tour Made in Scotland' (1803): 'It is indeed a melancholy thing to see a full-grown woman thus waiting, as it were, body and soul devoted to the poor beast; yet even this is better than working in a manufactory the day through' (*Journals of Dorothy Wordsworth*, ed. E. de Selincourt (2 vols; London, 1952), i. 218).

—and this once again reminds one of the soldier's desolate
solitude in Book Four. The kinship of girl and soldier becomes
overt in Wordsworth's revisions to both passages in the 1850
Prelude:

> the girl with pallid hands
> Was busy knitting . . .

> (*1850* ix. 514–15)

> Long were his arms, pallid his hands; his mouth
> Looked ghastly . . .

> (*1850* iv. 394–5)

In the 1805 poem their identity is implied but not made quite so
explicit, for just where one might establish the girl's ghostly
existence by substituting a few lines from Wordsworth's earliest
description of the soldier,

> the girl with her two hands
> Was busy knitting in a heartless mood
> Of solitude . . . *Her face was turn'd*
> *Towards the road, yet not as if she sought*
> *For any living thing. She appeared*
> *Forlorn and desolate, a girl cut off*
> *From all her kind, and more than half detached*
> *From her own nature*[24]

—Beaupuy directs Wordsworth's imaginative identification with
the girl into political idealism,

> —and at the sight my friend
> In agitation said, ' 'Tis against that
> Which we are fighting' . . .

In doing so, the girl loses her supernatural incipience to the
Revolution, while Wordsworth's political faith attains the power
and unanswerable logic of visionary insight:

> I with him believed
> Devoutly that a spirit was abroad
> Which could not be withstood, that poverty,
> At least like this, would in a little time
> Be found no more, that we should see the earth

---

[24] Passage from 'The Discharged Soldier', ll. 55–60 of the early text, ed. B.
Darlington, *BWS*, p. 434, changing the soldier's sex.

Unthwarted in her wish to recompense
The industrious, and the lowly child of toil,
All institutes for ever blotted out
That legalized exclusion, empty pomp
Abolished, sensual state and cruel power,
Whether by edict of the one or few—
And finally, as sum and crown of all,
Should see the people having a strong hand
In making their own laws, whence better days
To all mankind.

(ix. 520–34)

Wordsworth's recreation of his encounter with the hunger-
bitten girl is a perplexed spot of time that—perhaps unexpectedly
—finds a sublime counterpart in his memory of crossing the Alps
in Book Six, for in each case disappointed vision yields a compensating insight. In Book Nine the displaced imagination is manifest
as the 'spirit' of revolution; in Book Six, though, it finds no
correspondent home and issues as a usurping power which
Wordsworth acknowledges as the glory of his own soul (vi.
525–32). Retrospectively these two passages from *The Prelude*
identify imagination as the faculty which mediates the revolutionary motive to change and progress in 1792—'whence better
days | To all mankind'—and the visionary power Wordsworth
had come to recognize in 1804. Common to both is an aspiration
to redeemed life,

Effort, and expectation, and desire,
And something evermore about to be

(vi. 541–2)

—and Wordsworth concludes his hymn to imagination in Book
Six with a metaphorical allusion to the patriot army of 1792,
acknowledging its formative revolutionary impulse but discarding the mundane paraphernalia of politics:

The mind beneath such banners militant
Thinks not of spoils or trophies, nor of aught
That may attest its prowess, blest in thoughts
That are their own perfection and reward—. . .

(vi. 543–6)

In retrospect Wordsworth's 'men from far, with sound | Of
music, martial tunes, and banners spread' appear as emblems of

the self-sufficient power of the individual mind and, specifically, the imagination. With hindsight, too, Beaupuy's crusading purpose 'of benediction to the world' emerges as a further pattern for Wordsworth's intentions as editor of the *Philanthropist* during 1794, in which Godwinian theories of progress superseded revolution as the means to social amelioration; 'let the field be open and unencumbered, and truth must be victorious' (*E Y*, p. 125). Likewise, Wordsworth's realization of the inefficiency of *Political Justice* to that end was ultimately compensated by Coleridge's influence in 1797, and their mutual translation of regenerative possibility in mind and nature—the One Life which provided the original philosophic basis of *The Recluse*.

In that poem as still anticipated at the close of *The Prelude*, Book Thirteen, Coleridge and Wordsworth were to be 'joint labourers' in a work for man's 'redemption, surely yet to come' (xiii. 439–41). Joint labourers, that is, in the work to which Beaupuy was devoted when he met Wordsworth at Blois thirteen years earlier, and in pursuit of which Wordsworth too might have died,

> A poet only to myself, to men
> Useless, and even, belovèd friend, a soul
> To thee unknown.
>
> (x. 199–201)

Writing in 1804 Wordsworth presents Beaupuy as Coleridge's predecessor, a philosophic guide expounding his 'creed | Of zeal' with enthusiasm and self-devotion. The contrast with Coleridge's continuing failure to supply the philosophic hard core of *The Recluse* must have seemed sadly ironic, and it underlines the anxiety of Wordsworth's requests for his 'notes for the Recluse' (*E Y* p. 452) throughout this year. As anticipated by Coleridge, though, *The Recluse* was a poem which Wordsworth was uniquely unqualified to write. This was because the principle of Wordsworth's lasting commitment to the 'philosophic war' for man's redemption had never found an enduring justification in any single political or philosophic system. Looking back, his allegiance to republicanism, *Political Justice*, and even the idea of One Life could be seen to have usurped the promptings of personal vision as a means of access to redeemed existence—the invisible world that lies just beyond the point at which Beaupuy

wakened Wordsworth from his reverie, with a reminder of
political objectives:

> that poverty,
> At least like this, would in a little time
> Be found no more . . .

'A holy train | Or blest procession': Wordsworth, John Oswald, Henri Grégoire

> Such conversation under Attic shades
> Did Dion hold with Plato, ripened thus
> For a deliverer's glorious task, and such
> He, on that ministry already bound,
> Held with Eudemus and Timonides,
> Surrounded by adventurers in arms,
> When those two vessels with their daring freight
> For the Sicilian tyrant's overthrow
> Sailed from Zacynthus . . .
>
> (*P.* ix. 415–23)

Drawing on Plutarch's *Life of Dion*, Wordsworth makes a veiled
reference to the object and nature of the 'philosophic war' that he
had discussed with Beaupuy. As Wordsworth's revolutionary
mentor, Beaupuy finds his counterpart in Plato while Wordsworth—'ripened thus'—assumes Dion's role as liberator. The
implications of this are curious. In Book Nine, Beaupuy is (mistakenly) reported to have died 'Upon the borders of the unhappy
Loire', suppressing rebellion in the Vendée (ix. 431–2). The
parallel with Dion suggests that Wordsworth's own task lay
overseas, implicitly in a crusade to liberate Britain. If this was
what Wordsworth had in mind in 1792, the nature of his scheme
is best appreciated by substituting Wordsworth's ministry for
Dion's in his poem of 1816:

> Five thousand warriors—O the rapturous day!
> Each crowned with flowers, and armed with spear and shield,
> Or ruder weapon which their course might yield,
> To *London* advance in bright array.
> Who leads them on?—The anxious people see
> Long-exiled *William* marching at their head,
> He also crowned with flowers of *France*,
> And in a white, far-beaming, corslet clad!

Pure transport undisturbed by doubt or fear
The gazers feel; and, rushing to the plain,
Salute those strangers as a holy train
Or blest procession (to the Immortals dear)
That brought their precious liberty again.

(*P W* ii. 273–4, ll. 18–30)

At first sight this may appear ludicrous, but it is in fact a telling approximation to Wordsworth's idea of revolution in the second half of 1792. The revolutionary war against Britain—which the *Prelude* parallel with *Dion* implies—should not be lightly dismissed. David Erdman has drawn attention to Wordsworth's possible acquaintance with the anglo-Jacobin, John Oswald, who in Autumn 1792 was proposing a cross-channel attack from France to liberate the citizens of London:

You have named the proper enemy, King George. But you won't find him on the battlefields of Europe; you won't find him in the South Seas. Just reach across the channel and seize him by the throat! All that's needed is a stout military body to land in the Thames and spark the zeal of the London sans culottes, who are miserable and hate their tyrant.[25]

When Wordsworth returned to Paris late in 1792, news of an imminent British revolution was in the air. The frequent addresses from British radical clubs to the National Convention at this time appeared to promise its likelihood, and doubtless encouraged John Oswald's hopes of inciting 'the London sans culottes' to rebellion. Wordsworth could not have missed these exciting rumours and reports, and the disparity between his expectations at Paris and the reality he discovered in London would have dismayed him even before Britain entered the war against France. That event in turn was rendered all the more bitter because after mid-1792 Wordsworth had been thinking of the Revolution as a millenarian campaign for the liberation of Europe, and then the world. The reappearance of the patriot army at Blois as 'a holy train | Or blest procession' in *Dion* is wholly appropriate to Wordsworth's original conception of their purpose some twenty-four years earlier.

Up until 1792 Wordsworth had apparently not responded to the Revolution as a millennial epoch, although dissenters in Britain

---

[25] John Oswald, quoted in Erdman, 'not Napoleon', p. 94.

certainly had done. 'What an eventful period is this!' Richard Price exclaimed to the Revolution Society in November 1789: 'I am thankful that I have lived to it; and I could almost say, *Lord now lettest thou thy servant depart in peace, for mine eyes have seen thy salvation.*'[26] Two years later Joseph Priestley anticipated 'the Prospect of the general Enlargement of Liberty' as 'the happy state of things, distinctly and repeatedly foretold in many prophecies, delivered more than two thousand years ago'. As a necessarian and rational dissenter, for whom reason was 'the umpire in all disputes', Priestley welcomed the Revolution as 'a liberating of all the powers of man' that promised the future establishment of 'Truth' and 'universal peace' on earth.[27] As a believer in revealed religion, he could simultaneously interpret ultimate revelation as the consummation 'repeatedly foretold' in the scriptures. Priestley's millenarian idea of the Revolution was justified by his religion, his philosophic thinking, his liberal politics, and to a great extent this holistic certainty was his major intellectual legacy to Coleridge. After 1794 Coleridge's principal effort in his lectures and poetry was to discover a comparable unity of religion, philosophy, and politics, but by way of demonstrating the certainty of Priestley's 'happy state of things' in a 'blest future' yet to come.

That process of deferral, coupled with a renewed philosophic basis for hope, was sustained by Coleridge and Wordsworth in their scheme for *The Recluse* as a millenarian poem. However, superficial agreement on this plan in spring 1798 concealed differences in their respective approaches to it. Wordsworth's millenarian idea of revolution in 1792 has a direct link with his later response to Godwin, the *Philanthropist* project, and his own grandiose proposals for *The Recluse*. But Wordsworth's millenarianism, unlike Coleridge's, did not reflect the philosophic and religious concerns of rational dissenters nor did he share their belief in divine revelation. It was initially the product of personal experience and involvement at Blois, immediate and vulnerable rather than the lasting intellectual possibility it remained for Coleridge. This explains why, in later years, Wordsworth was

[26] Price, *Discourse*, p. 49.
[27] Joseph Priestley, *Letters to the Right Honourable Edmund Burke, Occasioned by his Reflections on the Revolution in France* (Birmingham, 1791), pp. 141, 143, 146.

drawn successively by the optimistic philosophy of *Political Justice*, and by Coleridge's apparent confidence as prophet of the millennium in 'Religious Musings'. Each bolstered the fundamental insecurity of Wordsworth's millenarianism. His reliance upon Coleridge for completion of *The Recluse* was, therefore, much more than a sad reminder of days at Alfoxden when that collaboration had seemed possible. Wordsworth's dependence upon Coleridge and the poem's millenarian purpose were inseparably involved, a memorial to his earlier experiences at Blois and, especially, to Michel Beaupuy and Henri Grégoire.

Grégoire had been elected Constitutional Bishop of Blois in February 1791, and served in the Constituent Assembly at Paris until it was dissolved the following September. He then came back to Blois where he became president of *Les Amis* two months later. On 21 September 1792 Grégoire returned to the central revolutionary government as delegate for Loire-et-Cher at the first sitting of the National Convention.[28] That same day he moved for the Convention to 'abolish the monarchy' and rejected a counter-proposal for discussion of the matter: 'What is the point of talk', he said,

when the whole world is in agreement anyway? Morally speaking, kings have always been a grotesque freak. The history of monarchy has been the martyrdom of entire nations; the tyrant's court has always been a playground for criminals, a slaughterhouse to which his own people are brought. Since we are all convinced that this is the case, why bother with further discussion? (*Moniteur*, xiv. 8)

Grégoire's motion was put to the vote without debate, and adopted with applause. Next day the *Moniteur* reported, '*La Convention nationale décrète que la royauté est abolie en France*' (*Moniteur*, xiv. 8). On 15 November Grégoire delivered another vehemently anti-monarchist speech, and the same day was voted President of the Convention.

Grégoire was, therefore, the immediate catalyst of the French Republic. Not only was he at Blois and taking a leading part in *Les Amis* while Wordsworth was in the city, he had already returned to Paris when Wordsworth passed through on his way home to England. Wordsworth's proximity to—and perhaps his

---

[28] For Grégoire, see W. Gibson, *Grégoire and the French Revolution* (London, 1932), and R. Necheles, *The Abbé Grégoire, 1787–1831* (Westport, Conn., 1971).

personal acquaintance with—the author of the French Republic explains his admiring reference to Grégoire as 'a man of philosophy and humanity' in his *Letter to the Bishop of Llandaff*. In his pamphlet, Wordsworth draws on Grégoire's speech of 15 November to justify Louis's execution. 'A bishop', he writes, ironically comparing Grégoire with the reactionary Richard Watson,

A man of philosophy and humanity as distinguished as your Lordship, declared at the opening of the national convention, and twenty-five millions of men were convinced of the truth of the assertion, that there was not a citizen on the tenth of august who, if he could have dragged before the eyes of Louis the corse of one of his murdered brothers, might not have exclaimed to him, Tyran, voilà ton ouvrage. (*Pr. W.* i. 32)

In the speech to which Wordsworth refers, Grégoire had actually identified those 'murdered brothers' as members of the patriot armies fighting against the royalists of Europe. 'Let me remind you of all those martyrs to the cause of Liberty,' Grégoire told the Convention, 'all those victims who have fallen over the last three years.—Is there a parent, or a friend of one of our dear brothers who sacrificed his life on the frontier, or on the *journée* of 10 August, who would not drag his corpse to the feet of Louis XVI and exclaim: Voilà ton ouvrage!' (*Moniteur*, xiv. 492).

As 'a man of philosophy and humanity', Grégoire appears to have had a striking influence upon Wordsworth during 1792, most probably after Beaupuy had left Blois in July. Beaupuy had successfully brought Wordsworth over to the cause; his sense of purpose and self-devotion had inspired Wordsworth's own patriotism, and his military calling shaped Wordsworth's idea of 'philosophic war' as a revolutionary crusade that might, ultimately, liberate Britain. Grégoire complemented Beaupuy's influence, and it was not an accident that Wordsworth recalled the passage in his speech concerning battles on the French frontiers. More specifically, Grégoire elaborated Beaupuy's revolutionary militarism on a universal and apocalyptic scale, and in doing so he provided a source for the millenarian claims of Wordsworth's poetry from 'Descriptive Sketches' onwards.

On 14 July 1792, *Fédération* day, Grégoire addressed *Les Amis*. This was two weeks before Beaupuy left Blois, and presumably by this time Wordsworth regarded himself as a patriot. The

Fédération would now have appeared significant to him as the anniversary of the Revolution, and also of the day he had first set foot in France in 1790. Wordsworth was most likely among *Les Amis* on this day, but even if he was not he could have read Grégoire's speech afterwards because *Les Amis* voted that it should be published. 'Mankind', Grégoire began, 'is burdened with chains, compelled to labour, to beg, to die for those few others who jeer at their misery but are protected by the laws of the land . . .'[29] He condemned monarchs for the suffering caused by their wars, such that the châteaux around Blois—'Romorantin, Vendôme, Blois & Chambou'—were still red with the blood of their victims. In contrast, the patriot armies were now fighting for 'la liberté de l'univers', and he foresaw the Revolution regenerating Europe and then the whole world:

The present augurs well for the future. Soon we shall witness the liberation of all humankind. Everything confirms that the coming revolution will set all of Europe free, and prove a consolation for the whole human race. Liberty has been fettered to thrones for far too long! She will burst those irons and chains and as she extends her influence beyond our horizons, will inaugurate the federation of all mankind![30]

Appropriately for 14 July, Grégoire's 'revolution prochaine' was a world-wide *Fédération* for which the patriot armies were fighting at that moment on the borders of France. Wordsworth anticipates a similar prospect in his revolutionary hymn at the conclusion of 'Descriptive Sketches', where 'Fire and Sword' purify the world of tyranny and oppression:

> Lo! from th'innocuous flames, a lovely birth!
> With it's own Virtues springs another earth:
> Nature, as in her prime, her virgin reign
> Begins, and Love and Truth compose her train . . .

(ll. 782–5)

By autumn 1792, when he was working on 'Descriptive Sketches', Wordsworth was certainly familiar with Paine's idea of Revolution as 'a renovation of the natural order of things' (*R M* i. 166), and probably also with his prophecy that 'the present generation will appear to the future as the Adam of a new world'

---

[29] *Discours sur la Fédération du 14 Juillet 1792, par M. Grégoire* (Orléans, 1792), 3 [cited hereafter as *Discours*].
[30] *Discours*, p. 11.

(*RM* ii. 290). The crucial point, though, is that Wordsworth's millenarianism dates from the second half of 1792, and evidence in 'Descriptive Sketches' and *A Letter to the Bishop of Llandaff* points to Grégoire's visionary republicanism as its immediate source. Up to that moment, Beaupuy and *Les Amis* ensured that Wordsworth's developing patriotism was republican in character, before the imprisonment of the royal family on 10 August. Grégoire's influential presence at Blois and his decisive role in establishing the republic in September would have provided a continuity in Wordsworth's experience, such that the declaration on 21 September appeared as the inevitable fulfilment of Grégoire's prophecies two months before. At just this time, too, news of the patriot victory at Valmy would have seemed to bring a European *Fédération* within the bounds of possibility. The coincidence of these two events is the 'lovely birth' celebrated by Wordsworth in 'Descriptive Sketches', and for the moment his optimism allowed him to view massacres at Paris and Orléans as 'a convulsion from which is to spring a fairer order of things' (*Pr. W.* i. 34). The grounds of doubt, however, had been sown.

'To Paris I returned': September–December, 1792

The state, as if to stamp the final seal
On her security, and to the world
Shew what she was, a high and fearless soul—
Or rather in a spirit of thanks to those
Who had stirred up her slackening faculties
To a new transition—had assumed with joy
The body and the venerable name
Of a republic. Lamentable crimes,
'Tis true, had gone before this hour—the work
Of massacre, in which the senseless sword
Was prayed to as a judge—but these were past,
Earth free from them for ever (as was thought),
Ephemeral monsters, to be seen but once,
Things that could only shew themselves and die.
    This was the time in which, enflamed with hope,
To Paris I returned.

(*P.* x. 24–39)

In *The Prelude*, Book Ten, Wordsworth's journey back to Paris is recalled as a triumphant return, 'a little month' after France's

'new transition' to a republic and the passing horror of the
September Massacres. He was certainly at Paris in time to hear
Grégoire denounce Louis to the convention on 15 November, but
since leaving Blois in September he had spent the intervening time
at Orléans. It was here that he heard how Grégoire 'stirred up' the
Convention on 21 September, and would have joined in celebrat-
ing the republic. But in Orléans, too, he witnessed 'the work | Of
massacre' at first hand and this, perhaps, was one 'mournful
calendar of true history' that was to haunt him when he visited the
scenes of the massacres at Paris (x. 69). Wordsworth's return to
Paris, 'enflamed with hope' should be seen against an erosion of
the more stable confidence he had shared with Beaupuy, when
'doubt [was] not' (ix. 411). The 'slackening faculties' of revolutionary government, 'lamentable crimes', and Wordsworth's
parenthetic hindsight 'as was thought' all combine to register an
emergent context of uncertainty. The first tremor of doubt, even
as France assumed the name of a republic, came with the news of
killings in Paris and violent riots at Orléans. These events provided much of the imagery in the closing lines of 'Descriptive
Sketches', which were composed during Wordsworth's second
stay at Orléans during September and October 1792.

  'I roam'd where Loiret's waters glide', Wordsworth writes
towards the end of 'Descriptive Sketches', 'Thro' rustling aspins
heard from side to side', and then—somewhat incongruously
—breaks off his lyrical description of the riverside at Orléans and
concludes his poem with a prophecy of revolutionary victory to
come:

> Liberty shall soon, indignant, raise
> Red on his hills his beacon's comet blaze;
> Bid from on high his lonely cannon sound,
> And on ten thousand hearths his shout rebound;
> His larum-bell from village-tow'r to tow'r
> Swing on th'astounded ear it's dull undying roar . . .
>
> (ll. 774–9)

Wordsworth's couplets work effectively in this declamatory climax of the poem, but their assertive movement is complicated by
certain details of imagery. The 'larum-bell', for instance, is not
pealing for victory but tolling out a warning; it is the tocsin
calling villagers to arms. Similarly, the 'indignant' vauntings of

'Liberty' appear in a context of civil dissent and strife, the sound of cannon echoing 'on ten thousand hearths'. Wordsworth's anthem to liberty is undercut by its own imagery, and points to a new complexity in his response to the Revolution after September 1792.

On 21 September the citizens of Orléans celebrated the recent successes of the army, and three days later 'l'établissement de la république française' was commemorated with a large procession and a bonfire. A member of the National Convention, Manuel, arrived and delivered a speech inviting 'all citizens to study and to observe the laws of the republic, and to cultivate the true virtues and spirit of republicanism'—sentiments which were welcomed by his audience.[31] However, these celebrations were overshadowed by very recent scenes of violence at Orléans, and Manuel had good reason to stress the importance of 'des lois républicains' in his speech.

On 30 August 1792 the citizens of Orléans demonstrated against the high price of bread. Further unrest came two weeks later, when a flour merchant was killed after he had insulted a crowd that gathered to watch his wagons unload. The mob then turned on other merchants, burning and looting their houses and killing thirteen people before the authorities acted to impose a curfew on 17 September: 'the *red flag* was raised, the members of three corps and a detachment of the garde nationale were called out, some on foot, some with horses, and with *two cannons*. They took up position in different quarters of the city and proclaimed *martial law*.'[32] The closing lines of 'Descriptive Sketches' were evidently drawn from Wordsworth's own experience of this unrest in the city: '[W]ar's discordant habits [gleam] thro' the trees', he writes, 'And the red banner mock[s] the sullen breeze' (ll. 746–7). But his intention in the poem was to sublimate these disconcerting events as the birth-pangs of the new republic,

[31] Bimbenet, v. 1225.
[32] Bimbenet, v. 1219. George Monro, the British spy at Paris, reported on 22 and 23 Sept. that 'Orléans is in an absolute state of civil war; the sections had suspended the Municipality, and they refused to comply with this suspension, and defended themselves in a house with cannon. A deputation of the National Convention have been sent.' See *The Despatches of Earl Gower*, ed. O. Browning (Cambridge, 1885), 225.

Yet, yet rejoice, tho' Pride's perverted ire
Rouze Hell's own aid, and wrap thy hills in fire.
Lo! from th'innocuous flames, a lovely birth!

(ll. 780–2)

—a vision that was symbolically enacted on 24 September when three members of the Convention arrived from Paris, removed the 'red banner' of martial law and substituted a pike decorated with a cap of liberty and tricolour ribbons.[33] However, Wordsworth had yet to come to terms with the more sinister massacres that had taken place at Paris between 2 and 6 September. It was the shadow of these 'lamentable crimes' that confronted him on his return to the capital in late October or early November.

James Watt, Junior, witnessed the massacres and on 5 September he wrote to his father:

I am filled with involuntary horror at the scenes which pass before me and wish they could have been avoided, *but at the same time I allow the absolute necessity of them.* In some instances the vengeance of the people has been savage and inhuman. They have dragged the dead naked body of the Princess de Lamballe through the streets & treated it with all sorts of indignities. Her head stuck upon a Pike was carried through Paris and shown to the King & Queen, who are in hourly expectation of the same fate.[34]

Wordsworth's immediate response to revolutionary violence in September 1792 very likely coincided with Watt's. Like Watt he would have been horrified at news of the massacres but he also seems to have been prepared to accept their 'necessity', and allow the end to justify the means. In *A Letter to the Bishop of Llandaff*, Wordsworth excuses the recent killings as 'a convulsion from which is to spring a fairer order of things', echoing his earlier sublimation of riot as 'th'innocuous flames' from which 'springs another earth' in 'Descriptive Sketches' (*Pr. W.* i. 34). But Wordsworth's experience differed importantly from Watt's in that he never saw the September Massacres at first hand. After his return to Paris he visited the scenes of the killings, and his subsequent brooding on their significance gave this moment the power of a spot of time when recreated in *The Prelude*, Book Ten:

This was the time in which, enflamed with hope,
To Paris I returned. Again I ranged,

[33] Bimbenet, v. 1223.
[34] Robinson, *CHJ*, p. 353.

More eagerly than I had done before,
Through the wide city, and in progress passed
The prison where the unhappy monarch lay,
Associate with his children and his wife
In bondage, and the palace, lately stormed
With roar of cannon and a numerous host.
I crossed—a black and empty area then—
The square of the Carousel, few weeks back
Heaped up with dead and dying, upon these
And other sights looking as doth a man
Upon a volume whose contents he knows
Are memorable but from him locked up,
Being written in a tongue he cannot read,
So that he questions the mute leaves with pain,
And half upbraids their silence. But that night
When on my bed I lay, I was most moved
And felt most deeply in what world I was;
My room was high and lonely, near the roof
Of a large mansion or hotel, a spot
That would have pleased me in more quiet times—
Nor was it wholly without pleasure then.
With unextinguished taper I kept watch,
Reading at intervals. The fear gone by
Pressed on me almost like a fear to come.
I thought of those September massacres,
Divided from me by a little month,
And felt and touched them, a substantial dread
(The rest was conjured up from tragic fictions,
And mournful calendars of true history,
Remembrances and dim admonishments):
'The horse is taught his manage, and the wind
Of heaven wheels round and treads in his own steps;
Year follows year, the tide returns again,
Day follows day, all things have second birth;
The earthquake is not satisfied at once'—
And in such way I wrought upon myself,
Until I seemed to hear a voice that cried
To the whole city, 'Sleep no more!' To this
Add comments of a calmer mind—from which
I could not gather full security—
But at the best it seemed a place of fear,
Unfit for the repose of night,
Defenceless as a wood where tigers roam.

(x. 38–82)

In October 1792 Wordsworth's hopes apparently faltered and then turned to fear as, alone in his room, he imagined 'those September massacres' until they assumed the frightening physical presence of 'a substantial dread'. That fear is the emotional charge which gave this moment its enduring power; as relived in *The Prelude*, though, it betrays a deeper sense of his own complicity in the killings as a patriot himself. His 'substantial dread' is the imagination's fearful manifestation of guilt, rather like the 'huge and mighty forms that do not live | Like living men' which troubled his childish dreams after stealing the boat on Ullswater. Moreover, that repressed guilt is the link connecting 'the fear gone by' and his proleptic assumption of responsibility for 'a fear [that was still] to come', the execution of Louis in January 1793. Unable or unwilling to confront his own conscience, it is projected in the voice he seems to hear crying '"Sleep no more!"' as Macbeth had done after assassinating Duncan (II. ii. 35).

On his return to Paris Wordsworth was certainly horrified at what had been done in the name of the Revolution. It is quite possible, too, that at this moment he would have seen the 'black' remains of the funeral pyres in the 'square of the Carousel' as substantial auguries of Louis's future fate, soon to be debated by the National Convention. But in Book Ten his transposition of 'fear gone by' on to the execution yet to come was made with the subsequent knowledge that these events marked the threshold of Robespierre's attempt to save the Revolution by means of terrorism. It was also nurtured by association with a formative trauma involving death and self-reproach: the loss of his father. The movement from 'enflamed' expectation to guilty self-implication in Book Ten is essentially the sequence of the spot in the *Two-part Prelude*, which recalls how the schoolboy's 'anxiety of hope' succeeded by his father's death led to a sense of 'chastisement' for bringing the sorrowful event about (*1799*, i. 353–7). As Wordsworth recalls this early loss, the child's bewildered self-blame is projected on to the 'indisputable shapes' of mist advancing over the landscape like the 'questionable shape' of Hamlet's father's ghost come to seek vengeance for his murder (I. iv. 43).[35]

In December 1783 Wordsworth had followed his father's body 'to the grave' (*1799*, i. 353). Nine years later, there was no

---

[35] See *BV*, p. 63, for a detailed discussion of Shakespeare's presence in this passage.

corresponding evidence of the deaths at Paris, the square appearing as 'a black and empty area then | . . . few weeks back | Heaped up with dead and dying' (x. 46–8). Into this awful vacancy press those figures of 'substantial dread' and also, perhaps, that childhood memory which came back upon him in 'remembrances and dim admonishments'. Significantly, at this point in Book Ten Wordsworth again alludes to *Hamlet*, in the 'little month' dividing him from the massacres as it does Hamlet from his father's death—'So excellent a king that was' (I. ii. 139, 147). In this particular speech, though, Hamlet has not as yet confronted old Hamlet's ghost; his self-reproach is fed not by frustrated vengeance but by his inability to prevent the march of events as his mother remarries—'But break, my heart, for I must hold my tongue' (I. ii. 159).

As Wordsworth recreates his feelings in that 'high and lonely room', the *Hamlet* echo amplifies the dim sense of *déjà vu* related to his childhood experience and articulates it with the immediate violence of massacre and regicide to create a recurring pattern of death and contingent guilt. It also defines Wordsworth's responsibility for revolutionary violence in his failure, so far, to act or speak out against it.

> An insignificant stranger and obscure,
> . . . and little graced with powers
> Of eloquence even in my native speech . . .
>
> (x. 130–2)

When 'wrought upon' imaginatively, this sense of powerlessness before an ineluctable repetition of fear 'gone by' in a fear 'to come' issues in a terrifying vision of cyclical violence:

> 'The horse is taught his manage, and the wind
> Of heaven wheels round and treads in his own steps;
> Year follows year, the tide returns again,
> Day follows day, all things have second birth;
> The earthquake is not satisfied at once'—
>
> (x. 70–4)

By externalizing his imaginative perception of pattern and return so that it becomes the nature of 'all things [to] have second birth', Wordsworth also sublimates his own complex sense of responsibility for the Revolution's deterioration into violence and terrorism. Later on in Book Ten Robespierre's execution appears as the ultimate confirmation of the destructive cycle, now the manifestation of 'eternal justice' and 'vengeance',

> 'Come now, ye golden times',
> Said I, forth-breaking on those open sands
> A hymn of triumph, 'as the morning comes
> Out of the bosom of the night, come ye.
> Thus far our trust is verified . . .'
>
> (x. 541–5)

His 'hymn', and the immediate setting on Leven Sands at low tide, call back the apocalyptic vision earlier in the book—' "the tide returns again, | Day follows day" '—and present the execution of Robespierre as a triumphant consummation. But in doing so, Wordsworth's joy at Robespierre's downfall is shown to lie not wholly in avenging the Terror, but also in fulfilling his own wish to have countered the violence as a man of decisive action in Paris late in 1792.

'Betimes next morning', Wordsworth continues after recalling his wakeful night of fear,

> to the Palace-walk
> Of Orleans I repaired, and entering there
> Was greeted, among divers other notes,
> By voices of the hawkers in the crowd
> Bawling, *Denunciation of the crimes
> Of Maximilian Robespierre.*
>
> (x. 83–8)

Louvet denounced Robespierre to the Convention on 29 October, accusing him of 'slandering the most committed patriots' by implicating them in 'the shocking days of the first week in September'. He claimed that Robespierre was fostering his own 'personality cult', presenting himself as 'the only virtuous man in France, the saviour of the people', and concluded his speech by accusing Robespierre of having 'évidemment marché au suprême pouvoir' (*Moniteur*, xiv. 344). Wordsworth's reconstruction of Louvet's 'charge' is deliberately placed after his terrifying reverie of 'a fear to come', by way of validating his claim that at this moment in 1792 he had 'in some sort' realized

That liberty, and life, and death, would soon
To the remotest corners of the land
Lie in the arbitrement of those who ruled
The capital city; what was struggled for,
And by what combatants victory must be won;
The indecision on their part whose aim
Seemed best, and the straightforward path of those
Who in attack or in defence alike
Were strong through their impiety—. . .

(x. 108–16)

Writing with hindsight Wordsworth presents the period of his return to Paris as a crucial turning-point in the Revolution, at which it might have been possible to ensure peaceful change rather than the terrorism that followed in 1793–4. At the time, of course, these long-term consequences of the 'struggle' for leadership of the Revolution would not have been apparent, but the immediate issue preoccupying the Convention in November–December 1792 certainly was. The debate about the fate of the 'unhappy monarch' highlighted the different tactics of the 'combatants' at Paris, as the 'indecisive' Gironde lost momentum to the 'straightforward path' advocated by Robespierre and his followers. The Jacobins sought immediate condemnation and execution of Louis, while the Gironde were concerned with the legality of proceedings and constitutional problems of bringing the former king to the bar. The argument forced delegates at the Convention to explain their political positions clearly, and Wordsworth most likely responded by taking stock of his own allegiance as well. The debate must also have convinced him that Louis's death was inevitable, and that Robespierre's ruthlessness would ultimately bring him to 'supreme power'.

On 13 November Saint-Just put the Jacobin position to the Convention by claiming Louis must be judged 'as an enemy' of France and as a 'tyrant'. 'For myself', he said, 'I can see no mean: this man must reign or die.'[36] On 3 December, shortly before Wordsworth left Paris, Robespierre took the same uncompromising stand: 'If Louis is acquitted, where then is the revolution? If Louis is innocent, all defenders of liberty are slanderers.' He

---

[36] M. Walzer, *Regicide and Revolution: Speeches at the Trial of Louis XVI*, trans. M. Rothstein (Cambridge, 1974), 121, 123 [cited hereafter as Walzer].

concluded his speech by contradicting his earlier plea for abolition of the death penalty in France: 'Louis must die because the
nation must live', he said; 'I ask that the National Convention
declare him, from this moment on, a traitor to the French nation,
a criminal toward humanity.'[37]

Robespierre and Saint-Just inevitably made more moderate
speakers appear to be defending the monarchy, and in comparison the legal and constitutional concerns of the Girondins would
certainly have appeared as 'indecision', but it was with them that
Wordsworth apparently sympathized as the 'best' hope for the
Revolution. Their position was clearly if pedantically explained
by Condorcet in a pamphlet circulated in Paris late in November.
A trial, he felt, was essential, for Louis had conspired 'against the
general safety of the state'. 'France has been betrayed', Condorcet
said, 'and it has the right to discover how far and by whom. May
such knowledge not be necessary to its safety and influence the
precautions it must take for its defense? Therefore, France has the
right to prosecute and judge Louis XVI, even if he enjoys absolute
inviolability.' At this point, though, a problem arose in that Louis
could not be tried by the Convention, which would 'be at once
legislator, accuser, and judge', and therefore 'violate the first
principles of jurisprudence'. Condorcet's solution was to propose
a 'tribunal' with a 'special jury . . . chosen by all the departments',
to ensure Louis an 'impartial trial' before the whole nation.[38]

When the Convention voted to execute Louis on 16–17
January 1793, a number of leading Girondins supported the
death penalty, vindicating Wordsworth's sense of their
indecisiveness. After the execution Wordsworth was to justify
Louis's death by claiming that he had occupied 'that monstrous
situation which rendered him unaccountable before a human
tribunal' (*Pr. W.* i. 32). In doing so, he was using Condorcet's
insistence upon constitutional form to excuse the policy of the
Jacobins, reconciling the divided arguments he had heard and
read at Paris in November 1792. At that time he was 'greatly
agitated' by the sectarian struggle for power, and had 'grieved' at
recent events. 'Yet did I grieve', he recalls in *The Prelude*, Book
Ten,

---

[37] Walzer, pp. 131, 138.
[38] For Condorcet, see Walzer, pp. 147, 150, 154.

> nor only grieved, but thought
> Of opposition and of remedies:
> An insignificant stranger and obscure,
> Mean as I was, and little graced with powers
> Of eloquence even in my native speech,
> And all unfit for tumult and intrigue,
> Yet would I willingly have taken up
> A service at this time for cause so great,
> However dangerous.

(x. 128–36)

'A service at *this* time', because looking back Wordsworth could see that the argument about Louis marked a transfer of initiative from the Gironde to Robespierre and his followers, who would later direct the Terror through the Committee of Public Safety established in April 1793. Rather than the military calling he had contemplated earlier at Blois, Wordsworth's idea of 'service' in Paris was as a decisive speaker in the National Convention— a more persuasive orator than Louvet, Gorsas, Condorcet and others had proved. Though 'little graced with powers | Of eloquence', he says,

> Inly I revolved
> How much the destiny of man had still
> Hung upon single persons

(x. 136–8)

—and in the 1850 *Prelude* adds,

> Nor did the inexperience of my youth
> Preclude conviction, that a spirit strong
> In hope, and trained to noble aspirations,
> A spirit thoroughly faithful to itself,
> Is for Society's unreasoning herd
> A domineering instinct, serves at once
> For way and guide . . .

(1850, x. 164–70)

Wordsworth's claim that 'the destiny of man had still | Hung upon single persons' represents a significant alteration in his idea of the Revolution late in 1792. It registers a depreciation of his former enthusiasm for revolutionary democracy, and anticipates his radical identity of 1793–5 which would look to the guidance of the 'single person', the 'sage' as the best hope for mankind. *Les Amis* and the patriot volunteers at Blois had impressed him as the popular manifestation of 'a cause | Good'; Beaupuy and Grégoire together offered the possibility of active commitment, and a millenarian optimism for the future. From November 1792 on Wordsworth apparently concentrated all these hopes and aspirations in his belief

> that the virtue of one paramount mind
> Would have abashed those impious crests, have quelled
> Outrage and bloody power
>
> (x. 179–81)

—and achieved a peaceful destiny for France. As he saw French democracy and republicanism overtaken by terror during the next year his confidence in revolutionary action grew weaker, and in 'A Night on Salisbury Plain' Wordsworth offers 'the labours of the sage' as an alternative means to achieve 'happiness and virtue' (Gill, p. 37, ll. 510–12). The poem qualifies his former admiration for

> one whom circumstance
> Hath called upon to embody his deep sense
> In action

—and substitutes the sage's 'gentle words' of philosophy as a guard against the 'self-consuming rage' of political violence. Between 1793 and 1795 Wordsworth was to find his sage in William Godwin, whose *Political Justice* offered the certainty of progress and perfectibility while repudiating any recourse to action in achieving that end. 'Man', said Godwin, 'is in reality a passive, and not an active being' (*PJ* i. 310). In this way, violence in France coupled with Wordsworth's vexed hopes of an active career as soldier, journalist, delegate, set his bearings towards Godwin as a new 'way and guide', the immediate successor to Beaupuy and Grégoire.

'Reluctantly to England', December 1792

By identifying with the Gironde in November 1792 Wordsworth must have hoped to see Louis removed by constitutional and legal means, not summary execution. Tom Paine had been in Paris since September, and he too sought to avoid Louis's death by proposing—somewhat oddly—that he be banished to America as 'the best, the most politic measure, that can be adopted'.[39] Late in 1792 Paine was the most prominent among a large group of expatriate radicals resident in Paris whose activities were centred upon White's Hotel—possibly the 'large mansion or hotel' in which Wordsworth stayed at this time. Some of them were known to Wordsworth, and they provide an important link between his weeks in the revolutionary capital and his return to London in December 1792.

On 6 November the patriot army built upon its success at Valmy with a further victory at the battle of Jemappes. Two weeks afterwards, on 19 November, the National Convention voted its Edict of Fraternity in which they promised 'help to all nations that wished to recover their liberty' (*Moniteur*, xiv. 517). For Wordsworth both of these developments would have been encouraging as a further fulfilment of Grégoire's 'coming revolution [which] will set all of Europe free'. Contemporary reports from London suggested that a British revolution was imminent too, just as Wordsworth was preparing for his journey back across the channel.

On 18 November 1792 the radicals at White's Hotel celebrated French successes with a dinner at which they toasted 'the French Republic . . . the French armies . . . the National Convention', as well as 'the coming Convention of England and Ireland; the union of France, Great Britain and Belgium, and may neighbouring nations join in the same sentiments'. They drew up an address to the National Convention, in which they congratulated France on 'fulfilling its great destinies', and looked forward to

a close union between the French republic and the English, Scotch, and Irish nations, a union which cannot fail to ensure entire Europe the enjoyment of the rights of man and establish on the firmest bases universal peace. We are not the only men animated by these sentiments. We doubt not that they would be also manifested by the great majority of our countrymen if public opinion were consulted, as it ought to be, in a national convention.[40]

Although Wordsworth's name is not included in the fifty signatures to this address, fifty more guests were also present at

[39] Thomas Paine, *Reasons for Wishing to Preserve the Life of Louis Capet, As Delivered to the National Convention* (London, 1793), 15–16.
[40] Alger, pp. 325–8, gives details of the White's Hotel dinner and petition.

White's Hotel on 18 November but did not sign. Wordsworth could well have been among them, and James Losh—who was also at Paris late in 1792—may have been there too. Both were acquainted with some who did sign the address: John Tweddell's brother Francis was first on the list; John Oswald was there and so was Losh's friend Dr William Maxwell. Wordsworth would certainly have approved their hopes for a 'close union' between France and Britain, and when the address was read out to the Convention on 28 November it was Henri Grégoire who, as president, replied on behalf of the French government. He anticipated the reconciliation of France with Britain, Scotland, and Ireland in 'two republics', and concluded to loud applause by telling the 'esteemed republicans' of White's Hotel that their 'celebration of the achievements of the French Revolution is the forerunner of future festivities in all countries' (*Moniteur*, xiv. 593).

The White's Hotel address echoes the sentiments of other petitions sent to the Convention in 1792 from radical societies in Britain. As Grégoire's reply shows, these addresses fostered the idea of an imminent British revolution, and further encouraged French hopes of liberating Europe. On 28 November the address from White's Hotel was immediately followed by a deputation from the SCI in London, delivered by the lawyer John Frost and Paine's friend Joel Barlow. 'After the example given by France,' Barlow said, 'future revolutions will be easy. It would not be extraordinary if, in a little while, congratulations were to arrive to a National Convention of England.' Barlow went on to read the SCI's address which claimed to express 'the opinions of the majority of the English nation' in celebrating the 'sacred cause' of the French Revolution. As a gesture of practical goodwill, he concluded, the SCI had sent a thousand pairs of shoes to be given 'aux soldats de la liberté' (*Moniteur*, xiv. 593–4). After prolonged applause, Grégoire once again replied: 'The spirits of Pym, of Hampden, and of Sidney hover above your heads', he said, 'and without doubt, the moment is at hand when the French Nation will send its own congratulations to the National Convention of Great Britain' (*Moniteur*, xiv. 594).[41]

---

[41] Goodwin, pp. 507–12, gives a detailed 'List of addresses from English reform societies to the French National Convention (November, December 1792)'.

In spite of Grégoire's optimism, Joel Barlow's speech and the radicals' petitions did not correspond to the political reality in Britain late in 1792. At this time the British government was responding with alarm to rumours of insurrection and incipient revolution in London. The army were called out, parliament was recalled for an extraordinary meeting on 13 December, and five days later Paine was tried in absence for seditious libel in *The Rights of Man, Part II*. He was found guilty and outlawed. In Paris, though, Wordsworth most likely shared the hopes of other expatriate radicals and joined Grégoire in looking forward to a future alliance between France and Britain. He must have felt himself at the hub of European politics, the very centre of contemporary affairs and revolutionary progress. Military successes and reports from London apparently confirmed all that he had seen and heard in recent months. The one event he would not have expected was Britain's alliance with the royalist coalition against France after February 1793. The excitement of Paris, and the promise of a British Convention provide the immediate background to his feeling of shock and betrayal when war became the reality he had to confront shortly after coming home in December 1792.

3

'Mr. Frend's Company'

Cambridge, Dissent, and Coleridge

Cambridge and dissent

> From the heart
> Of London, and from cloisters there, thou cam'st,
> And didst sit down in temperance and peace,
> A rigorous student. What a stormy course
> Then followed—
>
> (*P*. vi. 288–92)

Coleridge came up to Jesus College from the cloisters of Christ's Hospital in October 1791, and started his academic career with studious commitment:

I read Classics till I go to bed . . . If I were to read on as I do now—there is not the least doubt, that I should be Classical Medallist, and a very high Wrangler—but *Freshmen* always *begin* very *furiously*. I am reading Pindar, and composing Greek verse, like a mad dog. I am very fond of Greek verse, and shall try hard for the Brown's Prize ode. (*C L* i. 16–17)

The 'Greek verse' to which Coleridge refers was his Ode 'On the wretched lot of the Slaves in the Isles of Western India', for which he won the Browne Gold Medal in 1792.[1] Unlike Wordsworth at this time Coleridge had 'fastened on' slavery as a significant liberal issue, and his prize-winning poem foreshadows his *Lecture on the Slave Trade* of June 1795 which was subsequently published in the fourth number of the *Watchman*. Like Felix Vaughan, who left Jesus in 1790, Coleridge was also responsive to the political disadvantages of dissenters. On 24 January 1792 he wrote to his brother George, 'Mr. Frend's company is by no means invidious. On the contrary . . . Tho' I am not an *Alderman*, I have yet *prudence* enough to *respect* that *gluttony of Faith* waggishly yclept Orthodoxy.' (*CL* i. 20).

George had evidently heard about Frend's unitarianism and warned his brother to beware of him. He knew that if Coleridge were influenced by Frend to the extent that he refused to subscribe to the Thirty-nine Articles, he would forfeit his degree and the chance of a college fellowship. Hence Coleridge's waggish declaration of his 'orthodoxy'. As it turned out Coleridge did not sustain the studious promise of his first year at Cambridge, and he left Jesus in December 1794 without sitting his final examinations. The question of subscription on taking his degree did not arise. But George's worries about 'Mr. Frend's company' were confirmed in Coleridge's emergence as a unitarian, and by the course of his political career after leaving Cambridge. Frend's influence upon Coleridge, in turn, was conditioned by dissenters at Jesus College and in Cambridge town in the years leading up to the French Revolution. It is to this background that one must look for a fuller understanding of Coleridge's radical identity during the 1790s.

In the two decades before the fall of the Bastille, and in the period immediately following 1789, religious dissenters from Cambridge were closely connected with the movement for parliamentary reform in London. This involvement developed in two stages, the first of which appears in the formation of the Constitutional Society in April 1780, in which Cambridge men played an important part. The second period of influence is to be found in the sizeable Cambridge contingent among London radical circles and leading members of the Corresponding Society after 1792. The source of this Cambridge connection with metropolitan radicalism can be traced to a small but active group of dissenters in town and university back in the 1770s, and to one college in particular: Jesus.

During the 1770s and 1780s many dissenters and reformists were associated with Jesus College: among them were William Frend, Gilbert Wakefield, Robert Robinson, Felix Vaughan, George Dyer, and—a little later—Coleridge. George Dyer celebrated Wakefield's 'ample mind' and Frend's 'gen'rous name, | Glowing with freedom's sacred flame' in his 'Ode on Peace'.[2] He reserved a whole stanza, though, in praise of the 'peaceful virtues'

---

[1] For a translation of Coleridge's Ode, see A. Morrison, 'Samuel Taylor Coleridge's Greek Prize Ode on the Slave Trade' in J. R. Watson (ed.), *An Infinite Complexity: Essays in Romanticism* (Edinburgh, 1983), 145–60.

[2] 'Ode on Peace, Written, in Part, in Jesus College Garden', in George Dyer, *Poems* (London, 1792), 17–18.

of Robert Tyrwhitt, unitarian, former fellow of Jesus College, and a constant presence at Cambridge until his death in 1817.

In a footnote to his 'Ode on Peace' Dyer recollected that Tyrwhitt 'was the first who endeavoured to restore religious liberty to the University of Cambridge'.[3] In 1771–2 he had collaborated with John Jebb of Peterhouse in petitioning the university senate for annual examinations and removal of subscription at graduation. His first petition was submitted in June 1771. It failed, as did a second on 6 December. Further attempts were made by Jebb on 8 May 1772, three on the following 12 May, one on 15 December 1773, another on 11 May 1774, and his last in 1775. All were rejected without explanation or outvoted, but Dyer mentions that the proposals for examination reform caused a 'great ferment' at Cambridge and were 'supported by some of the most learned members of the University, and countenanced by the Chancellor'.[4] All was not lost, for failure at Cambridge was to have a beneficial effect on the campaign for parliamentary reform in London.

The petitions at Cambridge in the early 1770s were complemented by applications to the House of Commons for repeal of the Test Acts. In April 1771 Jebb travelled to London, and in July he attended the first meeting of the Feathers Tavern Committee which had been elected to raise a petition to parliament. Jebb composed the *Circular Letter* which formed the petition, but when presented to the Commons on 6 February 1772 it was ordered to lie on the table without discussion. In 1775 he resigned his Church of England living, 'fully satisfied . . . that the almighty author of the universe is, in the strictest sense of the expression, ONE'.[5] Undergraduates had been barred from attending his lectures on the Greek Testament since 1768 because of his unorthodox opinions, but Jebb did not leave Cambridge until 1776 when he moved permanently to London. Thereafter he was a 'constant attendant' at the Essex Street unitarian chapel and in April 1780 became 'one of the most zealous' founding members of the SCI.[6]

---

[3] Dyer, *Poems*, p. 18.

[4] George Dyer, *History of the University and Colleges of Cambridge* (2 vols; London, 1814), i. 124, 126–7.

[5] John Jebb, 'A Short State of the Reasons for a Late Resignation' in *The Works of John Jebb*, ed. J. Disney (3 vols; London, 1787), ii. 206 [cited hereafter as Jebb, *Works*].

[6] 'Memoir' in Jebb, *Works*, i. 1–227.

In Coleridge's lecture *On the Present War* Jebb appears as a prophet who had predicted William Pitt's repressive policies of 1795. 'The penetration of the great and good Dr. Jebb foresaw his Apostacy', Coleridge told his audience at Bristol '—and he is said to have been greatly agitated. "Elisha settled his countenance stedfastly on Hazael, and the Man of God wept. And Hazael said, Why weepeth my Lord? And he answered, because I know the evil that thou wilt do!"' (*Lects. 1795*, p. 65). In 1782 Pitt had proposed an enquiry into parliamentary representation, but two years later he had deserted the cause of reform. Coleridge's source for Jebb's prophecy appears in his *Letter to the Secretary to the Society for Constitutional Information*, 20 July 1784: 'Heaven grant the constitution may meet with friends of a very different spirit', Jebb had written there, 'or, english liberties will soon become an empty name!'[7] His *Letter* was reprinted in Jebb's *Works*, edited by John Disney and published in 1787, one year after Jebb's death. Coleridge was evidently familiar with Jebb's writings, and would also have heard about 'the great and good Dr. Jebb' from Frend and Dyer, from Wakefield who had been Jebb's student, and from his original colleagues and friend at Jesus, Robert Tyrwhitt.

Whereas Jebb left Cambridge for London, Tyrwhitt stayed on at Jesus College. In 1777 he resigned his fellowship, 'conceiving that it bound him to attendance upon the established service of the church in the college-chapel, which he could not conscientiously comply with'.[8] But he never left the college, as Frend would later be forced to do, and continued there as 'an unobtrusive Unitarian'. 'Mr T dined in the common hall & retired with the rest to the Combination room', Frend recalled in 1835, 'but in no case did he ever bring forward his particular religious opinions. He never went to Chapel or to any church except St Marys where the liturgy is not used & he preached there when it came to his turn. Two of his sermons are printed & in them his Unitarian sentiments are not disguised.'[9] Dyer claimed that Tyrwhitt's name was 'justly revered in the university, and never to be mentioned by the friends of liberty but in terms of

[7] Jebb, *Works*, iii. 381.
[8] Theophilus Lindsey, *An Historical View of the State of the Unitarian Doctrine and Worship* (London, 1783), 466–7.
[9] L-B Dep. 71, fo. 206. William Frend to Lady Byron, 15 Nov. 1835.

respect'.[10] Although he was discreet, Tyrwhitt gathered a circle of friends who shared his political and religious opinions making Jesus College a sympathetic environment for dissenters at Cambridge in the 1780s. The group that met over tea in his rooms on Sunday, 8 October 1788 was to have a direct influence on Coleridge only a few years later:

Lord's day. After service Frend, Barham, Paulus, Dyer, another, and myself [Robert Robinson], drank tea with the venerable Mr. Tyrwhitt. He is the grandson of Gibson, bishop of London, and stood full in the path to preferment: but conscience forbad: he resigned all, even his fellowship, and now lives in college, as in an hotel, a tranquil life of literary labour, and universal beneficence. Here I procured an MS. which Mr. Frend had taken out of the public library for me.[11]

Tyrwhitt and Robert Robinson were senior tea drinkers; Frend and Dyer were younger disciples. Robinson had been at Cambridge as long as Tyrwhitt, but while the latter remained quietly in his college Robinson was active among dissenters and reformists in and around Cambridge. He was a self-taught man who had started life as an apprentice hairdresser in London in 1749. He had then moved to Norwich as a Methodist preacher, from where he subsequently travelled to Cambridge and settled down as the Baptist minister of St Andrew's in 1761. He knew both Tyrwhitt and Jebb during the 1770s and was 'very attentive' in supporting their graces to the university senate, as well as the Feathers Tavern petition to the Commons.[12]

In 1774 Robinson published his Arcana, or the Principles of the Late Petitioners to Parliament, 'collecting all the old arguments in his mind', as George Dyer said, 'but giving a new turn to the controversy'.[13] He emphasized that the 'practice of judging for themselves is coeval with mankind, to be traced up to the most remote antiquity', and 'gave a new turn' to the dissenters' argument by claiming that

whoever looks attentively will find that the leading principles of the petitioners, as far as they relate to the subject in question, are the allowed

[10] George Dyer, Memoirs of the Life and Writings of Robert Robinson (London, 1796), 78 [cited hereafter as Robinson Memoirs].
[11] Robinson Memoirs, p. 315.
[12] Robinson Memoirs, pp. 11–31.
[13] Robinson Memoirs, p. 80. See also G. Hughes, With Freedom Fired: The Story of Robert Robinson, Cambridge Non-Conformist (London, 1955), 46.

or professed principles of all mankind, and it will be easy from hence to infer that universal toleration, when thoroughly understood, will meet with less opposition than may at first seem from all ranks of men; all men, statesmen, merchants, churchmen, and princes above all, will find their account in it.[14]

It is a short step from allowing the 'leading principles of the petitioners' to be the 'principles of all mankind', to inferring with Tom Paine that 'universal toleration' is in fact a right of man. If 'all men . . . find their account' in judging for themselves, the judgement of all men must be allowed as equal, and not reserved to an aristocracy of 'statesmen, merchants, churchmen, and princes'. 'The right of private judgment is the very foundation of the reformation', Robinson writes elsewhere in *Arcana*, 'and without establishing the former in the fullest sense, the latter can be nothing but a faction in the state, a schism in the church'.[15]

Robinson's *Arcana* represents the political radicalism of religious dissent which was subsequently to appear particularly ominous to Edmund Burke when coupled with the dissenters' admiration for the French Revolution. During the 1780s, though, Robinson had taken practical steps to consolidate links between Cambridge dissent and parliamentary reform by founding the Cambridge Society for Constitutional Information. The object of this society, not surprisingly, 'was the same as that established in London by Dr. Jebb, Major Cartwright, Capel Lofft, and others. On the formation of the London constitutional society in April 1780, Capel Lofft sent Robinson a copy of their address, and an account of their proceedings: these served as models for the constitutional society at Cambridge.'[16] Robinson himself explained in a letter that, like its parent in London, the Cambridge society was composed of dissenters and whig freeholders from the surrounding neighbourhood:

[By] a constitutional society of freeholders, which I had the pleasure of forming amongst a few dissenters, and which is multiplied into a very large body of freeholders of liberal sentiments, a great respectability, because a great political weight, is acquired to the dissenters of both town and country. We meet once a quarter at an inn, and dine together,

---

[14] Robert Robinson, *Arcana, or the Principles of the Late Petitioners to Parliament* (Cambridge, 1774), 56, 109–10 [cited hereafter as *Arcana*].

[15] *Arcana*, p. 33.

[16] *Robinson Memoirs*, pp. 193–4.

—a part of us, I mean: and there, as the complaisance of the company often gives me the chair, I preach civil and religious liberty, and often, when tea comes, theology—not *points*, but general, and, I judge, useful truths.[17]

Besides strengthening links between Cambridge dissenters and liberals and their counterparts in London, the Cambridge Constitutional Society was also fruitful in that it fostered 'a very large body' of liberals in the vicinity of the town. In so doing, Robinson helped to establish a local readership for Benjamin Flower's influential newspaper, the *Cambridge Intelligencer*, which first appeared in July 1793 and to which Coleridge contributed. The liberal circles with which Robinson was associated in the 1770s and 1780s also attracted a young graduate from Emmanuel College: George Dyer.

During 1784 Robinson published *A Political Catechism*, which consisted of a series of political dialogues between a father and his son, George. Perhaps this is significant, for Robinson was a formative influence upon Dyer's political and religious ideas at this time. They were first acquainted in 1777 when Dyer was studying in Emmanuel College, along with William Taylor who was to be Wordsworth's schoolmaster at Hawkshead. On graduating in 1778 Dyer worked as an usher at Dedham grammar school, but he later returned to Cambridge where he lived with Robinson 'not simply as tutor to his family, but with the view of profiting by his doctrine and learned conversation'. In 1781 Dyer preached as a baptist in Oxford—'with no very happy results' —but in the following decade he moved with Robinson towards unitarianism. Joseph Priestley was convinced that Robinson was 'of the unitarian faith' when he died on a visit to Birmingham in 1790. His lasting importance for Dyer appears in his references to Robinson's works in his own pamphlets, and in the extensive *Memoirs* of Robinson published by Dyer in 1796.[18]

Two years after Robinson's death Dyer left Cambridge for London. Between 1792 and 1795 he published four political pamphlets which drew upon his Cambridge background while

---

[17] *Robinson Memoirs*, p. 194.
[18] For Dyer and Robinson, see *Robinson Memoirs*, p. 124; Dyer's obituary in *Gentleman's Magazine*, NS xv (May, 1841), 545; E. A. Payne, 'The Baptist Connections of George Dyer', *Baptist Quarterly*, x (1940–1), 265. For Priestley on Robinson, see *Robinson Memoirs*, pp. 397–8.

responding to the more radical aspirations of the Corresponding Society and Paine's *Rights of Man*. 'That there are individuals', Dyer says in the second edition of his *Inquiry into the Nature of Subscription*, 'both among the dissenters and of the establishment, who may with me approve a republican as the most complete form of government, I cannot entertain a doubt'—and he adds later, 'what short of a national convention can remedy the evil? Heaven crown the wishes of constitutional reformers with success!'[19] Dyer's estimate of British republican opinion in 1792 coincided with the optimistic addresses sent to the National Convention late in 1792, which Wordsworth had witnessed before his return to London. But by confounding the hopes of 'constitutional reformers' with the establishment of a British convention, Dyer's pamphlet would also have appeared to substantiate Burke's suspicions in his *Reflections* and encouraged the reactionary alarm that developed during the winter of 1792–3.

Eight months after the *Reflections* appeared, Priestley's house and laboratory in Birmingham had been wrecked by a 'church and king' mob. Burke contended that 'the celebration of the 14th of July, and the libels of Thomas Paine, were the causes of the riots', implicitly recognizing Priestley as a revolutionary and the disturbances as a valid form of protest. Dyer offered an alternative version of the same event when he suggested that the 'disorders . . . were promoted by men, who supposed themselves complying with the wishes of the government'.[20] Whether or not Dyer was correct, it is clear that after 1790 dissenters were faced with increasing opposition which could extend to physical violence. As revolution in France and reaction at home led Dyer, Price, Priestley, and others into political conflict, at Cambridge William Frend was brought to trial for the publication of his pamphlet *Peace and Union* in February 1793. Thinking back on his trial, Frend wondered why he had not been prosecuted when his *Thoughts on Subscription* had first appeared in 1788: 'Why was it not then done? the answer is obvious. The publick mind had not then been poisoned by proclamations: the terms jacobin,

---

[19] George Dyer, *An Inquiry into the Nature of Subscription* (2nd edn; London, 1792), pp. xxiv, 276 [cited hereafter as Dyer, *Inquiry*].
[20] For Burke on Priestley, see *Parl. Hist.* xxix. 1394. For Dyer's response, Dyer, *Inquiry*, p. 288.

republican, and leveller had not been familiarized to an english ear . . .' (Sequel, p. 5).

By 1793, as Frend says, religious dissent and political radical-ism had become synonymous, and unitarianism was readily confounded with violent revolutionary conspiracy. In this climate of opinion, the defeat of Fox's motion in the Commons on 11 May 1792 effectively discouraged hopes for repeal of the Test Acts by petition. But dissenters still had everything to gain from a reform of parliament itself, and this explains why Dyer, Frend, Vaughan, and other dissenting contemporaries were attracted to the Constitutional and Corresponding Societies in London during 1794–5.

In his pamphlet The Complaints of the Poor People of England Dyer mentions that while in London he had 'almost constantly attended' a committee 'formed of delegates from various societies'.[21] This was most probably connected with the SCI, of which Dyer was a member, but could equally well have been the Corresponding Society's central Committee of Correspondence in which he also had influential acquaintances and contacts. In either case, Dyer's involvement with metropolitan reform groups would explain his enthusiasm for 'promoting a NATIONAL FREEDOM' by

establishing book societies through the kingdom, whose sole object might be the distribution of small political pamphlets among the lower ranks of people, such as 'a political Dialogue' lately published, and printed for Mr. Johnson, St. Paul's Church Yard; The Patriot also, printed for Mr. Robinson, Paternoster Row; and cheap editions of Mr. Paine's Rights of man. Parents also, in helping forward the same design, should turn their attention to the HOPES OF THE NATION, the rising generation. The true female character also should be asserted, and the rational woman, rescued from the insolence of tyrant man, should instil into young minds the rights of man and the rights of woman. See Mr. Locke's Treatise on Education, and an elegant and judicious perform-ance, entitled, A Vindication of the Rights of Woman, part 1. ch. 2 by Mrs. Mary Wollstonecraft. Mr. Robinson's judicious Plan of Lectures on the principles of non-conformity, would well employ dissenting ministers.[22]

---

[21] George Dyer, The Complaints of the Poor People of England (2nd edn; London, 1793), 81 [cited hereafter as Dyer, Complaints].
[22] Dyer, Inquiry, pp. 356–7n.

Dyer's scheme for 'book societies' acknowledges the influence of Robinson and the activities of the SCI and its Cambridge associate during the 1780s. It also responds to the fresh impetus for political education in the London Corresponding Society, in Paine's *Rights of Man*, and in a number of other pamphlet replies to Burke. Like Dyer, when Frend arrived in London during autumn 1793 he too moved to the centre of metropolitan radical life. He met Godwin regularly, and by late 1794 he was actively involved as a leader of the Corresponding Society. In March 1795 he joined the organizing committee of the Society's fund to defray the costs of defendants acquitted in the 1794 treason trials and the expenses of individuals still held in prison. Other members of this committee included Dr William Maxwell, who in 1792 had attempted to supply the French army with English-made daggers; Gilbert Wakefield, who by now was acquainted with Coleridge; Wordsworth's friend James Losh, a member of the SCI and of the Friends of the People; and the veteran Major John Cartwright. Out of a total of sixteen members on this committee, at least eight were Cambridge men.[23]

By 1794–5, therefore, there was a very considerable Cambridge element among the leadership of the Corresponding Society, which also overlapped with Godwin's intellectual circle of friends. Coleridge first met Godwin in December 1794, and his acquaintance with Dyer and Frend suggests that while in town he was moving exceptionally close to the Constitutional and Corresponding Societies as well. Two months later Wordsworth met Godwin and Dyer at Frend's house in Buckingham Street. That Coleridge and Wordsworth should both have been among the same company within weeks during the winter of 1794–5 was due in part to Godwin's contemporary notoriety. Their near coincidence was also a result of the dominant Cambridge presence in metropolitan radical circles that had developed over the previous decades, such that they had mutual friends and contacts long before they met each other. At this moment in February

---

[23] For Frend's subscription, see *Morning Chronicle* (23 Mar. 1795). His own list of subscribers survives in CUL Add. MSS 7886/288, and among them are Sir Francis Burdett, Horne Tooke, and William Maxwell. For Maxwell, see Godwin, pp. 242–3, and Alger, pp. 345–6. Dyer remembered introducing 'Mr. C' to Wakefield in a letter of 24 May 1836 to a Mr Carey of the British Museum; the letter is now in the archives of Emmanuel College, Cambridge.

1795, however, Coleridge was reacting unfavourably to Godwin in his earliest Bristol lectures, whereas Wordsworth had been drawn to Godwin as an admirer of *Political Justice*. Intellectually, they appeared to be moving in contrary directions. In Coleridge's case, the reasons for this can be found in his experiences at Cambridge and the company of William Frend back in 1792–3.

'Mr. Frend's company'

Towards the end of his life Frend recollected his student days at Christ's College, which he entered in Michaelmas Term 1776, and the lasting memory of his 'much valued Tutor' William Paley.[24] Paley had been a fellow at Christ's since 1766 and was ordained the following year, but he nevertheless held liberal views on toleration and subscription. He sympathized with Jebb and Tyrwhitt but declined to join the Feathers Tavern petition on the grounds that he 'could not afford to keep a conscience', a policy that was rewarded when Paley became Archdeacon of Carlisle in August 1782. Frend was, at first, similarly prudent. He graduated as second wrangler, was ordained and elected to a fellowship at Jesus during 1779–80. Besides teaching mathematics and philosophy he held the livings of two parishes near Cambridge at Long Stanton and Madingley, where he established a Sunday School for the village children.

Although Frend must have known about the dissenters' petitions to the university as an undergraduate, he does not appear to have entered the controversy or to have held unorthodox beliefs. He recalled that, when first elected to his fellowship, he had viewed Robert Tyrwhitt 'with no small degree of aversion' and that their 'acquaintance was slight' until Frend's religious beliefs altered.[25] Shortly after his trial Frend said that his faith 'probably was first shaken by learning the hebrew language, and consequently by paying a greater attention to the scriptures' (*Sequel*, p. 104). By June 1787 he had 'ceased to officiate in the church of England'. He resigned his two livings later on in that year, and in 1788 published a polemical defence of his unitarianism in *An Address to the Inhabitants of Cambridge*, in which he declared

---

[24] L-B Dep. 71, fo. 201. Frend to Lady Byron, 29 Dec. 1831.
[25] L-B Dep. 71, fo. 206. Frend to Lady Byron, 15 Nov. 1831.

the trinity to be 'rank nonsense' and trinitarians 'highly criminal'.[26]

Unlike Robert Tyrwhitt, who remained unobtrusively at Jesus, Frend was active outside the college and

became a pretty constant attendant at Robinson's meeting, established a theological lecture at a private house in the town, and occasionally delivered expository discourses at Fen-Stanton, in Huntingdonshire, in a meeting room belonging to John Curwan ... an old acquaintance of Robinson's, who had lately embraced the doctrine of the unitarians.[27]

Through his friendship with Tyrwhitt and Robinson, Frend must also have met Dyer at this time and in 1788 he corrected the proofs for the first edition of Dyer's *Inquiry into the Nature of Subscription*. In addition to publishing and lecturing, Frend now entered the university debate about dissent. He contemplated submitting his own petition to the senate in 1787, and the following year published his pamphlet *Thoughts on Subscription to Religious Tests*. Frend's new willingness to participate in this controversy cost him his tutorship, like John Jebb who had been prohibited from lecturing on the Greek Testament twenty years previously. The dismissal was confirmed on 29 December 1788, so that Frend was now in the same position as Robert Tyrwhitt: forbidden to teach but permitted to reside in college as a fellow.

Soon after resigning his church livings, Frend had made his first visit to the Essex Street chapel on 30 December 1787. Here he met the most prominent unitarians of the day, among them Theophilus Lindsey and Joseph Priestley. On 31 December 1787 Lindsey wrote to one William Tayleur mentioning that Frend 'was at our chapel yesterday' and that he 'had some conversation with him afterwards'.[28] In 1788 Lindsey saw Frend's *Thoughts on Subscription* through the press, and passed a copy to Priestley. 'I like Mr. Frend's Second Address no less than his first,' Priestley told Lindsey in January 1789, 'I greatly admire his spirit and ability, and hope much from him.' Frend's knowledge of Hebrew encouraged Priestley to invite his collaboration on a new translation of

---

[26] See Frend's letter to the *Public Advertiser* (20 June 1788), and William Frend, *An Address to the Inhabitants of Cambridge* (St Ives, 1788), 5, 7.

[27] *Robinson Memoirs*, pp. 315–6.

[28] *The Letters of Theophilus Lindsey*, ed. H. McLachlan (Manchester, 1920), 126–7.

the scriptures, Frend's task being 'the historical books'.[29] He worked on this translation throughout 1790 and 1791 only to have his manuscript 'lost', as he said later, 'in the flames enlightened by the blind zeal of the church at Birmingham' (*Sequel*, p. 111).

Frend's loss in the riots of 1791 doubtless gave impetus to his strictures on mob violence in *Peace and Union*, an attitude which Coleridge also shared in his political lectures. Wordsworth mentioned the outrageous treatment of 'the philosophic Priestley' as 'a traitor or a parricide' in his *Letter* (*Pr. W.* i. 38), but the matter was to preoccupy Coleridge up to five years later when he alluded to the 'Birmingham Riots' in his *Moral and Political Lecture*, in the 'Introductory Address' to *Conciones ad populum*, in 'Religious Musings', and in his 'Essay on Fasts' in the second issue of the *Watchman* (*Lects. 1795*, pp. 10, 38; *Watchman*, p. 53). Frend would certainly have encouraged Coleridge to read Priestley during 1792 and 1793, and Priestley's high standing among Cambridge liberals and dissenters at that time appears from an inscription for an inkstand presented to him on his emigration to America in April 1794:

To JOSEPH PRIESTLEY, LL.D., &c., on his departure into exile, from a few Members of the University of Cambridge, who regret that this expression of their esteem should be occasioned by the ingratitude of their country.

Wm. Frend, James Losh, John Tweddell, Godfrey Higgins.[30]

All four signatories were to witness Wordsworth's introduction to Godwin in February 1795. More immediately, their esteem for Priestley was shared by Coleridge, who lamented his exile 'o'er the ocean swell' in a sonnet published in the *Morning Chronicle* on 11 December 1794, ten days before his own meeting with Godwin. In 'Religious Musings', which was apparently begun on Christmas Eve 1794, Priestley appears with Coleridge's other political, spiritual, and philosophic heroes as a member of the 'elect' alongside Milton, Newton, Hartley, and Franklin:

> Lo! Priestley there, Patriot, and Saint, and Sage,
> Whom that my fleshly eye hath never seen
> A childish pang of impotent regret

[29] J. T. Rutt, *The Life and Correspondence of Joseph Priestley* (2 vols; London, 1832) ii. 18, 24 [cited hereafter as *Priestley Life*].

[30] *Priestley Life*, ii. 225.

1. *The Exalted Reformer*. Joseph Priestley burned in effigy by a Church and King mob, from the *Bon Ton Magazine*, i. p. 167. A crowd feeds the flames with a portrait of Oliver Cromwell, *The Rights of Man*, Toasts, Sermons, and Priestley's translation of the Bible to which William Frend contributed a translation of the Old Testament.

Hath thrill'd my heart. Him from his native land
Statesmen blood-stain'd and Priests idolatrous
By dark lies mad'ning the blind multitude
Drove with vain hate: calm, pitying he retir'd,
And mus'd expectant on these promis'd years.

(ll. 387–94)

In May 1796 Lamb was to boast a 'transient superiority' over
Coleridge in that he had actually 'seen priestly' (Marrs, i. 12). For
Coleridge, however, Priestley's exile signified much more than
government intolerance and national ingratitude. Coming within
months of Frend's banishment from Cambridge, it constituted a
major loss of intellectual and spiritual leadership for which
Coleridge's own efforts as a lecturer during 1795 would offer
some redress in furthering the cause of progress and reform, and
countering the popularity of Godwin's godless *Political Justice*.
Priestley's departure and Godwin's atheism consequently served
to focus Coleridge's radical identity, providing a demarcation
between the formative period at Jesus College and Coleridge's
swift emergence as an active political figure in 1795. However,
the initial displacement in Coleridge's development from 'furious
freshman' to political lecturer appears in Frend's trial at Cambridge in May 1793, and it is from these proceedings that
Coleridge's debt to Frend can be traced most clearly.

The man whose company Coleridge had found 'by no means
invidious' in January 1792 was a convinced unitarian, embittered
by the loss of his tutorship which he blamed upon 'ecclesiasti-
cal tyranny' of the university. He was a close acquaintance of
Priestley, angered by the government's hostility to dissenting
opinion which only served to highlight the civil and religious
liberties gained in France after 1789. While Coleridge was en-
joying 'Mr. Frend's company' during 1792, and composing his
'Ode on the Slave Trade', the political mood of Cambridge was
following London in becoming markedly less tolerant of dissenters and reformists. On 22 June 1792 the university sent a loyal
address to the king, and during the following winter there were
riots in the town in the course of which a dissenting meeting-
house was attacked. As elsewhere throughout the country an
'Association for the Preservation of Liberty and Property against
Republicans and Levellers' was founded, and on 20 December
112 publicans declared their intention to report conversation,

pamphlets, and books 'of a treasonable or seditious tendency' to the local magistrates. On the last day of the year an effigy of Tom Paine was burnt on Market Hill. It was against this background of hostility and impending crisis that Coleridge's radicalism began to take a distinctive form.[31]

On 5 February 1793 Coleridge wrote to Mrs Evans in London enclosing 'a little work of that great and good man, Archdeacon Paley—it is entitled motives of Contentment—addressed to the poorer part of our fellow Men' (*CL* i. 48). His professed admiration for Paley echoes Frend's estimate of his own 'much valued Tutor', but the pamphlet otherwise seems an unlikely index to Coleridge's sympathies at this moment. 'Frugality itself is a pleasure', according to Paley, and a little later in his pamphlet he enquires what the 'poor man' could discover 'in the life . . . of the rich that should render him dissatisfied with his own?'[32]

As a 'compleat Necessitarian' in December 1794 Coleridge's position contradicted Paley by identifying moral character with 'the circumstances of life' (*CL* i. 137). In his *Moral and Political Lecture*, too, he was to make an identical point by way of his question, 'can we wonder that men should want humanity, who want all the circumstances of life that humanize?' (*Lects. 1795*, p. 10). Coleridge was not yet a necessitarian in February 1793, but there is little reason to suppose that he was attracted by Paley's 'motives of Contentment' other than as, perhaps, a prudent text to recommend to the mother of Mary Evans with whom he was in love.[33] This likelihood is corroborated by a letter Coleridge wrote two days later, this time to Mary herself. In it Coleridge mentions a second, different pamphlet of pressing relevance to contemporary affairs.

'Have you read Mr. Fox's letter to the Westminster Electors?' he asked Mary, 'It is quite the *political Go* at Cambridge, and has converted many souls to the Foxite Faith' (*CL* i. 51). Fox's *Letter*

---

[31] For Cambridge during 1792–3, see Gunning, i. 256–79.

[32] William Paley, *Reasons for Contentment Addressed to the Labouring Part of the British Public* (London, 1793), 11, 14.

[33] Cf. William Hazlitt's memory of Coleridge's attitude to Paley in January 1798: 'He mentioned Paley, praised the naturalness and clearness of his style, but condemned his sentiments, thought him a mere time-serving casuist, and said that "the fact of his work on Moral and Political Philosophy being made a text-book in our Universities was a disgrace to the national character."' See 'My First Acquaintance with Poets', Howe, xvii. 114.

was a follow-up to his speech in parliament on 13 December 1792, in which he had condemned the Commons' 'zealous concurrence' with the contemporary rumour

that there exists at this moment an insurrection in this kingdom. An insurrection! Where is it? Where has it reared its head? Good God! an insurrection in Great Britain! No wonder that the militia were called out, and parliament assembled in the extraordinary way in which they have been. But where is it?[34]

This alarm of insurrection in December 1792 was largely a response to the reform societies' admiring addresses to the French government, coupled with the recent Edict of Fraternity at the National Convention.[35] As Fox's speech indicates, the panic was misplaced and can also be attributed to hearsay and to misleading newspaper reports which Fox believed the government had deliberately encouraged to give grounds for a policy of repression. 'Dangers, which they considered as distant,' he alleged, 'they were not displeased that the public should suppose near, in order to excite more vigorous exertions.'[36] In his pamphlet *Letter* Fox identified the government's ulterior motive in exciting hostility towards reformists, and religious dissenters in particular:

But are there, in truth, no evils in a false alarm, besides the disgrace attending those who are concerned in propagating it? Is it nothing to destroy peace, harmony and confidence, among all ranks of citizens? Is it nothing to give a general credit and countenance to suspicions, which every man may point as his worst passions incline him? In such a state, all political animosities are inflamed. We confound the mistaken speculatist with the desperate incendiary. We extend the prejudices which we have conceived against individuals to the political party or even to the religious sect of which they are members. In this spirit a judge declared from the bench, in the last century, that poisoning was a Popish trick, and I should not be surprised if Bishops were now to preach from the pulpit that sedition is a Presbyterian or a Unitarian vice. Those who differ from us in their ideas of the constitution, in this paroxysm of alarm we consider as confederated to destroy it. Forbearance and toleration have no place in our minds; for who can tolerate opinions, which

---

[34] *Parl. Hist.* xxx. 14.

[35] See Chapter 2.

[36] C. J. Fox, *A Letter from the Right Honourable Charles James Fox to the Worthy and Independent Electors of the City and Liberty of Westminster* (London, 1793), 13–14 [cited hereafter as Fox, *Letter*].

according to what the Deluders teach, and rage and fear incline the Deluded to believe, attack our Lives, our Properties, and our Religion? This situation I thought it my duty, if possible, to avert, by promoting an inquiry.[37]

Fox's pamphlet found a ready welcome in Cambridge, which suggests that it articulated a widely felt unease about the government's domestic policies and its intentions towards France in the days just before the outbreak of war in February 1793. Wordsworth echoed Fox in his *Letter to the Bishop of Llandaff* when he enquired if 'the house of the philosophic Priestley' would have been destroyed had the people been left 'to the quiet exercise of their own judgment' (*Pr. W.* i. 37–8). The 'Deluders' to whom Fox refers are also the prototypes of Coleridge's 'Statesmen blood-stain'd and Priests idolatrous' in 'Religious Musings', whose 'dark lies' had incited the Birmingham riots of 1791. More immediately, the 'paroxysm of alarm' had ensured Paine's conviction for seditious libel at the trial conducted on 18 December 1792. Coleridge, too, would soon have first-hand evidence of repression in action, for a few days after he had recommended 'Mr. Fox's letter' to Mary Evans, William Frend became a target for the prejudice and hostility Fox had warned against in his pamphlet.

Peace and Union was published at St Ives near Cambridge on 12 or 13 February 1793. Within ten days the Master and fellows of Jesus College met and passed resolutions condemning Frend for 'prejudicing the clergy in the eyes of the laity, of degrading in the publick esteem the doctrines and rites of the established church, and of disturbing the harmony of society' (*Account*, p. x). Copies of this resolution and the offending pamphlet were sent to the Vice-Chancellor and to the Bishop of Ely, thereby starting the proceedings which led to Frend's trial the following May.

The similarities between Fox's *Letter* and Frend's *Peace and Union* in responding to a contemporary sense of crisis explain the popularity of both at Cambridge. The two pamphlets were published within days of each other, and, as the debate in the Commons on 13 December 1792 had already demonstrated, they both 'came forth at à time when the public mind was filled with the strongest apprehensions of dangerous plots against the peace

[37] Fox, *Letter*, pp. 14–15.

of the kingdom, and insurrections were supposed ready to break out in every quarter' (*Account*, pp. 85–6). In the opening paragraph of *Peace and Union*, Frend described the present state of the country and the supposed threat of violence which had prompted him to write his pamphlet:

The royal proclamations and the number of associated bodies on various pretexts in different parts of the kingdom are a sufficient proof, that the minds of men are at present greatly agitated; and that the utmost rigour of government, aided by the exertions of every lover of his country, is necessary to preserve us, from falling into all the horrours attendant on civil commotions. (*P&U*, p. 1)

Frend claimed that Britain was split into two camps, represented by the 'advocates for a republick' and defenders of the constitution (*P&U*, p. 2). The actual position, however, was rather less clearly cut. Dyer and Wordsworth were relatively outspoken in admitting their republicanism during 1792–3, and the 'associated body' of reformers in the Corresponding Society were careful to sidestep the issue of republicanism in *The Rights of Man* by calling for a peaceful reform of the parliamentary system rather than a more fundamental change in the form of government. Frend was probably closer to the actual state of affairs early in 1793 when he said

There is no subject, on which the contending parties are so much at variance, as on that of parliamentary reform. On the one hand it is asserted, that the constitution, as settled at the revolution, must remain inviolate; on the other, that corruptions of government render a reform in the representation of the people, and the duration of parliaments absolutely necessary. (*P&U*, p. 5)

This was a fair analysis of the aims of the reformists, and the objections of Edmund Burke. Frend's purpose in *Peace and Union* was to preserve the country from 'the horrours attendant on civil commotions' and, as he put it, bring 'Republicans and Anti-Republicans' together to resolve their differences peaceably. 'I resolved to address the contending parties', Frend recollected after his trial, 'with a view of bringing them together, to consult for the common good' (*Account*, p. ii). In the same spirit, Fox had sought to avoid 'rage and fear' by discussion, and an 'avowed negociation' between Britain and France to avoid the calamity of war.

Coleridge and others at Cambridge were sufficiently impressed by Fox's *Letter* to be converted to the 'Foxite Faith', and their reaction to *Peace and Union* was equally favourable. Frend was to tell Lady Byron that his pamphlet 'excited no small sensation at the time [of] the first edition'.[38] It too became the '*political Go*' and '*Frend for Ever!!!*' was chalked up on college walls.[39] If Frend had gone no further than to agree with Fox on the importance of peaceful negotiation and warn against the ill-advised policies of the government, he would probably have escaped prosecution. Frend's downfall lay in his unequivocal support for parliamentary reform, and his readiness to draw comparisons between Britain in 1793 and the recent course of the French Revolution:

From neglecting to examine and correct the abuses, prevailing through length of time in an extensive empire, we have seen a monarch hurled from his throne, the most powerful nobility in Europe driven from their castles, and the richest hierarchy expelled from their altars. Had the monarch seasonably given up some useless prerogatives, he might still have worn the crown; had the nobility consented to relinquish those feudal privileges, which were designed only for barbarous ages, they might have retained their titles; could the clergy have submitted to be citizens, they might still have been in possession of wealth and influence. The proper time to correct any abuse, and remedy any grievance, is the instant, they are known. (*P&U*, p. 43)

Frend's warning that the government should immediately reform would have appeared especially ominous in the light of his comments on the recent trial and execution of Louis XVI. 'No englishman need be alarmed at the execution of an individual at Paris', he wrote;

Louis Capet was once king of France, and entitled to the honours due to that exalted station. The supreme power in the nation declared, that France should be a republick: from that moment Louis Capet lost his titles. He was accused of enormous crimes, confined as a state prisoner, tried by the national convention, found guilty, condemned, and executed. What is there wonderful in all this? (*P&U*, p. 45)

For those who were less sympathetic to revolutionary justice the execution of Louis was a disquieting event, and Frend's support for the National Convention was deliberately provocative.

---

[38] L-B Dep. 71, fo. 114. Letter of 7 Jan. 1838.
[39] F. Knight, *University Rebel: The Life of William Frend, 1757–1841* (London, 1971), 140.

Wordsworth took a similar attitude in his *Letter to the Bishop of Llandaff*, sneering at 'the idle cry of modish lamentation' that followed Louis's death and claiming that his crimes justified his execution (*Pr. W.* i. 32). Frend's experience at Cambridge suggests that Wordsworth might have been prosecuted too, had he published his pamphlet; it may well have been news of Frend's trial which decided him against publication in spring 1793. The Vice Chancellor's statement at the conclusion of the proceedings reveals that the authorities regarded Frend's vindication of the French government as a justification for similar proceedings in London.

Frend and Wordsworth coincided in approving Louis's execution, and they both condemned British participation in the European war against France. In the second appendix to *Peace and Union* Frend described his meeting with a group of poor market women from Fen-Stanton, where he sometimes lectured. Frend says that the encounter 'made an impression on [his] mind, which all the eloquence of the houses of lords and commons cannot efface'—much as Wordsworth's meeting with the 'hunger-bitten girl' in a lane near Blois struck him as an image of injustice. 'At this moment', Frend continues, 'perhaps the decree is gone forth for war. Let others talk of glory, let others celebrate the heroes, who are to deluge the world with blood, the words of the poor market women will still resound in my ears, we are sconced three-pence in the shilling, one fourth of our labour. For what!' (*P&U*, p. 49). Frend's concern with the economic distresses of war aligns him with the mainstream of contemporary opposition, with Wordsworth in his *Letter* and Dyer in *Complaints of the Poor*. It also anticipates his commitment to the democratic aspirations of the Corresponding Society in 1794. On 1 May 1795 John Thelwall used *Peace and Union* in one of his lectures, quoting the 'very affecting circumstance' of the market women from 'the excellent pamphlet of Citizen *Frend*' as evidence of the domestic suffering caused by war.[40] Frend was genuinely horrified by the 'assassinations, murders, massacres, burning of houses, plundering of property, open violations of justice, which have marked the progress of the French revolution' (*P&U*, p. 1). Nevertheless his support for reform, his professed

[40] John Thelwall, 'Second Lecture on the Causes of the Present Dearness and Scarcity of Provisions', *Tribune*, ii. 32.

indifference to Louis's death and opposition to the war placed him at the forefront of radical opinion early in 1793, and this was sufficient to ensure his prosecution by the university.

On 4 March the Vice-Chancellor's committee decided to prosecute, but details of their decision were withheld despite Frend's enquiries. Five days afterwards Frend wrote to the *Morning Chronicle* requesting the editors to stop printing letters in his defence, which he believed encouraged 'still more the malice of [his] enemies'.[41] He consulted a lawyer, who could find no 'doctrine or opinion' in *Peace and Union* 'as could render [Frend] infamous in any legal sense' (*Account*, pp. xvi–xvii). Nevertheless, the treatment he received at Jesus College was markedly prejudiced, in that he was required to 'remove from the precincts of the college' on 4 April, some three weeks before he received a summons to the court on 24 April (*Account*, p. xx). Only three fellows voted against his expulsion—Thomas Newton, Gervase Whitehead, and William Otter—but Robert Tyrwhitt was to support Frend throughout his trial by sitting next to him in the court and offering his advice.

The proceedings began on 3 May 1793. Frend insisted that the court should comply with all forms of correct procedure, and on one occasion demanded 'that the accuser might not be permitted to speak till he had put on his proper academical habit' (*Account*, p. 7). His intention was to frustrate the trial and make his prosecutors look foolish, and a report in the *Morning Chronicle* on 28 May shows that he succeeded:

On the day of Mr. FREND's defence, the young men in the gallery occasionally expressed by their usual tokens their approbation of the defendant, and their scorn for his accusers . . . This . . . kindled vehement indignation in the Seniors. Mr. FARISH, the Proctor, called out to Dr. MILNER, 'Mr. Vice-Chancellor, I see a young man clapping his hands in the gallery.' 'I hope you know him,' quoth Mr. Vice-President, 'Yes, Sir,' said the Proctor, and hurried into the gallery to seize the supposed delinquent. As soon as he had apprehended his man, he said, 'Sir, you were clapping your hands;' to which the young gentleman replied, with a smile, 'Ah! Sir, I wish I could,' which increased the zealous Proctor's wrath, and it might have gone hard with the luckless undergraduate, if he had not shewn that his left arm was disabled . . .[42]

---

[41] *Morning Chronicle* (9 Mar. 1793). Background details about the prosecution appear in *Account*, pp. xi–xiii.

[42] *Morning Chronicle* (28 May 1793).

Frend had spoken in his own defence on 24 May, and Henry Gunning claimed that the 'delinquent' who applauded his speech and then changed places with 'the luckless undergraduate' was Coleridge (Gunning, i. 299–300). The speech lasted three hours and drew applause from the gallery, and—as the *Morning Chronicle* report indicates—particularly impressed Coleridge. The most emotive strategy of Frend's defence was to recall the initial welcome for the French Revolution at Cambridge in 1789: 'I did rejoice at the success of the french revolution', he said:

and is there an englishman, who did not exult on this occasion? At what period did I rejoice? was it not at the time when every good man rejoiced with me, when tyranny received a fatal blow, when despotism was overthrown by the united efforts of all orders of men in an extensive empire? Was it not, Sir, at the time when that horrid dungeon was destroyed, in which had been tormented so many victims of caprice and effeminate cruelty? Was it a crime, Sir, to rejoice, when the whole nation was of one mind, and this university thought it a duty to impress the sentiment on our young men, by giving them as a proper subject for their talents, the taking of the bastile? (*Account*, p. 92)

Frend was deliberately reminding the Vice-Chancellor of the time when John Tweddell had been awarded a university prize for a speech in which he hailed the 'deeds of glory' in France. In doing so he also emphasized the degree to which good men who still retained their French sympathies in 1793 were now, as Wordsworth put it in his *Letter*, subject to widespread 'odium' (*Pr. W.* i. 49). While indicating his support for France, however, he admitted that the September Massacres were 'dreadful outrages' that had disgraced a 'noble cause', and concluded his defence with the tactful observation that 'silence on french affairs, is most adviseable' (*Account*, p. 92). Later that same day he was judged guilty of transgressing the university's statute *De concionibus*, which dated from 1608. The statute specifically forbade

that any person shall, in any sermon, in drawing out any theses, in public lectures, or in any other public manner, within our university, teach, or treat of, or defend any thing against the religion, or any part of it, received and established in our kingdom by public authority. . . . Whoever shall do the contrary shall, upon the order of the Chancellor with the assent of the major part of the heads of colleges, retract and confess his error and temerity . . .[43]

[43] See B. R. Schneider, *Wordsworth's Cambridge Education* (Cambridge, 1957), 115.

When asked if he wished to retract Frend declared—no doubt to great applause from the gallery—that he 'would sooner cut off this hand than sign the paper' (*Account*, p. 176). On 30 May he was banished from the university, and after an unsuccessful appeal Frend was forced to quit Jesus College on 27 September when the gates were chained up to prevent him entering (*Account*, p. xlii).

Although the statute *De concionibus* dealt with religious matters, Henry Gunning was correct when he recalled that 'the great object in prosecuting Frend was of a political rather than of a religious character' (Gunning, i. 303). The Vice-Chancellor's closing speech to the court indicates that the university had proceeded against Frend out of the contemporary crisis of alarm which *Peace and Union* was intended to resolve:

Were not the times, when the pamphlet appeared, most critical? Did the author inculcate the necessity of peace and good order? When the national convention of france had filled up the measure of their crimes, by murdering the king, and destroying all lawful government, and their deliberations breathed nothing but atheism and anarchy, did he inculcate a respect for the king and parliament of this country, and for the reformed religion, and the functions of the clergy as established by law? In a word, was it not his plain object to teach the degraded laity, that they were sitting like brute beasts under an usurped authority. (*Account*, pp. 181–2)

The most casual reading of *Peace and Union* would have revealed that Frend had not incited the 'degraded laity' to rebellion. His intention was precisely the opposite, in that he denounced 'assassinations, murders, massacres' and hoped to prevent 'civil commotions'. The Vice-Chancellor's allusions to French 'atheism and anarchy' and to the 'brute beasts' of Britain are clear echoes of Burke's *Reflections*—'a church pillaged', 'civil and military anarchy', 'swinish multitude'—and a measure of the extent to which the recent 'paroxysm of alarm' had accelerated political reaction. His comments to the unruly 'young men in the gallery' were intended to justify the trial, but also provide a final identification of Frend as a victim of the panic and suspicion that Fox had warned against in his *Letter to the Westminster Electors*:

He would not, he said, animadvert on the noisy and tumultuous irregularities of conduct by which the proceedings on some of the former court days had been interrupted. He informed them, that their passions and affections had been founded upon some vague ideas, that the accused person had been persecuted. It was necessary to advertise them of their danger, when this country had just escaped an alarming crisis, and every attempt to punish libellous attacks on the constitution and the government was called a species of persecution, and contrary to the imprescriptible rights of man. (*Account*, p. 185)

For Coleridge, Frend's trial was first evidence of the repression that would be sustained against the democratic reform movement in years to come. Its immediate consequence at Cambridge, however, was to encourage and unite the friends of liberty in university and town. Henry Gunning said that the prosecution had been 'instituted against the prevalence of Jacobinism in the University', and that the Vice-Chancellor had boasted that he did not ' "believe Pitt was ever aware of how much consequence the expulsion of Frend was: it was the ruin of the Jacobinical party as a *University thing* "'(Gunning i. 308–9). The trial was certainly of 'consequence' in Cambridge, but it did not 'ruin' the 'Jacobins' at the university as the Vice-Chancellor was pleased to think. On the contrary the proceedings gave them a focus and a cause, and their noisy support was evident in court. As might be expected, there was a renewed demand for the controversial pamphlet and Benjamin Flower published a second edition of *Peace and Union* in July 1793. On 20 July he also published the first issue of his weekly newspaper, the *Cambridge Intelligencer*, which was to circulate throughout the Midlands and East Anglia and enjoy a success that Flower himself claimed was 'almost unparalleled in the history of provincial news papers'.[44] Flower published extracts from *Peace and Union* in the paper during 1793, not just because he had a vested interest in sales but because, as he said, Frend's 'remarks appear to us of such importance, that we shall occasionally lay them before our readers'.[45] By the end of the year, too, Frend's own *Account of the Proceedings* appeared on the Cambridge bookstalls, so that, although he had been forced to move to London, his reputation and opinions endured.

Coleridge was a regular reader of the *Cambridge Intelligencer* and Flower was to advertise and publish some of his earliest writings, among them *The Fall of Robespierre* in September

[44] *Cambridge Intelligencer* (8 Mar. 1794).
[45] *Cambridge Intelligencer* (10 Aug. 1793).

1794. But for Coleridge the year after Frend's trial until his meeting with Southey at Oxford in June 1794 was restless and unhappy. Between 2 December 1793 and 8 April 1794 he enlisted in the King's Light Dragoons as Silas Tomkyn Comberbache without, apparently, pausing to consider his possible involvement in the war with France. Why did he do so? The explanation that he offered George Coleridge was that he had incurred debts (*CL* i. 67), but financial worries were also compounded by what he termed his 'Debauchery'. Writing to George in February 1794 from his billet at Henley-on-Thames, Coleridge explained how 'a multitude of petty Embarrassments' had exhausted his funds:

So small a sum remained, that I could not mock my Tutor with it—My Agitations were delirium—I formed a Party, dashed to London at eleven o'clock at night, and for three days lived in all the tempest of Pleasure —resolved on my return—but I will not shock your religious feelings—I again returned to Cambridge—staid a week—such a week! Where Vice has not annihilated Sensibility, there is little need of a Hell! On Sunday night I packed up a few things,—went off in the mail—staid about a week in a strange way, still looking forwards with a kind of recklessness to the dernier resort of misery—An accident of a very singular kind prevented me—and led me to adopt my present situation—(*CL* i. 68)

This account of the matter is inconsistent and vague, but he was evidently recalling a period of considerable personal upset. Coleridge's 'petty Embarrassments' were only part of a deeper anguish: 'I am not, what I was:—*Disgust—I feel*, as if it had —jaundiced all my Faculties' (*CL* i. 67). Many years afterwards Coleridge described his experiences as a dragoon to William Godwin, who recorded what Coleridge had said. There is no mention of financial difficulties in Godwin's version of the episode, but Coleridge's memory of 'Vice' and thoughts of suicide apparently remained clear:

1793 wins a prize for the best Greek ode—never told his love—loose in sexual morality—spends a night in a house of ill fame, ruminating in a chair: next morning meditates suicide, walks in the park, enlists, sleeps 12 hours on the officer's bed, & upon awaking is offered his liberty, which from a scruple of honour he refuses —marched to Reading—dinnerless on Christmas day, his pocket having been picked by a comrade

1794 discharged by lord Cornwallis, after having been 4 months a
   horse-soldier—returns to Cambridge—[46]

Whatever actually happened on that night Coleridge claimed
to have spent 'ruminating in a chair', he evidently enlisted as a
dragoon at a moment of extreme distress. His debts contributed
to his unhappiness, and it seems likely that this was exacerbated
by his unrequited love for Mary Evans and self-disgust at his
encounters with prostitutes. The army was an alternative to his
thoughts of suicide, a way to lose himself and escape the stress of
his immediate past. Furthermore, this trauma of sexual revulsion
may offer a source for the lifelong uneasiness about sensual
experience that Norman Fruman has described as Coleridge's
'debilitating struggle with *le diable au corps*', one of the earliest
manifestations of which appears in Coleridge's rejection of
Political Justice as 'a Pander to Sensuality' (*CL* i. 199) and
'Principles so lax as to legalize the most impure gratifications'
(*Lects. 1795*, p. 165).[47] By indicting Godwin's philosophy as
sexually licentious—'th'imbrothell'd Atheist'—Coleridge sublimated his awareness of personal weaknesses and, in his political
and religious lectures of 1795, consolidated his own identification with christian morality and continence.

Coleridge's enlistment kept him away from Cambridge
throughout the Lent Term of 1794. On his return to Jesus he was
summoned before the Master and fellows, and sentenced to 'a
month's confinement to the precincts of the College' (*CL* i. 80).
Sometime during that month he decided to make a tour of Wales
with his acquaintance Joseph Hucks, and the two probably left
Cambridge on 15 June and arrived in Oxford two days later.
Coleridge visited his old friend from Christ's Hospital, Robert
Allen, and by 19 June Allen had introduced him to his own friend
at Oxford, Robert Southey. From that moment Coleridge's
radical career was under way.

[46] Godwin's MS biographical notes on Coleridge's life up to 1799, A-S Dep. c.
604/3.
[47] See N. Fruman, 'Coleridge's rejection of nature and the natural man' in R.
Gravil, L. Newlyn, and N. Roe (eds), *Coleridge's Imagination: Essays in Memory of
Peter Laver* (Cambridge, 1985), 69–78.

'Frendotatoi meta Frendous': Coleridge in 1794

Following Coleridge's unhappy months as a 'horse-soldier', his high-spirited letter to Southey on 6 July 1794 marks a reappearance of the former self who had cheered and clapped William Frend in the university court during May 1793:

> It is *wrong*, Southey! for a little Girl with a half-famished sickly Baby in her arms to put her head in at the window of an Inn—'Pray give me a bit of Bread and Meat'! from a Party dining on Lamb, Green Pease, & Sallad—Why?? Because it is *impertinent* & *obtrusive!*—I am a Gentleman!—and wherefore should the clamorous Voice of Woe *intrude* upon mine Ear!? (*C L* i. 83)

Coleridge's anecdote is clumsily playful, but it also serves as a reminder of Frend's despairing words at the conclusion of *Peace and Union*: 'Alas! my poor countrymen, how many years calamity awaits you before a single dish or a glass of wine will be withdrawn from the tables of opulence' (*P&U*, p. 49). In his defence speech, however, Frend was careful to appear less outspoken, and he did so by claiming that his opinion was 'the same with that of the bishop of Llandaff, . . . That the rich shall not oppress the poor, nor the poor riotously attack the rich, that they shall be all equal in our courts of judicature, these are the true principles of equality' (*Account*, pp. 90–1).

Richard Watson, bishop of Llandaff, was a fellow of Trinity College, Cambridge, and retired Professor of Divinity, so that Frend was aligning himself with a prestigious member of the university. At one time Watson had taken a progressive and liberal attitude to dissent and reform, but the publication of his *Sermon to the Stewards of the Westminster Dispensary* in January 1793 announced his unequivocal support for the establishment, and drew Wordsworth's reply in his *Letter*. Frend's invocation of Watson seems most likely to have been a bluff, and the genuine voice of his opinions is heard elsewhere in his speech where he defends his unitarianism. It was at the intersection of his religious dissent with his politics that Frend located 'the true principles of equality', and here too that one can identify his presence behind Coleridge's political and religious character. 'I have been represented as an heretick, deist, infidel, atheist,' Frend complained:

> Shall he, Sir, be esteemed an infidel, who, for the second article of his creed, grounds his hope of salvation solely on Jesus Christ? Who looks

upon his saviour as a person sent from heaven to be the means of the greatest happiness to mankind? We may boast of our knowledge of and acquaintance with god, we may confound every gainsayer on the terms of our salvation, yet, if we neglect the principle of universal benevolence, our faith is vain, our religion is an empty parade of useless and insignificant sounds. That every christian is bound to entertain sentiments of universal benevolence, to love his fellow creatures of every sect, colour or description, is the third grand point of my faith. If any one, Sir, should ask me, to what sect I belong? my answer is, my sect is not confined to age, colour, or country. I am a firm believer in the truths revealed by God, but I usurp no authority over another man's conscience. Our lord and saviour Jesus Christ is the head of my sect, he has laid down the rules of its faith and discipline. (*Account*, pp. 89–90)

The articles of Frend's creed all became 'grand points' of Coleridge's unitarianism although he could of course have found similar statements elsewhere, most notably perhaps in Priestley's *General View of the Arguments for the Unity of God*. But Frend's principle of 'universal benevolence' without which 'religion is an empty parade of useless and insignificant sounds' has a more obviously seminal bearing upon Coleridge's 'sacred sympathy' in 'Religious Musings', man's access to 'the present God',

> whose presence lost,
> The moral world's cohesion, we become
> An Anarchy of Spirits!

> (ll. 158–60)

Frend's 'benevolence' and Coleridge's 'sympathy' are vital reconciling principles of faith, and a justification for the liberty of conscience Frend claimed in his defence speech. From 1794 onwards, however, Coleridge's radical dissent moved beyond conscientious opposition to the establishment, in an effort to realize the political, social, and philosophical context of his unitarianism as a complex but coherent whole. The history of this intellectual and imaginative reconciliation is 'Religious Musings', and its consummation appears in Coleridge's transfiguring of Frend's tolerant society in a 'blest future' of 'pure FAITH',

> each heart
> Self-govern'd, the vast family of Love
> Rais'd from the common earth by common toil
> Enjoy the equal produce.

> (ll. 353–6)

Coleridge's first approach to that millenarian ideal dates from his meeting with Southey in June 1794, and their plan for Pantisocracy. In its earliest conception Pantisocracy was 'a scheme of emigration on the principles of an abolition of individual property' that would be established in America on the banks of the River Susquehannah (*CL* i. 96–7). For Coleridge, however, its equalitarian principles were not wholly political or economic, but religious and emotional as well: Pantisocracy was to be a 'family of Love' or, as he put it in a letter to Southey on 18 September 1794, 'frendotatoi meta frendous. Most friendly where all are friends' (*CL* i. 103). Coleridge's pun on Frend's name was, I think, a deliberate acknowledgement. His letters of summer 1794 alternate between excited anticipation of 'the pure System of Pantocracy' (*CL* i. 84), and a parallel concern to explain its systematic perfection through the workings of personal friendship to 'universal benevolence'. 'The ardour of private Attachments makes Philanthropy a necessary *habit* of the Soul', he told Southey on 13 July 1794:

I love my *Friend*—such as *he* is, all mankind are or *might be*! The deduction is evident—. Philanthropy (and indeed every other Virtue) is a thing of *Concretion*—Some home-born Feeling is the *center* of the Ball, that, rolling on thro' Life collects and assimilates every congenial Affection. (*C L* i. 86)

Pantisocracy was to be a model society, a '*center*' from which the cumulative momentum of affection would proceed to the regeneration of 'all mankind'. But there is of course no obvious inevitability about this process at all. On the contrary, Coleridge's manifesto implies an underlying emotional insecurity (already evident in the disastrous horse-soldier episode) as a primary condition of his lifelong need to 'collect and assimilate' disparate experience into an ideal whole. In the months after his first meeting with Southey, Coleridge's anxiety for certainty was satisfied by David Hartley's demonstration of human perfectibility in his christian and necessarian *Observations on Man*, to the extent that Coleridge announced himself 'a compleat Necessitarian' on 11 December 1794 (*CL* i. 137). Looking further ahead, Hartley would provide the philosophic buttress to Coleridge's argument for the 'universal efficiency' of religion in his 1795 lectures. A major encouragement in this direction was George

Dyer's enthusiastic welcome for the Pantisocracy scheme when he first met Coleridge late in August 1794.

In his letter of 1 September 1794 Coleridge told Southey he had breakfasted 'with Dyer, Author of the Complaints of the Poor, —on Subscription, &&c—I went—explained our System—he was enraptured—pronounced it impregnable—He is intimate with Dr Priestley—and doubts not, that the Doctor will join us' (*CL* i. 97–8). Dyer's happy response is understandable for Pantisocracy was very much akin to his own idea of 'mankind, as a family' in *An Inquiry into the Nature of Subscription*. He took this ideal from the 'infant state of society' coeval with the 'Patriarchal Ages', in which Dyer claimed

there would be no opposition of interests; no exclusive privileges would be enjoyed; no invidious distinctions kept up. In proportion to the smalness of these societies, and the narrowness of their territories, the fraternal spirit would exert itself in all its simplicity and glory. Primitive societies would naturally put this question, Are we not all brethren?[48]

The resemblances between Pantisocracy and Dyer's 'primitive society' are, perhaps, not surprising given Coleridge's evident familiarity with Dyer's pamphlet 'on Subscription'. A continuing link between the two appears in Coleridge's essay 'Enthusiasm for an Ideal World' in *The Friend*, where he recalls that the 'little society' of Pantisocracy 'was to have combined the innocence of the patriarchal age with the knowledge and genuine refinements of European culture' (*Friend*, i. 224). Among other influences on Coleridge's plan of emigration the example of Joseph Priestley would have counted for a great deal. He had left for America in April 1794, and settled near the Susquehannah—the site that Coleridge and Southey were to choose for Pantisocracy. The exciting possibility that 'the Doctor', and perhaps Dyer too, might join the community would have hardened Coleridge's resolve to go—and it explains his scorn for Southey's plan to try out the scheme in Wales: 'pardon me—it is nonsense—We must go to America' (*CL* i. 132).[49]

Pantisocracy was the fruit of Coleridge's first friendship with

[48] Dyer, *Inquiry*, p. 13.
[49] For a wider discussion of the intellectual context of Pantisocracy, see J. R. MacGillivray, 'The Pantisocracy Scheme and its Immediate Background' in *Studies in English by Members of the University of Toronto* (Toronto, 1931), 131–69. See also E. Logan, 'Coleridge's Scheme of Pantisocracy and American Travel Accounts', *PMLA* xlv (Dec. 1930), 1069–84.

Southey; the scheme fostered his acquaintance with Dyer in London, and it also helps clarify Coleridge's attitude to Godwin at this time. Southey's allegiance to *Political Justice* can be dated from November and December 1793 when he borrowed both volumes from the Bristol Library, and wrote to his friend Horace Bedford recommending him to read them too.[50] It seems likely that, when discussing the equalitarian ideal of Pantisocracy with Coleridge, Southey would have followed Godwin in arguing that 'private considerations must yield to the general good' (*PJ* i. 165). Coleridge would have responded, with Dyer, that 'exclusive privileges' were in any case 'invidious' under God. He would also have insisted that love and friendship were the means to human regeneration, and in this respect Coleridge was fundamentally at odds with Godwin's disinterested rationalism in *Political Justice*.

The philosophic bases of Southey's and Coleridge's respective ideas of Pantisocracy were contradictory, and contributed to the disintegration of the scheme during the Autumn of 1794. In his Bristol lectures the following year, however, Coleridge returned to this issue and used it to sharpen his critique of *Political Justice*, arguing that, whereas Godwin's philosophy 'builds without a foundation' in human nature, 'Jesus knew our Nature . . . the Love of our Friends, parents and neighbours lead[s] us to the love of our Country to the love of all Mankind. The intensity of private attachment encourages, not prevents, universal philanthropy—' (*Lects. 1795*, p. 163). Jesus' human wisdom recalls the affective '*Concretion*' of Pantisocracy, and in so doing it highlights the vexed frontier between Coleridge's unitarianism and Godwinian rationalism in their rival definitions of human benevolence. Coleridge's first letter to Southey opens by acknowledging this difference between them: 'You are averse to Gratitudinarian Flourishes—else would I talk about hospitality, attentions &c &c' (*CL* i. 83). He could joke with his new friend in July 1794, but he would soon regard Godwin's ideas as a genuine threat to society, religion, and morals. In this way Coleridge's dissenting inheritance from Cambridge came to bear directly upon contemporary radical affairs in 1794–5, specifically in his efforts to counter the popularity of *Political Justice* and its influence among members of the democratic reform movement.

[50] See Curry, i. 40, and G. Whalley, 'The Bristol Library Borrowings of Southey and Coleridge, 1793–8', *The Library*, 5s, iv (1949), 114–32.

Coleridge and Godwin first met on 21 December 1794 in company with Richard Porson and Thomas Holcroft, both of whom Coleridge already knew (*CL* i. 138–9). Godwin noted in his diary that their conversation turned upon 'self love & God', with Coleridge perhaps invoking Priestley and Hartley, Frend and Dyer to confound Godwin's arguments from *Political Justice* and Holcroft's 'incessant Metaphysics' and '*Atheism*'.[51] Such an idea of their talk is only my speculation, but it draws some substance from Coleridge's subsequent dating of 'Religious Musings' to Christmas Eve of 1794, three days after the meeting. This suggests that his poem was originally conceived as a further reply to Godwin and Holcroft, and that Coleridge's meditation on politics, philosophy, and religion in the poem as composed over the next two years was an elaboration of its primary anti-Godwinian initiative. In this respect 'Religious Musings' also complements Coleridge's lectures delivered at Bristol during 1795, in which he developed his argument with Godwin, and established his own relation to the democratic reform movement and to its leading spokesman John Thelwall.

At the close of his third *Lecture on Revealed Religion*, delivered on 26 or 29 May 1795, Coleridge explained that he had 'dwelt the more particularly on . . . Christ's character and doctrine because the Stoical Morality which disclaims all the duties of Gratitude and domestic Affection has been lately revived in a book popular among the professed Friends of civil Freedom—' (*Lects. 1795*, p. 164). During 1794–5 *Political Justice* had a demonstrable influence among radical intellectuals in London: James Losh, John Tweddell, Basil Montagu, William Frend, William Mathews, and Wordsworth were all frequently in Godwin's company at this time, and sympathetic to his ideas. More disturbing, from Coleridge's point of view, would have been the popularity of *Political Justice* among working men such as John Binns and Francis Place who formed the leadership of the London Corresponding Society during 1795.[52] But most insidious of all was

[51] For Coleridge's and Godwin's meeting, see GD vi; for Coleridge's estimate of Holcroft's intellect and conversation, CL i. 138–9, and Chapter 5 below.

[52] Thale, p. 93 and n., points out that Thelwall's earliest offer to 'read political Lectures' to the Corresponding Society on 14 Nov. 1793 cited *Political Justice* as his text, although he was soon delivering his own material. The issue of Godwin's influence on the leadership and members of the Society is discussed more fully in Chapter 5 below.

John Thelwall's use of Godwinian principles in his lectures at Beaufort Buildings. On 16 May 1795, for instance, Thelwall announced his intention of 'popularising those ideas [he believed] to be true', and proceeded to condemn '*sorrow* and *regret*' as 'weaknesses' and quote Godwin in denouncing gratitude as 'a vice': 'If gratitude . . . has a tendency to draw the human mind from the consideration of the whole, and to fix it, from a principle of self love, upon a few individuals, then I shall be obliged to conclude that gratitude is no virtue, but that, on the contrary, it is an enemy to that great fountain of all virtue—Justice!' (*Tribune*, i. 229).

Ten days after this lecture was published in Thelwall's journal the *Tribune*, Coleridge delivered his anti-Godwinian lecture at Bristol evidently as a direct reply to Thelwall's 'popularizing' of *Political Justice* 'among the professed Friends of civil Freedom'. Coleridge's differences with Godwin consequently issued as part of a wider dialogue with John Thelwall and the reform movement during 1795, that would eventually lead to personal correspondence and, in 1797, to their meeting at Nether Stowey. Coleridge's and Thelwall's mutual awareness throughout these years will be discussed in a subsequent chapter, but for now it is sufficient to indicate the swiftness with which Coleridge had developed from distracted undergraduate early in 1794 to take a prominent and active role in contemporary radical affairs. By the end of 1795 and the debate about Pitt's and Grenville's repressive 'Gagging Acts', Coleridge's stature was comparable to—and certainly not less than—that of leading figures of metropolitan radicalism such as Godwin and Holcroft, Thelwall, Dyer, and Coleridge's former hero at Jesus College, William Frend. It was Coleridge's considerable reputation in these London circles that also proved to be one factor in attracting Wordsworth to Bristol in August 1795.

4

'War is Again Broken Out'

Protest and Poetry, 1793–1798

'Let others talk of glory . . .'

'Lordynges . . . ther is ful many a man that crieth "Werre!
werre!" that woot ful litel what werre amounteth. Werre at
his bigynnyng hath so greet an entryng and so large, that
every wight may entre whan hym liketh, and lightly fynde
werre; but certes what ende that shal therof bifalle, it is nat
light to knowe. For soothly, whan that werre is ones bigon-
ne, ther is ful many a child unborn of his mooder that shal
sterve yong by cause of thilke werre, or elles lyve in sorwe
and dye in wrecchednesse.'

(Chaucer, 'The Tale of Melibee')

The struggle which was beginning, and which many thought
would be brought to a speedy close by the irresistible arms of
Great Britain being added to those of the Allies, I was
assured in my own mind would be of long continuance, and
productive of distress and misery beyond all possible cal-
culation. This conviction was pressed upon me by having
been a witness, during a long residence in revolutionary
France, of the spirit which prevailed in that country.

(Wordsworth, 'Advertisement' to 'Guilt and Sorrow', 1842)

When Wordsworth returned to London in December 1792 one
event that would have concentrated his attention was the trial of
Paine for seditious libel in *The Rights of Man*. With hindsight this
prosecution can be seen to have initiated years of systematic
repression, but for Wordsworth at the time it provided immediate
evidence that reformists and French sympathizers were under
attack from the government. Paine had been living in France since
the previous September, from where he sent a letter to the
Attorney-General, Lord Kenyon, claiming that his trial was
'against the rights' of the English people; 'though you may not
choose to see it,' he added, 'the people are seeing it very fast, and

the progress is beyond that you may choose to believe'.[1] The rapid growth of the London Corresponding Society and massive circulation of *The Rights of Man* were evidence of the progress Paine had in mind, and had been cited as such in the fraternal addresses from British radical societies to the National Convention. But it must soon have been apparent to Wordsworth that the actual state of affairs in Britain was more complicated and less promising than his recent experiences at Paris had led him to believe.

Thomas Erskine acted in Paine's defence on 18 December, and spoke out in court against the injustice of the proceedings: 'I say, if the man upon trial were stained with blood instead of ink,—if he were covered over with crimes of which human nature would start at the naming, the means employed against him would not be the less disgraceful.'[2] The trial was over in a single day. Paine was found guilty without the jury retiring to consider their verdict, and his conviction marked one climax of what Erskine termed the 'ridiculous panic' that had been growing throughout the previous year. That same panic, Erskine later recalled, led Britain to war with France; Fox's warnings about the 'paroxysm of alarm' in his pamphlet *Letter* proved well founded.

In his brilliant analysis of *The Causes and Consequences of the Present War with France*, Erskine traced the source of the conflict to the first Royal Proclamation against Seditious Writings on 21 May 1792. This, he said, was 'the first act of government regarding France and her affairs':

The proclamation had unquestionably for its object to spread the alarm against French principles; and, to do it effectually, all principles were considered as French by his Majesty's ministers which questioned the infallibility of their own government, or which looked towards the least change in the representation of the people in Parliament. . . . The spirit which became prevalent about this time, which bore down everything before it, and prepared the nation for war, was an absolute horror of everything connected with France . . . It confounded the casual intemperance of an enlarged and warm zeal for the freedom and happiness of mankind with a tendency to universal anarchy.[3]

---

[1] *State Trials*, xxii. 397–8.
[2] *State Trials*, xxii. 468.
[3] Thomas Erskine, *A View of the Causes and Consequences of the Present War with France* (London, 1797), 13, 15, 18. This book was in the package sent to Wordsworth by James Losh, 20 Mar. 1797. See *EY*, p. 186n., and Chapter 7 below.

As the months passed this 'alarm' was further excited by the September Massacres and French Republic, by the Edict of Fraternity, and by the apparent willingness of British reformists to welcome French assistance. Crisis came in December when French ships sailed into the River Scheldt, contravening a British treaty with Prussia by which the navigation had been closed to international trade. The French ambassador in London was told that the British government regarded this action as 'the formal declaration of a design to extend universally the new principle of Government adopted in France, and to encourage disorder and revolt in all countries'.[4] When news of Louis's execution arrived on 24 January, the ambassador was dismissed. He returned to Paris on 1 February, and on the same day the National Convention voted for war. After debating Louis's death, the Scheldt, and the Edict of Fraternity, the British government considered itself at war with France. Less than two months had passed since Wordsworth's return.

'And now the strength of Britain was put forth', Wordsworth recalls in *The Prelude*, Book Ten,

> In league with the confederated host;
> Not in my single self alone I found,
> But in the minds of all ingenuous youth,
> Change and subversion from this hour.
>
> (x. 229–33)

It was a dismaying moment for anyone who believed

> That if France prospered good men would not long
> Pay fruitless worship to humanity
>
> (x. 222–3)

—and in Cambridge the undergraduates expressed their disapproval by supporting William Frend, who had condemned the war in *Peace and Union*: 'Let others talk of glory, let others celebrate the heroes, who are to deluge the world with blood' (*P&U*, p. 49). For Wordsworth's 'single self', however, war proved rather more disturbing than this recollection of 'change and subversion' suggests. It was a violent deflection of his experiences and expectations in the previous year, 'a stride at once | Into

---

[4] *Morning Chronicle* (17 Jan. 1793).

another region' (x. 240–1). Had he stayed longer in France he might have assimilated war as 'progress on the self-same path' with the patriot armies he had admired at Blois. But by quitting Paris for London in December 1792 he moved from a city that anticipated European liberation to one gripped by reactionary panic; he lost a personal community with revolutionary progress, and returned to his native country where those same values now isolated him in opposition.

Against this background of complex personal dislocation Wordsworth's memory of war as a 'shock | Given to [his] moral nature' appears most starkly, not just as a 'lapse | [Or] turn of sentiment' but a devastating disappointment (x. 233–6). Subsequent passages in Book Ten present this moment in February 1793 as a threshold of discouragement that would eventually lead Wordsworth to *Political Justice* as

> the philosophy
> That promised to abstract the hopes of man
> Out of his feelings . . .

> (x. 806–8)

An immediate consequence of the war was Wordsworth's close alignment with the democratic reform movement in its campaign for parliamentary reform, and in opposing the government's policies of war and repression. 'The friends of liberty congratulate themselves upon the odium under which they are at present labouring,' he writes in his *Letter*, 'nor are they disheartened by the diminution which their body is supposed already to have sustained' (*Pr. W.* i. 49). In this respect his position early in 1793 resembles that of James Losh who with George Tierney drafted the petition from the Friends of the People that was presented to the Commons by Charles Grey on 6 May. Wordsworth was in town at this time, and was acquainted with Losh, so that his name may have been among the petitioners although the list has apparently been destroyed.[5] Nevertheless, it is clear that, for Wordsworth in his *Letter* and for Losh as a member of the Friends of the People, war with France and reform at home were decisive factors in their political allegiances during 1793.

---

[5] For Losh, see H. Lonsdale, *The Worthies of Cumberland* (6 vols; London, 1867–75), iv. 190, and Goodwin, pp. 280–1. Losh's petition was among those destroyed in the fire of 1834; personal correspondence with Clerk of the Records, House of Lords, 23 Sept. 1983.

Coleridge's early response to the war is less immediately apparent. He makes no mention of it in surviving letters from 1793, but his connection with Frend and enthusiasm for Fox's *Letter to the Westminster Electors* ('the *political Go*') had a formative influence upon his position in his 1795 lectures. In his *Letter to the Westminster Electors* Fox sought to prevent hostilities by an 'avowed negociation' between the two governments.[6] No negotiation took place, and exactly two years later Coleridge recalled this moment—and Fox's pamphlet—in his lecture *On the Present War*. 'On a subject so universally discussed it would be a vain endeavour to adduce any new argument', he told his audience: 'The War might probably have been prevented by Negociation: Negociation was never attempted. It cannot therefore be *proved* to have been a *necessary* war, and consequently it is not a just one' (*Lects. 1795*, p. 54). The corollary was that France had been unjustly provoked into a war of self-defence, and Coleridge subsequently argued that British aggression had forced Robespierre to adopt terrorism as a means to consolidate the French war effort and eliminate 'those who were inclined to mutiny' (*Lects. 1795*, p. 74). At the same time, he believed that the cost of maintaining the conflict might force violent revolution in Britain at a period when 'The Example of France' had become a '"Warning to Britain"' (*Lects. 1795*, p. 6). During 1795 the expense and upheaval of war coincided with food shortages, and led to riots throughout the country: 'Oppression is grievous—the oppressed feel and are restless', Coleridge warned; 'Such things *may* happen' (*Lects. 1795*, p. 48).[7] In concluding his lecture *On the Present War*, he loads all responsibility for 'the peculiar horrors of the present' upon the British government's policy of war:

Our national faith has been impaired; our social confidence hath been weakened, or made unsafe; our liberties have suffered a perilous breach, and even now are being (still more perilously) undermined; the Dearth, which would otherwise have been scarcely visible, hath enlarged its terrible features into the threatening face of Famine; and finally, of US will justice require a dreadful account of whatever guilt France has perpetrated, of whatever miseries France has endured. Are we men?

---

[6] Fox, *Letter*, p. 24. See also Coleridge's references to Fox in his 'Review of the Motions . . . for a Peace with France', *Watchman*, pp. 16–22.

[7] For these riots see *MWC*, pp. 70–2, 156–7, and Goodwin, p. 360.

Freemen? rational men? And shall we carry on this wild and priestly War against reason, against freedom, against human nature? If there be one among you, who departs from me without feeling it his immediate duty to petition or remonstrate against the continuance of it, I envy that man neither his head or his heart! (*Lects.* *1795*, p. 74)

Coleridge maintained his opposition to the war throughout the next three years and, as Hazlitt recalled, delivered an impressive sermon upon 'the fatal effects of war' as a candidate for the unitarian ministry at Shrewsbury in January 1798 (Howe, xvii. 108). Equally consistent was his belief that war and violent revolution would only be prevented by 'cultivating benevolent affections' contingent upon religion. Over the same period Wordsworth assumed a succession of political and philosophic identities, moving from republicanism through Godwinian rationalism to the One Life, whereas Coleridge's experience was of intellectual assimilation and relative continuity. This difference between them underlines Wordsworth's memory of Coleridge's 'regulating influence' after June 1797, and of Dorothy's companionship as a 'saving intercourse | With [his] true self' (*P.* x. 907, 914–15). But the crisis of war also had a fruitful effect in Wordsworth's development as poet of social and political protest in 'Salisbury Plain', and ultimately has a bearing on *The Borderers* and his poetry of human suffering in 'The Ruined Cottage' as well. Coleridge praised Wordsworth as 'the best poet of the age' having read the earlier poem (*CL* i. 215–16 and n.); he thought *The Borderers* 'absolutely wonderful' (*CL* i. 325), and Dorothy says that he was 'much delighted' with 'The Ruined Cottage' when it was read to him at Racedown (*E Y*, p. 189). Looking back over their respective literary and philosophic responses to war since February 1793, one can see a potential for the creative exchange that would accompany and sustain their early friendship five years later.

Comfortable words for a comfortless world

It is the nature of man to die.
(Paine, *Rights of Man*, 1791)

We die, my friend.
(Wordsworth, 'The Ruined Cottage', 1797)

In the second part of *The Rights of Man* Paine condemned 'the present old governments' of Europe for perpetuating a 'continual system of war and extortion':

What inducement has the farmer, while following the plough, to lay aside his peaceful pursuit, and go to war with the farmer of another country? or what inducement has the manufacturer? What is dominion to them, or to any class of men in a nation? Does it add an acre to any man's estate, or raise its value? Are not conquest and defeat each of the same price, and taxes the never-failing consequence? (*R M* ii. 191)

Paine's humanitarian and economic arguments for peace in *The Rights of Man* were widely read during 1792, and influential thereafter as the two cornerstones of radical opposition to the war with France. An early example of Painite protest was Frend's appendix to *Peace and Union*, 'The Effect of War on the Poor', which was published days after hostilities began in February 1793: 'What must be their fate, when we suffer under the most odious scourge of the human race, and the accumulation of taxes takes away half of that daily bread, which is scarce sufficient at present for their support?' (*P & U*, pp. 47–8). Shortly afterwards Joseph Gerrald repeated Paine's argument, in almost identical terms, at the opening of his pamphlet *A Convention the Only Means of Saving us from Ruin*. 'War is again broken out,' Gerrald begins:

From the Streights of Gibraltar to the bottom of the Baltic all Europe is involved in military operations. The plough is abandoned, and the loom stands still; fleets are equipped and armies levied, to disturb peaceful communities, and to lay waste the earth. ... [I]t is the blood of the peasant and the manufacturer which flows in the battle; it is the purse of the tradesman and the artificer which is emptied in the contest.[8]

---

[8] Joseph Gerrald, *A Convention the Only Means of Saving us from Ruin* (London, 1793), 1.

Coleridge's and Wordsworth's preoccupation with the economics and hardship of war between 1793 and 1795 locates both of them in the mainstream of contemporary protest. In his *Letter to the Bishop of Llandaff* Wordsworth joins Gerrald, Frend, and Paine in describing the government's policy as 'an infatuation which is now giving up to the sword so large a portion of the poor and consigning the rest to the more slow and more painful consumption of want' (*Pr. W.* i. 49). Two years later, in *On the Present War*, Coleridge elaborates the argument into a self-perpetuating cycle of war, economic decline, crime, and persecution:

War ruins our Manufactures; the ruin of our Manufactures throws Thousands out of employ; men cannot starve: they must either pick their country-men's Pockets—or cut the throats of their fellow-creatures, because they are Jacobins. If they chuse the latter, the chances are that their own lives are sacrificed: if the former, they are hung or transported to Botany Bay. (*Lects. 1795*, p. 68)

While Coleridge and Wordsworth can be seen to coincide with the general terms of Painite opposition, each makes a distinctly individual use of them. In 'Religious Musings' Coleridge presents a litany of sufferings that issue from 'scepter'd Glory's goredrench'd field', as the prelude to divine retribution promised in Revelations. But he does so by way of recommending patience to brake the progress of war, ruin, and hunger to crime and violence:

> Rest awhile
> Children of Wretchedness! More groans must rise,
> More blood must steam, or ere your wrongs be full.
> Yet is the day of Retribution nigh:
> The Lamb of God hath open'd the fifth seal:
> And upward rush on swiftest wing of fire
> Th'innumerable multitude of Wrongs
> By man on man inflicted! Rest awhile,
> Children of Wretchedness! The hour is nigh . . .
>
> (ll. 313–21)

Back in 1789 Richard Price had welcomed the French Revolution as the coming of the millennium; seven years later Coleridge's poem offers a consolation and a promise, but defers that consummation to a 'blest future' yet to come. Both Price and Coleridge interpreted the present in the light of Revelations, and

Coleridge's footnote to the passage above specifically directs his readers to 'the sixth Chapter of the Revelation of St. John the Divine'. This sustained effort of christian optimism connects Coleridge's protest with Price's *Nunc dimittis*, but also serves to distinguish Coleridge's intellectual and religious approach to contemporary crisis from Wordsworth's more obviously emotional response.

The related issues of war, poverty, and social disruption link Wordsworth's *Letter*, 'A Night on Salisbury Plain', and the 1795 revision of that poem, and 'The Ruined Cottage' in 1797–8. But, while Wordsworth's opposition was consistent throughout this period, his political and philosophic allegiances changed, as did his treatment of human suffering in his writing. His earliest expression of protest was *A Letter to the Bishop of Llandaff*, written as a reply to Richard Watson's reactionary Appendix to his *Sermon to the Stewards of the Westminster Dispensary*, dated 25 January 1793. Watson expressed his horror at Louis's execution, at the 'sanguinary, savage, more than brutal' establishment of the French republic, and aligned himself with Burke in defence of the British constitution: 'Wise men have formed it, brave men have bled for it, it is our part to preserve it.' 'I think it far too excellent', he says elsewhere, in a calculated swipe at members of the Corresponding Societies; 'I think it far too excellent to be amended by peasants and mechanics'.[9]

To be effective Wordsworth's *Letter* must have been written shortly after Watson's pamphlet appeared, probably during February 1793.[10] Wordsworth draws upon his experiences in France, and specifically from Grégoire's speech of 15 November 1792, to defend the republic and justify Louis's death (*Pr. W.* i. 32–4). Arguing as 'the advocate of republicanism', he criticizes monarchy, the parliamentary and legal systems, the 'infatuation' of war, and expresses his support for 'the general call for a parliamentary reform' (*Pr. W.* i. 48–9). While looking back to his year in France, therefore, Wordsworth's republican manifesto also reveals his swift reaction to contemporary crisis in Britain

[9] Richard Watson, *A Sermon Preached Before the Stewards of the Westminster Dispensary, with an Appendix* (2nd edn; London, 1793), pp. 23, 32, 38.

[10] My dating follows Owen's and Smyser's argument for composition in Feb. or Mar. 1793, based on the contemporaneity of allusions in the *Letter* (*Pr. W.* i. 20–1). Mark Reed's suggestion of 'June or, at the latest, shortly after' seems rather too late in view of Wordsworth's topical comments on Louis and the war; Reed, pp. 25, 142.

after his return. In doing so, his *Letter* establishes the context of protest that gives impetus to his narrative of hardship and suffering in 'Salisbury Plain'.

In 'Salisbury Plain' the Female Vagrant tells of her lost home, of war, and the death of her husband and children ' "all in one remorseless year" ' (Gill, p. 31, l. 320). Wordsworth's concluding stanzas draw out the political and social implications of the woman's tale, in his denunciation of warmongering 'present old governments':

> Say, rulers of the nations, from the sword
> Can ought but murder, pain, and tears proceed?
> Oh! what can war but endless war still breed?
>
> (Gill, p. 37, ll. 507–9)

Work on the earliest surviving manuscript of the poem was probably completed in 1793, certainly by spring 1794 (*E Y*, p. 120; Gill, pp. 5, 7), and it shows Wordsworth drawing upon the idiom of contemporary anti-war protest. The Female Vagrant's story dramatically realizes Joseph Gerrald's vision of 'fleets . . . equipped and armies levied, to disturb peaceful communities, and to lay waste the earth'. Similarly, Wordsworth's allusion to Milton's sonnet 'On the Lord General Fairfax'—'what can war but endless war still breed'—also serves to reiterate Paine's attack on the 'continual system of war and extortion' in *The Rights of Man*.

However, 'Salisbury Plain' is poetry not a polemical pamphlet, and as Mary Jacobus has shown it also has important precursors in eighteenth-century humanitarian verse such as Langhorne's 'Country Justice', Goldsmith's 'Deserted Village', and the 'Winter' tragedy in Thomson's 'Seasons'.[11] She also rightly points out that the Female Vagrant is a major development upon the 'tragic super-tragic' portrayal of the destitute woman in 'An Evening Walk', especially so in Wordsworth's new preoccupation with the woman's inner life. ' "Oh dreadful price of being! to resign | All that is dear in being" ': her words are a lament for her dead family, but also suggest that the ' "dreadful price" ' of that loss has worked a change of self:

---

[11] See M. Jacobus, *Tradition and Experiment in Wordsworth's Lyrical Ballads, 1798* (Oxford, 1976), 133–58 [cited hereafter as Jacobus].

'Some mighty gulf of separation passed
I seemed transported to another world:
A dream resigned with pain when from the mast
The impatient mariner the sail unfurled,
And whistling called the wind that hardly curled
The silent seas. The pleasant thoughts of home
With tears his weather-beaten cheek impearled:
For me, farthest from earthly port to roam
Was best; my only wish to shun where man might come.'

(Gill, p. 33, ll. 370–8)

The two opening lines would have gained a topical resonance
from the practice of transporting convicts and reformists to
Botany Bay although that recognition devolves upon the
woman's '"gulf of separation"' as a state of mind, registering her
passage through suffering to '"another world"' of dream-like
abstraction. The sailor's bustling activity contrasts with the
woman's lifelessness, his impatient purpose to return home ironically emphasizing her distracted alienation from all humankind,
her '"only wish to shun where man might come"'.

Wordsworth's achievement in the earliest version of 'Salisbury
Plain' is limited by conventional Spenserian verse, frequent use of
personifications and generally unwieldy syntax. Nevertheless, the
stanza discussed above represents a new insight into the nature of
suffering and a first step towards the articulate restraint of 'The
Ruined Cottage'. Mary Jacobus and others have acknowledged
the poem's importance in this respect, but have been at a loss to
account for Wordsworth's emergent stature as a poet of human
suffering at this moment in 1793. It is worth recalling, by way of
comparison, that Southey and Coleridge did not develop in this
way. A passage from 'Joan of Arc' that appeared in the first issue
of the *Watchman* offers some parallels with Margaret's circumstances in 'The Ruined Cottage', but the extract from 'Religious
Musings' published as 'The Present State of Society' in the second
issue reveals no advance on the melodramatic verse in 'An
Evening Walk':

O wretched Widow who in dreams dost view
Thy Husband's mangled corse—and from short doze
Start'st with a shriek! or in thy half thatch'd cot,
Wak'd by the wintry night-storm, wet and cold,
Cow'rst o'er thy screaming baby!

(*Watchman*, p. 65)

Why, then, did Wordsworth's poetry evolve from a comparably extravagant sensationalism to the Female Vagrant's '"dream resigned with pain"' in the earliest version of 'Salisbury Plain' of 1793? Mary Jacobus's suggestion that 'he grew more concerned with—perhaps simply more aware of—human feeling' is doubtless correct, but it does not explain his achievement in the poetry. A subsequent comment, however, offers more purchase in returning to 'anti-war protest, as well as the more general humanitarian protest of the period' as 'the chief impulse behind *Salisbury Plain*'.[12] It is in this context that Wordsworth's growing awareness of human feeling becomes more readily explicable, and here too that a source for the distinctively Wordsworthian poetry of 'Salisbury Plain' and 'The Ruined Cottage' can be found.

E. P. Thompson has suggested that government-sponsored alarm and repression in 1792 responded to a 'sea-change in the attitudes of the inarticulate—or in the structure of feeling of the poor' that disposed them to 'harbour and tolerate the seditious' (*M W C*, p. 127). The idea is attractive although a restructuring of feeling among the inarticulate is extremely difficult to assess two centuries afterwards, hence Thompson's canny resort to Ariel's mysterious 'sea-change'. On the other hand, it is demonstrable that the 1790s saw an alteration in the structure of feeling for the poor and disenfranchised among articulate liberals, radicals, and dissenters. This is evident in a sympathetic emotional identification with social victims that is very different, for example, from the patronizing attitude of the SCI to 'the *poor* Man' in the 1780s.[13] It was this change in articulated political and social feeling that led to government reaction, and which also offered an enabling pattern for Wordsworth's poetic development after 1793.

In September 1792 Thomas Cooper published his pamphlet *Reply to Mr. Burke's Invective Against Mr. Cooper and Mr. Watt* as a defence against Burke's speech in the Commons on 30 April, in which he had denounced Cooper's and Watt's address to the Jacobins at Paris. Given Wordsworth's certain knowledge of their visit to Paris, and the likelihood of his meeting with Watt during 1792, it is not unreasonable to assume his familiarity with

[12] See Jacobus, pp. 140, 142–3.
[13] See Chapter 1 above.

Cooper's pamphlet following his return to London.[14] If he did read it, he would have come across this remarkable attack upon forced recruitment for the army and navy:

A still more flagrant Instance of Cruelty and Injustice toward the Poor, is the Practice of *Impressing*. The Labour of the poor Man, constitutes the whole of his Wealth, and his domestic Connections almost the whole of his happiness. But on a sudden under the dubious authority of a Press Warrant, he is cut off from his peaceful habitation and domestic Society, and forcibly dragged on board the floating Prison of a Tender: he is compelled to labour in the dreadful Service of murdering his fellow Creatures at the command of his Superiors, and paid such scanty Wages, not as he can earn or deserves, but as the niggardly System of Government Finance thinks fit to allow. His Family meanwhile, who look up to him for Comfort and Subsistance, ignorant of his Misfortune, are anxiously expecting his wonted return; perhaps their homely repast for the night depended on his earnings for the day; but his usual hour of return to his family is gone by; each passing footstep, each noise of distant Similarity is eagerly listened to in vain; Hope, still draws out the lengthened evening till a sleepless night of lamentation and despair succeeds the dreary melancholy hours, of successive disappointment and fruitless expectation. The next or succeeding day brings the mournful tidings of his destiny, and leaves the widowed wife (perhaps the pregnant Mother) to eke out a comfortless existence under the accumulated pressure of Want, and Labour, and Sorrow, and Disease.[15]

Cooper initially follows Paine in pointing to the economic hardship caused by 'pressing' and the 'dreadful Service' of military life. He goes on, though, to develop the thrust of Painite protest by exploring the human cost of war—not on the battlefield—but in the disruption of 'peaceful habitation and domestic Society'. In doing so, political argument merges with and finds a larger significance in Cooper's elegiac sympathy with the abandoned family: 'each passing footstep, each noise of distant Similarity is eagerly listened to in vain.' The ultimate price of 'Cruelty and Injustice toward the Poor' emerges in the distracting experience of 'successive disappointment and fruitless expectation', and the 'comfortless existence' of the 'widowed wife'. Or, to put it in slightly different terms, the radical idiom of *The*

---

[14] For Watt and Wordsworth in France, see Chapter 2 above.
[15] Thomas Cooper, *A Reply to Mr. Burke's Invective Against Mr. Cooper and Mr. Watt* (Manchester, 1792), 72–3.

Rights of Man gives place to the insight of the imaginative poet.

Leaving aside the question of Wordsworth's familiarity with Cooper's *Reply*, the similarities of theme and treatment in pamphlet and poetry are striking. The widow's 'comfortless existence' foreshadows the Female Vagrant's loss of '"all that is dear is being"' through the deaths of her loved ones. The fate of Cooper's recruit, 'compelled to labour in the dreadful Service of murdering his fellow Creatures . . . and paid such scanty Wages' is a pattern for the sailor's story in the 1795 revision of 'Salisbury Plain', pressed into service 'to rouze the battle's fire' then discharged penniless by the 'slaves of Office' into a life of crime (Gill, p. 125, ll. 81, 91). But Cooper's pamphlet is perhaps most impressive for anticipating Robert's enlistment, and the story of Margaret's 'successive disappointment and fruitless expectation' in 'The Ruined Cottage':

> —Yet ever as there passed
> A man whose garments shewed the Soldier's red
> Or crippled Mendicant in Sailor's garb,
> The little Child who sate to turn the wheel
> Ceased from his toil, and she with faltering voice,
> Expecting still to learn her husband's fate,
> Made many a fond inquiry; and when they
> Whose presence gave no comfort were gone by,
> Her heart was still more sad.
>
> (Butler, pp. 70, 72, ll. 498–506)

My point is not to offer Cooper's *Reply* as one more source or analogue for 'The Ruined Cottage', the plot and details of which were, as James Butler says, 'common knowledge' among Wordsworth's associates at the time (Butler, p. 6). Contrasts between poem and pamphlet are equally valuable in clarifying the relation between them, and 'The Ruined Cottage' diverges most obviously from Cooper's protest in relegating 'the plague of war' to a past 'now ten years gone', and elaborating the widow's 'comfortless existence' as the substance of the pedlar's narrative of Margaret's suffering. The motive to sympathy as effective protest in pamphlets by Paine, Frend, Gerrald, Cooper, and others consequently also appears as an initiating prompt for Wordsworth's imaginative mediation with social victims and outcasts. Thereafter Wordsworth's poetry evolves as an inverse ratio of its explicit political purpose until in 'The Ruined Cottage' the 'Cruelty and Injustice' that had preoccupied Cooper has receded into a background of incidental detail. The successive stages of this development can be traced through the revised 'Salisbury Plain' of 1795, *The Borderers*, and the 'Baker's Cart' fragment of late 1796–7.

During 1794 and 1795 Wordsworth's reading of *Political Justice* and *Caleb Williams*, as well as his friendship with Godwin, encouraged him to revise 'Salisbury Plain' such 'that it may be looked on almost as another work', as he told Francis Wrangham on 20 November 1795. 'Its object is partly to expose the vices of the penal law', he added, 'and the calamities of war as they affect individuals' (*E Y*, p. 159). Wordsworth had attacked the judicial system as a 'thorny labyrinth of litigation' in his *Letter* (*Pr. W.* i. 47), and the Female Vagrant's story turned on 'the calamities of war'. Two years later his major alteration in 'Adventures on Salisbury Plain' was to add the discharged sailor's narrative, which focuses his new concern with the causes of crime, the status of punishment, and the psychology of guilt.[16]

Wordsworth's sailor is a benevolent man betrayed into crime and then punished by the society he has served: he is discharged with no quittance, murders to provide for his family, and is finally executed by 'the slaves of Office' whose negligence forced him to commit the crime in the first place. An immediate influence upon 'the vices of the penal law' as represented in the sailor's story was Godwin's necessarian argument that criminal behaviour was the product of circumstances, and that punishment was consequently a violation of justice: 'The assassin cannot help the murder he commits any more than the dagger' (*PJ* ii. 690). Besides coinciding with Godwin late in 1795, Wordsworth would also have agreed with Southey that 'society makes the crime and then punishes it' (Curry, i. 41), and with Coleridge in *On the Present War*:

And if in the bitter cravings of Hunger the dark Tide of Passions should swell, and the poor Wretch rush from despair into guilt, then the

---

[16] Stephen Gill's Introduction to *The Salisbury Plain Poems* discusses the extent to which the MS 'Adventures of Salisbury Plain', which dates from c. 1799, may represent Wordsworth's revised poem of 1795 (Gill, pp. 9–12). See also J. Wordsworth, 'Startling the Earthworms', *TLS* (3 Dec. 1976).

GOVERNMENT indeed assumes the right of Punishment though it had neglected the duty of Instruction, and hangs the victim for crimes, to which its own wide-wasting follies and its own most sinful omissions had supplied the cause and the temptation. (*Lects. 1795*, p. 70)

'Adventures on Salisbury Plain' presents much that Wordsworth, Coleridge, and Southey held in common when they first met at Bristol late in August–September 1795, specifically their mutual opposition to war and criticisms of criminal law. But Wordsworth's concerns in the poem also extend beyond political and social protest, to the sailor's state of mind in his 'rush from despair into guilt'.

Like the Female Vagrant the sailor carries 'a perpetual weight' upon his spirit (Gill, p. 146, l. 558), the self-alienating knowledge of his own guilt. A gibbet with a hanging corpse rouses 'a train | Of the mind's phantoms' (Gill, p. 126, ll. 114–22), and the sight of a father striking his son's 'batter'd head' reminds him of how the blood 'Flow'd from the spot where he that deadly wound | Had fix'd on him he murder'd' (Gill, p. 149, ll. 644–5). The sailor's 'inward trouble' appears in his guilty association of ideas and images, but his anguish is also a threshold to compassionate understanding and the Wordsworthian intuition that such human wisdom is attained through the experience of suffering. ' " 'Tis a bad world, and hard is the world's law" ', he says by way of reconciling father and son:

> 'Each prowls to strip his brother of his fleece;
> Much need have ye that time more closely draw
> The bond of nature, all unkindness cease,
> And that among so few there still be peace:
> Else can ye hope but with such num'rous foes
> Your pains shall ever with your years increase.'
> While his pale lips these homely truths disclose,
> A correspondent calm stole gently on his woes.

> (Gill, p. 149, ll. 658–66)

The sailor's 'homely truths' develop Paine's admonition that man should see 'his species, not with the inhuman idea of a natural enemy, but as kindred' (*RM* ii. 182), and they validate Wordsworth's Godwinian critique of 'penal law'. But 'the bond of nature' and sanctity of 'kindness' represent compassionate virtues that are alien to the rational perfectibility of *Political*

Justice, in which Wordsworth had nevertheless found an intellectual justification for his radicalism in recent months. 'Adventures on Salisbury Plain' achieves a superficial if unstable reconciliation of contradictory philosophies, and in doing so it registers deeper 'contrarieties' that led to the moral 'despair' recalled by Wordsworth in *The Prelude*, Book Ten. I shall come back to this moment later, but here I want to claim that it was productive rather than disabling, and that Wordsworth's 'despair' establishes a continuity between philosophic tensions implicit in 'Adventures on Salisbury Plain' and their creative resolution in *The Borderers*.

Wordsworth wrote *The Borderers* out of disenchantment with *Political Justice*, but his play does more than expose the inadequacies of Godwin's philosophy. Herbert, his daughter Matilda, and her lover Mortimer represent the 'bond of nature' or human kindness, threatened by Rivers's conspiracy to betray all three by persuading Mortimer to murder Herbert. But while Rivers invokes Godwin's ideal 'independent intellect' to justify killing, he is not strictly a Godwinian type at all. His character is in fact a perverse concentration of the frailties of human nature he claims to despise. In his youth he had been 'the pleasure of all hearts', potentially a good and benevolent man like the sailor in 'Adventures on Salisbury Plain' or, as Rivers acknowledges, like Mortimer too. Rivers and the sailor are both betrayed into crime; both murder an innocent man. In the poem the sailor's remorse issues as compassion for a destitute soldier, for the Female Vagrant, and in his comfortable words of reconciliation for the father and son. Rivers's discovery that he had been deceived into committing murder results in a collapse of self—'I could not support the change; | I sunk into despair'—until his pride resurrects itself in acts of 'power and terror' and his arrogant self-assertion as

> a being who had passed alone
> Beyond the visible barriers of the world
> And travelled into things to come.

(Osborn, p. 238, IV. ii. 143–5)

Throughout the play Rivers's claims to independence from 'the uses of the world' are ironically qualified by the 'invisible barrier' of his own character, as manifest through his obsession with the past and compulsion to deceive Mortimer into re-enacting it.

Rivers may paraphrase *Political Justice* but he is actually a figure of *un*reason:

> my sleep was linked
> To purposes of reason—my very dreams
> Assumed a substance and a character.

(Osborn, p. 238, IV. ii. 123–5)

In the end *The Borderers* is anti-Godwinian to the extent that it shows the workings of human nature as ineluctably 'accidental' and irrational. Its epitome is not a critique of the 'independent intellect', but the limitless human potential to good or evil that is best expressed by the sailor's stricken recognition in 'Salisbury Plain': ' "What hearts have we!" ' Rather than indicating a 'transition in [Wordsworth's] soul' accompanying his 'moral despair', *The Borderers* is continuous with the ' "dreadful price of being" ' experienced by the Female Vagrant and the sailor in successive versions of 'Salisbury Plain'. Mortimer is doomed, like them, to a life withdrawn from his kind,

> a wanderer on the earth,
> A shadowy thing . . .
> Living by mere intensity of thought,
> A thing by pain and thought compelled to live . . .

(Osborn, p. 294, V. iii. 265–6, 272–3)

His final words stand as his epitaph, but also as a testament to Cooper's 'comfortless existence' as quotidian reality. The 'sea-change' in political feeling that formerly inspired pamphlets and poems of protest has found its ultimate expression in Wordsworth's tragic vision of human life.

'Jacobin' poems?

> I have seen the Baker's horse
> As he had been accustomed at your door
> Stop with the loaded wain, when o'er his head
> Smack went the whip, and you were left, as if
> You were not born to live, or there had been   5
> No bread in all the land. Five little ones,
> They at the rumbling of the distant wheels
> Had all come forth, and, ere the grove of birch
> Concealed the wain, into their wretched hut

They all return'd. While in the road I stood   10
Pursuing with involuntary look
The Wain now seen no longer, to my side
[   ] came, a pitcher in her hand
Filled from the spring; she saw what way my eyes
Were turn'd, and in a low and fearful voice   15
She said—that wagon does not care for us—
The words were simple, but her look and voice
Made up their meaning, and bespoke a mind
Which being long neglected, and denied
The common food of hope, was now become   20
Sick and extravagant,—by strong access
Of momentary pangs driv'n to that state
In which all past experience melts away,
And the rebellious heart to its own will
Fashions the laws of nature.   25

(MH, pp. 5–6)

The 'Baker's Cart' fragment was probably composed between
late 1796 and March 1797. It immediately precedes work on 'The
Ruined Cottage' and anticipates some details and circumstances
of the later poem. A first glance might also suggest that Wordsworth's fragment corresponds to Coleridge's account of 'helpless
Women . . . "Bold from despair and prostitute for Bread"' in *On
the Present War* (*Lects. 1795*, p. 69). But the 'Baker's Cart' has no
political or social purpose comparable to Coleridge's lecture or to
Wordsworth's own earlier poetry of protest. The wain is 'loaded'
as usual, the land is evidently one of plenty, and the horse is
'accustomed' to stop at the door of the hut. It is the violation of
that customary routine—'Smack went the whip'—that prompts
Wordsworth's interest, which turns upon the figure left behind 'as
if | [She] were not born to live, or there had been | No bread in all
the land'. '[A]s if': Wordsworth gestures towards famine as a
possible explanation for what has happened, but apparently by
way of showing that it is not so in this case. The 'Five little ones'
come out expectantly when the wagon is heard, and silently retire
into their hut before it has disappeared again. Their pathetic
appeal, which in 1793 Paine, or Frend, or Cooper, or Wordsworth might have used for protest, now elicits no comment at all.

Up to line 10, the poem describes a routine inexplicably upset
as the wain moves off, drawing after it Wordsworth's 'involuntary look'. The following lines mediate between the poet's blank

confusion and the woman's state of mind, so that the poem as a whole moves from incidental disruption to inner derangement. The 'Smack' of the whip drives off the horse, but it finds a further report in the woman's 'sick and extravagant' mind,

> driv'n to that state
> In which all past experience melts away,
> And the rebellious heart to its own will
> Fashions the laws of nature.

Her wilful fashioning of those 'laws' appears in her simple words '—that wagon does not care for us—', irrationally attributing her own desolation to the wain's desertion of routine. But in doing so she also identifies Wordsworth's 'law of nature' in the human kindness or 'care' which her existence has been denied.

The 'Baker's Cart' opens with an incident that apparently has potential for protest: ' "'Tis against that | Which we are fighting" ', Beaupuy might have said. Rather than finding its meaning in famine or poverty, though, it turns inwards to discover a heart goaded into strife against its own nature. This imaginative involution from external circumstances to inner life is a paradigm for Wordsworth's larger development from poet of protest to poet of human suffering that I have been tracing in this chapter so far. It also offers a clue to understanding the perplexed response to some of the poems Wordsworth wrote during the next two years, when they were published in the first edition of *Lyrical Ballads* in September 1798.

Dr Burney reviewed *Lyrical Ballads* for the *Monthly Review* in June 1799. He was confused by most of the poems, but 'The Last of the Flock' caused him particular difficulty. "We are not told how the wretched hero of this piece became so poor', Burney says:

He had, indeed, ten children: but so have many cottagers; and ere the tenth child is born, the eldest begin to work, and help, at least, to maintain themselves. No oppression is pointed out; nor are any means suggested for his relief. If the author be a wealthy man, he ought not to have suffered this poor peasant to part with *the last of the flock*. What but an Agrarian law can prevent poverty from visiting the door of the indolent, injudicious, extravagant, and, perhaps, vicious? and is it certain that rigid equality of property as well as of laws could remedy this evil?[17]

---

[17] *Monthly Review*, xxix (June 1799), 207.

It is easy to laugh at Burney, but his misreading of 'The Last of the Flock' does help to define the relation of some of Wordsworth's ballads to contemporary ideas of 'Jacobin' poetry. Three points that Burney makes are correct: 'We are not told how the wretched hero . . . became so poor', he says. 'No oppression is pointed out; nor are any means suggested for his relief.' His mistake was to anticipate Wordsworth's concern with 'oppression' and 'relief', and that the poem would advocate a 'levelling' Agrarian law: he was looking for a protest poem, and was puzzled to find that Wordsworth's ballad frustrated his expectations.[18]

Burney's comments on 'The Last of the Flock' may well have been influenced by an article upon 'Jacobin Poetry' in the second issue of the *Anti-Jacobin; or, Weekly Examiner* which appeared on 27 November 1797. The purpose of this discussion was to define a particular treatment of suffering figures characteristic of 'Jacobin' poetry, by way of ridiculing the political motives of the poet:

A human being, in the lowest state of penury and distress, is a treasure to a [poet] of this cast—He contemplates, he examines, he turns him in every possible light, with a view of extracting from the variety of his wretchedness, new topics of invective against the pride of property. He indeed (if he is a true Jacobin) refrains from *relieving* the object of his compassionate contemplation; as well knowing that every diminution from the general mass of human misery, must proportionably diminish the force of his argument.[19]

The *Anti-Jacobin* took Southey's 'Widow' as an example of this 'Jacobin' mode, and parodied its clumsy and inappropriate sapphic metre in 'The Friend of Humanity and the Knife-grinder'. Like Wordsworth's beggar in 'An Evening Walk', Southey's widow is described with melodramatic relish and then abandoned to her misery and death. The *Anti-Jacobin* parody indulges a comparable wish to contemplate wretchedness, and wittily frustrates it. The poem forms a dialogue in which the Friend of

---

[18] Back in 1793 Wordsworth explained his attitude to Agrarian law in his *Letter*: 'I am not an advocate for the agrarian law', he said, 'but I contend that the people amongst whom the law of primogeniture exists, and among whom corporate bodies are encouraged and immense salaries annexed to useless and indeed hereditary offices, is oppressed by an inequality in the distribution of wealth which does not necessarily attend men in a state of civil society' (*Pr. W.* i. 43–4).

[19] *Anti-Jacobin; or, Weekly Examiner* (2 vols.; London, 1799), i. 70.

Humanity repeatedly interrogates the knife-grinder to extract his 'Pitiful story',

> 'Tell me, Knife-grinder, how you came to grind knives?
> Did some rich man tyranically use you?'

—but his solicitude is rebuffed by the knife-grinder's tale of tavern brawls and the stocks, and by his concluding remark: '"for my part, I never love to meddle | With Politics, Sir."' The Friend of Humanity reproaches him as a '"Wretch! whom no sense of wrongs can rouse to vengeance"', overturns his grinding-wheel, *'and exit in a transport of republican enthusiasm and universal philanthropy'.*[20]

The *Anti-Jacobin* parody of 'The Widow' is amusing and, in this instance, rightly sends up Southey's experiments with metre. It is also particularly astute for identifying a treatment of human suffering that is common to 'Jacobin' or protest poetry, and Wordsworth's 'tragic super-tragic' in *The Prelude*, Book Eight:

> Then, if a widow staggering with the blow
> Of her distress was known to have made her way
> To the cold grave in which her husband slept,
> One night, or haply more than one—through pain
> Or half-insensate impotence of mind—
> The fact was caught at greedily, and there
> She was a visitant the whole year through,
> Wetting the turf with never-ending tears,
> And all the storms of heaven must beat on her.

> (viii. 533–41)

'The fact was caught at greedily': in 'An Evening Walk' 'distress' is the material for sensational elaboration not compassionate understanding, and in protest poetry it feeds 'invective against the pride of property'. In each case the human experience is subordinate to an ulterior motive, but in 'The Last of the Flock' this is apparently not so—hence Dr Burney's bafflement. The shepherd is in 'the lowest state of penury and distress' as the *Anti-Jacobin* required. Wordsworth's encounter with the weeping man leads to the questions expected of a friend to humanity,

> I follow'd him, and said, 'My friend
> What ails you? wherefore weep you so?'

> (ll. 15–16)

[20] *Anti-Jacobin*, i. 72. For 'The Widow' and 'An Evening Walk', see *MH*, p. 63.

—apparently to 'extract . . . the variety of his wretchedness'. But no political 'invective' follows. In 'The Last of the Flock' Wordsworth seems deliberately to conform to the *Anti-Jacobin* pattern of protest poetry, only to disappoint the anticipated attack on 'pride of property'. As in the earlier 'Baker's Cart' fragment, Wordsworth's concern in 'The Last of the Flock' appears where he diverges from the circumstantial 'fact' of distress towards an imaginative understanding of the shepherd's existence.

Burney's literal observation that 'the author . . . ought not to have suffered this poor peasant to part with *the last of the flock*' may, as Mary Jacobus says, be a 'naïve' index of Wordsworth's success 'in making us respond to the poetry of passion as if to passion itself'.[21] But when read in the light of contemporary expectations about political poetry, his comment is the less simplistic for indicating Wordsworth's larger success in realizing the imaginative potential of protest in his poems of 1797–8. Clearly, this approach is effective for only some of the poems Wordsworth published in *Lyrical Ballads*; it is not possible to read 'The Idiot Boy' or 'The Complaint of a Forsaken Indian Woman' as modified social protest, although the emotional and imaginative concerns of both poems might be related back through 'The Ruined Cottage' and 'The Female Vagrant' to the compassionate politics of earlier years. The milieu of protest does have a bearing, though, on a poem Wordsworth wrote at about the same time as the 'Baker's Cart' late in 1796 or early 1797, 'Old Man Travelling':

> The little hedge-row birds,
> That peck along the road, regard him not.
> He travels on, and in his face, his step,
> His gait, is one expression; every limb,
> His look and bending figure, all bespeak   5
> A man who does not move with pain, but moves
> With thought—He is insensibly subdued
> To settled quiet: he is one by whom
> All effort seems forgotten, one to whom
> Long patience has such mild composure given,   10
> That patience now doth seem a thing, of which
> He hath no need. He is by nature led

[21] *Jacobus*, p. 205.

To peace so perfect, that the young behold
With envy, what the old man hardly feels.
—I asked him whither he was bound, and what   15
The object of his journey; he replied
'Sir! I am going many miles to take
'A last leave of my son, a mariner,
'Who from a sea-fight has been brought to Falmouth,
'And there is dying in an hospital.'   20

As with his comments on 'The Last of the Flock', Burney misreads 'Old Man Travelling' as a poem of protest—this time against the war with France. '[F]inely drawn', he says, 'but the termination seems pointed against the war; from which, however, we are now no more able to separate ourselves, than Hercules was to free himself from the shirt of Nessus'—and he adds by way of a final perverse hint: 'The old traveller's son might have died by disease.'[22] The mariner is evidently ' "dying in an hospital" ' of war wounds, but his father's mild words are not explicitly 'pointed against the war' at all. Burney is wide of the mark, but his comments once again suggest how 'Old Man Travelling' is related to protest poetry, while transcending the political and social focus of that genre.

The shepherd in 'The Last of the Flock' and the woman in the 'Baker's Cart' are consumed and distracted by their experiences; like Mortimer they are beings 'by pain and thought compelled to live'. Wordsworth's old man resembles Mortimer as 'a shadowy thing', but he has passed the boundary of anguished consciousness to exist in profound passivity, 'insensibly subdued | To settled quiet'. His self-resignation leads to transcendence of self, 'by nature led' Wordsworth writes,

> To peace so perfect, that the young behold
> With envy, what the old man hardly feels.

His quietus is enviable but it is not explicable. Wordsworth's questions, 'whither . . . and what | The object of his journey', seek a rational understanding of the old man's existence, and his reply yields a few circumstantial details that are irrelevant to the preceding imaginative 'sketch'. The same might be said of 'The Discharged Soldier' and 'The Leech-gatherer' in each of which an imaginative comprehension of the solitary figure is accompanied

[22] *Monthly Review*, xxix (June 1799), 209.

by what Jonathan Wordsworth has called 'the border compulsion to ask questions':

> While thus we travelled on I did not fail
> To question him of what he had endured
> From war & battle & the pestilence
>
> (*B W S*, p. 436, ll. 136–8)

—and, in the later poem,

> 'How is it that you live, and what is it you do?'
>
> (l. 119)

Such questioning may reflect Wordsworth's intuition that the old man, the soldier, and the leech-gatherer possess an ultimate wisdom beyond the bourn dividing life and death, but his inter-rogation might formerly have been designed to 'extract' a tale comparable to those of the sailor and Female Vagrant in 'Salis-bury Plain'. Looking back over Wordsworth's development after 1793, the most characteristic perceptions and strategies of his imaginative poetry can be seen to have evolved out of political and social protest, as much as from eighteenth-century literary precursors such as Langhorne, Goldsmith, Thomson. In that process the political imperative is succeeded by imaginative re-ceptivity as the dominant mode of Wordsworth's writing, and the social victim gradually transformed into a figure of monitory wisdom. So it is that Thomas Cooper's unhappy conscript, 'cut off from his peaceful habitation and domestic Society' and put to 'murdering his fellow Creatures', returns as if from another world in the ghostly form of Wordsworth's discharged soldier:

> He was in stature tall,
> A foot above man's common measure tall,
> And lank, and upright. There was in his form
> A meagre stiffness. You might almost think
> That his bones wounded him. His legs were long,
> So long and shapeless that I looked at them
> Forgetful of the body they sustained.
> His arms were long & lean; his hands were bare;
> His visage, wasted though it seem'd, was large
> In feature; his cheeks sunken; and his mouth
> Shewed ghastly in the moonlight. From behind
> A mile-stone propp'd him, & his figure seem'd

Half-sitting & half-standing. I could mark
That he was clad in military garb,
Though faded yet entire. His face was turn'd
Towards the road, yet not as if he sought
For any living thing. He appeared
Forlorn and desolate, a man cut off
From all his kind, and more than half detached
From his own nature.

(BWS, p. 434, ll. 41–60)

The conscript who was forcibly separated from his family is transfigured in Wordsworth's soldier as 'a man cut off | From all his kind', and almost abstracted from 'his own nature' altogether. His ghastly figure has acquired an emblematic presence beyond the 'simple fact' of his personal history, placing him in a distinguished line that includes the 'olde man' resting at the stile in Chaucer's 'Pardoner's Tale':

'Thus walke I, lyk a restelees kaityf,
And on the ground, which is my moodres gate,
I knokke with my staf, bothe erly and late,
And seye "Leeve mooder, leet me in!
Lo how I vanysshe, flessh, and blood, and skyn!
Allas! whan shul my bones been at reste?"'

(ll. 728–33)

—And Spenser's 'dead-living swaine' Malegar in *The Faerie Queene*:

As pale and wan as ashes was his looke,
His bodie leane and meagre as a rake,
And skin all withered like a dryed rooke . . .

(II. xi. 22)

Finally, as has often been pointed out,[23] the soldier's 'uncouth shape' recalls Milton's Death at the gates of Hell in *Paradise Lost*,

If shape it might be called that shape had none
Distinguishable in member, joint, or limb,
Or substance might be called that shadow seemed

(ii. 667–9)

---

[23] For example in *BV*, p. 13, and, more recently, L. Newlyn, *Coleridge, Wordsworth, and the Language of Allusion* (Oxford, 1986), 30.

—but, as Wordsworth was well aware, Milton had also embedded a republican barb in his description of this figure:

> black it stood as night,
> Fierce as ten Furies, terrible as hell,
> And shook a dreadful dart; what seemed his head
> The likeness of a kingly crown had on.

(ii. 670–3)

Milton would have claimed the authority of Revelations 6: 2 for Death's 'kingly crown', although his anti-monarchist jibe at the Restoration is obvious and might also extend to a grisly joke at the expense of Charles I who had lost his crown along with his head. Wordsworth's discharged soldier shares the permanent significance of all the deathly archetypes mentioned above. No longer the focus of protest, he is a symbolic figure uniting the kingly perpetrators and manifold victims of war in a common destiny: 'the great day of wrath' promised in Revelations 6: 17. But for Wordsworth the encounter with the soldier also served to waken, 'in [his] own despite', memories of the shock and disappointment that followed his return from France in December 1792. As he contemplates the soldier, Wordsworth's 'mingled sense | Of fear and sorrow' arises, in part, from that recollection. It also betrays his recognition of the soldier as a harbinger of 'the day of vengeance' for which he had prayed when war began exactly five years previously in February 1793:

> I left the shady nook where I had stood
> And hailed the Stranger. From his resting-place
> He rose, & with his lean & wasted arm
> In measured gesture lifted to his head
> Returned my salutation.

(BWS, p. 435, ll. 85–9)

With the soldier's 'measured' acknowledgement the poet of social protest first emerges as prophet of apocalypse, translating 'Effort, and expectation, and desire' from the revolutionary milieu of 1792–3 as a prerogative of the imagination 'And something evermore about to be' (P. vi. 541–2). 'I returned | The blessing of the poor unhappy man', Wordsworth writes, 'And so we parted': his 'ghastly' encounter with the soldier was in fact a moment of benediction, an unexpected earnest of his own future calling as a writer.

5

'A Light Bequeathed'

Coleridge, Thelwall, Wordsworth, Godwin

'Giving a tongue to misery': Coleridge and Thelwall in 1795

> Ah, quiet dell! dear cot, and mount sublime!
> I was constrain'd to quit you. Was it right,
> While my unnumber'd brethren toil'd and bled,
> That I should dream away the trusted hours
> On rose-leaf beds, pamp'ring the coward heart
> With feelings all too delicate for use? . . .
> I therefore go—and join head, heart, and hand,
> Active and firm, to fight the bloodless fight
> Of Science, Freedom, and the Truth in Christ.[1]

'Reflections on Entering into Active Life' was written shortly after Coleridge's marriage to Sara Fricker on 4 October 1795. The poem celebrates the happiness of their early marriage, but with an intimation of disturbance—

> We could hear
> (At silent noon, and eve, and early morn)
> The sea's faint murmur

—that was realized with Coleridge's return to Bristol in November, where he resumed the 'bloodless fight' of lecturing that he had been conducting since the beginning of the year. 'Reflections' is a personal poem, but it also responds to external pressures that Coleridge felt had 'constrained' him to return to his public, political life at Bristol.

The conflicting motives to participation in the battle for 'Freedom, and the Truth', or withdrawal into private life were not peculiar to Coleridge on his honeymoon in 1795. Coleridge's experience was common to all friends of liberty over the previous two years, as a reaction to the government's repressive policies. In

---

[1] *Monthly Magazine*, ii (July–Dec. 1796), 732. On 20 Mar. 1796 James Losh sent Wordsworth a parcel of books containing this volume of the *Monthly Magazine* (*LD* ii; *EY*, p. 186n.).

May 1794 the leaders of the Corresponding and Constitutional Societies had been arrested and imprisoned in the Tower and Newgate Jail. Habeas Corpus was suspended on 23 May, and the prisoners were held over the summer until formally charged with treason on 2 October. Thomas Hardy, Horne Tooke, and John Thelwall were then brought to trial and acquitted during the next two months; after Thelwall's acquittal on 5 December, the other prisoners were freed without trial. The experience nevertheless encouraged Thomas Hardy, who had founded the London Corresponding Society in January 1792, to resign from the society and concentrate on rebuilding his shoemaking business. John Thelwall also retired from the Corresponding Society, and explained his reasons for doing so at the mass meeting in Copenhagen Fields, 26 October 1795. 'I have of late ceased to be a member of the society that called this meeting', Thelwall said:

The plain fact is, Citizens, that the advice of certain friends, in whose judgment and whose patriotism I can confide, some reflections upon late perversions of the law, the desire of frustrating future attempts to check the progress of liberty by charges of constructive and accumulative treason, and the consequent precautions of personal prudence, have prevented me of late from acting as a member of the London Corresponding Society

—but he added: 'I have always retained the most inviolable attachment to the *principles* for which you associate.'[2]

Had the verdict on 5 December 1794 turned against Thelwall he would presumably have been executed, hence his 'precautions of personal prudence' in quitting the society. He was afraid that 'wayward passions' and 'imprudences' of other members could lead to a second prosecution, which might be successful. But Thelwall's retirement from the Corresponding Society was not the end of his political career. He ceased 'acting as a member', but his activities had not ceased altogether. After 6 February 1795 he resumed his lectures at Beaufort Buildings, Strand, believing that 'a mind trusting only to itself, and independent of the humours and sentiments of others, may in some circumstances of society, do more service to the cause of liberty and justice . . .' (*Tribune*, i.

---

[2] John Thelwall, *Peaceful Discussion, and not Tumultuary Violence the Means of Redressing National Grievances* (London, 1795), 1–2 [cited hereafter as *Peaceful Discussion*].

332). Although he was acting independently Thelwall remained the most prominent radical figure in London during 1795, and claimed an average attendance at his lectures of over five hundred people per night (*Tribune*, ii. vi). But, while his reformist principles were unaltered by the treason trials, he was now conscious of the dangers faced in publicizing them. Government spies attended his lectures, and so consistently misrepresented him in their reports that he was obliged to hire a shorthand writer to take transcripts which were later published in the *Tribune*. He took care to strengthen his hat against assassins, carried 'a short tuck-stick', and preferred to walk down the middle of the street at night to avoid attack.[3]

Thelwall's wish to further the cause of reform and his fears for his own safety illustrate the dilemma confronting friends of liberty in 1794–5. While he no longer belonged to the Corresponding Society in 1795, Thelwall was undeterred in his support for its activities. 'The shopkeeper, the mechanic, the poor ploughman, all suffer together', he told the crowd on 26 October 1795, 'and to reform the corruption which is destroying us is a common cause, in which we ought all to unite heart and hand together; for there is no other way to work out our political salvation.'[4] The following month Coleridge left Clevedon to 'join head, heart, and hand' with his 'unnumber'd brethren', in the fight for 'political salvation'. Like Thelwall, Coleridge had faced a hostile audience intent on disrupting his lectures. '[T]he opposition of the Aristocrats is so furious and determined', he told George Dyer in February 1795, 'that I begin to fear, that the Good I do is not proportionate to the Evil I occasion—Mobs and Mayors, Blockheads and Brickbats, Placards and Press gangs have leagued in horrible Conspiracy against me . . . and . . . were scarcely restrained from attacking the house in which the "damn'd Jacobine was jawing away"' (*CL* i. 152). Later in the same letter, he told Dyer that he had been '*obliged* to publish' his *Moral and Political Lecture*, 'it having been confidently asserted that there was Treason in it' (*CL* i. 152). For the same reason, Thelwall

---

[3] *The Life of John Thelwall by his Widow* (London, 1837), 135 [cited hereafter as *Thelwall Life*], and *Recollections of the Life of John Binns, . . . written by Himself* (Philadelphia, 1854), 44 [cited hereafter as *Binns*].
[4] *Peaceful Discussion*, p. 9.

employed his shorthand writer to guard against over-zealous informers.

Coleridge's lecturing activities at Bristol very closely resembled those of Thelwall in London. In 1795 both were lecturing independently of the popular reform societies, while making a common cause with them in the campaign for reform and an end to the war with France. Furthermore, they kept a close eye on each other throughout the year and appear to have had a considerable mutual influence. Coleridge's response to Thelwall's popularizing of *Political Justice* has already been mentioned in Chapter 3, and later on in 1795 the Two Bills prompted a further exchange between Bristol and London that led to Coleridge's and Thelwall's personal acquaintance and growing friendship during the next two years.

The Two Bills were designed to suppress the reform movement as a whole, though the immediate pretext was an attack on the king's carriage at the opening of parliament on 29 October. A large crowd gathered, shouting 'Down with Pitt!', 'No war!', 'No king!', 'No Pitt!', 'Peace!', 'Bread!', and a stone broke a window in the king's carriage as it drove past. 'My Lord, I, I, I've been shot at!', George reputedly exclaimed as he arrived at the House of Lords (*MWC*, p. 158). Grenville's 'Treasonable Practices' Bill sought to make all criticism of the king and his heirs and successors, whether spoken or written, a treasonable offence. Pitt's 'Seditious Meetings' Bill was intended to limit the size of public meetings called 'for the alteration of matters established in church and state', and rendered all such meetings liable to the control of magistrates. The Bill was deliberately framed to prevent the Corresponding Society holding mass meetings such as that on 26 October 1795, and to stop Thelwall's lectures at Beaufort Buildings. Both acts were passed into law on 18 December 1795, a date already significant in the radical calendar as the third anniversary of Paine's trial in 1792.

On 9 December 1795 Thelwall attacked the Treason Bill. '*Hume* might have been hanged for his "Idea of a Free Commonwealth"', he told his audience, 'as *Godwin* has shewn in his "Considerations"—The future venders of that work may be hanged, drawn and quartered, as Coleridge has shewn in his "Protest"' (*Tribune*, iii. 159). Thelwall was thinking of Coleridge's condemnation of the Bill in *The Plot Discovered*, which was probably published at Bristol between 4 and 6 December:[5]

To promulge what we believe to be truth is indeed a law beyond law; but now if any man should publish, nay, if even in a friendly letter or in social conversation any should assert a Republic to be the most perfect form of government, and endeavour by all argument to prove it so, he is guilty of High Treason . . . (*Lects. 1795*, p. 289)

Thelwall responded swiftly to Coleridge's pamphlet, probably because of Coleridge's reference to his London lectures as the ostensible target of the Seditious Meetings Bill. 'Nothing could make [Thelwall] of importance but that he speaks the feelings of multitudes', Coleridge said, then went on to enquire whether Thelwall could effectively oppose the government if he were merely 'an unsupported malcontent'. 'William Pitt knows', Coleridge continued, 'that Thelwall is the voice of tens of thousands' (*Lects. 1795*, p. 297).

Oddly enough, Thelwall construed Coleridge's comments in *The Plot Discovered* as a personal attack. Reports to this effect reached Coleridge, prompting his letter of April 1796 which led to a regular correspondence over the next year and, ultimately, to Thelwall's visit to Stowey and Alfoxden in July 1797. 'Pursuing the same end by the same means we ought not to be strangers to each other', Coleridge's letter begins:

—I have heard that you were offended by the manner in which I mentioned your name in the Protest against the Bills—I have looked over the passage again, and cannot discover the objectionable sentence. The words 'unsupported Malcontent' are caught up from the well-known contemptuous pages of Aristocratic Writers & turned upon them: they evidently could not be spoken in my own person, when 5 or 6 lines below, I affirm that you are the 'Voice of Tens of Thousands' —certainly therefore not 'an unsupported Malcontent.' . . .
—When I recited the Protest, the passage was 'unsupported Malcontents' meaning myself & you—but I afterwards was seized with a fit of modesty & omitted myself—(*CL* i. 204–5)

Despite Coleridge's 'fit of modesty', his letter reveals that in 1795–6 he identified his own political lecturing with Thelwall's —and that Thelwall took a reciprocal interest in Coleridge's

---

[5] See P. Kitson, 'Coleridge's *The Plot Discovered*: A New Date', *N&Q* (Mar. 1984), 57–8.

activities at Bristol. The campaign against the Treason and Seditious Meetings Bills clarifies Coleridge's relation to Thelwall; it also helps to place him within the wider context of liberal and reformist opinion at this time, and to establish a link with his former mentor at Cambridge, William Frend.

On 12 November 1795 Thelwall spoke at the General Meeting of the Corresponding Society in Copenhagen Fields. This meeting had been called to vindicate the society from any connection with the attack on the king's coach on 29 October, and to demonstrate public opposition to the Two Bills. The society's 'Address to the King' was drawn up by Thelwall, who also read it aloud to the crowd. 'Parliamentary corruption, and an unjust and ruinous war, have reduced us to beggary and famine', Thelwall said, 'and when we call for the reformation of the *one*, and the relinquishment of the *other*, Bills are brought into Parliament *by your Majesty's ministers*, which make it FELONY and HIGH TREASON to give *a tongue to those miseries* we cannot but feel!!!'[6] Five days later Coleridge attended a meeting at the Bristol Guildhall 'convened by public Advertisement', to

'congratulate his Majesty on his late providential escape from the attack and insult offered to his person, and to shew their utmost abhorrence of such proceedings . . . [and] at the same time, to implore his Majesty to remove the present heavy Calamities and Distresses of the People, by restoring to them the Blessings of Peace.' (Lects. 1795, p. 359)

An account of the proceedings at Bristol was published on 23 November in a London newspaper, the *Star*. After a loyal address had been approved, an amendment was proposed 'to beseech his Majesty to restore the Blessings of Peace to his faithful People' (*Lects. 1795*, p. 359). At this the Guildhall became 'extremely agitated', but after some time Coleridge succeeded in making himself heard. He condemned the attack on the king, but like Thelwall was more concerned 'to give *a tongue to those miseries* we cannot but feel':

He began by expressing his astonishment at the paradoxes he had heard: he said, that the whole business was a paradox. If the outrage on his Majesty's person was a great evil (and it certainly was) the best method

---

[6] *The Speech of John Thelwall at the Second Meeting of the London Corresponding Society, November 12, 1795* (London, 1795), 5–6.

2. James Gillray, *Copenhagen House*. John Thelwall appears on the right foreground addressing the assembled citizens at the mass meeting of the London Corresponding Society, 12 November 1795. The speaker on the left is John Gale Jones, and in the background is Richard 'Jacobin' Hodgson, the radical hatter from Westminster. Joseph Priestley appears in the centre foreground facing Thelwall, and the two urchins playing democratic roulette in front of him look like Coleridge, left, and Southey, right. 'Citizen Wordsworth' sits in the tree behind John Gale Jones.

to disapprove of it, and to prevent a repetition of such evils, was to remove the cause: the insult would never have been offered, if the people had not been rendered outrageous by their sufferings under the present cruel, sanguinary, and calamitous war. They had been cajoled into an approbation of it, at its commencement: and they had felt their error. . . . Mr. C. contended that the poorest subjects had the most at stake, they had 'their all'. 'Though the war,' said he, 'may take much from the property of the rich, it left them much: but a PENNY taken from the pocket of a poor man might deprive him of a dinner.'

He was here authoritatively stopped . . . (*Lects. 1795*, p. 361)

The chairman evidently wanted to avoid trouble, but the *Star* reported Coleridge's speech as 'the most elegant, the most pathetic, and the most sublime Address that was ever heard, perhaps, within the walls of that building' (*Lects. 1795*, p. 361). By the end of 1795 Coleridge was a confident and experienced public speaker, and his Guildhall speech reveals how very close he was to John Thelwall's position on the war, the attack on the king, and the Two Bills. His reference to the calamitous effects of war also recalls the conclusion to William Frend's *Peace and Union*: 'What must be their fate, when we suffer under the most odious scourge of the human race, and the accumulation of taxes takes away half of that daily bread, which is scarce sufficient at present for their support?' (*P&U*, pp. 47–8). *Peace and Union* had appeared in February 1793. Its publication coincided with the 'commencement' of the French war, and it is likely that Coleridge was thinking of Frend's appendix to his pamphlet, 'The Effect of War on the Poor', when he referred to the nation having been 'cajoled into an approbation' of the conflict. Moreover, while Coleridge was voicing his opposition in the Bristol Guildhall, Frend was furthering the same cause in London too.

During 1794–5 the imprisonment, prosecution, and subsequent resignation of the founding members of the Corresponding Society was compensated by the emergence of a second generation of leaders. Among them were William Frend, Francis Place, and John Binns, all three of whom were also prominent in the radical intellectual circles associated with Godwin and Holcroft—where Wordsworth could also be found up until August 1795. On 7 December Frend was present at the last mass meeting of the Corresponding Society in Marylebone Fields, and he spoke from the tribune alongside Thelwall. The artist Joseph

Farington was in the crowd, and he subsequently described Frend's appearance and speech upon the Two Bills in his diary:

Friend,—he spells his name *Frend*,—is a gentlemanlike looking Man: of good stature and bulk; apparently about 34 or 5 years of age: Dark hair witht. powder.—He stated to the poeple [*sic*] that the Bill of rights, limited even the power of parliaments, any act of which, inconsistent with the principles of the constitution, would be waste paper, and should be disregarded; and the Juries, before whom persons may be brought, under the provisions of the proposed Bills, were bound as Englishmen to shew their contempt of the bills, by acquitting the accused persons; unless they had been guilty of some offence which is at present considered criminal.—This was the principal point of his speech.—He was dressed in blue with a white waistcoat; and seemed in appearance ill suited to those about him . . . [7]

Frend's own prosecution at Cambridge would have lent impetus to his instruction that juries should acquit 'accused persons', in contempt of the Bills. Farington disapproved of Thelwall —'a little, and very mean looking Man'—and seems to have regarded Frend as a gentleman who had fallen into bad company. He nevertheless followed the debate about the Two Bills over the next weeks, and eight days after they passed into law he reported that 'poeple of property are in general in favor of Government; as are also respectable people of a lower class'.[8] The Two Bills also united 'unrespectable' opposition to the government. Mrs Thelwall recalled the 'ferment' during November and December 1795, the 'union of heart' among reformists, and the renewed co-operation between Whigs and the popular societies at this moment.[9] On 16 November the Duke of Bedford and Fox addressed the Whig Club in New Palace Yard, both wearing the radical uniform favoured by Thelwall, Frend, and—in 1796—by Coleridge. Farington attended this meeting too:

A little after 12 the Hustings being prepared. The Duke of Bedford &c. came upon it. Much hallooing & clapping on their appearance. The Duke was dressed in a Blue Coat & Buff waistcoat with a round Hat. His Hair cropped and without powder.—Fox also cropped, and without

[7] *The Diary of Joseph Farington*, ed. K. Garlick, A. Macintyre, and K. Cave (16 vols published; New Haven and London, 1978–84), ii. 428 [cited hereafter as *Farington Diary*].

[8] *Farington Diary*, ii. 455.

[9] *Thelwall Life*, p. 397.

powder, His Hair grisly grey . . . After much acclamation Fox adressed [*sic*] the multitude stating the loss of the liberties of the people, if the Bill passed, and calling upon them to come forward and support a Petition to the House of Commons against it.[10]

On the following day Coleridge made his sublime speech in the Bristol Guildhall, responding to a widely felt sense of crisis that united the Whig Club and the London Corresponding Society in condemnation of the government. His opinions at this moment coincided with those of John Thelwall in identifying the war as the cause of public unrest, and with Frend and Fox in opposing the Two Bills. All four agreed on the need to petition king and Commons. The Prospectus to the *Watchman* was the product of these months of crisis and unity: '[*The Watchman's*] chief objects are to co-operate (1) with the WHIG CLUB in procuring a repeal of Lord Grenville's and Mr. Pitt's bills, now passed into laws, and (2) with the PATRIOTIC SOCIETIES, for obtaining a Right of Suffrage general and frequent' (*Watchman*, p. 5).

When Coleridge was 'constrained' to quit Sara and Clevedon early in November 1795, his career as a political radical was about to reach its peak. His participation in the Guildhall meeting and his lecture *The Plot Discovered* aligned him with liberals and reformists in Bristol and London. Thelwall's awareness of Coleridge coupled with the report of Coleridge's speech in the *Star* suggest that he was becoming a prominent figure in contemporary opposition, and was by no means a minor provincial, 'a sort of little Bristol Thelwall' as E. P. Thompson once suggested.[11] There can be no doubt, either, that Wordsworth was acquainted with Coleridge's reputation while in London earlier in 1795. On 24 October he told Mathews that 'Coleridge was at Bristol part of the time [he] was there', which implies that both had already heard of him before Wordsworth's departure from London in August (*E Y*, p. 153).

Just over a month after Wordsworth's letter to Mathews, Azariah Pinney wrote to Racedown telling Wordsworth about the recent proceedings in the Guildhall. 'I am afraid you will think me tedious', he told Wordsworth,

[10] *Farington Diary*, ii. 404. Coleridge told Josiah Wade that he had 'preached in coloured Cloths' at Nottingham in Jan. 1796 (*CL* i. 180), and he later recalled in *Biographia* that he had worn 'a blue coat and white waistcoat' when 'preaching' on his *Watchman* tour (*BL* i. 179).

[11] In 'Disenchantment or Default?', p. 159.

in detailing the particulars of a meeting, the effective result of which is likely to be so nugatory—I think the Oppositionists deserve great credit for their peaceful and orderly behaviour on that day—I am glad to see so many petitions preferred, of the same nature, as I flatter myself they will now be attended to; for if the contrary be the case, I dread the consequence—the murmurs of the people will for a time be suppressed by the military forces but whenever circumstances shall favour resistance, their complaint will burst forth with the whirlwind's fury—I have not yet heard one argument that I have even thought plausible in favr. of the Convention bill: all I can learn from its supporters and advocates, is, that the Times justify the measure. Pray let me know what you think of it; but I can almost anticipate your sentiments.[12]

Pinney assumes Wordsworth's agreement in opposition, but his letter also conveys a mixture of optimism and despondency. He flattered himself the petitions 'will now be attended to', but also admitted the 'effective result' of the Guildhall meeting was likely to be 'nugatory'. Pinney's letter is important in registering a last moment of concerted effort to reform, and a simultaneous awareness of defeat. The same disenchantment is betrayed in Coleridge's Prospectus to the *Watchman*, where even as he announced his willing co-operation he confessed the cause lost, the Bills 'now passed into laws'. His call for 'a Right of Suffrage general and frequent' reiterates the demands of dissenters and reformists since the 1770s, but in doing so at this moment seems correspondingly hopeless.

The Two Bills succeeded in suppressing the reform movement, and there were no more mass meetings after December 1795. In the following year the London Corresponding Society was split by quarrels over tactics and finances, and its membership gradually declined (Goodwin, pp. 402–3). John Thelwall undertook a series of lectures at Norwich in June 1796, but when he tried to continue at Yarmouth and Wisbech he was threatened by pressgangs of sailors and was forced to give up (Goodwin, pp. 404–5). Coleridge's *Watchman* tour in the Midlands and North offers a parallel to Thelwall's efforts in East Anglia, and his 'preaching' was received more kindly. Writing from Birmingham on 18 January, Coleridge told Josiah Wade: 'Yesterday I preached twice, and, indeed, performed the whole service, morning and

---

[12] BUL, Pinney Family Letter Book 13. See also R. Woof, 'Wordsworth and Coleridge: Some Early Matters', *BWS* 79–82.

afternoon. There were about fourteen hundred persons present, and my sermons, (great part extempore) were *preciously peppered with Politics*. I have here, at least, double the number of subscribers, I had expected' (*CL* i. 176). Coleridge apparently obtained one thousand subscriptions for the *Watchman* on this tour (*BL* i. 184), but the number was insufficient to cover printing expenses. '—In short,' he told Thomas Poole on 5 May 1796, 'my tradesmen's Bill[s] for the Watchman, including what Paper I have bought since the seventh number, the Printing, &c— amount to exactly five pounds more than the whole amount of my receipts' (*CL* i. 208). On Friday, 13 May the tenth issue appeared, but carried Coleridge's announcement on the final page that 'This is the last Number of the WATCHMAN' (*Watchman*, p. 374). One month earlier Thelwall had stopped publishing his *Tribune* in London.

For Coleridge and Thelwall the winter of 1795–6 was to prove the last moment when a concerted effort for reform seemed practicable. Each maintained his opposition hereafter, but the displacement of political possibility set them on course for Alfoxden in July 1797 when their discussions would turn upon poetry as much as on politics. Azariah Pinney rightly anticipated Wordsworth's opposition to the Two Bills in November 1795, but Wordsworth had already moved away from the centre of radical life in London to live with Dorothy at Racedown Lodge in Dorset. The autumn and winter of 1795–6 was a decisive period for him too, but for rather different reasons.

'Cautious William': Wordsworth in 1794

On 23 May 1794 Richard Wordsworth wrote to William advising him about the dangers of declaring his politics. 'I hope you will be cautious in writing or expressing your political opinions', he warned. 'By the suspension of the Habeas Corpus Acts the Ministers have great powers' (*EY*, p. 121n.). Richard had not lost any time before contacting his brother, for the Acts had been suspended that very day—shortly after the leaders of the Corresponding and Constitutional Societies had been arrested and detained. On 28 May Dorothy reassured Richard that she could answer 'for William's caution about expressing his political opinions', and added: 'He is very cautious and seems well aware of the dangers of a contrary conduct' (*E Y*, p. 121).

Five days before, and at the very moment Richard was writing his warning letter, 'cautious' William had declared to William Mathews that he belonged to 'that odious class of men called democrats, and of that class [would] forever continue' (*E Y*, p. 119). To call oneself a 'democrat' in 1794 meant that one held a number of specific political opinions. In *The Voice of the People*, Citizen Richard Lee offered this definition: 'DEMOCRAT,—one who maintains the rights of the people; an enemy to privileged orders, and all monarchial encroachments, the advocate of peace, œconomy, and reform.'[13] Wordsworth's opinions in 1794 coincided exactly. On 8 June he wrote again to Mathews:

I disapprove of monarchical and aristocratical governments, however modified. Hereditary distinctions and privileged orders of every species I think must necessarily counteract the progress of human improvement: hence it follows that I am not amongst the admirers of the British constitution. (*E Y*, pp. 123–4)

A year earlier the lawyer John Frost had been jailed and pilloried for expressing similar opinions—while drunk—in a coffee-house. 'I am for equality', he allegedly announced to an informer; 'I can see no reason why any man should not be on a footing with another; it is every man's birth-right . . . the constitution of this country is a bad one.'[14] Wordsworth may well have been thinking of Frost's fate when he referred to the government's repressive 'auxiliaries' of 'imprisonment and the pillory' in his *Letter* (*Pr. W*. i. 36). He decided not to publish his pamphlet in 1793, but his letters to Mathews in 1794 were less circumspect about declaring his political opinions. The post was not secure and Wordsworth's expressed disapproval of monarchy, aristocracy, and the constitution would have been sufficient to attract an informer's attention if the letters had fallen into the wrong hands. In his *Narrative of Facts Relating to a Prosecution for High Treason*, Thomas Holcroft mentioned the non-delivery of a letter he had sent to his son and daughter: 'as several of their letters addressed to me have miscarried,' he wrote, 'it is not improbable that it has

---

[13]   Richard Lee, *The Voice of the People* (London, 1795), unpaginated.
[14]   Cited in *Tribune*, ii. 225, and see also *The Trial of John Frost for Seditious Words* (London, 1794), 12, and *State Trials*, xxii. 476.

already been read, by the agents of ministry.'[15] By disclosing his democratic ideas in a letter, Wordsworth risked a similar 'miscarriage' of his own correspondence.

Suppose that Wordsworth had been visited by the 'agents of ministry' at Windy Brow in 1794, or later on in London: his acquaintance with Nicholson, his two visits to France, the closing lines of 'Descriptive Sketches', the manuscripts of his pamphlet 'by a Republican' and of 'Salisbury Plain' would all have appeared as evidence of an increasingly 'seditious' tendency in Wordsworth's opinions since 1791. Although there is no surviving evidence that Wordsworth's letters were opened, by July 1797 his name was familiar to the chief Bow Street magistrate and spymaster Richard Ford, as the 'Spy Nozy' affair reveals. Sometime after 1793, it seems, their paths had crossed though when and where is not apparent.[16] Wordsworth's letter of 8 June 1794 was particularly indiscreet, for besides declaring his democratic sympathies he also discussed plans for the *Philanthropist*—the political journal he hoped to co-edit with Mathews.

At the outset of their scheme, Wordsworth promised to devote 'every additional energy in [his] power' to furthering the cause of peaceful reform in the *Philanthropist*. Although short of money and unable to travel to London, he was anxious to deflect the possibility of violent change in Britain: 'Aware of the difficulty of this', he wrote to Mathews,

it seems to me that a writer who has the welfare of mankind at heart should call forth his best exertions to convince the people that they can only be preserved from a convulsion by oeconomy in the administration of the public purse and a gradual and constant reform of those abuses which, if left to themselves, may grow to such a height as to render, even a revolution desirable. (*E Y*, p. 124)

As a democrat Wordsworth looked for an extended suffrage, parliamentary reform, 'oeconomy', and an end to the French war. But the *Philanthropist* scheme also provides clear evidence of William Godwin's influence in Wordsworth's reference to 'Hereditary distinctions and privileged orders . . . [which] must necessarily counteract the progress of human improvement'. The

[15] Thomas Holcroft, *A Narrative of Facts Relating to a Prosecution for High Treason* (London, 1795), 22 [cited hereafter as *Holcroft Narrative*].

[16] See Chapter 7 below for Spy Nozy's interference with John Thelwall's post at Nether Stowey.

Philanthropist was to be a Godwinian journal that would 'diffuse by every method a knowledge of those rules of political justice, from which the farther any government deviates the more effectually must it defeat the object for which government was ordained' (*E Y*, p. 124).

Wordsworth's letter of 8 June 1794 reveals him moving away from his former belief in revolutionary change; his support for parliamentary reform remained consistent and reflected the aspirations of other good men at this moment, but his intellectual justification for social progress was now derived from *Political Justice*. In the plan for the *Philanthropist* Wordsworth had also recovered a possibility for personal 'exertion' in the cause of human regeneration that had eluded him at Paris late in 1792. Like *A Letter to the Bishop of Llandaff*, the *Philanthropist* was never published. It does, however, mark an important development in Wordsworth's thought that was to lead him towards Godwin and his associates in London in 1795. It also indicates —if only in prospect—that Wordsworth seriously considered joining Coleridge, Thelwall, and others in working for the peaceful 'political salvation' of the country. Whereas Coleridge's efforts were rooted in his religious belief, Wordsworth's were vindicated by *Political Justice*. To establish Wordsworth's intellectual debt to Godwin and the significance of their friendship, it is necessary to assess Godwin's stature on the contemporary radical scene and the extent of his influence in *Political Justice*.

Tom Paine's 'Ardent friend'

> —there was not a person almost to be met with in town or village who had any acquaintance with modern publications, that had not heard of the Enquiry concerning Political Justice . . .
>
> (William Godwin, ?1807)[17]

In the first edition of *Political Justice* Godwin opposed all forms of political association, and advocated instead the 'uncontrolled exercise of private judgment' as the means to the moral and intellectual improvement of mankind (*PJ* i. 158, 163). 'Human beings should meet together, not to enforce, but to enquire', he said, for 'Truth disclaims the alliance of marshalled numbers' (*PJ*

[17] A-S Dep. c. 531. Autobiographical fragment.

i. 216). The influence of truth on the human mind was necessary and irresistible, its ultimate triumph inevitable. Not surprisingly, then, Godwin regarded the 'alliance of marshalled numbers' in the L CS and S CI as needless. Unlike his friend Thomas Holcroft, who had been a leading member of the S CI since 1792, Godwin never joined the metropolitan reform societies and he 'frequently endeavoured to dissuade [John Thelwall] from continuing [his] Lectures' (*Tribune*, ii. viii). In Godwin's opinion, mass meetings and crowded lecture halls hindered the process of private judgement by inflaming the 'passions' of those who attended. They also provoked the government into repressive measures that prevented 'enquiry' and the dissemination of truth. In *Political Justice* Godwin advocated a radical quietism:

The complete reformation that is wanted, is not instant but future reformation. It can in reality scarcely be considered as of the nature of action. It consists in an universal illumination. Men feel their situation, and the restraints, that shackled them before, vanish like a mere deception. When the true crisis shall come, not a sword will need to be drawn, not a finger to be lifted up. (*PJ* i. 222–3)

There was to be no recourse to action at the moment of 'true crisis', since the gradual process of 'universal illumination' had already completed the necessary regeneration of the human mind. Godwin never defined any precise point in the future when this might be achieved, which was one cause of Coleridge's and Southey's reservations about *Political Justice* in 1795. Nevertheless, Godwin saw the efforts of the reform societies, and Thelwall's lectures, as redundant to the 'complete reformation that is wanted'.

As the author of *Political Justice* Godwin is frequently dismissed as an intellectual elitist, a theoretician who held aloof from the activities of the friends of liberty during the 1790s.[18] This was certainly the opinion of the government. Although the cabinet considered prosecuting Godwin on 25 May 1793, they

[18] See, for example, 'Bliss was it in that Dawn: The Matter of Coleridge's Revolutionary Youth', *TLS* (6 Aug. 1971) 931: 'Godwin, with his aloof elitism and his canny avoidance of persecution, ...' Compare *MWC*, p. 107: 'William Godwin's *Political Justice* . . . was confined to a small and highly literate circle', and especially Thompson's footnote, 'Godwin's philosophical anarchism reached a working-class public only after the [Napoleonic] Wars'. In fact, John Thelwall was using Godwin's ideas in his public lectures of 1795, and 'the working-class public' had access to *Political Justice* two decades earlier than Thompson suggests.

did not believe that *Political Justice* would achieve a circulation comparable to Paine's *Rights of Man*. Pitt cynically commented that '"a three guinea book could never do much harm amongst those who had not three shillings to spare"'.[19] *Political Justice* was 'safe' because expensive, and its appeal seemed limited to intellectuals.

Wordsworth's account of his Godwinian self in *The Prelude* appears to vindicate Pitt's judgement, by emphasizing the philo-sophic abstraction of *Political Justice* and playing down its significance in the political context of 1793–5:

> the dream
> Was flattering to the young ingenuous mind
> Pleased with extremes, and not the least with that
> Which makes the human reason's naked self
> The object of its fervour.
>
> (x. 814–18)

But Wordsworth was somewhat disingenuous when he wrote these lines, recalling Godwin's philosophy as a work of callow intellect that appealed only to the young and naïve. *The Prelude* does not suggest the complex significance of *Political Justice* for Wordsworth and his contemporaries between 1793 and 1795; although he does describe the intellectual confusion to which Godwin led him, he remains silent about the wider implications of his 'despair' as a moment in his political life. In fact, Pitt misjudged Godwin's status as a radical figurehead and the extent to which his ideas infiltrated the popular reform movement.

On 10 October 1824, 'in the sixty-ninth year of [his] age', Godwin composed a short fragmentary account of his reasons for writing *Political Justice*, which had first appeared thirty-one years earlier. 'No man perhaps has at any time been animated with a more earnest spirit of philanthropy, than I was in the composition of that work', he recalled. But the fragment ends with Godwin's realization that his efforts had long been forgotten, that he was now 'a prey to poverty and destitution'. 'I may be the martyr of this work', he wrote,

but, if I am, I cannot repent that I produced it. My martyrdom, if such it shall prove, will not be a scene of eclat, acted before the eyes of

---

[19] D. Locke, *A Fantasy of Reason: The Life and Thought of William Godwin* (London, 1980), 60.

thousands, & cheered by the applauses of multitudes of admirers. If I am left to perish, it will be in obscurity solitude & destitution, cheered only by the consciousness of good intentions, & the hope that I shall have neither lived nor written in vain.[20]

Godwin's unexpressed wish was that he too might have shared in the 'martyrdom' of Hardy, Thelwall, and other friends of liberty in 1794, 'a scene of eclat, acted before the eyes of thousands, & cheered by the applauses of multitudes of admirers'. The most remarkable fact is that he did not. Godwin escaped prosecution for treason and sedition, while Thomas Holcroft—a far less important figure on the radical scene—became a martyr to the cause of reform and liberty. Although Godwin never joined the Corresponding and Constitutional Societies, he knew most of the leading members personally and later wrote about the defendants at the treason trials as '[his] particular friends', adding that 'more than half of them were known to [him]'.[21] Like Coleridge and Thelwall in 1795, Godwin was independent of the radical societies only to the extent that he did not pay a subscription to one or other of them. It is time for Godwin's 'aloof elitism', and the question of his status as a political radical in the 1790s, to be reconsidered.

On 7 November 1791 Godwin wrote to Paine 'soliciting the advantage of [his] personal acquaintance':

I regard you, sir, as having been the unalterable champion of liberty in America, in England & in France, from the purest views to the happiness and the virtue of mankind. I have devoted my life to these glorious purposes, & am at this moment employed upon a composition, embracing the whole doctrine of politics, & in which I shall endeavour to convince my countrymen of the mischiefs of monarchial government, & of certain other abuses not less injurious to society. I believe that a cordial & unreserved intercourse between men employed in the same great purposes, is of the utmost service to their own minds & to their cause. . . .

I am, sir, already the ardent friend of your views, your principles & your mind

WG.[22]

---

[20] A-S Dep. c. 537. Godwin's reflections on his own life, dated 10 Oct. 1824.
[21] A-S Dep. c. 531.
[22] A-S Dep. b. 227/2 (b). Draft letter to Paine, omitting Godwin's deletions.

Godwin introduces himself as Paine's disciple, presenting *Political Justice* as a sequel to *The Rights of Man*. When he announced that he too had 'devoted [his] life to these glorious purposes', he was not exaggerating for Paine's benefit. Godwin had also been an 'unalterable champion of liberty' since 1789, although his long-standing commitment has been underestimated. This in turn has produced confusion about Godwin's significance to Wordsworth in 1794–5.

Joseph Ritson refers to 'Citizen Godwin' in his letters, and with justification. Although Godwin had serious reservations about the popular reform movement, he nevertheless took a close interest in its activities. On 4 November 1789 he had joined Price and the Revolution Society at its commemorative dinner in the London Tavern. He was evidently acquainted with members of the society and some of those present at that dinner—Kippis, Tooke, Lofft, Brand Hollis, Robinson, and Fawcett—were also connected with the SCI. He joined the Revolution Society dinner on 14 July 1790 to celebrate the first anniversary of the fall of the Bastille, and he heard Priestley preach the funeral sermon for Price, 1 May 1791 (GD ii, iii). Rather than holding aloof, Godwin was at the centre of dissenting and radical life from the very beginning of the French Revolution.

On 27 February 1791 Godwin called on Paine, but probably found that he was not at home. On 2 March he was reading the first part of *The Rights of Man* but he did not actually meet Paine until 4 November. On that day both were in the company dining at the London Tavern, along with Pétion, Tooke, and Priestley. Three days later Godwin wrote the letter of introduction quoted above, and on 13 November they met over dinner at Joseph Johnson's bookshop in St Paul's Churchyard. 'Dine at Johnson's' he wrote in his diary, 'with Paine, Shouet & Wolstencraft; talk of monarchy, Tooke, Johnson, Voltaire, pursuits & religion' (GD iv). This was Godwin's first meeting with Mary Wollstonecraft, whose *Vindication of the Rights of Men* had been published by Johnson in December 1790. At this time she was working on her *Vindication of the Rights of Women*, but Godwin was apparently most interested in talking to Paine. In his *Memoir* of Mary, Godwin recalled that he had

little curiosity to see Mrs. Wollstonecraft, and a very great curiosity to see Thomas Paine. Paine, in his general habits, is no great talker; and, though he threw in occasionally some shrewd and striking remarks, the conversation lay principally between me and Mary. I, of consequence, heard her, very frequently when I wished to hear Paine.

Time would change Godwin's estimate of Mary, but in November 1791 he was at work on *Political Justice* and evidently anxious to discuss politics with the author of *The Rights of Man*. On the other hand, the *Memoir* also suggests that Paine himself was a disappointment. Godwin had declared himself an 'ardent friend' to Paine's 'views', 'mind', and 'principles' only to find that he 'occasionally' said something worth hearing but was in general 'no great talker'.[23]

There are no further meetings with Paine recorded in Godwin's diary after the dinner at Johnson's. He read the second part of *The Rights of Man* on 16 February 1792, the day of publication. When Paine's trial for sedition came on at the Old Bailey on 18 December, Godwin was in the visitors' gallery. Like Thomas Erskine, he was shocked by the proceedings and condemned the trial in a letter to the *Morning Chronicle*:

Good God! what species of monster is this Thomas Paine, that all the rules of equity cease to be rules the moment he is the subject of animadversion? I was myself present at the trial of this man. We all know by what means a verdict was procured: by repeated proclamations, by all the force, and all the fears of the kingdom being artfully turned against one man.[24]

Although the immediate occasion of this letter was Paine's trial, Godwin's principal concern was the 'absurd and barbarous' alarm raised during 1792 by the government and John Reeves's 'Society for the Preservation of Liberty and Property against Republicans and Levellers'. From the earliest stages of repression, Godwin's response to political intimidation was to defend the 'advocates of Reform'.[25] During 1793 he visited Thomas Muir and Thomas Fysshe Palmer, imprisoned in the Woolwich hulks while awaiting transportation (7 Dec., G D v), and the following year he called on Joseph Gerrald and William Winterbotham in Newgate (7 April, and subsequently, G D v). Finally on 21

---

[23] See William Godwin, *Memoirs of the Author of 'A Vindication of the Rights of Women'* (London, 1798), 94.
[24] Godwin, *Uncollected Writings*, p. 116.
[25] Godwin, *Uncollected Writings*, p. 115.

October 1794 Godwin published his *Cursory Strictures on the Charge Delivered by Lord Chief Justice Eyre to the Grand Jury*, exposing the shortcomings of the government's case in the forthcoming treason trials and making a significant contribution to the acquittals of Hardy, Tooke, and Thelwall. Godwin may not have enjoyed a 'martyrdom' himself, but he did help to ensure that the defendants lived to experience 'the applauses of multitudes of admirers'.

By the end of 1794 Godwin was known as the author of *Political Justice* and of *Caleb Williams*, and he was also one of the most visible and active political figures in London. Some years later he recollected the notoriety that *Political Justice* had brought him:

—there was not a person almost to be met with in town or village who had any acquaintance with modern publications, that had not heard of the Enquiry concerning Political Justice or that was not acquainted in a great or small degree with the contents of that work—I was no where a stranger—the doctrines of that work (though, if any book ever contained the dictates of an independent mind, mine might pretend to do so) coincided in a great degree with the sentiments then prevailing in English society; & I was every where received with curiosity & kindness—If temporary fame ever was an object worthy to be coveted by the human mind, I certainly obtained it in a degree that has seldom been exceeded.[26]

This curious passage was written when 'temporary fame' had deserted Godwin, and perhaps he was exaggerating the extent of his former popularity. Hazlitt's essay on 'Mr. Godwin' in *The Spirit of the Age* nevertheless gives a similar account: 'no one was more talked of, more looked up to, more sought after', Hazlitt remembered (Howe, xi. 16). Godwin's memory that he was 'no where a stranger' suggests that he was widely known, but also that those who had read *Political Justice* tended to be acquainted 'with modern publications' anyway. The extent to which his ideas influenced the members of the popular societies—those without three shillings to spare and who maybe could not read—is more difficult to judge.

In *The Spirit of the Age* Hazlitt describes the impact of *Political Justice* upon radical intellectuals:

[26] A-S Dep. c. 531.

No work in our time gave such a blow to the philosophical mind of the country as the celebrated *Enquiry concerning Political Justice*. Tom Paine was considered for the time as a Tom Fool to him; Paley an old woman; Edmund Burke a flashy sophist. Truth, moral truth, it was supposed, had here taken up its abode; and these were the oracles of thought. . . .—Mr. Godwin indulged in extreme opinions, and carried with him all the most sanguine and fearless understandings of the time.

(Howe, xi. 17)

The appearance of *Political Justice* on 14 February 1793 was especially opportune. The September Massacres and the recent execution of Louis inevitably raised doubts about the regeneration of France, especially among those who had looked for peaceful constitutional change. At a single stroke *Political Justice* reasserted the perfectibility of mankind: 'No mind', Godwin claimed, 'can be so far alienated from truth, as not in the midst of its degeneracy to have incessant returns of a better principle' (*PJ* i. 29). Paine had been in France since September 1792, and in February 1793 his 'ardent friend' emerged as his successor as intellectual leader to 'the philosophic mind of the country'. Hazlitt's recollection suggests that he carried radical opinion with him like a metaphysical Pied Piper: 'I am studying such a book!' Southey wrote in November 1793, 'I am inclined to think man is capable of perfection.'[27] His welcome for Godwin's philosophy came immediately after his despair following the execution of Brissot in October, and anticipates Wordsworth's response in 1794. But the appeal of *Political Justice* was not confined to the philosophic minds of undergraduates, or intellectuals disenchanted by events in France and Britain.

In May 1795 Coleridge was to warn his listeners at the Assembly Coffee-house in Bristol that 'the Stoical Morality which disclaims all the duties of Gratitude and domestic Affection has been lately revived in a book popular among the professed Friends of civil Freedom—'(*Lects. 1795*, p. 164). The immediate cause for Coleridge's worry was Thelwall's use of Godwin's strictures against gratitude in a lecture earlier that month. He was also in a position to know the real extent of Godwin's popularity among the intellectual leaders of the reformists, and hence his likely influence on the movement as a whole. In December 1794 he dined with Godwin and Holcroft, and presumably heard

[27] Bod. MS English Letters c. 22.

about sales of *Political Justice* and the progress of truth from the author himself. Godwin's diary shows that in 1794 he had been sought out by Wordsworth's acquaintances James Losh, John Tweddell, William Mathews, and the Oxford classicist Richard Porson.[28] Two months after Coleridge's dinner Wordsworth met Godwin at William Frend's house, 27 February 1795. While in London, Coleridge might also have heard about the influence of *Political Justice* among rank-and-file working-class members of the Corresponding Society from George Dyer and from Frend, both of whom were friends of Godwin and closely involved with the Society's activities. He had also talked to Perry and Grey, editors of the *Morning Chronicle* in which *Cursory Strictures* had recently appeared (*C L* i. 138). When Coleridge said that *Political Justice* was 'popular among the professed Friends of civil Freedom', his word carried authority. Thirty years later Hazlitt was to confirm that 'wherever liberty, truth, justice was the theme, [Godwin's] name was not far off' (Howe, xi. 16).

Godwin might criticize the 'alliance of marshalled numbers', but Coleridge and Hazlitt suggest that some members of the reform movement responded to his ideas and adopted those appropriate to their aims. But while Godwin and the reformists shared a belief in the future reformation of society, their grounds for doing so were of course very different. In particular, Godwin rejected all exertion to that end: 'The complete reformation that is wanted', he said, 'can in reality scarcely be considered as of the nature of action.' John Thelwall defined this paradox of *Political Justice* most succinctly. '[I]n the midst of the singularities with which that valuable work abounds,' Thelwall wrote in *The Tribune*, 'nothing is perhaps more remarkable than that it should at once recommend the most extensive plan of freedom and innovation ever discussed by any writer in the English language, and reprobate every measure from which even the most moderate reform can rationally be expected' (*Tribune*, ii, p. vii).

In pin-pointing this 'remarkable singularity' of *Political Justice*, Thelwall reveals why Godwin has been regarded as an

---

[28] Losh and Tweddell first appear in Godwin's diary on 3 Feb. 1794, and Porson on 1 Dec. William Mathews is first mentioned as attending a dinner at Thelwall's house on 10 Dec. 1794, shortly after Thelwall's acquittal. The diary actually reads 'Matthews' not 'Mathews', but on 15 Aug. 1795 he writes 'Wordsworth and Matthews', suggesting that he usually spelt the name with two t's.

armchair agitator, a mere theoretician. Yes, Godwin did 'reprobate' all forms of political action, but Thelwall's subsequent
claim that Godwin scrupulously avoided 'all popular intercourse'
was not quite true (*Tribune*, ii. p. xv). He reserved his independence from the reform movement but made his own contribution
to its 'glorious purposes' of liberty and truth, such that his ideas
had a wider currency and influence than the government expected. *Political Justice* did not remain the property of an elite,
but spread among the popular societies influencing their thinking
and the direction of the reform campaign. This did not happen
through Godwin's passive process of enquiry, but because some
of his disciples took 'every measure' to propagate Godwin's
principles in pamphlets, lectures, journals—much to Coleridge's
dismay. One such disciple was John Thelwall; another might
have been Wordsworth in his *Philanthropist*. Thelwall's use of
Political Justice in his lectures clarifies the nature of Godwin's
popular influence in 1795, and also offers a model for Wordsworth's intentions for the *Philanthropist*. Paradoxically, the
principal message of both was to urge the need for a Godwinian
passivity as a response to terrorism in France and ministerial
provocation at home. In the end this was disabling to any
possibility of progress and change, and would lead both Thelwall
and Wordsworth to a crisis of confidence in political reformation,
and in *Political Justice* itself, late in 1795–6.

'Scattering the seeds of justice': Thelwall, Godwin, and Wordsworth's 'Philanthropist'

> there is some reason in the language of reformers
> (Wordsworth to Mathews, 24 Dec., 1794; *EY*, p. 137)

Early in the first volume of *Political Justice*, Godwin claimed that
his system was an 'all comprehensive scheme, that immediately
applies to the removal of counteraction and contagion, that
embraces millions in its grasp, and that educates in one school the
preceptor and the pupil' (*PJ* i. 27). The 'uncontrolled exercise of
private judgment' was a fundamental principle of *Political Justice*, that eliminated the roles of teacher and pupil. Godwin
anticipated an immaculate triumph of truth, but there is a step
missing between the enlightenment of the individual mind and the
'grasp' of his scheme upon 'millions'. As Thelwall pointed out,

Godwin announced 'the most extensive plan of freedom and innovation', only to reprobate all means of realizing his vision. '[A] distant prospect, which we are never to reach,' Coleridge observed, 'will seldom quicken our footsteps, however lovely it may appear' (*Lects. 1795*, p. 44). There was, in fact, a place for the Godwinian 'preceptor' and this was one function of Wordsworth's *Philanthropist*.

Godwin's principal method of reformation was rational enquiry: 'Human beings should meet together, not to enforce, but to enquire', he said (*PJ* i. 216). Both Godwin and Holcroft were members of a small society devoted to this end, The Philomatheans.[29] John Binns, one of the leaders of the London Corresponding Society in 1795, was also a member and he recalled their meetings in his *Recollections*:

> William Godwin and Thomas Holcroft were among the most powerful and admired writers of their day. Their style ... was vigorous and captivating, yet were they among the most diffuse and tiresome of speakers. I was one of an association, 'The Philomathean Society', of which they were both members. The number was limited to twenty-one. The Society met once a fortnight, to debate a subject previously proposed. So prolix were both these gentlemen, that a committee of the society was instructed to buy, and did buy, two fifteen minute glasses, the society having adopted a rule, that no member should speak for a longer time. I have no recollection ever to have seen either of those glasses turned when any member, other than Godwin or Holcroft rose to speak.[30]

If Binns was right there must have been a great deal of enforcing, and not much room for enquiry, when Godwin or Holcroft rose to speak. Coleridge mentioned the unedifying 'fierceness and *dogmatism*' of Holcroft's conversation in a letter to Southey (*CL* i. 138); in *My First Acquaintance with Poets* Hazlitt recalls Coleridge being asked 'if he was not much struck *with* [Holcroft],

---

[29] So, apparently, was John Thelwall. See his *Ode to Science. Recited at the Anniversary Meeting of the Philomathian Society, June 20, 1791, By Brother Thelwall* (London, 1791):

> Hail Philomathians! then; and may the name
> (As with prophetic joy my soul forsees)
> Thro' distant ages hallow'd shine.
> Hail Candidates for guiltless fame!

[30] Binns, p. 45. Godwin's diary contains frequent references to 'Philomaths', which obviously denotes a meeting of the society. Wordsworth's membership is discussed later in this chapter.

and he said, he thought himself in more danger of being struck *by him*' (Howe, xvii. 112). But Binns's *Recollections* does more than substantiate Coleridge's and Hazlitt's anecdotes. Binns's presence among The Philomatheans establishes a direct link between Godwin and the Corresponding Society—with 'those who had not three shillings to spare'.

John Binns was a plumber's labourer, a self-taught man. He was chairman of the General Committee of the LCS at the mass meeting in Copenhagen Fields on 26 October 1795, and would obviously have known many of the leaders and ordinary members of the society. On 26 October, for example, he spoke on the tribune alongside John Gale Jones, John Thelwall, Francis Place, William Frend, Richard 'Jacobin' Hodgson, 'and other able and well-known popular speakers'.[31] Leaving aside Frend and Thelwall, Jones was a 'shabby, genteel' surgeon, Place a breeches-maker, Hodgson a hatter. When Farington attended the meeting on 7 December 1795, he reported Jones to be an orator of 'genius' and 'imagination', compared to Thelwall who was only a 'ready speaker'.[32]

Godwin knew many of these men personally, and they in turn had read *Political Justice*. Francis Place's *Autobiography* recalls that, during 1794–5, 'Binns used to leave his work as soon as he could, and came to me to read, whilst I worked, and thus we both obtained knowledge at the same time'.[33] One of the books they read and discussed was certainly *Political Justice*. Binns admired Godwin's writing, and Place actually devised his own work ethic from Godwin's principles. Having read *Political Justice* in 1793, he had used it to justify setting up his own business:

The fear of doing injury to others by contracting debts . . . is a proper feeling . . . Mr. Godwins book extinguished this fear in me. It led me to reason on the matter and convinced me that a man might turn others to account in every kind of undertaking without dishonesty, that the ordinary tricks of tradesmen were not necessary, and need not be practised. This was to me the most grateful kind of knowledge I could acquire and I resolved to lose no time in putting it in practice . . .[34]

---

[31] Binns, p. 53.
[32] *Farington Diary*, ii. 429.
[33] *The Autobiography of Francis Place*, ed. M. Thale (Cambridge, 1972), 143–4 (cited hereafter as Place).
[34] Place, p. 137.

Place wasn't being ironic: his *Autobiography* treats his early struggles as a journeyman tailor with high seriousness. His business acumen, though, was inconsistent with Godwin's concept of the 'general good': Godwin sought disinterestedness, but Place selfishly 'turned others to account'. Coleridge might well have claimed that Place's loss of the 'proper' fear of debt confirmed his worries about the moral shabbiness of *Political Justice*: 'In this System a man may gain his self-esteem with little Trouble, he first adopts Principles so lax as to legalize the most impure gratifications, and then prides himself on acting up to his Principles' (*Lects. 1795*, pp. 164–5).

The mention of Godwin in Place's *Autobiography* is important. Although he does not say that *Political Justice* influenced his political development, Place shows that it did make an impact upon working men—those whom Pitt thought could not afford the book. He recalls that in spring 1793 a 'good workman who was constantly employed' at breeches-making 'might earn a guinea a week, but scarcly any one was fully employed'.[35] Nevertheless, his poverty did not stop him reading Godwin. The majority of members of the LCS would perhaps have been illiterate, unlike Place and Binns, but by examining Godwin's influence on the leadership it is possible to establish what use was made of *Political Justice* in the popular societies and in the campaign for reform. At the same time, Wordsworth's intentions for his journal emerge more clearly.

Thelwall and Godwin were good friends—until they quarrelled over Godwin's *Considerations on Lord Grenville's and Mr. Pitt's Bills* late in 1795. Thelwall mentioned their 'frequent friendly conversations' in *The Tribune*, but he added: [Godwin] has frequently endeavoured to dissuade me from continuing my Lectures, by arguments, strong and convincing I suppose to him, though to me they appeared visionary and futile' (*Tribune*, ii, pp. vii–viii). Godwin's argument would have been that reform, and the wholesale regeneration of mankind, could be achieved without Thelwall's lectures which aroused the passions of his audience but did not enlighten their minds. Thelwall would have countered that Godwin's 'extensive plan of freedom' was futile unless measures were taken to achieve it: 'what can be so

---

[35] Place, p. 112.

important as to generalise, by the most expeditious means, those maxims and principles by which the science of politics can be rendered most subservient to its great end—the interest and happiness of the whole?' (*Tribune*, ii. p. xi). Thelwall saw himself as a teacher—'not so much . . . the reaper who goes into the field to collect the harvest of opinion, as the sower, whose business it is to scatter the seed' (*Tribune*, ii. p. xiv). Despite their differences over the means to achieve progress, though, Thelwall and Godwin coincided on the 'great end' of politics and the 'seed' that needed to be scattered among the people. 'However [Godwin] and myself may differ as to the *means* of reform', Thelwall wrote, 'there are certain *principles* of politics and morality upon which we are very well agreed, and particularly upon those maxims which define *justice* as the sole basis of *virtue*, and the promotion of the *general good*, as the sole criterion of justice' (*Tribune*, iii. 103). He accepted the essential principles of *Political Justice*, but demanded the 'most expeditious means' of communicating them to the people. Thelwall's method was lecturing, Wordsworth's was to be the *Philanthropist*.

When Thelwall was arrested on 12 May 1794 the government confiscated three coach-loads of his property, which they intended to examine for evidence to substantiate a charge of treason. Thelwall later said: 'it is impossible for me to state the whole of my loss: but among the books of considerable value which I have lost, are Godwin's Political Justice, and Darwin's elegant Poem the Botanic Garden. Two books, to replace which alone, the reader will recollect, will cost me near four pounds' (*Tribune*, i. 91). He never recovered his books, but the influence of *Political Justice* is apparent in some of his lectures in 1795. 'Citizens,' Thelwall announced to his audience at Beaufort Buildings on 16 May, 'It is not often that I enter upon any subject in this dry and abstract manner' (*Tribune*, i. 231). He had been attacking the 'pretended virtues' of what he termed the 'retrospective system', which he defined as nationality, 'the spirit of party' in politics and religion, and social '*proscription*' or inequality (*Tribune*, i. 226–7). In place of these he advocated the 'Prospective Principle of Virtue', which he drew straight from *Political Justice*. Godwin said: 'If justice have any meaning, it is just that I should contribute every thing in my power to the benefit of the whole' (*PJ* i. 81)—and Thelwall followed by telling his listeners that justice 'is a supreme virtue . . . justice embraces the whole universe . . . it is the elementary principle of justice that you should do all the good to all human beings that you have the power of doing' (*Tribune*, i. 230).

On 16 May 1795 Thelwall was offering Godwin's visionary prospect of a scheme that 'embraces millions in its grasp', but by enforcing the principles of *Political Justice* he believed he was providing a means to its 'great end—the interest and happiness of the whole'. He went on to condemn the 'retrospective' virtues of '*sorrow* and *regret*' as 'weaknesses, which it is no further necessary for me to dwell upon'—much as Wordsworth's Rivers would rail against 'compassion' and 'pity' in *The Borderers*. Thelwall then turned to gratitude, and claimed that a 'chain of serious reasoning' had 'induced [him] to consider it as a vice' (*Tribune*, i. 229)—a statement which prompted Coleridge's reply at Bristol later in the month. In London, though, Thelwall's use of Godwin probably had a stabilizing influence during the months of crisis late in 1795. As such, his efforts correspond exactly to Coleridge's wish to 'regulate the feelings of the ardent . . . that so we may not be the unstable Patriots of Passion or Accident' (*Lects. 1795*, p. 5), and to Wordsworth's hope to 'establish freedom with tranquillity' (*E Y*, p. 124).

In his speech to the London Corresponding Society at Copenhagen Fields on 26 October 1795, Thelwall outlined the general purpose of his lectures. 'Extensive circulation is undoubtedly my object,' he said, 'for he who disseminates right principles and right sentiments . . . most widely among the common people, is the best friend to the peace and happiness of Society'. He went on to attack the war and the high price of bread: 'there was never a period in which the great mass of the people were abandoned to a fifth part of the misery, or treated with a fifth part of the neglect and injustice, which they are obliged to endure at this hour . . .' But he added, 'it is the system you must reform, not wreak your revenge upon individuals'. Thelwall's overriding concern on 26 October was to counsel 'the common people' against violence, pointing—once again like Coleridge—to the 'misfortunes [which] have fallen upon a neighbouring country, . . . from being . . . less influenced by principle than by faction'. He was apprehensive that, if the reformists were provoked into violent opposition, the government would use such disturbance as a pretext for establishing their own system of terror:

Yes, Citizens, conspiracies there are; but they are not the friends of liberty who are the conspirators, but the friends of the tottering cause of despotism and corruption. Those are the wretches who will conspire together, in the vain hope of making the friends of liberty, by plunging them into tumult and disorder, the instruments of their detestable machinations.[36]

He had just escaped with his life from the treason trials, and had no reason to suppose that the government had been deflected from its conspiratorial policies. Three days later the response to the assault on the king's coach was to prove Thelwall right. A royal proclamation on 4 November claimed the incident had been provoked by 'divers inflammatory discourses' delivered on 26 October, and the government acted by bringing the Two Bills before parliament.[37]

Ironically, Thelwall had repeatedly emphasized the need for *Peaceful Discussion, and not Tumultuary Violence [as] the Means of Redressing National Grievances*. His message was thoroughly Godwinian: 'Adhere then to reason and to the principles of truth and justice; for these are the principles of Liberty', he told the assembled citizens: 'The real lover of mankind must therefore labour to redress their wrongs by purifying the fountains of political dispensation. What are these impure and polluted fountains? Parliamentary Corruption!—the system of Cabinet intrigue!—the system of Rotten Boroughs!'[38] His speech confirms his continuing support for parliamentary reform, but he was advocating a Godwinian process of 'enquiry' as the means to purify the 'retrospective' system of government: 'be assured, it is by discussion of principle alone, by laying the axe of reason to the root of the tree of corruption, that the blasting foliage of luxury, and the poisonous fruit of oppression can be destroyed.'[39] Thelwall's rhetoric was violent, but he was actually agreeing with Godwin that in 1795 reform could no longer 'be considered as of the nature of action'. His message got through. In a pamphlet

---

[36] Quotations from Thelwall are from *Peaceful Discussion*, pp. iv, 3, 7–8, 10, 12.
[37] *Parl Hist*. xxxii. 243.
[38] *Peaceful Discussion*, p. 11.
[39] *Peaceful Discussion*, p. 11.

Account of the meeting in Copenhagen Fields, Citizen Richard Lee commented that

the proceedings of this day . . . prove to the satisfaction of every reflecting, impartial, and disinterested mind, that it is by the persevering efforts of *reason only*, they can ever hope to defend and preserve that inestimable jewel, LIBERTY; and that tumult and disorder are the detestable engines to which their base and bitter enemies alone can wish them to resort.[40]

Lee thought that 26 October had been 'A DAY WELL SPENT'. If it was a triumph for Binns, Jones, Thelwall, Place, and Frend, it was Citizen Godwin's day too.

Paradoxically, Thelwall had 'generalized' the very principle which he felt disabled Godwin's 'extensive plan of freedom and innovation'. During 1795 he used *Political Justice* as a counterpoise to crisis, and had scattered the seeds of justice as widely as he would have wished. Politically and intellectually, though, he had worked himself into a corner by effectively declaring himself, and the reform movement, redundant. In April 1796 he was forced to leave his lecture hall in Beaufort Buildings, and the same month ceased publication of the *Tribune*. After the mass meetings of October and December 1795, the winter marked the demise of Thelwall as a radical leader and the beginning of the end of the popular reform movement. The Two Bills were a significant factor in this, but Thelwall's speeches late in 1795 show that he had reached a point of crisis—almost of self-contradiction—that has significant implications for Wordsworth's 'perplexity' at this time as well. When Wordsworth told Mathews in June 1794 that he intended 'to diffuse by every method a knowledge of those rules of political justice', his plan anticipated Thelwall's lectures and speeches the following year. It was to lead Wordsworth to a very similar end.

Godwin's Wordsworth: 'The Philanthropist', 1794

> But when events
> Brought less encouragement . . . evidence
> Safer, of universal application, such
> As could not be impeached, was sought elsewhere.
>
> (P. x. 779–80, 788–90)

[40] Richard Lee, *Account of the Proceedings of a Meeting of the London Corresponding Society, Monday, October 26, 1795* (London, 1795), 3.

By mid-1793 war with France had brought Wordsworth close to despair, and this is registered in the closing stanzas of 'A Night on Salisbury Plain':

> Say, rulers of the nations, from the sword
> Can ought but murder, pain, and tears proceed?
> Oh! what can war but endless war still breed?
>
> (Gill, p. 37, ll. 507–9)

Faced with continuing war Wordsworth confessed his need for a philosophical guide comparable to Beaupuy, but who would enable him to sustain the optimism they had shared in 1792 in the less auspicious climate of 1793:

> [W]hence but from the labours of the sage
> Can poor benighted mortals gain the meed
> Of happiness and virtue, how assuage
> But by his gentle words their self-consuming rage?
>
> (Gill, p. 37, ll. 510–13)

When Wordsworth completed this early version of his poem at Windy Brow in spring 1794, he had found his 'sage' in William Godwin. The 'gentle words' of *Political Justice* offered exactly what Wordsworth had asked for—a scheme for 'poor benighted mortals' to gain 'happiness and virtue'.

It is difficult to ascertain precisely when Wordsworth first read Godwin's book. *Political Justice* appeared in February 1793, but there is no clear indication that he had read it until just over a year later. On 17 February 1794 Wordsworth wrote to Mathews, who had just returned from Portugal, asking about the political state of that country:

What remarks do you make on the Portuguese? in what state is knowledge with them? and have the principles of free government any advocate there? or is Liberty a sound of which they have never heard? Are they so debased by superstition as we are told, or are they improving in anything? I should wish much to hear of those things . . . (*EY*, p. 113)

All these questions sound rather odd until one turns to Godwin's discussion of 'sincerity' in *Political Justice*. He had used Portugal as a test case to answer his question, 'Ought I explicitly to declare the sentiments I entertain?' (*PJ* i. 272). The alternatives were a sincere declaration of opinion, or concealment. 'The arguments in favour of concealment in this case are obvious,' Godwin claimed:

> [Portugal] is subject to a high degree of despotism, and, if I delivered my sentiments in this frank manner, especially if along with this I were ardent and indefatigable in endeavouring to proselyte the inhabitants, my sincerity would not be endured. In that country the institution of the holy inquisition still flourishes, and the fathers of this venerable court would find means effectually to silence me, before I had well opened my commission. (*PJ* i. 273)

It seems certain that Godwin had 'told' Wordsworth that the Portuguese were 'debased by superstition', and Wordsworth's references to the Godwinian ideals of 'knowledge' and 'improvement' in his letter reinforce this likelihood. His question to Mathews, 'have the principles of free government any advocate there?', would arise from Godwin's conclusion

> that a person so far enlightened upon these subjects, ought by no consideration to be prevailed upon to settle in Portugal; and, if he were there already, ought to quit the country with all convenient speed. His efforts in Portugal would probably be vain; but there is some other country in which they will be attended with the happiest consequences.
> (*PJ* i. 280–1)

Wordsworth's letter to Mathews offered a chance to check Godwin's claim about Portugal. However his true interest in Godwin's comments actually lay elsewhere, in their relevance to his own position and that of other friends of liberty in Britain in 1794. Godwin believed that there might yet be hope for Portugal as a result of 'efforts' made in 'some other country': 'These great and daring truths ought to be published in England, France and other countries; and the dissemination that will attend them here, will produce a report and afford an example, which after some time may prepare them a favourable reception there' (*PJ* i. 281). But in 1794 the dissemination of 'great and daring truths' in England was unlikely to produce the 'report' that Godwin intended. Rather than preparing for a 'favourable reception' of truth in England or elsewhere, the reformer would be sent to Botany Bay—or worse. Contemporary Britain was subject to an equally 'high degree of despotism', and the dilemma of all friends of liberty had been precisely formulated in Godwin's question: 'Ought I explicitly to declare the sentiments I entertain?'

In August 1793 Thomas Muir was sentenced to fourteen years' transportation, and the following month Thomas Fysshe Palmer was banished for seven years. On 5 and 6 December the first British Convention at Edinburgh was forcibly dispersed; the secretary, William Skirving, and two Corresponding Society delegates Maurice Margarot and Joseph Gerrald were among those arrested. The following January Judge Braxfield sentenced Skirving and Margarot to fourteen years at Botany Bay for conspiring to '"subvert"' the country '"by intimidation, force and violence"' (Goodwin, pp. 304–6). Gerrald received an identical sentence in March. Wordsworth's comment on these trials appears at the end of 'Salisbury Plain', where he turns the charge of intimidation, force, and violence upon Braxfield and the government:

> Insensate they who think, at Wisdom's porch
> That Exile, Terror, Bonds, and Force may stand:
> That Truth with human blood can feed her torch,
> And Justice balance with her gory hand . . .
>
> (Gill, p. 37, ll. 514–17)

In spring 1794 the process of repression continued with the arrests of Hardy, Tooke, Thelwall, and other leading reformists. On 13 May a government 'Committee of Secrecy' met, and three days later submitted a report on the popular societies which detailed their development, the influence of Paine, and the various addresses sent to the National Convention. The committee also reported that the LCS had been organizing a second British Convention with the intention of subverting the constitution, and superseding the authority of the Commons. The government acted by suspending Habeas Corpus on 23 May. As Holcroft said, at this moment in 1794 'the tempest of insurrection and anarchy was so confidently affirmed to be rising, and raging, that the House of Commons voted the suspension of the Habeas Corpus bill, on the affirmation that dangerous and treasonable conspiracies did actually exist!'[41]

By May 1794 Wordsworth had presumably abandoned any plan to publish *A Letter to the Bishop of Llandaff*, but Godwin's question 'Ought I explicitly to declare the sentiments I entertain?'

---

[41] *Holcroft Narrative*, p. 13.

must have preoccupied him throughout this spring of arrests and trials. During May, though, his dilemma was resolved when Mathews wrote proposing that they collaborate on a journal. On 23 May Wordsworth replied assuring his friend that he wished 'most heartily to be engaged in something of that kind' (*E Y*, p. 118). He had already decided what sort of 'monthly miscellany' it was going to be. He asked Mathews, 'in what do we . . . suppose ourselves the most able either to entertain or instruct?', and straightaway answered his own question:

Of each others political sentiments we ought not to be ignorant; and here at the very threshold I solemnly affirm that in no writings of mine will I ever admit of any sentiment which can have the least tendency to induce my readers to suppose that the doctrines which are now enforced by banishment, imprisonment, &c, &c, are other than pregnant with every species of misery. (*E Y*, p. 119)

At the 'threshold' of their scheme Wordsworth proposed a political journal through which he could voice his opposition. His reference to 'banishment, imprisonment, &c, &c' recalls the lines from 'Salisbury Plain', and also indicates that the recent trials and transportation had hardened his commitment to the radical cause. His letter leaves Mathews no room for argument. 'In a work like that of which we are speaking', he told his friend,

it will be impossible (and indeed it would render our publication worthless were we to attempt it,) not to inculcate principles of government and forms of social order of one kind or another. I have therefore thought it proper to say this much in order that if your sentiments or those of our coadjutor are dissimilar to mine, we may drop the scheme at once. (*E Y*, p. 119)

Wordsworth's 'principles of government and forms of social order' sound vague, and perhaps he intended to wait for Mathews's reply before going into greater detail. In this letter, though, he declares himself a 'democrat', and would have looked for 'the rights of the people . . . peace, oeconomy, and reform'. He returns to the 'principles' of their journal later on, but this time his comments are based upon *Political Justice*:

I should principally wish our attention to be fixed upon life and manners, and to make our publication a vehicle of sound and exalted Morality. All the periodical miscellanies that I am acquainted with, except one or two of the reviews, appear to be written to maintain the existence of prejudice and to disseminate error. To such purposes I have already said I will not prostitute my pen. (*E Y*, p. 119)

He had actually said he would never condone the government's repressive policies, although here he defines those policies as 'prejudice' and 'error'. While responding to the crisis facing the reform movement, he was now thinking in Godwinian terms. The 'sound and exalted Morality' he had in mind would be drawn from *Political Justice*.

At the opening of *Political Justice* Godwin summarized his reasons for believing in the 'improvement' and perfectibility of mankind. 'The probability of this improvement will be sufficiently established', Godwin claimed,

if we consider, FIRST, that the moral characters of men are the result of their perceptions: and, SECONDLY, that of all the modes of operating upon mind government is the most considerable. In addition to these arguments it will be found, THIRDLY, that the good and ill effects of political institution are not less conspicuous in detail than in principle; and FOURTHLY, that perfectibility is one of the most unequivocal characteristics of the human species, so that the political, as well as the intellectual state of man, may be presumed to be in a course of progressive improvement. (*PJ* i. 11)

Godwin's 'argument' rests upon the necessary influence of 'perception' to the formation of 'moral character', and this was the fundamental assumption of Coleridge's and Southey's idea of Pantisocracy. By asserting perfectibility as 'one of the most unequivocal characteristics of the human species', it necessarily followed that mankind 'may be presumed to be in a course of progressive improvement'. Given the extensive influence of government upon mind, any improvement in the 'political institution' would lead to a corresponding change in individuals. A little later on, Godwin enlarges this point to include 'three principal causes by which the human mind is advanced towards a state of perfection': 'literature, or the diffusion of knowledge through the medium of discussion, whether written or oral; education, or a scheme for the early impression of right principles upon the hitherto unprejudiced mind; and political justice, or the adoption of any principle of morality and truth into the practice of a community' (*PJ* i. 19).

'Literature, Education, and *Political Justice*' would have been a fine motto for the *Philanthropist*; Godwin's theory and

Wordsworth's scheme for a journal coincide exactly. Ideally, Godwin believed that 'the hitherto unprejudiced mind' should be the focus of his educative scheme, but he also recognized its impossibility. 'Where must the preceptor himself have been educated', he enquired, 'who shall thus elevate his pupil above all the errors of mankind?' (*PJ* i. 25). Having admitted this obstacle, he simply denied the need for teacher or pupil: 'Where can a remedy be found for this fundamental disadvantage? where but in political justice, that all comprehensive scheme, that immediately applies to the removal of counteraction and contagion, that embraces millions in its grasp, and that educates in one school the preceptor and the pupil?' (*PJ* i. 27). The problem of 'education' is dismissed in a rhetorical question, and a confident assertion of the 'comprehensive scheme'. John Thelwall was alive to this 'fundamental disadvantage' of *Political Justice*, and less sanguine about the 'grasp' of Godwin's system. Thelwall saw his lectures as an efficient means to mass enlightenment and Wordsworth's *Philanthropist* was to have an identical function. It allowed him to express his political opposition to the government, and to call for change and improvement. In 1794 Godwin's philosophy boosted Wordsworth's political confidence once more, and with this his millenarian optimism of 1792 revived as well.

On 8 June Wordsworth wrote again to Mathews, telling him that 'a more excellent system of civil policy might be established', but he added that 'in [his] ardour to attain the goal, [he did] not forget the nature of the ground where the race is to be run' (*EY*, p. 124). Despite his wish for change, this letter also registers Wordsworth's doubts about the extent and speed of reformation needed: 'The destruction of those institutions which I condemn appears to me to be hastening on too rapidly. I recoil from the bare idea of a revolution; yet, if our conduct with reference both to foreign and domestic policy continues such as it has been for the last two years how is that dreadful event to be averted?' (*EY*, p. 124). This sounds curiously moderate after his condemnation of monarchy and 'the infatuation profligacy and extravagance of men in power' earlier in his letter. The Terror in France was an obvious reason for Wordsworth's 'recoil from the bare idea of a revolution'—and these fears would have been exacerbated by a recent discovery of arms at Edinburgh on 15 and 16 May. Robert Watt, an ex-government informer, had planned an armed insurrection to seize the Lord Provost, Braxfield, and other Scottish judges as hostages, and demand that the king dismiss the government and end the war (Goodwin, pp. 334–6). The preparations for this coup appeared to vindicate ministerial fears of a violent uprising, and a second British Convention which Thomas Hardy had proposed in a 'Circular Letter' sent to provincial corresponding societies in April 1794. In fact, Watt's plot may have been a misguided attempt to act as an *agent provocateur* and restore his credibility with the government. Coleridge evidently believed so and told Southey in September that 'Watt was a villain—and became a Traitor, that when matters were to a head, he might have the Merit of being an *Informer*' (*CL* i. 106). Thomas Holcroft was confident that 'no insurrection, or shade of insurrection, has appeared on the part of the people wishing reform'—but he went on to recall that 'Many surmises and tales prevailed, during the summer of the memorable 1794'.[42]

If Wordsworth had heard about Watt's preparations, his fears about the 'destruction' of institutions and possible revolution are understandable. As in his May letter to Mathews, his more elaborate proposals for the *Philanthropist* in June reveal a continuing sense of crisis. Having acknowledged revolution as a potential threat that he would wish to avoid, he turns that possibility against the government:

it seems to me that a writer who has the welfare of mankind at heart should call forth his best exertions to convince the people that they can only be preserved from a convulsion by oeconomy in the administration of the public purse and a gradual and constant reform of those abuses which, if left to themselves, may grow to such a height as to render, even a revolution desirable. (*E-Y*, p. 124)

When Wordsworth wrote this, he was thinking of the causes of Revolution in France in 1789. Thelwall was to make a similar point (with some irony) in a lecture of March 1795, drawing parallels between the *ancien régime* and contemporary Britain:

If, I say . . . the *despotism* of France was overthrown on account of the abject misery into which the mass of the people were plunged by the profligate expenditure of the public money in foreign exploits and crusades, and the eventual embarrassments of the revenues of that country, it is the duty of ministers to take care that the orderly,

---

[42] *Holcroft Narrative*, pp. 12, 19.

benevolent and just government of England is not overthrown by a system of war and taxation inevitably tending to reduce the people and the revenues to the same calamitious situation. (*Tribune*, i. 55)

Wordsworth and Thelwall agreed that the expense of the French war would bankrupt the country, and that the pattern of events which had led to revolution in 1789 was being repeated in Britain—at the very moment when revolution had become synonymous with violence.

Coleridge was to use the 'Example of France' as a warning to British reformists in his *Moral and Political Lecture*, but in the belief that 'French Freedom is the Beacon, that while it guides us to Equality should show us the Dangers, that throng the road' (*Lects. 1795*, p. 6). Wordsworth made a similar remark in his letter to Mathews, 8 June 1794, developing this idea of France as a caution to Britain: 'I deplore the miserable situation of the French', he wrote, 'and think we can only be guarded from the same scourge by the undaunted efforts of good men in propagating with unremitting activity those doctrines which long and severe meditation has taught them are essential to the welfare of mankind' (*E Y*, pp. 124–5). His reliance on the 'efforts of good men' to ensure peaceful change anticipates Thelwall's and Coleridge's purposes in lecturing during 1795. As a Godwinian, though, Wordsworth in 1794 condemned public meetings and lectures; he was probably thinking of Thelwall's activities in London when he told Mathews: 'when I observe the people should be enlightened upon the subject of politics, I severely condemn all inflammatory addresses to the passions of men, even when it is intended to direct those passions to a good purpose' (*EY*, p. 125).

Two years earlier the excited and emotional scenes at *Les Amis* had brought Wordsworth over to the revolutionary cause. By June 1794 his position was precisely the opposite. His hopes were now rooted in a patient passivity, and in anticipation of the gradual but inevitable triumph of political justice. Following Godwin's belief that reformation 'can in reality scarcely be considered as of the nature of action', Wordsworth's 'undaunted efforts' and 'unremitting activity' were to promote peaceful 'enquiry'. 'Freedom of inquiry is all that I wish for', he told Mathews, 'let nothing be deemed too sacred for investigation; rather than restrain the liberty of the press I would suffer the most atrocious doctrines to be recommended: let the field be open and unencumbered, and truth must be victorious' (*EY*, p. 125). He was echoing Godwin almost word for word, in a passage from *Political Justice* that provides the theory and the title of Wordsworth's journal:

The revolutions of states, which a philanthropist would desire witness, or in which he would willingly co-operate, consist principally in a change of sentiments and dispositions in the members of those states. The true instruments for changing the opinions of men are argument and persuasion. The best security for an advantageous issue is free and unrestricted discussion. In that field truth must always prove the successful champion. If then we would improve the social institutions of mankind, we must write, we must argue, we must converse. To this business there is no close; in this pursuit there should be no pause. (*PJ* i. 202)

Wordsworth's *Philanthropist* was to be a vehicle for 'investigation' and 'unrestricted discussion', but it also had a definite purpose and a contemporary relevance. As the government seemed to be pushing the country towards a 'convulsion', Godwin's principles might counteract that danger and 'establish freedom with tranquillity'. The *Philanthropist* was a means for 'benighted mortals [to gain] the meed | Of happiness and virtue' —but it was also something more.

'I know that the multitude walk in darkness', Wordsworth wrote to Mathews. 'I would put into each man's hand a lantern to guide him' (*EY*, p. 125). He was echoing Isaiah 9: 2: 'The people that walked in darkness have seen a great light: they that dwell in the land of the shadow of death, upon them hath the light shined.' For Wordsworth in 1794, the 'great light' was the 'universal illumination' anticipated by Godwin. As a prophet of Godwinian enlightenment Wordsworth's *Philanthropist* was the 'lantern' which would lead the benighted people of Britain—'the land of the shadow of death'—to future reformation. The plan for the *Philanthropist* is a first utterance of Wordsworth's prophetic wish. It is heard again early in 1800, in the 'Prospectus' to *The Recluse*:

> Come thou, prophetic spirit, soul of man,
> Thou human soul of the wide earth, that hast
> Thy metropolitan temple in the hearts
> Of mighty poets; unto me vouchsafe

> Thy foresight, teach me to discern, and part
> Inherent things from casual, what is fixed
> From fleeting, that my song may live, and be
> Even as a light hung up in heaven to chear
> The world in times to come.
>
> <div align="center">(<i>B V</i>, p. 389, ll. 55–63)</div>

In June 1794 Godwin's 'rules of immutable justice' offered Wordsworth the certainty he had lacked when he wrote 'A Night on Salisbury Plain', and for which he later prayed in his 'Prospectus' to *The Recluse*. *Political Justice* enabled him to maintain the 'solicitude for all' that he first experienced in France in 1792, and to revive the millenarian hopes of that time. Godwin was the heir to Beaupuy and Grégoire, redefining 'l'esprit réligieux de la Revolution' in the necessary bias to perfectibility of the human mind. In this respect the *Philanthropist* is an important transitional stage in Wordsworth's millenarianism, linking the French Revolution with his later hopes for *The Recluse*. Wordsworth's journal represents the point at which the revolutionary motive to regeneration was assumed in the rational working of the individual mind. The ensuing failure of Wordsworth's confidence in *Political Justice* consequently appears as a drawn-out repetition of the 'shock | Given to [his] moral nature' when war began in 1793. It constituted the deepest level of his 'despair' recalled in *The Prelude*, Book Ten, and was the primary condition of his need for a permanent basis for hope,

> to discern, and part
> Inherent things from casual, what is fixed
> From fleeting . . .

With the execution of Robespierre in July 1794 and the acquittals at the Old Bailey later in the year, Wordsworth felt a confidence in the future that he would not regain until the months at Alfoxden with Coleridge and Dorothy in 1797–8. Ironically, Wordsworth's acquaintance with Godwin himself was to be a major factor in the collapse of the certainty he had found in *Political Justice*.

'Barricadoing the road to truth': Wordsworth's Godwin, London 1795

> I had done a great deal with my Political Justice, but also
> much harm—Oh, that it had been possible for such a man as
> Wordsworth to have taken my place!
>
> (William Godwin, ?1804)[43]

Wordsworth's scheme for the *Philanthropist* was never realized.
There may have been further plans laid after Wordsworth's letter
of June 1794, but by 7 November both editors had lost interest.
'The more nearly we approached the time fixed for action,'
Wordsworth told Mathews, 'the more strongly was I persuaded
that we should decline the field' (*E Y*, p. 134). He implies that they
had fixed a date for publication and goes on to tell Mathews of
his continuing 'determination' to work for a newspaper, which
may have a bearing on his possible connection with the *Philanthropist* published by Daniel Isaac Eaton in London between
March 1795 and January 1796.[44] For the moment, however,
their project was abandoned. There were several reasons for this.
Wordsworth was reluctant to leave Keswick for London: in May
he told Mathews he could not afford to do so, and after September he was obliged to look after Raisley Calvert who was dying of
consumption (*E Y*, pp. 118, 135). The *Philanthropist* could never
have been a practical scheme with its editors at different ends of
the country, and the political circumstances which had influenced
Wordsworth's idea for a journal had also changed.

During the summer Robespierre's execution revived Wordsworth's hopes for France, which devolved, in turn, upon the
political situation in Britain. Shortly after his 'hymn of triumph'
over Robespierre in *The Prelude*, Book Ten, he remembers that

> through zeal,
> Such victory [he] confounded in [his] thoughts
> With one far higher and more difficult:
> Triumphs of unambitious peace at home,
> And noiseless fortitude.
>
> (x. 589–92)

---

[43] A-S Dep. b. 229/2. Fragmentary notes on the back of a letter to Godwin from his
brother John, 2 Feb. 1804.

[44] See Appendix, 'Wordsworth and Eaton's *Philanthropist*', below.

The hint is slight, but enough to suggest that *The Prelude* leaves much unsaid about his hopes for a comparable but 'higher' triumph in Britain. Wordsworth had opposed 'banishment, imprisonment, &c, &c' ever since Muir and Palmer were sentenced in mid-1793. His joy at the outcome of the 1794 treason trials appears in a letter written on Christmas Eve of that year—the very moment when Coleridge, apparently, began 'Religious Musings'. 'I rejoice with you on the acquittal of the prisoners', he wrote to Mathews:

The late occurrences in every point of view are interesting to humanity. They will abate the insolence and presumption of the aristocracy by shewing it that neither the violence, nor the art, of power can crush even an unfriended individual, though engaged in the propagation of doctrines confessedly unpalatable to privilege; and they will force upon the most prejudiced this conclusion that there is some reason in the language of reformers. . . . To every class of men occupied in the correction of abuses it must be an animating reflection that their exertions, so long as they are temperate will be countenanced and protected by the good sense of the country. (*EY*, p. 137)

In December 1794 Wordsworth would have counted himself among the 'unfriended individuals' engaged 'in the correction of abuses'. Wordsworth's *Letter*, 'Salisbury Plain', and the idea of the *Philanthropist* had each a specific social and political purpose—even though none of them had yet been published. Wordsworth's renewed confidence late in 1794 has an immediate bearing on his return to London in February 1795 and his possible activities there in the following months. For the moment, while he nursed Raisley Calvert, the most 'animating reflection' of all would have been William Godwin's contribution to the acquittals in his *Cursory Strictures*.

Chief Justice Eyre delivered his charge of high treason to the grand jury on 2 October 1794, and the indictment against the twelve defendants was read four days later. It was only now that Godwin's friend Thomas Holcroft surrendered to the authorities and was imprisoned in Newgate. Before doing so he had written to Godwin, who was staying with Dr Parr in Warwickshire, asking for assistance. Godwin later recalled what followed. 'I left Dr. Parr on Monday, the 13th', he wrote:

I reached town on Monday evening, & having fully revolved the subject, & examined the doctrines of the Lord Chief Justice's Charge to the

Grand Jury, I locked myself up on Friday & Saturday, & wrote my Strictures on that composition, which appeared at full length in the Morning Chronicle of Monday, & were transcribed from thence, into other papers—[45]

The publication of *Cursory Strictures* was a setback for the prosecution, and useful support for the defendants. It was one of the most immediately influential pamphlets published during the 1790s and to this extent, perhaps, is comparable to Burke's *Reflections* and Paine's *The Rights of Man* in its impact upon contemporary affairs. The government was sufficiently alarmed to try to prevent sales of the pamphlet; a copy of *Cursory Strictures* survives in the Treasury Solicitor's files, and on its cover is written: 'Recvd from H Barlow who bought it at Kearsley's . . . K promised immed.y to stop the Sales—23d: Octr. 1794. 8 p.m.'[46] Wordsworth's admiration for *Political Justice* and his interest in the trials would have encouraged him to read *Cursory Strictures*. Given its wide circulation in the *Morning Chronicle* and other papers, and as a separate pamphlet, he very likely saw it during November or December 1794; as Mrs Thelwall recalled, the pamphlet was read 'with avidity' and circulated rapidly 'throughout the kingdom'.[47]

Godwin's argument was that Eyre's charge had no basis in established law or legal precedent, which defined treason as '"levying war against the King within the realm, and the compassing or imagining the death of the King"'.[48] He went on to expose Eyre's 'new and imaginary treason of conspiring to

---

[45] A-S Dep. c. 531. Godwin's subsequent comments on Horne Tooke's trial in this manuscript reveal the almost farcical nature of the proceedings—almost, were it not that the defendants' lives depended on the outcome of the trials:

During the progress of these trials I was present at least some part of every day—Hardy's trial lasted eight, & Horne Tooke's six days—Among the many atrocities witnessed on that occasion, perhaps the most flagitious was the speech of the attorney-general, now lord Eldon, at the close of the trial of that extraordinary man—in his peroration he burst into tears, & intreated the jury by their verdict to vindicate his character & fame; he urged them by the consideration of his family to cooperate with him in leaving such a name behind to his children as they should not look upon as their disgrace—it was in the close of this year that I first met with Samuel Taylor Coleridge . . .

[46] TS 11 952 3496 (3). Coleridge's *Fall of Robespierre* had been on sale at Kearsley's bookshop since 11 Oct. or thereabouts (*CL* i. 117).

[47] *Thelwall Life*, p. 214.

[48] William Godwin, *Cursory Strictures on the Charge Delivered by Lord Chief Justice Eyre to the Grand Jury, October 2, 1794* (London, 1794), 4 [cited hereafter as *Cursory Strictures*].

subvert the Monarchy'. 'The remainder of the charge', Godwin claimed,

is made up of hypothesis, presumption, prejudication, and conjecture. There is scarcely a single line that is not deformed with such phrases as 'public notoriety,' 'things likely,' 'purposes imputed,' 'measures supposed,' and 'imaginary cases.'

The plain reason of all this is, that the Chief Justice suspected, that the treason described in the statute 25 Edward III, and those founded upon precedent, or deducible from adjudged cases, even with the addition of the Chief Justice's new constructive treason, founded, as he confesses, upon no law, precedent, or case, and which therefore is in reality no treason, did not afford a sufficient ground of crimination against the prisoners. He is therefore obliged to leave the plain road, and travel out of the record.[49]

But Godwin's pamphlet did more than reveal the weakness of Eyre's case against the defendants. Inevitably, and perhaps ironically, Godwin was defending the activities of the reform societies he had claimed were unnecessary in *Political Justice*. He mocked the 'easy and artful manner in which the idea of treason is introduced' in Eyre's charge:

First, there is a 'concealed purpose,' or an insensible 'degeneracy,' *supposed* to take place in these associations. Next, that 'concealed purpose,' or insensible 'degeneracy,' is *supposed* to tend directly to this end, the 'subversion of the Monarchy.' Lastly, a 'conspiracy to subvert the Monarchy,' is a treason, first discovered by Chief Justice Eyre in 1794, never contemplated by any lawgiver, or included in any statute. Deny the Chief Justice any one of his three assumptions, and his whole deduction falls to the ground. Challenge him, or any man living, to prove any of them; and you require of him an impossibility. And it is by this sort of logic, which would be scouted in the rawest graduate in either of our Universities, that Englishmen are to be brought under the penalties of treason![50]

His conclusion was inevitable: 'If any of the prisoners now under confinement had acted according to all the enumerations of his imaginary cases, it may safely be affirmed, that, upon any sober trial upon a charge of High Treason, they must infallibly be acquitted.'[51]

Horne Tooke read *Cursory Strictures* while detained in the

[49] *Cursory Strictures*, p. 10.
[50] *Cursory Strictures*, pp. 13–14.
[51] *Cursory Strictures*, p. 19.

Tower. He immediately saw that Godwin had demolished the charge, and exclaimed to Jeremiah Joyce, ' "By G—d . . . this lays Eyre completely on his back." '[52] When Hardy, Tooke, and Thelwall were acquitted and the other prisoners were freed, Godwin became a hero of the reform movement. He had attended each of the trials at the Old Bailey, and recalled that, when he met Tooke in May 1795, 'he called the author to him, & taking his hand, conveyed it suddenly to his lips, vowing that he could do no less by the hand which had given existence to that production' (GD vi; entry made 29 January 1809). This was the time recollected by Hazlitt when Godwin 'blazed as a sun in the firmament of reputation' (Howe, xi. 16). He was the celebrated author of *Political Justice* and *Caleb Williams*, and the outspoken defender of the friends of liberty in *Cursory Strictures*. It was at this moment, too, that Wordsworth first met Godwin.

On 7 November 1794 Wordsworth told Mathews that he had begun 'to wish much to be in town', and enquired about the possibilities of 'procuring a similar occupation' to Mathews's post as parliamentary reporter for the *Telegraph* (*E Y*, p. 136). As he heard news of the acquittals, the pull of politics and London must have grown stronger. After the death of Raisley Calvert in January 1795 he left Penrith for Newcastle where he visited Dorothy, and by the end of February he was in London. Like Coleridge the previous December, he was attracted to the most prominent reformists and intellectual radicals of the day—and it was not long before he met them. On Friday, 27 February Godwin wrote in his diary, 'tea Frend's w. H[olcrof]t., Losh, Tweddel, Jona. Raine, Edwards, Wordsworth, Higgins, French & Dyer' (G D vii)—and the following day his diary notes that 'Wordsworth calls'. Wordsworth's meeting with Godwin marked the beginning of an acquaintance that lasted until Godwin's death in 1836. More immediately, though, he joined Godwin's circle of friends which in 1795 included the most well-known radicals in the country. The next months mark Wordsworth's closest connection with the popular reform movement, and with the Godwinian element among its leadership. That mixture of Godwinian philosophy and reformist politics led John Thelwall towards confusion and self-contradiction later in

---

[52] *Thelwall Life*, pp. 213–14.

1795, and it was to have similar consequences for three young Cambridge men present at Frend's tea-party: Wordsworth, Losh, Tweddell. On 27 February Wordsworth must have felt himself at the very centre of contemporary radical affairs, and this sense of participation in current political and intellectual controversy was to render his subsequent disillusionment all the more bitter. It would be compounded, too, by a growing sense of disappointment in Godwin as a person. To understand Wordsworth's experiences in 1795–6, how they resemble and differ from those of Losh and Tweddell, it is necessary to take a closer look at the company he met at William Frend's house on 27 February.

Wordsworth may have been introduced to the company by Tweddell or Losh. The political trajectory of these three follows a similar pattern from Cambridge to Godwin's circle in 1795. Tweddell had welcomed the French Revolution in his prize speech in October 1790, days after Wordsworth's return home from France. Losh visited Paris late in 1792 when Wordsworth was also there, and they may have travelled back together.[53] Like Wordsworth, Losh and Tweddell were drawn to Godwin and *Political Justice* early in 1794; they dined with him at James Mackintosh's house on 3 February, and met on a number of occasions later in the year.[54] Tweddell wrote to Isabel Gunning that he found *Political Justice* 'a very able book', and added that it contained 'much truth mixed with much absurd paradox . . . It is much talked of, and deserves to be talked of.'[55] Henry Gunning, no relation of Isabel, recalled that, 'The acquittal of Hardy and Horne Tooke . . . afforded the highest gratification to Tweddell . . . [He] took every opportunity of speaking his sentiments most freely, and, to those who watched the signs of the times, most indiscreetly' (Gunning, ii. 87). Wordsworth's and Tweddell's opinions—and their lack of caution in expressing them—coincided exactly in 1794–5. James Losh would have agreed with them too, and his activities between 1793 and 1795

---

[53] Reed, p. 139, cites J. R. MacGillivray's suggestion that Wordsworth's comment to Losh about seasickness, 11 Mar. 1798, recalls a channel crossing together in Dec. 1792 (*EY*, p. 213).

[54] Also present at Mackintosh's dinner on 3 Feb. were Dr Samuel Parr, tutor to John Tweddell and Joseph Gerrald, Robinson the publisher of *Political Justice*, and Joseph Johnson. Godwin says they talked of 'passions'.

[55] G. Paston, 'The Romance of John Tweddell' in *Little Memoirs of the Eighteenth Century* (London, 1901), 342–3 [Cited hereafter as Paston, 'Tweddell'].

had extended to personal involvement in contemporary reformist politics.

While Wordsworth was writing his *Letter to the Bishop of Llandaff* in 1793, Losh was drafting the petition of the Society of the Friends of the People presented to the Commons on 6 May. He was a close friend of Felix Vaughan, and after Vaughan's death in 1799 recalled how they 'went the summer [legal] circuit together in 1794' with another young lawyer called Charles Ward: 'we excited great dread among the creatures of administration, and were, I believe, generally considered as three men likely to make a noise in the political world . . .' (LD iv). Later that year, Vaughan acted for the defence in the treason trials and was for a time thought to have written *Cursory Strictures*.[56] James Losh, for his part, joined a Corresponding Society committee to organize a subscription to pay the defendants' expenses. Other members included William Maxwell, William Frend, Major Cartwright, Gilbert Wakefield, and Godfrey Higgins; George Dyer was very likely involved as well.[57]

The group of friends Wordsworth met on 27 February included Cambridge contemporaries whose experiences since 1790 had been very similar to his own. During the next few months Losh, Tweddell, and Wordsworth would be moving in the same circles, presumably seeing each other with mutual friends such as William Mathews, Basil Montagu, and Francis Wrangham, who had met Coleridge the previous September (CL i. 107). The company at Frend's house also included some more senior radical figures—Godwin, Holcroft, Dyer, and Frend himself, all four of whom were acquainted with Coleridge too. Holcroft had been released without trial on 1 December and two weeks later met Coleridge, who disliked his conversation and atheism but accepted an invitation to 'dine with him and Godwin' (CL i. 138–9). Coleridge also knew Dyer by February 1795, and was corresponding with him about his lectures at Bristol. Dyer had taken copies of *The Fall of Robespierre* and *A Moral and Political Lecture*, while Coleridge in turn had read Dyer's *Complaints of*

---

[56] *Thelwall Life*, p. 214.

[57] The subscription and committee members were announced in the *Morning Chronicle* on 23 Mar. 1795: 'The British Nation will not suffer men to be finally crushed by Expence, who have risen superior to false accusation.' Two months later £1429. 3s. had been raised. See also Chapter 3 above.

the Poor People of England and placed an order for ten copies of his *Dissertation on Benevolence* with Joseph Cottle (*CL* i. 152). When Wordsworth met Dyer on 27 February, he was actually preparing the *Dissertation* for publication. In his pamphlet Dyer was concerned (among other things) with the 'inconveniences and losses' incurred by the defendants in the treason trials, and mentioned the subscription organized by Frend, Losh, Higgins, and the others:

It is with pleasure, [the author] has been given to understand, that a plan is now forming among some respectable persons, to bring before the publick several of the above cases; and it is to be hoped, the plan will comprehend every case of real distress throughout the country connected with pretended treasons or sedition. But feeble subscriptions will produce little benefit to the numerous sufferers, and reflect little honour on the publick. What has been said concerning the places of confinement, the abodes, or the publications of the above persons, were meant as hints to benevolent readers. [58]

The plan 'now forming among some respectable persons' was not advertised until 23 March, when the subscription was announced in the *Morning Chronicle*. Dyer must therefore have been writing this final section of his *Dissertation* in the weeks immediately before this announcement, and had heard about or was actually involved in the scheme. It is virtually certain that the discussion on 27 February would have turned upon the recent treason trials. Holcroft's imprisonment and forthcoming *Narrative of Facts Relating to a Prosecution for High Treason* would have been mentioned; so would *Cursory Strictures*, and Dyer's *Dissertation*. It is also likely that the plan for a subscription was discussed, since at least three of the committee were present. Perhaps it was at Frend's house, and in Wordsworth's company, that Dyer was first 'given to understand' that the plan was 'forming' and said he would refer to it in his forthcoming pamphlet.

One could go on at considerable length listing mutual acquaintances, activities, connections and publications that emanated from the group Wordsworth joined at Frend's house. For Losh, Tweddell, and Wordsworth it was a reunion, a political homecoming, and for Wordsworth it was also the first

---

[58] George Dyer, *A Dissertation on the Theory and Practice of Benevolence* (London, 1795), 101 [cited hereafter as Dyer, *Dissertation*].

opportunity to meet his 'sage', William Godwin. With hind-sight, though, the most significant factor was the number of those present who already knew Coleridge. The tea-party at Frend's consequently has a direct bearing upon Wordsworth's subse-quent development from Godwinian radical to poet; it marks the beginning of the end of his Godwinian allegiance, and perhaps the first moment when he heard about Coleridge. His growing disillu-sion with Godwin in the coming months would set him on course for Bristol, Racedown, and, ultimately, Alfoxden between 1795 and 1797. For the moment, though, he was undoubtedly very excited to meet his intellectual hero and arranged to call on him the following day.

Godwin's references to Wordsworth in his diary between February and August 1795 are brief and not especially helpful. However, an interesting pattern does emerge if one lists all the meetings that followed their introduction on 27 February:

[Feb.]	28.	Sa.	Wordsworth calls . . .
[Mar.]	10.	Tu.	Wordsworth breakfasts . . .
[Mar.]	25.	W.	Wordsworth, M[athews?] & Fawcet call . . .
[Mar.]	31.	Tu.	Wordsworth & M[athews?] call . . .
[Apr.]	9.	Thu.	Wordsworth breakfasts . . .
[Apr.]	22.	W.	Wordsworth . . .
[July]	14.	Tu.	Call on Wordsworth.
[July]	29.	W.	Call on Wordsworth . . . nah.
[Aug.]	15.	Sa.	Wordsworth & Matthews call, nah.
[Aug.]	18.	Tu.	Call on Wordsworth nah.

(GD vii)

At first sight this appears to be limited to meetings, and failed encounters. On 29 July Wordsworth was most likely visiting Cobham with Wrangham and Montagu, and by 18 August had perhaps left for Bristol (Reed, p. 166). But between late April and July a change seems to have taken place in their relationship. Until April Wordsworth was calling regularly on Godwin, but there-after seems to have been less concerned to do so. Godwin, on the other hand, started to call on Wordsworth in July and August—twice finding him not at home. It would be easy to read too much into this. Robert Woof is, perhaps, right in suggesting that the frequency of Wordsworth's early visits may be attributed to his living in Godwin's neighbourhood in Somers Town; there-after he moved to share Montagu's rooms at Lincoln's Inn, and his visits became less convenient (Reed, p. 164). This is quite possible, but the change could also be attributed to a gradual cooling of Wordsworth's enthusiasm for *Political Justice* and its author. After Wordsworth's welcome for *Political Justice* in 1794 Godwin himself was most likely a great disappointment, and especially so in his conversation.

At least four of Wordsworth's recorded meetings with Godwin took place on a Tuesday. This was also the day on which the Philomathean Society met for debates and discussion, and there is evidence that Wordsworth and William Mathews attended. 'Pray write to me at length and give me an account of your proceedings in the society', Wordsworth wrote to Mathews on 21 March 1796 (*EY*, p. 169). He does not go into details, but the Philomatheans seem a likely possibility for the society he had in mind. On Tuesday, 10 March Wordsworth breakfasted with Godwin, and that day Godwin also noted in his diary, 'Philomaths: soldier v. priest'. The subject is somewhat out of character with others debated, which included animals, marriage, metaphysics, Christian morality, self love, capital punishment. Wordsworth's early ideas for a career had included both soldier and priest; moreover, Beaupuy and Bishop Grégoire had represented the revolutionary embodiment of both professions for Wordsworth in 1792. Without more evidence, it is impossible to do more than suggest that Wordsworth attended one or two meetings of the Philomatheans and possibly suggested the subject for discussion on 10 March. His connection with Godwin, the letter to Mathews of March 1796, and the 'soldier v. priest' debate all point to the likelihood of Wordsworth's presence. If he did hear Godwin and Holcroft speaking to the society, his account of Godwin's philosophy and his perplexed disillusion in *The Prelude*, Book Ten, becomes more readily understandable.

John Binns remembered Godwin's and Holcroft's 'diffuse and tiresome' speeches to the society in his *Recollections*. His memory is corroborated by Hazlitt, who discussed Holcroft's conversation with Coleridge when visiting Alfoxden in May 1798:

I complained that he would not let me get on at all, for he required a definition of every the commonest word, exclaiming, 'What do you mean by a *sensation*, Sir? What do you mean by an *idea*?' This, Coleridge said, was barricadoing the road to truth:—it was setting up a turnpike-gate at every step we took. (Howe, xvii. 112)

Holcroft's 'dogmatism of conversation', as Coleridge termed it, was also characteristic of Godwin. In November 1800 Lamb wrote to Thomas Manning about his new friend John Rickman who, Lamb said, 'can talk Greek with Porson, politics with Thelwall, conjecture with George Dyer, nonsense with me' and, he added, 'Does not want explanations, translations, limitations, as Professor Godwin does when you make an assertion' (Marrs, i. 244). Wordsworth's memory of his 'ready welcome' for *Political Justice* in *The Prelude,* Book Ten, recalls his enthusiasm for the *Philanthropist* scheme in 1794, through which he hoped to 'Build social freedom on its only basis: | The freedom of the individual mind' (x. 824–5). His ensuing perplexity appears to have stemmed in part from his discovery the following year that Godwin's methods of 'enquiry' offered no such 'freedom' to the mind. His 'sage' turned out to be a nit-picking pedant, who

> sacrificed
> The exactness of a comprehensive mind
> To scrupulous and microscopic views
> That furnished out materials for a work
> Of false imagination, placed beyond
> The limits of experience and of truth.
>
> (x. 843–8)

As Book Ten makes clear, though, Wordsworth initially followed Godwin's hair-splitting method of reasoning. It was this process of taking 'scrupulous and microscopic views' of man, politics, society, that eventually led to disillusionment:

> Thus I fared,
> Dragging all passions, notions, shapes of faith,
> Like culprits to the bar, suspiciously
> Calling the mind to establish in plain day
> Her titles and her honours, now believing,
> Now disbelieving, endlessly perplexed
> With impulse, motive, right and wrong, the ground
> Of moral obligation—what the rule,
> And what the sanction—till, demanding proof,
> And seeking it in every thing, I lost
> All feeling of conviction, and, in fine,
> Sick, wearied out with contrarieties,
> Yielded up moral questions in despair . . .
>
> (x. 888–900)

In 1794 Godwinian rationalism had appeared to Wordsworth as a 'lantern' that would guide humanity to peaceful reformation, much as Thelwall later thought Godwinian 'enquiry' could ensure the peaceful triumph of reform. Godwin led Thelwall to a dead-end as a political activist. For Wordsworth in 1795, the 'road to truth' turned out to be 'barricadoed' by the author of *Political Justice* himself.

The account of Wordworth's disenchantment with Godwin in Book Ten traces an experience that lasted over a year, and it juxtaposes Godwinian rationalism and human nature as the basis of his intellectual and moral conflict. The 'weary labyrinth' that led him towards despair, however, recalls the pedantic arguments of Godwin and Holcroft in private conversation and at the Philomathean Society. In retrospect, then, Wordsworth's meetings with Godwin in 1795 mark the high point of his allegiance to the author of *Political Justice*, but also the gradual erosion of his former confidence in his 'sage'. The apparent shift in their relation between April and July may therefore register a change in Wordsworth's estimation of Godwin as a man and thinker. When he wrote to Mathews in March 1796, his enquiry about 'the society' is undercut by two further questions: 'Are your members much encreased? and what is of more consequence have you improved I do not ask in the [art] of speaking, but in the more important one of thinking?' (*E Y*, p. 169).

Wordsworth's friends Mathews and Montagu were still regularly in Godwin's company at this moment, and his slighting questions indicate his distance from their intellectual circle. His reference to the 'art of thinking' perhaps also anticipates 'Anecdote for Fathers' as a humorous deflation of the overworked Godwinian intellect, that would 'think, and think, and think again', but whose enquiries,

> five times did I say to him,
> 'Why? Edward, tell me why?'
>
> (ll. 47–8)

—merely prompt the child's whimsical answer. The final stanza of the ballad makes Wordsworth's point in showing how 'the art of thinking' is also '*how the art of lying may be taught*'. Another ballad, 'Expostulation and Reply', turns upon the incessant questioning of 'Matthew',

'Why William, on that old grey stone,
'Thus for the length of half a day,
'Why William, sit you thus alone,
'And dream your time away?

'Where are your books? that light bequeath'd
'To beings else forlorn and blind!
'Up! Up! and drink the spirit breath'd
'From dead men to their kind.'

(ll. 1–8)

The irony of the second stanza debunks Matthew's bookish-
ness, but it also consigns Godwin and Wordsworth's former
Godwinian self to one common intellectual grave. The '"light
bequeath'd | To beings else forlorn and blind"' recalls Words-
worth's former belief in *Political Justice* as a 'lantern' that would
lead 'benighted mortals' to 'happiness and virtue'. Here, though,
that lantern is an *ignis fatuus* exhaled from the dead upon
'"their kind"' whom Matthew represents. The ballad counters
Matthew's questionings with the 'wise passiveness' of a receptive
mind,

'Think you, 'mid all this mighty sum
'Of things for ever speaking,
'That nothing of itself will come,
'But we must still be seeking?

'—Then ask not wherefore, here, alone,
'Conversing as I may,
'I sit upon this old grey stone,
'And dream my time away.'

(ll. 25–32)

In 1798 Wordsworth's confidence in passivity and reverie had
been achieved over two years in which he had taken stock of his
intellectual and emotional being, and had benefited from the
company of Dorothy and Coleridge while at Racedown and
Alfoxden. None of his Godwinian contemporaries in 1795
achieved a comparable self-transformation, but Wordsworth's
development can best be appreciated in the light of their less
fruitful experiences of disillusion with Godwin and politics over
the same period.

6

'A Sympathy with Power'

Imagining Robespierre

Wordsworth's 'hymn of triumph'

> O friend, few happier moments have been mine
> Through my whole life than that when first I heard
> That this foul tribe of Moloch was o'erthrown,
> And their chief regent levelled with the dust.

(P. x. 466–9)

So Wordsworth tells Coleridge of his feelings when he heard of
the death of Robespierre in summer 1794, while crossing the
Leven Sands. 'Great was my glee of spirit, great my joy', he
recalls. Coleridge's reaction to the news was different. He immediately collaborated with Southey on a tragedy, *The Fall of
Robespierre*, and he continued to explore Robespierre's character
and motives in his political lectures of 1795. Coleridge's interest
in Robespierre was shared by John Thelwall, and both agreed
that William Pitt wanted Robespierre's political acumen.
Coleridge went further, though, and used Robespierre as a foil in
his developing idea of the imagination during 1795–6. When he
wrote about Robespierre's death in *The Prelude* Wordsworth
knew that Coleridge had not shared his feelings at the time, and
that his friend's complex response to the Jacobin leader was
ultimately of the greatest importance to himself.

As remembered in Book Ten, Robespierre perished 'by the
might | of [his] own helper', in confirmation of Wordsworth's
own vision of cyclical and self-consuming violence,

> 'Year follows year, the tide returns again,
> Day follows day, all things have second birth'

(x. 72–3)

—hence his 'hymn of triumph', his sense of personal vindication:
' "Come now, ye golden times", | Said I.' But the 'golden times' did
not come immediately. France did not recover the revolutionary

idealism of former years, and no longer provided a model for political and social change in Britain. Despite his 'hymn of triumph' and apparently renewed confidence in the future, the Terror marked the end of Wordsworth's belief in revolution as a means to political and social regeneration. Between 1794 and 1795 he found compensation in *Political Justice*, until that too led him to the 'moral despair' recalled in Book Ten.

In *The Prelude* Wordsworth claims that

> then it was
> That thou, most precious friend, about this time
> First known to me, didst lend a living help
> To regulate my soul.

> (x. 904–7)

Coleridge and Wordsworth first met at Bristol in late August or September 1795, but they had no obvious mutual influence until two years later. Nevertheless, Wordsworth deliberately presents Coleridge as a redeeming figure in Book Ten, the successor to his schoolmaster and poetic mentor, William Taylor, whose grave Wordsworth visited on the day he had heard of Robespierre's execution back in August 1794. When Wordsworth reminded Coleridge of that day, he did so in the knowledge that Robespierre's downfall was a threshold to their early meetings and mutual commitment to poetry in June 1797. Looking back, his 'hymn of triumph' over Robespierre was also an anthem to the 'golden times' at Racedown and Alfoxden, then three years in the future.

'Excess of glory obscured': Robespierre, Pitt, and Godwin

Many years after the French Revolution, William Godwin looked back to the time when he had 'blazed as a sun in the firmament of reputation' as the author of *Political Justice*. For Godwin 1794 was memorable not for the Terror in France and the execution of Robespierre, but for the treason trials in London, 'an attempt to take away the lives of men by a constructive treason, & out of many facts no one of which was capital, to compose a capital crime—the name of the man in whose mind the scheme of this trial was engendered was Pitt—'.[1] He was recalling the moment

---

[1] A-S Dep. c. 531.

3. Sketch of a trial at the Old Bailey drawn by John Thelwall while imprisoned in the Tower of London during 1794.

when his demolition of the charge of 'constructive treason' in *Cursory Strictures* had enhanced his notoriety and made him a hero of the reform movement. In Book Ten of *The Prelude* Wordsworth also remembers the government's 'attempt to take away the lives of men' by perverting the forms and rule of law. 'Our shepherds', he says,

> at that time
> Thirsted to make the guardian crook of law
> A tool of murder
>
> (x. 645–7)

—and this memory, in turn, recalls his nightmare dreams of the massacres at Paris earlier in Book Ten,

> Such ghastly visions . . . of despair,
> And tyranny, and implements of death . . .
>
> (x. 374–5)

The implied similarity between the British 'tool of murder' and French 'implements of death' was deliberate. Unlike Godwin, Wordsworth did not believe that the scheme of the treason trials had been 'engendered' in Pitt's mind. Pitt had no capacity for originality; he was an imitator, and a foolish one at that,

> Though with such awful proof before [his] eyes
> That he who would sow death, reaps death, or worse,
> And can reap nothing better, childlike longed
> To imitate—not wise enough to avoid.
>
> (x. 648–51)

The 'awful proof' Wordsworth had in mind was the violent repression in France, which culminated in Robespierre's death on 28 July 1794. In spite of this example the British government had persisted in 'composing a capital crime', as Godwin put it, and charged the reformists with treason. In Book Ten, Wordsworth draws a direct analogy between the 'unjust tribunals' of Paris and those at the Old Bailey, and also implies that by 'sowing death' like Robespierre the British government would have risked a similar downfall.

Wordsworth's recollection of the treason trials in *The Prelude* was written during August 1804, exactly ten years after the event. The date is important, for his portrayal of Pitt and his government as imitators of Robespierre has a curious link with work on the last seven stanzas of 'Ode'—'Intimations'—in spring of the same year. In stanza seven of his 'Ode' Wordsworth had described the four-year-old child's restless urge to imitate, 'fit[ting] his tongue'

> To dialogues of business love or strife
> But it will not be long
> Ere this be thrown aside
> And with new joy and pride
> The little actor cons another part
> Filling from time to time his humourous stage
> With all the persons down to palsied age
> That Life brings with her in her Equipage
> As if his whole vocation
> Were endless imitation.[2]

(ll. 97–107)

The child's 'joy and pride' at adopting a succession of adult roles is ironic, for the 'earnest pains' of his imitation hasten the loss of his own childhood and draw him to the 'prison-house' of adult life. In *The Prelude*, Book Ten, though, Wordsworth's 'little actor' is William Pitt; his wilful 'conning the part' of Robespierre leads—literally—to the prison-houses of Newgate and the Tower. The child in the 'Ode' impatiently throws aside one 'part' to adopt another, innocently aware that he is at strife with himself. Pitt, on the other hand, had only one vocation: to imitate the man whose execution should have stood as a warning example,

> Though with such awful proof . . . childlike longed
> To imitate—not wise enough to avoid.

The idea of Pitt as a perverse child is peculiar to Wordsworth in 1804, but he was not alone in interpreting the British repression as an imitation of the Terror in France. Besides recalling the child from 'Intimations', the passage from *The Prelude*, Book Ten, was almost certainly influenced by Wordsworth's reading of *Conciones* and also, perhaps, by John Thelwall's *Tribune*. In 1795 Coleridge and Thelwall agreed that Pitt was in every way inferior to Robespierre; furthermore, their attitudes to Robespierre himself also closely coincided.

---

[2] Quoted from the text in J. Curtis, *Wordsworth's Experiments with Tradition: The Lyric Poems of 1802* (Ithaca and London, 1971), 167.

On 23 May 1795 the *Tribune* contained Thelwall's third lecture on 'The Prospective Principle of Virtue', which drew upon his reading of *Political Justice*. Wordsworth was in London at this time and, given his friendship with Godwin and his democratic politics, he may well have been among the audience at Beaufort Buildings when Thelwall made a sustained 'comparison between the character of Robespierre and the immaculate minister of this country' (*Tribune*, i. 254). Thelwall argued that the arrests of 1794, the suppression of Habeas Corpus, the charges and trials were a policy of terrorism copied from the French, in the hope of suppressing all opposition to the government. 'I will ask you', Thelwall said,

what might have been the situation of this country, if the late prosecutions had succeeded? . . . who knows, when you once begin a system of massacre, and especially *legal* massacre, for opinion, where you can stop? I do not believe that *Robespierre* meditated, in the first instance, those scenes of carnage into which he at last was plunged. . . . I have strong suspicions in my mind, that, if they had touched the life of an individual who stood at the bar of the Old Bailey, the gaols of London (and we all know we have abundance) would have been as crammed as ever the prisons of Paris were, even in the very dog-days of the tyranny of Robespierre. (*Tribune*, i. 258)

Since Thelwall's life had depended on the outcome of 'the late prosecutions' his suspicions were understandable, and were shared by others as well. The government had been frustrated by the acquittals at the Old Bailey, and Thelwall developed his argument further by attacking Pitt as an unsuccessful imitator of Robespierre. He outlined their political characters, but to the disadvantage of

that Minister who, without the energy of Robespierre, has all his dictatorial ambition; who, without the provocations which Robespierre and his faction experienced, has endeavoured, vainly endeavoured, to carry into execution the same system of massacre for opinion, of sanguinary prosecution for proclaiming truth, of making argument High Treason, and destroying every individual who dared to expose his conduct, or oppose his ambitious views. (*Tribune*, i. 254)

Thelwall damns Pitt for endeavouring to execute a 'system of massacre for opinion', and—ironically enough—for failing to succeed in his ambition. At the same time, he almost acquits

Robespierre who had introduced his system of terror after 'provocations'. The provocation Thelwall had in mind was the European coalition against France, which he believed had encouraged the leaders of the republic to adopt extreme and violent policies. In *The Prelude* Wordsworth makes an identical point,

> And thus beset with foes on every side,
> The goaded land waxed mad
>
> (x. 311–12)

—and at the end of his lecture 'On the Present War' in *Conciones* Coleridge takes the argument full circle by identifying Pitt, not Robespierre, as ultimately responsible for the Terror in France:

It was a truth easily discovered, a truth on which our Minister has proceeded, that valour and victory would not be the determiners of this War. *They* would prove finally successful whose resources enabled them to hold out the longest. The commerce of France was annihilated . . . Immense armies were to be supported . . . Alas! Freedom weeps! The Guillotine became the Financier-General.—That dreadful pilot, Robespierre, perceived that it would at once furnish wind to the sails and free the vessel from those who were inclined to mutiny.—Who, my Brethren! was the cause of this guilt, if not HE, who supplied the occasion and the motive? (*Lects. 1795*, p. 74)

One month after Britain joined the war against France the patriot armies under General Dumouriez were defeated at Neerwinden in Holland, while the simultaneous rebellion in the Vendée put the republic at risk from within. Coleridge's analysis of the financial ruin caused by maintaining large armies at a time when war sapped commerce and trade was insightful. Throughout 1793 inflation and the shortage of goods meant that prices rose steeply, adding in turn to unrest at Paris and elsewhere in the country. In response, the National Convention sought to consolidate the powers of central government. Representatives were sent to the armies and into the provinces to bolster revolutionary enthusiasm, recruit soldiers, and root out counterrevolutionaries. The Revolutionary Tribunal was set up at Paris, and on 6 April the Committee of Public Safety was established to direct executive government and policy. As Coleridge indicated, the machinery through which the Terror was implemented was set up in spring 1793 as a response to threats inside, and from outside, the republic. He had substantial grounds for his claim that, by maintaining a war of attrition against France, Pitt had in fact supplied the 'occasion and the motive' for the Terror. In 1795 Coleridge and Thelwall agreed that Robespierre had been 'provoked' into violence. At the same time, their need to condemn the repressive policies of the British government led both to compare Pitt unfavourably with Robespierre. Like their analyses of the immediate causes of the violence in France, their perceptions of Robespierre's character and motives are also strikingly similar.

Robespierre's execution was first reported in the London *Times* on 16 August.[3] Six days later Southey wrote to Horace Bedford telling him that, with Coleridge, he had written 'a tragedy upon [Robespierre's] death in the space of two days' (Curry, i. 72–3). This 'tragedy' was *The Fall of Robespierre*, and Southey continued his letter by giving his 'opinion of this great man', whom he believed had been 'sacrificed to the despair of fools and cowards':

> Coleridge says 'he was a man whose great bad actions cast a dis[astrous] lustre over his name.' He is now inclined to think with me that the [actions?] of a man so situated must not be judged by common laws, that Robespierre was the benefactor of mankind and that we should lament his death as the greatest misfortune Europe could have sustained . . .
>
> (Curry, i. 73)

Coleridge's idea of Robespierre during 1794–5 was more complex than Southey suggests; in none of his surviving writings does he hail Robespierre as 'the benefactor of mankind', although he may have done so in conversation. Southey's letter does, however, anticipate Coleridge's dedication to the play where he says that he has 'endeavoured to detail . . . the fall of a man, whose great bad actions have cast a disastrous lustre on his name' (*CPW* ii. 495). In the opening speech of the play, Robespierre is described as

> Sudden in action, fertile in resource,
> And rising awful 'mid impending ruins;
> In splendor gloomy, as the midnight meteor,
> That fearless thwarts the elemental war
>
> (*CPW* ii. 496)

[3] N. Ascherson (ed.), *The French Revolution; Extracts from 'The Times', 1789–1794* (London, 1975), 114–15.

—and just visible through the gloom is Milton's 'dread commander' in *Paradise Lost*

> above the rest
> In shape and gesture proudly eminent
> Stood like a tower; his form had yet not lost
> All her original brightness, nor appeared
> Less than archangel ruined, and the excess
> Of glory obscured . . .
>
> (i. 589–94)

Robespierre's awful stature recalls Satan's towering presence, his 'disastrous lustre' the obscured glory of the fallen archangel. Rather than seeing Robespierre as 'the benefactor of mankind' as Southey had done, Coleridge presents him as the heroic rebel undaunted by the ruin brought upon himself. Like Satan he retains traces of his 'original brightness' in his resourcefulness and swiftness to action. Despite the obvious debt to Milton, *The Fall of Robespierre* reveals Coleridge's genuine interest in Robespierre's character and motives, subsequently explored with greater insight in his lectures of 1795. There is also evidence that the similarity between Coleridge's and Thelwall's ideas of Robespierre may have been influenced by Thelwall's reading of the play, providing a first instance of the mutual awareness that developed during 1795.

In late September 1794 five hundred copies of *The Fall of Robespierre* were published at Cambridge by Benjamin Flower. At least 125 copies were sent to London, one hundred to Kearsley the bookseller, and twenty-five to George Dyer (*CL* i. 117). Dyer was a friend of Thelwall's and may have sent a copy to him in the Tower. This would explain what appear to be echoes of Coleridge's play in Thelwall's lecture 'On the Prospective Principle of Virtue':

Robespierre had a soul capacious, an imagination various, a judgement commanding, penetrating, severe. Fertile of resources, he foresaw, created, and turned to his advantage all the events that could possibly tend to the accomplishment of his designs. The mind of Pitt is barren and inflated, his projects are crude, and his views short sighted. (*Tribune*, i. 259)

Thelwall's lecture develops Coleridge's idea of Robespierre as 'Sudden in action, fertile in resource', into a Machiavellian hero who turns all to his advantage. Thelwall's purpose was to present Pitt in a relatively unfavourable light and he did so by stressing Robespierre's resourceful energy and the quality of his mind. Where Robespierre was vital and creative, Pitt's mind was 'barren and inflated', lifeless and flatulent. Where Robespierre could foresee and manipulate events to his advantage, Pitt was myopic and his politics inept. 'Having viewed these facts,' Thelwall concluded, 'it is impossible to doubt which of these characters we must prefer.'

This lecture was delivered and published in London during May 1795, some eight months after the publication of *The Fall of Robespierre* and almost a year after the death of Robespierre himself. Three months previously, in February 1795, Coleridge had delivered 'three political Lectures' at Bristol (*CL* i. 152). One of these was his *Moral and Political Lecture*, published in February and later expanded to form the 'Introductory Address' to *Conciones* which was published the following December. One of Coleridge's major additions in his 'Introductory Address' was a history of the different factions that had recently held power in France. Like Thelwall, Coleridge emphasizes Robespierre's ruthlessness, but he was also concerned to explore his motives:

Robespierre . . . possessed a glowing ardor that still remembered the *end*, and a cool ferocity that never either overlooked, or scrupled, the *means*. What that *end* was, is not known: that it was a wicked one, has by no means been proved. I rather think, that the distant prospect, to which he was travelling, appeared to him grand and beautiful; but that he fixed his eye on it with such intense eagerness as to neglect the foulness of the road. (*Lects. 1795*, p. 35)

In the 'Introductory Address' the Machiavellian politician turns visionary, and Coleridge implies that Robespierre might have redeemed himself had his 'grand and beautiful' prospect ever been realized. This idea of Robespierre was probably influenced by Coleridge's reading of his speeches to the National Convention, from which he had already drawn material for *The Fall of Robespierre*. In his major speech on political morality, delivered 5 February 1794, Robespierre defended the original ideals of the French Revolution but countenanced violence as a means of ensuring the rights of man. 'What is the objective toward which we are reaching?' Robespierre asked, and then declared the aim of the Revolution to be 'The peaceful enjoyment of liberty and equality; the reign of that eternal justice whose laws are engraved not on marble or stone but in the hearts of all men, even in the heart of the slave who has forgotten them or of the tyrant who disowns them'.[4] In reaffirming the principles of 1789 Robespierre also defined the 'distant prospect' to which Coleridge refers in his 'Introductory Address'. But within minutes of advocating the 'peaceful enjoyment of liberty and equality', Robespierre claimed that, only by 'sealing our work with our blood, we may witness at least the dawn of universal happiness —this is our ambition, this is our aim'.[5] He then described the 'goadings' and 'provocations' the republic had endured from its enemies:

Externally all the despots surround you; internally all the friends of tyranny conspire; they will conspire until crime is deprived of all hope. It is necessary to annihilate both the internal and external enemies of the republic or perish with its fall. Now, in this situation your first political maxim should be that one guides the people by reason, and the enemies of the people by terror. . . . Terror is only justice that is prompt, severe, and inflexible; it is thus an emanation of virtue . . .[6]

Robespierre's speech vindicates Coleridge's idea of his contradictory motives, 'His cool ferocity that persuaded murder, | Even whilst it spake of mercy' (*CPW* ii. 516). The abstract bases of Robespierre's 'maxim'—'reason', 'justice', 'virtue'—also correspond to those of *Political Justice*,

> the philosophy
> That promised to abstract the hopes of man
> Out of his feelings

—and for Coleridge in 1795 this abstraction from human nature was the fundamental weakness of Godwin's system. As I suggested in Chapter 4, an identical realization on Wordsworth's part was one contributing factor in the dissolution of his own faith in *Political Justice*. By invoking 'reason' and 'justice' to excuse terrorism, therefore, Robespierre is another ancestor of

---

[4] P. Beik (trans. and ed.), *The Documentary History of Western Civilisation: The French Revolution* (London, 1971), 278 [cited hereafter as Beik].

[5] Beik, p. 279.

[6] Beik, p. 283.

Rivers who attempts a similar rational justification of murder in *The Borderers*. In *The Prelude* Wordsworth further identified Robespierre's politics with Godwin's philosophy by using the Terror as an extended and internalized metaphor for the misguided Godwinian 'reasonings' which preceded his work on *The Borderers* in 1796—a point to which I shall return shortly.

　Robespierre's 'great bad actions' did not merely challenge Coleridge's and Wordsworth's allegiance to the French Revolution. As Coleridge realized, and as Robespierre's speech shows, the *'end'* that he had in view was true to the ideals of 1789 which had been shared by all good men since. Those ideals were betrayed, though, by the *'means'* he had adopted to realize them. Both Coleridge and Wordsworth discovered in Robespierre an alarming, distorted version of themselves. Although the Terror ceased with Robespierre's death, his shadow endured long afterwards, to be reincarnated by Wordsworth in 1796–7 as Rivers. Coleridge's self-recognition in Robespierre had a formative influence on his idea of imagination in 1795, and ultimately contributed to the 'living help' he was able to offer Wordsworth in 1797.

Coleridge and the politics of imagination

During 1794 the 'rules of political justice' offered Wordsworth and some of his Cambridge contemporaries certainty and guidance at a time when all seemed tending to 'depravation'. As editor of the *Philanthropist* Wordsworth conceived himself as a Godwinian sage and prophet, propagating Godwin's philosophy of necessary progress and passivity to 'establish freedom with tranquillity' (*E Y*, p. 124). In 1795 Coleridge assumed an identical role, but for him the only 'gentle words' that might prevent violent revolution were those of religion:

In that barbarous tumult of inimical Interests, which the present state of Society exhibits, *Religion* appears to offer the only means universally *efficient*. The perfectness of future Men is indeed a benevolent tenet, and may operate on a few Visionaries, whose studious habits supply them with employment, and seclude them from temptation. But a distant prospect, which we are never to reach, will seldom quicken our footsteps, however lovely it may appear; and a Blessing, which not ourselves but *posterity* are destined to enjoy, will scarcely influence the actions of *any*—still less of the ignorant, the prejudiced, and the selfish. (*Lects. 1795*, pp. 43–4)

Like Thelwall, Coleridge realized that Godwin had neglected the means to achieve his vision of perfectibility. Religion, however, offered the certainty of 'an infinitely great revolution hereafter', simultaneously the establishment of a just society and the promised millennium. This, he believed, might serve as a popular restraint—'Rest awhile | Children of Wretchedness!'—which was exactly how Wordsworth and Thelwall responded to *Political Justice* between 1794–5. But the function of religion was not limited to a palliative for misery. It also comprised a genuine alternative to the bogus prospect of perfection offered by the 'studious visionaries' of the Philomathean Society, the 'dim-eyed Sons of Blasphemy' with whom Wordsworth was connected in 1795. Coleridge's means of attaining that 'distant prospect' was a function of his idea of benevolence, which provided the impetus to progress and perfectibility that he believed *Political Justice* lacked.

In his defence speech to the university court in May 1793, William Frend had listed the principal 'articles of his creed' as a unitarian dissenter. 'We may boast of our knowledge of and acquaintance with god,' Frend had said,

we may confound every gainsayer on the terms of our salvation, yet, if we neglect the principle of universal benevolence, our faith is vain, our religion is an empty parade of useless and insignificant sounds. That every christian is bound to entertain sentiments of universal benevolence, to love his fellow creatures of every sect, colour or description, is the third grand point of my faith. (*Account*, pp. 89–90)

For Frend, 'universal benevolence' was the reconciling expression of faith and the foundation of his hope for salvation. From present human love he construed the terms of future regeneration, and this complex idea of benevolence was inherited and developed by Coleridge after 1794. It underlies his idea of Pantisocracy as a '*center*' from which restoration might proceed by assimilation and expansion, and this process was reinforced by Hartley's belief that 'vice originates not in the man, but in the surrounding circumstances' (*Lects. 1795*, p. 12).[7] On these grounds Coleridge could offer a necessary and Christian

[7] See Chapter 3 above.

alternative to Godwin in his 1795 lectures. Ultimately, though, Frend's definition of benevolence as an expansive and regenerative power lies behind Coleridge's evolving idea of imagination during the same year. The contemporary political context and the awful figure of Robespierre were to prompt Coleridge's reformulation of 'the third grand point of [Frend's] faith' in the restless, progressive faculty of imagination.

'It is melancholy to think', Coleridge wrote to George Dyer on 10 March 1795,

that the best of us are liable to be shaped & coloured by surrounding Objects—and a demonstrative proof, that Man was not made to live in Great Cities! Almost all the physical Evil in the World depends on the existence of moral Evil—and the long-continued contemplation of the latter does not tend to meliorate the human heart.—The pleasures, which we receive from rural beauties, are of little Consequence compared with the Moral Effect of these pleasures—beholding constantly the Best possible we at last become ourselves the best possible. In the country, all around us smile Good and Beauty—and the Images of this divine καλοκἀγαθόν are miniatured on the mind of the beholder, as a Landscape on a Convex Mirror. (CL i. 154)

Dyer had written complaining of 'languor' and 'illiberal feelings' caused by living in London, drawing Coleridge's comments on the necessary influence of 'surrounding Objects' to moral good or evil. 'God love you, my very dear Sir!', Coleridge continued, 'I would that we could form a Pantisocracy in England, and that you could be one of us!—The finely-fibred Heart, that like the statue of Memnon, trembles into melody on the sun-beam touch of Benevolence, is most easily jarred into the dissonance of Misanthropy' (CL i. 155). Coleridge's image of mind as the 'Convex Mirror' of a Claude glass is passive and reflective: the 'finely-fibred Heart', though 'easily jarred', is vital and responsive to 'the sun-beam touch of Benevolence' and becomes a power to moral good in itself. This letter to Dyer reveals Coleridge moving on from the essentially mechanical 'leading idea' of Pantisocracy, 'to make men necessarily virtuous by removing all motives of Evil', to discover a living principle of amelioration in the workings of the 'heart' that he would later attribute specifically to the imagination. This development was also shared by George Dyer early in 1795, and suggests a considerable mutual influence during these months.

Dyer's *Dissertation on the Theory and Practice of Benevolence* was published in March 1795, and contains passages strikingly akin to Coleridge's thinking at this time:

The GOOD MAN from the appearances of nature derives tender affections, generous principles, and humane conduct. From the glowing and variegated scenes around him he derives something which warms his heart, and throws a smile over his countenance. The imbecility of the beings, to whom by his very nature he is related, does but strengthen his heart, and when he takes a gloomy view of things, the exertions of benevolence raise his spirit. The good man thus acquires universal tenderness.[8]

One might easily mistake this for a passage from one of Coleridge's lectures or letters of 1795. Given Coleridge's friendship with Dyer since August 1794, their correspondence and familiarity with each other's publications, the parallels between the two are perhaps not surprising. Both were concerned to redefine the possibility of progress in a non-political context; Dyer appropriates the contemporary liberal label 'The GOOD MAN' to this end, discarding politics for the benevolent tendency to good in 'the appearances of nature'. A comparable development appears in Coleridge's discussion of 'thinking and disinterested Patriots' in his *Moral and Political Lecture* and the 'Introductory Address' to *Conciones*.

Coleridge's patriots were the reformists Joseph Gerrald, Thomas Muir, Thomas Fysshe Palmer, and Maurice Margarot, all of whom had been tried for sedition during 1793–4 and transported to Botany Bay. In his *Moral and Political Lecture* Coleridge was silent about their political activities as members of reformist societies, and principally concerned to define his ideal of progressive 'intellect':

These are the men who have encouraged the sympathetic passions till they have become irresistible habits . . . Accustomed to regard all the affairs of man as a process, they never hurry and they never pause; theirs is not that twilight of political knowledge which gives us just light enough to place one foot before the other; as they advance, the scene still opens upon them, and they press right onward with a vast and various landscape of existence around them. Calmness and energy mark all their actions, benevolence is the silken thread that runs through the pearl chain of all their virtues. Believing that vice originates not in the man, but

---

[8] Dyer, *Dissertation*, p. 19.

OMNE SOLUM FORTI PATRIA.

I.KAY 1794.

JOSEPH GERRALD

A Delegate to the British Convention.

4. Profile of Joseph Gerrald, one of Coleridge's 'thinking and disinterested Patriots'. Frontispiece to *The Trial of Joseph Gerrald* (1794).

in the surrounding circumstances; not in the heart, but in the under-standing; he is hopeless concerning no one . . . (*Lects.* 1795, p. 12)

The reference to 'sympathetic passions' and the origin of vice in circumstances recall Coleridge's theory of Pantisocracy in 1794; the 'vast and various landscape' corresponds to Dyer's 'glowing and variegated scenes' in his *Dissertation*. Coleridge differs im-portantly from Dyer, however, in emphasizing onward 'process' and 'advance' within this vibrant landscape; his patriots 'press right onward', he says, with 'calmness and energy' and 'benev-olence' as their guiding principle. But, like Godwin in *Political Justice*, Coleridge lacks for the moment any motive to this progress beyond his assertion that true patriots are 'Accustomed to regard the affairs of man as a process'. The patriot 'looks forward with gladdened heart to that glorious period when Justice shall have established the universal fraternity of Love', Coleridge claims, and then adds,

These soul ennobling views bestow the virtues which they anticipate. He whose mind is habitually imprest with them soars above the present state of humanity, and may be justly said to dwell in the presence of the most high. Regarding every event even as he that ordains it, evil vanishes from before him, and he views with naked eye the eternal form of universal beauty. (*Lects.* 1795, p. 13)

Here, the working of 'Justice' to 'universal fraternity' is in fact less significant than the patriot's happy anticipation of that state. The emphasis is less on immediate fulfilment than aspiration. The patriot 'looks forward with gladdened heart', his foresight is 'soul ennobling', soaring above quotidian existence to participate 'in the presence of the most high'. Coleridge starts in the twilight world of 'political knowledge' to end with a vision of God, viewing 'with naked eye the eternal form of universal beauty'.

   In February 1795 Coleridge followed Price, Priestley, and Frend in identifying political and social regeneration with divine revelation, but he also located the revolutionary motive to pro-gress within the visionary power of the individual mind. At thi' moment, though, he wanted philosophical support for his clair as the *Critical Review* pointed out: 'he has not stated, in a ' sufficiently scientific and determinate,' the reviewer noted principles to which, as he expresses it, he now procee most *important point*' (*Lects.* 1795, p. 2). One of ' overriding concerns hereafter would be to identify religious and philosophic grounds for certainty, and in *Religious Musings* he would marshal the 'systems' of Hartley, Berkeley, and Priestley to this end. But the *Critical Review* had in fact pin-pointed a fundamental weakness in Coleridge's visionary politics. Ultimately, visionary revelation—'Regarding every event even as he that ordains it'—is not philosophically or rationally 'determinate'. By translating revolutionary 'process' as a function of that revelation, therefore, Coleridge abandoned possible certainty of proof and this disability was one reason for his failure to supply Wordsworth with any coherent philosophic framework for *The Recluse*. More immediately fruitful, however, was his identification of imagination as the focus of his hopes for the amelioration of mankind. A crucial factor in doing so was Coleridge's self-perception in Robespierre.

In their various lectures during 1795 Coleridge and Thelwall both presented Robespierre as a man of vision, although their purposes in doing so were ultimately different. Thelwall claimed Robespierre had a 'capacious' soul, a 'varied' imagination, and that Pitt was in every way his inferior. Coleridge would have agreed, but he found the paradoxes of Robespierre's character and motives equally fascinating. Where Thelwall was content to describe, Coleridge was concerned to analyse. Thelwall's Robespierre was of political significance only, but Coleridge's Robespierre had a direct bearing on his thinking about imagination in 1795. Coleridge's earliest definition of imagination comes at the beginning of his *Lecture on the Slave Trade*, delivered 'by particular desire' on 16 June 1795. 'To develope the powers of the Creator', Coleridge says,

is our proper employment—and to imitate Creativeness by combination our most exalted and self-satisfying Delight. But we are progressive and must not rest content with present Blessings. Our Almighty Parent hath therefore given to us Imagination that stimulates to the attainment of *real* excellence by the contemplation of splendid Possibilities that still revivifies the dying motive within us, and fixing our eye on the glittering Summits that rise one above the other in Alpine endlessness still urges us up the ascent of Being, amusing the ruggedness of the road with the beauty and grandeur of the ever-widening Prospect. Such and so noble are the ends for which this restless faculty was given us—but horrible has been its misapplication. (*Lects. 1795*, pp. 235–6)

This passage foreshadows the definitions of primary and secondary imagination in *Biographia Literaria*, but its seminal significance lies in its immediate implications in 1795 rather than in anticipating Coleridge's position twenty years later. In 'the contemplation of splendid Possibilities that still revivifies the dying motive within us' Coleridge recalled his 'soul ennobling views' that 'bestow the virtues which they anticipate' in *A Moral and Political Lecture*. There, however, he had lacked any explanation for that attainment and his most significant development in his *Lecture on the Slave Trade* was to define imagination as the progressive and God-given power that 'stimulates' to excellence through 'contemplation of splendid Possibilities'. The imagination emerges as the faculty that sustains the dying motive to progress 'up the ascent of being' to reveal—in the end—'the eternal form of universal beauty'. It was this translation of 'splendid Possibilities' from revolutionary politics to the 'restless faculty' of mind that offered Coleridge a counterbalance to disappointment through years when Wordsworth—who had made a parallel investment of hope in *Political Justice*—suffered a period of despair. That transition, in turn, was conditioned by Coleridge's insight into Robespierre's 'horrible misapplication' of imagination during the Terror.

By the end of 1796 Coleridge had identified the cause of Robespierre's downfall in his lack of patience. 'Permit me', Coleridge wrote to John Thelwall on 17 December 1796, 'as a definition of this word to quote one sentence from my first Address, . . . "Accustomed to regard all the affairs of Man, as a Process, they never hurry & they never pause." In his not possessing *this* virtue, all the horrible excesses of Robespierre did, I believe, originate' (*C L* i. 283). Coleridge's definition of patience comes from his discussion of 'thinking and disinterested Patriots', with whom he evidently identified himself, in his 'Introductory Address' and *A Moral and Political Lecture*. Like Robespierre these patriots were distinguished by their foresight and vision, but also for the restraint which he had not possessed. 'Calmness and energy mark all their actions', Coleridge had said in February 1795, while their visionary and progressive intellects identify them as prototypes of his elect in 'Religious Musings',

> Who in this fleshly World . . .
> Their strong eye darting thro' the deeds of Men

Adore with stedfast unpresuming gaze
Him, Nature's Essence, Mind, and Energy!
And gazing, trembling, patiently ascend
Treading beneath their feet all visible things
As steps, that upward to their Father's Throne
Lead gradual . . .

(ll. 52–9)

Robespierre, in comparison, was too presumptuous. He might have belonged among the elect but for the impatience which betrayed his own vision and usurped God's providence. His imagination had slipped the control of love, which alone could have reconciled Robespierre's efforts to the 'distant prospect' he had in view and avoided the excesses of the Terror. As it was, Robespierre remained unregenerate, a patriot manqué, a damaged version of Coleridge himself. In the 'Introductory Address' Robespierre appears as a grotesque parody of the 'disinterested Patriots' and the elect, divided against himself and his country. 'His dark imagination was still brooding over supposed plots against freedom', Coleridge said, '—to prevent tyranny he became a Tyrant—and having realized the evils which he suspected, a wild and dreadful Tyrant. . . . he despotized in all the pomp of Patriotism, and masqueraded on the bloody stage of Revolution, a Caligula with the cap of Liberty on his head' (*Lects. 1795*, p. 35).

Coleridge drew this passage from the first act of *The Fall of Robespierre*. In the 'Introductory Address' the theatrical metaphor works to highlight the contradictory fragments of Robespierre's political personality, a tyrant ruling in the name of liberty. Coleridge coined a new word—'despotize', meaning to act the part of a despot—to define the split in Robespierre's psyche which he attributed to impatience, equivalent for Coleridge to a lack of faith.[9] Not surprisingly, Coleridge found a similar dislocation in *Political Justice*, 'a book which builds without a foundation, [and] proposes an end without establishing the means' (*Lects. 1795*, p. 164), whereas Robespierre 'remembered the *end*' but was unscrupulous about the '*means*' adopted to achieve it (*Lects. 1795*, p. 35). Robespierre's politics and

---

[9] See my note, 'Robespierre's Despotism and a word Coined by Coleridge', *N&Q* (Aug. 1981), 309–10.

Godwin's philosophy failed to 'develope the powers of the Creator' and were inevitably self-defeating. Robespierre rushed headlong to attain his 'distant prospect', and the spectacle horrified and fascinated Coleridge. At the other extreme was 'dimeyed' Godwin, the 'studious visionary' who denied the existence of God and passively awaited the triumph of political justice in 'a distant prospect, which we are never to reach'. Coleridge's perception of an underlying similarity between Robespierre and Godwin fed his doubts about the moral effects of *Political Justice* and its popularity among reformists. His deepest fear, I think, was that Godwin's abstract and unprincipled philosophy might lead to political and social breakdown, and ultimately to violence like that witnessed in France. As it turned out, *Political Justice* had a restraining effect upon the reform movement late in 1795, and Coleridge's worries never became a reality. But they did have an imaginative fruition in Wordsworth's *Borderers* and later on in *The Prelude*, Book Ten.

In Book Ten Wordsworth recalls the 'miserable dreams' that he experienced during the Terror:

> Such ghastly visions had I of despair,
> And tyranny, and implements of death,
> And long orations which in dreams I pleaded
> Before unjust tribunals, with a voice
> Labouring, a brain confounded . . .
>
> (x. 374–8)

His night-visions of despair and confusion before those 'unjust tribunals' subsequently reappear in Wordsworth's recollection of his Godwinian speculations about society and human nature. 'Thus I fared', he says,

> Dragging all passions, notions, shapes of faith,
> Like culprits to the bar, suspiciously
> Calling the mind to establish in plain day
> Her titles and her honours . . .
>
> (x. 888–92)

Here Wordsworth is prosecutor, judge, and defendant, divided against himself over the 'bar' of self-inquisition. He is endlessly prevented from reaching a verdict,

> by reasonings false
> From the beginning, inasmuch as drawn

Out of a heart which had been turned aside
From Nature by external accidents,
And which was thus confounded more and more,
Misguiding and misguided

(x. 883–8)

—in exactly the way that Coleridge believed Robespierre had
been confounded by the means he had adopted to save France.
With the republic threatened with invasion and rebellion, he had
been pushed into terrorism to protect the Revolution: 'And thus
beset with foes on every side', Wordsworth says in Book Ten,
'The goaded land waxed mad' (x. 311–12). A little later in the
same book, Wordsworth again connects the Terror with his
Godwinian thinking by using identical language to define his
intellectual confusion. '[M]y mind was both let loose,' he recalls,
'Let loose and goaded'—and the deliberate link with the 'goaded
land' is confirmed by these being the only two usages of 'goaded'
in Wordsworth's poetry. 'I took the knife in hand', he continues,

And, stopping not at parts less sensitive,
Endeavoured with my best of skill to probe
The living body of society
Even to the heart.

(x. 872–6)

The guillotine has become a surgeon's knife, and the surgeon is
Wordsworth himself performing a grotesque anatomy by vivisec-
tion upon the 'living body of society', as Robespierre had sought
to purge the internal enemies of France and 'seal our work with
our blood'. Through a series of deliberate and striking verbal
parallels the madness of the 'goaded land' is internalized as the
self-consuming disturbance of Wordsworth's mind,

now believing,
Now disbelieving, endlessly perplexed
With impulse, motive, right and wrong

(x. 892–4)

—until he 'Yielded up moral questions in despair', bringing ruin
upon himself as Robespierre had done. However, Wordsworth's
extinction as a Godwinian being carries an intimation of future
restoration in its echo of Matthew 27: 50, 'Jesus, when he had
cried again with a loud voice, yielded up the ghost'—but the

resurrection was to follow. For Wordsworth in *The Prelude* despair gives way to Dorothy's healing presence, Coleridge's friendship, and, under their influence, his own reincarnation as a poet:

> 'Come now, ye golden times',
> Said I, forth-breaking on those open sands
> A hymn of triumph . . .

Book Ten of *The Prelude* imaginatively associates Robespierre's politics with Godwin's philosophy, Wordsworth's confused Godwinian self with the author of the Terror: both 'by the might | Of their own helper [were] swept away' (x. 548–9). Wordsworth wrote this section of *The Prelude* in 1804, but it apparently insists that some realization of the deathly potential of *Political Justice* originally contributed to his moral 'despair'. Moreover, the very nature of that despair seems to have fostered Wordsworth's subsequent receptivity to Coleridge's ideas when they met in June 1797.

In *The Prelude* Wordsworth confounds Robespierre with Satan, 'Chief regent' of the 'foul tribe of Moloch', the serpent that marred the Revolution with violence. But his effort to damn Robespierre momentarily relaxes at one point where he admits that even during the 'rage and dog-day heat' of the Terror he had found

> Something to glory in, as just and fit,
> And in the order of sublimest laws.
> And even if that were not, amid the awe
> Of unintelligible chastisement
> [He] felt a kind of sympathy with power—
>
> (x. 412–16)

Wordsworth's 'kind of sympathy with power' ironically resembles his 'ready welcome' for *Political Justice* in 1794 as a means to prevent the 'scourge' of violence afflicting Britain (*E Y*, p. 124). In *The Prelude* he recalls Godwin's philosophy as an 'unimpeachable' power

> To look through all the frailties of the world,
> And, with a resolute mastery shaking off
> The accidents of nature, time, and place,
> That make up the weak being of the past,

> Build social freedom on its only basis:
> The freedom of the individual mind,
> Which, to the blind restraint of general laws
> Superior, magisterially adopts
> One guide—the light of circumstances, flashed
> Upon an independent intellect.

(x. 820–9)

The 'resolute mastery' and magisterial guidance recall Wordsworth's confident assertion of the 'rules of political justice' in his
letter to Mathews of 8 June 1794 (*EY*, p. 124). Four months
before Wordsworth wrote that letter, in his speech on political
morality Robespierre had made an equally sweeping claim for
'virtue and equality' which he identified as the 'soul of the
republic'. Robespierre too had 'shaken off' the frailties of feeling
and other 'accidents' of human nature, to present republican
virtue as 'a compass to direct you through the tempest of the
passions and the whirlwind of the intrigues that surround you.
You have the touchstone with which you can test all your laws, all
the propositions that are laid before you'.[10] Moments later
Robespierre used that 'touchstone' to justify his ruthless equation
of terrorism with justice. In *The Prelude* Wordsworth presents
Political Justice as a similar touchstone, 'to the blind restraint of
general laws | Superior': where Robespierre had openly advo-
cated the use of violence, Wordsworth hints darkly at the similar
end to which Godwinian rationalism tended. He does so by
defining Godwin's philosophy,

> —the light of circumstances, flashed
> Upon an independent intellect

—in words taken from the mouth of a man who would persuade
murder. As is well known, these lines originally appeared in *The
Borderers* where Rivers congratulates Mortimer for killing
Herbert:

> You have obeyed the only law that wisdom
> Can ever recognize: the immediate law
> Flashed from the light of circumstances
> Upon an independent intellect.
> Henceforth new prospects ought to open on you,
> Your faculties should grow with the occasion.

(Osborn, p. 210, III. v. 30–5)

---

[10] Beik, p. 281.

However, the 'new prospects' and growing 'faculties' contingent upon Rivers's 'immediate law' ironically also correspond to the 'ever-widening Prospect' and restlessly progressive faculty of imagination in Coleridge's *Lecture on the Slave Trade*. The anti-Godwinian thrust of Wordsworth's irony in *The Borderers* lies in the conditional 'ought to open', 'should grow', and in the immediate context of the play where no 'prospect' appears except a mutual bond in guilt. In the character of Rivers Wordsworth had, in fact, realized Coleridge's perception of the similarities between Godwin's arrogant abstraction and Robespierre's visionary politics. By working through his doubts about Godwin and political revolution in *The Borderers*, Wordsworth effectively cleared his mind of the intellectual debris of the previous five years. When he completed his play in spring 1797, he was ready to respond to the help and guidance Coleridge could now bring him. The nature of that help and of Wordsworth's receptivity to it are revealed, perhaps unexpectedly, by Wordsworth's renewed interest in mathematics sometime in 1796 and in his portrait of a misanthropic solitary in 'Lines left upon a Seat in a Yew-tree', which was composed between April and June 1797 just before Coleridge arrived at Racedown.

Mathematics, the 'lost man', and Coleridge's 'living help'

> What then remained in such eclipse, what light
> To guide or chear? The laws of things which lie
> Beyond the reach of human will or power,
> The life of Nature, by the God of love
> Inspired . . .

(P. xi. 96–100)

Wordsworth's memory of the 'despair' to which *Political Justice* led him is also a recollection of self-discovery and renewal that would lead to his emergence as poet and friend of Coleridge. As I suggested in Chapter 5, his dissatisfaction with Godwin can be dated from his months in London in 1795; rather than culminating in a single moment of crisis and breakdown, the process of disillusion extended well over a year and was accompanied by Wordsworth's search for a philosophical alternative to Godwinian rationalism. In *Prelude* Book Ten this need led Wordsworth, initially, to a return upon his Cambridge self and a revived interest in mathematics. 'I lost | All feeling of conviction', he recalls in *The Prelude*,

> and, in fine,
> Sick, wearied out with contrarieties,
> Yielded up moral questions in despair,
> And for my future studies, as the sole
> Employment of the inquiring faculty,
> Turned towards mathematics, and their clear
> And solid evidence.
>
> (x. 897–904)

The 'evidence' he had in mind was the objective certainty offered by 'the elements | Of geometric science' (vi. 136–7) as a counterpoise to Godwin's legacy of intellectual and moral confusion. Wordsworth's recourse to mathematics at this moment was, literally, a return to basics but it was also the start of his self-reconstitution as a poet. The significance of mathematics in this process is revealed in his recollected fondness for such studies in *Prelude*, Book Six. 'I had stepped | In these inquiries but a little way', he recalls there, but had found 'Enough to exalt, to chear me and compose' (vi. 137–8, 141). In what follows he explains the power of geometry to sustain and calm, in a passage that has important implications for his post-Godwinian self of 1796. 'I meditated', Wordsworth says,

> Upon the alliance of those simple, pure
> Proportions and relations, with the frame
> And laws of Nature—how they could become
> Herein a leader to the human mind—
> And made endeavours frequent to detect
> The process by dark guesses of my own.
> Yet from this source more frequently I drew
> A pleasure calm and deeper, a still sense
> Of permanent and universal sway
> And paramount endowment in the mind,
> An image not unworthy of the one
> Surpassing life, which—out of space and time,
> Nor touched by welterings of passion—is,
> And hath the name of, God. Transcendent peace
> And silence did await upon these thoughts
> That were a frequent comfort to my youth.
>
> (vi. 143–59)

Here, geometry is recalled as an analytical science of 'Proportions and relations' that correspond with 'the frame | And laws of Nature'. In establishing such certainty, though, geometry also offered intellectual stimulus—'a leader to the human mind' —in Wordsworth's 'meditation' and 'dark guesses of [his] own'. Furthermore the sense of 'permanent and universal sway' afforded by geometry as a manifestation of the mind's 'paramount endowment', constituted an image of transcendent order and power which 'hath the name of, God'. Wordsworth was writing Book Six in spring 1804, and at that moment presented the geometric intellect as correspondent to the 'paramount endowment' assumed by imagination in Book Thirteen, to perceive 'an under-presence, | The sense of God' (xiii. 71–2). The source of his identification of geometry with the visionary imagination can be traced eight years earlier in Wordsworth's 'turn towards mathematics' in 1796, which offers an emergent parallel with Coleridge's experience immediately before his meeting with Wordsworth at Racedown. The evidence, oddly enough, appears through Wordsworth's friendship with Basil Montagu after 1795.

Wordsworth first met Basil Montagu 'by an accident' in London early in 1795; they spent 'some months together' before Wordsworth left for Bristol in August, and Montagu subsequently considered his meeting with Wordsworth 'the most fortunate event of [his] life'.[11] Wordsworth helped Montagu out of certain 'wild' habits, and subsequently took Basil Montagu, Junior, to Racedown leaving his father free to develop his legal career. Their early friendship was encouraged by a mutual admiration for *Political Justice*, although Montagu's personal acquaintance with Godwin apparently dated from July 1795 and flourished during the following autumn and winter after Wordsworth's departure. Godwin's diary shows him to have been frequently in Montagu's company at this time, often with Francis Wrangham and William Mathews present too. Like Wordsworth, Montagu seems to have attended the Philomathean society, Godwin noting on 23 February 1796 'tea Montagu's . . . Philomaths, property' (GD vii), and he sent Wordsworth the

---

[11] DC MS A/Montagu B/26. 'Basil Montagu's Narrative of the Birth and Upbringing of his son.'

second edition of *Political Justice* in March. When Wordsworth visited London the following June, he stayed in Montagu's chambers, and renewed his acquaintance with Godwin on at least four occasions (*E Y*, p. 170n.).

By mid-1796, however, Wordsworth's enthusiasm for *Political Justice* had cooled; he told Mathews in March that Godwin's 'second preface' was 'a piece of barbarous writing' and that he had not been encouraged to read any further (*E Y*, p. 170). Montagu, on the other hand, seems to have remained a firm Godwinian until summer 1797 when he visited Wordsworth and Coleridge at Stowey (Reed, p. 204). At this time he told Azariah Pinney he no longer agreed 'with Mr. Godwin . . . that all men are Benevolent & Wise & that restrictions are useless':

If man be benevolent & wise: it certainly is unnecessary that there should be Promises, Gratitude, Restraints, Law, Religion &c: But he is short sighted & selfish, & without these restraints he is a Monster—It is a specious system, it is addressed to the most flattering of the passions: & is not easily refuted, because it requires some knowledge of human nature . . .[12]

Montagu's revised opinion of Godwin in 1797 coincided exactly with Wordsworth's and Coleridge's, and undoubtedly reflected their influence. He might well have been thinking of Rivers when he described man 'without restraints' as 'a Monster'; Coleridge had criticized Godwin's ignorance of human nature in his 1795 lectures, and the same realization had fed Wordsworth's doubts about *Political Justice*. Finally, in defining *Political Justice* as 'a specious system . . . addressed to the most flattering of the passions', Montagu anticipates Wordsworth's memory of Godwin's 'flattering dream' in *The Prelude*. Given Wordsworth's and Coleridge's bearing upon Montagu's 'fluctuating opinions on Morals' in 1797, it is significant that among his papers are some sheets that elaborate connections between geometry and imagination. These appear to date from 1796–7 and may possibly represent some 'mathematical' collaboration between

---

[12] Basil Montagu to Azariah Pinney, undated letter watermarked 'Russell & Co 1797', BUL, Pinney Papers, Domestic Box R/3, Miscellaneous papers of Basil Montagu. Montagu refers to his 'residence at Alfoxden', which could be his visit of July–Aug. 1797, or more likely his extended stay the following Nov.–Dec., which would mean the letter was probably written early in 1798. In either case, though, his revised opinion of Godwin dates from summer 1797.

Wordsworth and Montagu during these two years, perhaps on Wordsworth's visit to London in June 1796 or Montagu's short stay at Racedown in March 1797 (Reed, pp. 182–5, 194).

Wordsworth's account of 'geometric science' in *The Prelude*, Book Six, anticipates the visionary imagination in Book Thirteen and, ultimately, Coleridge's 'primary imagination' in *Biographia*. Basil Montagu's manuscript scheme for the 'Proper Mode of teaching Geometry' and its relation to the developing imagination of a child, is perhaps closer to Coleridge's idea of 'Creativeness by combination' in his *Lecture on the Slave Trade* and to the 'secondary imagination' in *Biographia*. 'If I am to imagine', Montagu writes,

> *or form an image*, by putting things together in my mind, in an arrangement different from that in which I have beheld them, & thus create a whole which I have not seen, out of parts which I have seen; the distinctness of the original conceptions will be equally subservient to this process. By appealing in this manner to his senses, & making him feel the firmness of the ground on which he treads, one might probably instruct a boy, at an early age, in the elements of Geometry, so as rarely to give him disgust, & frequently great satisfaction.[13]

Montagu argues that geometry would foster 'distinct & deep . . . impressions of sense' in the child, which in turn would feed the imagination or 'power of abstraction'. His theory corresponds to Wordsworth's memory in *The Prelude*, Book Six, that geometry encouraged his own efforts 'to detect | The process by dark guesses of [his] own', leading him also to a sense of 'universal sway'. Although there is no certain evidence to connect Montagu's papers on geometry with Wordsworth's 'turn towards mathematics', their mutual concern with what Montagu termed 'the irresistible force of Mathematical Evidence' suggests its likelihood. Possibly Wordsworth and Montagu were both interested in young Basil's education, and the best method of teaching him mathematics. For both Wordsworth and Montagu, though, the significance of geometry lay in establishing fundamental impressions from which the imaginative 'process' could begin. In outline at least this foreshadows Wordsworth's portrait of the early years of his Pedlar:

[13] BUL, Pinney Papers, Domestic Box R/3. Ten sheets of comments on the teaching of maths and geometry, undated but watermarked 'E&P1796'. The writing is all in Montagu's hand.

> deep feelings had impressed
> Great objects on his mind with portraiture
> And colour so distinct that on his mind
> They lay like substances & almost seemed
> To haunt the bodily sense. He had received
> A precious gift for as he grew in years
> With these impressions would he still compare
> All his ideal stores, his shapes & forms
> And being still unsatisfied with aught
> Of dimmer character he thence attained
> An *active* power to fasten images
> Upon his brain & on their pictured lines
> Intensely brooded even till they acquired
> The liveliness of dreams.
>
> (Butler, p. 341)

Wordsworth substitutes 'deep feelings' for Montagu's 'deep . . . impressions of sense', but the progression from a formative 'substantial impression' to an '*active* power' is essentially the same. As Jonathan Wordsworth says, *The Pedlar* is Wordsworth's most confident statement of the philosophy of One Life, and reflects Coleridge's influence in providing 'a philosophical basis for his response to Nature' (*MH*, pp. 200–1). In doing so Coleridge gave Wordsworth creative access to his own experience; but when he subsequently wrote about the growth of the Pedlar's mind he seems to have drawn upon his idea of the geometric intellect to provide a coherent pattern for that development, while discarding the framework of mathematical theory.

In the Second Book of *The Two-part Prelude*, Wordsworth's concern was to emphasize a comparable continuity and unity of progression in his own mind, and he contrasts the 'false distinctions' created by analytical reason:

> But who shall parcel out
> His intellect by geometric rules,
> Split like a province into round and square? . . .
> Thou, my friend, art one
> More deeply read in thy own thoughts, no slave
> Of that false secondary power by which
> In weakness we create distinctions, then
> Believe our puny boundaries are things
> Which we perceive, and not which we have made.

To thee, unblinded by these outward shews,
The unity of all has been revealed . . .

(1799, ii. 242–4, 249–56)

Wordsworth's hymn of thanks to his friend and philosophic guide represents a reaction from his mathematical self of 1796, rejecting geometric rules as reductive and divisive and celebrating the revealed 'unity of all'. But, although he presents that self as misguided in *The Two-part Prelude*, his development between 1796 and 1798 suggests the contrary, and that his recourse to mathematics had prepared his receptivity to Coleridge's thinking in the first place.

The Prelude, Book Six, and Montagu's 'Mode of teaching Geometry' indicate that Wordsworth's renewed interest in mathematics had two immediate effects. One was to regain the 'clear | And solid evidence' which Godwinian abstraction had denied him, and was effectively a return upon his own experience and senses, 'making him feel the firmness of the ground on which he [trod]'. Secondly, in those 'elements | Of geometric science' he rediscovered a 'guiding light' for his own 'dark guesses' or insights, now allied once more 'with the frame | And laws of Nature' as 'the rules of political justice' had not been. In this respect mathematics reinforced Dorothy's influence in maintaining a 'saving intercourse | With [his] true self', and that of 'Nature's self' in reviving 'the feelings of [his] earlier life' (x. 914–15, 924). Although not mentioned as such in *The Two-part Prelude*, or in Book Ten of the 1805 poem, Wordsworth eventually recognized that geometry held a redemptive possibility, a paradigm of the visionary and creative powers of his own imagination. In 1796 geometry was Wordsworth's intellectual bridge from Godwin to One Life, a further redefinition of revolutionary possibility in the relation of mind to nature. Coleridge enabled Wordsworth to move on from this point, to reformulate his revolutionary and Godwinian solicitude for man as a corollary of his own visionary fondness for nature. Wordsworth's recognition of this potential, just before Coleridge's arrival at Racedown, appears in his 'Lines Left upon a Seat in a Yew-tree'. This poem is also an epitaph for a generation of good men like Coleridge and himself who had lost confidence in politics and *Political Justice*, but without discovering a consoling 'light | To guide [and] chear' as they had done.

The reclusive solitary in Wordsworth's 'Lines' is a study of disappointment exacerbated by a simultaneous awareness of possible—but unattainable—fulfilment:

> —He was one who own'd
> No common soul. In youth, by genius nurs'd,
> And big with lofty views, he to the world
> Went forth, pure in his heart, against the taint
> Of dissolute tongues, 'gainst jealousy, and hate,
> And scorn, against all enemies prepared,
> All but neglect: and so, his spirit damped
> At once, with rash disdain he turned away,
> And with the food of pride sustained his soul
> In solitude.—Stranger! these gloomy boughs
> Had charms for him; and here he loved to sit,
> His only visitants a straggling sheep,
> The stone-chat, or the glancing sand-piper;
> And on these barren rocks, with juniper,
> And heath, and thistle, thinly sprinkled o'er,
> Fixing his downward eye, he many an hour
> A morbid pleasure nourished, tracing here
> An emblem of his own unfruitful life:
> And lifting up his head, he then would gaze
> On the more distant scene; how lovely 'tis
> Thou seest, and he would gaze till it became
> Far lovelier, and his heart could not sustain
> The beauty still more beauteous. Nor, that time,
> Would he forget those beings, to whose minds,
> Warm from the labours of benevolence,
> The world, and man himself, appeared a scene
> Of kindred loveliness: then he would sigh
> With mournful joy, to think that others felt
> What he must never feel: and so, lost man!
> On visionary views would fancy feed,
> Till his eye streamed with tears. In this deep vale
> He died, this seat his only monument.
>
> (ll. 12–43)

Like the royalist officer in *Prelude*, Book Nine, the 'lost man' is self-consumed and ruined by his arrogance and 'contempt', and this issues in a sort of diseased paralysis. The officer's sword

> was haunted by his touch
> Continually, like an uneasy place
> In his own body

$$(\text{ix. } 162-4)$$

—but never drawn from its scabbard. Similarly, the 'Yew-tree' solitary is haunted by his own frustrated powers of intellect and vision, nourishing a 'morbid pleasure' in discovering 'emblem[s] of his own unfruitful life'. Both soldier and solitary are harmless brothers of Rivers in *The Borderers*, the disgruntled intellectual who expresses his contempt in murderous conspiracy. It would be wrong, though, to regard the recluse in 'Lines' simply as a victim of Godwinian rationalism, a desiccated intellect. The poignancy of his isolation stems from his awareness of a genial possibility that is withheld:

> lifting up his head, he then would gaze
> On the more distant scene; how lovely 'tis
> Thou seest, and he would gaze till it became
> Far lovelier, and his heart could not sustain
> The beauty still more beauteous.

His heart responds to the beauteous scene but cannot escape its own solipsism, remaining a 'sordid solitary thing', wanting the power to 'sacred sympathy' of 'Religious Musings'. He is an inarticulate visionary who has withdrawn from 'the world' to exist in a limbo between the potential politics had once seemed to hold and an alternative communion he cannot attain:

> Nor, that time,
> Would he forget those beings, to whose minds,
> Warm from the labours of benevolence,
> The world, and man himself, appeared a scene
> Of kindred loveliness: then he would sigh
> With mournful joy, to think that others felt
> What he must never feel: and so, lost man!
> On visionary views would fancy feed,
> Till his eye streamed with tears.

For George Dyer in 1795, the 'GOOD MAN' had derived 'tender affections, generous principles, and humane conduct' from 'the appearances of nature', a regenerate harmony of 'man, nature, and society' that also harks back to Paine's democracy of 'kindred' in *The Rights of Man*. 'There is no time', Dyer says in his *Dissertation*, in which we range with so much advantage to ourselves through the walks of creation, as that, in which we contemplate the character of Benevolence. In whatever point of the universe we take our stand, and to whatever spot we turn our eyes, how fertile and glowing the landscape! In a system so contrived, that one part sheds its influence on, and promotes the harmony of, the other, this cannot be otherwise: There is a kind of voice that speaks through the universe.[14]

Between 1795 and 1796 Coleridge was to offer Dyer's benevolent access to universal harmony as the One Life of 'Religious Musings', Dyer's 'kind of voice' as the omnipresence of God:

> 'Tis the sublime of man,
> Our noontide Majesty, to know ourselves
> Parts and proportions of one wond'rous whole:
> This fraternises man, this constitutes
> Our charities and bearings. But 'tis God
> Diffused through all, that doth make all one whole . . .

> (ll. 135–40)

Wordsworth's 'lost man' in his 'Lines Left upon a Seat in a Yew-tree' cannot attain this benevolent and fraternizing knowledge of 'God | Diffused through all'. He is similarly unable to connect 'the labours of benevolence' with a transcendent communion in One Life, which was central to Coleridge's and Dyer's political thought and also recalls Frend's defence speech back in 1793: 'if we neglect the principle of universal benevolence, our faith is vain, our religion is an empty parade of useless and insignificant sounds'. For Coleridge in June 1795 'the principle of universal benevolence', the knowledge of 'one wond'rous whole', was a prerogative of the imagination. In Wordsworth's 'Lines' the visionary power appears as a function of 'fancy', although in the didactic conclusion to the poem—possibly added later— Wordsworth identifies 'the holy forms | Of young imagination' as a corrective to his solitary's intellectual pride. One should, perhaps, be careful not to overstress parallels in Coleridge's and Wordsworth's thinking about the politics of imagination and nature between 1795 and 1797, but the similarities are often insistent. As Jonathan Wordsworth pointed out some time ago in *The Music of Humanity*, 'That Coleridge should have evolved a philosophical belief which Wordsworth assimilated is perhaps

---

[14] Dyer, *Dissertation*, p. 15.

not very surprising. That he should also have been the first to portray the central Wordsworthian mystical experience is quite extraordinary' (*MH*, p. 193).

It is equally surprising, too, that just before Coleridge's visit to Racedown Wordsworth should have reached a point where he was in need of precisely the intellectual and philosophic guidance that Coleridge could bring him. Coleridge's 'living help' recollected in *The Prelude*, Book Ten, was to provide a vocabulary and philosophy that enabled Wordsworth to articulate his own 'visionary views' as his misanthropic recluse could never do. In giving Wordsworth imaginative access to his own 'mystical experience', Coleridge also allowed him to reconstitute the revolutionary hopes he had first experienced in France during 1792 in the relation of his own mind to

> The life of Nature, by the God of love
> Inspired
>
> (xi. 99–100)

—and specifically in the act of self-communion celebrated by Coleridge at the end of 'France, an Ode':

> Yes! while I stood and gaz'd, my temples bare,
> And shot my being thro' earth, sea, and air,
> Possessing all things with intensest love,
> O Liberty, my spirit felt thee there!

These final lines of Coleridge's 'Ode' are his most confident assertion of the One Life as a redemptive possibility that might replace his former hopes that France would 'compel the nations to be free'. His act of participation and possession is also personal and private, an act of faith. Nevertheless, it was this belief that was to provide the philosophical basis for *The Recluse* as first planned by Coleridge and Wordsworth in spring 1798. Their mutual certainty at this moment explains Wordsworth's initial confidence in the scheme: 'I know not any thing which will not come within the scope of my plan', he told James Webbe Tobin on 6 March (*E Y*, p. 212). 'The Ruined Cottage' and 'Pedlar' doubtless made up the '1300 lines' of verse Wordsworth claimed to have completed towards *The Recluse* at this moment. But in 1798 Wordsworth came rather closer to his idea of *The Recluse* as a poem that would reconcile 'Nature, Man, and Society' in a very different work: 'Tintern Abbey'.

7

Inner Emigrants

Kindly Interchange, Rash Disdain

'The new recluse'

Where—where—if this mad violence on the one hand, and
this criminal supineness on the other, continue—where is
manly reason to cast the anchor of sustaining hope? or,
rather, whither to *spread the sail* for consolatory refuge.[1]

Violent intimidation and repressive legislation forced John
Thelwall to abandon his political lectures. He was obliged to
leave his home and lecture hall in Beaufort Buildings, Strand, in
April 1796 and the same month ceased to publish his *Tribune*.
From this moment Thelwall was in retreat. He attempted 'to
revive discussion' in lectures 'at Yarmouth, Lynn, Wisbeach,
Derby, Stockport, and Norwich' in 1796–7, but later recalled
that at 'four of these places he narrowly escaped assassination . . .
by the sailors, the armed associators, and the Inniskilling dragoons, by whom he was successively attacked'.[2] 'Such was the
conclusion of [my] political career', he admitted.

Thelwall's withdrawal from political life was to take him to
Nether Stowey and Alfoxden in July 1797. He contemplated
settling there 'In philosophic amity to dwell' with Coleridge,
Thomas Poole, 'Allfoxden's musing tenant, and the maid | Of
ardent eye',

> With kindly interchange of mutual aid,
> To delve our little garden plots, the while
> Sweet converse flow'd, suspending oft the arm
> And half-driven spade, while, eager, one propounds,
> And listens one, weighing each pregnant word,
> And pondering fit reply, that may untwist

[1] John Thelwall, *An Appeal to Popular Opinion Against Kidnapping and Murder
in a Narrative of the Late Atrocious Proceedings, at Yarmouth* (2nd edn; London,
1796), 67.
[2] John Thelwall, *Poems, Chiefly Written in Retirement* (2nd edn; Hereford,
1801), p. xxx [cited hereafter as Thelwall, *Poems*].

The knotty point—perchance, of import high—
Of moral Truth . . .[3]

But on 21 August Coleridge wrote advising Thelwall to delay his return to Stowey; 'I am afraid, that even riots & dangerous riots might be the consequence', he told Thelwall,

—come! but not yet!—come in two or three months—take lodgings at Bridgewater—familiarize the people to your name & appearance—and when the *monstrosity* of the thing is gone off, & the people shall have begun to consider you, as a man whose mouth won't eat them—& whose pocket is better adapted for a bundle of sonnets than the transportation or ambush-place of a French army—then you may take a *house*—but indeed—I say it with a very sad, but a very clear conviction—at *present* I see that much evil & little good would result from your settling here. (*C L* i. 343–4)

Coleridge had got cold feet, and was anxious to keep Thelwall at a distance. His apparently light-hearted reference to Thelwall as bloodthirsty Jacobin betrays his uneasiness, and at this moment would not have drawn a smile from his correspondent either. During 1796–7 Thelwall was a well-known but isolated figure; even Coleridge, Wordsworth, and Poole, all of whom sympathized with his opinions and his dilemma, did not want him in the neighbourhood of Stowey. Instead, he eventually settled at Llyswen in South Wales where he tried to make a living by farming and was visited by Wordsworth, Coleridge, and Dorothy in August 1798 (*E Y*, p. 222). However, local hostility was subsequently aggravated, as he said, 'by the most pointed and inflammatory allusions from the pulpit', and Thelwall was forced to leave the village.

In the Prefatory Memoir to his *Poems, Chiefly Written in Retirement* Thelwall described himself as 'The new Recluse':[4] a restless pariah comparable to the figure imaginatively realized by Coleridge in his Ancient Mariner, denied even the barren repose of Wordsworth's 'lost man'. His experience of political reaction was an extreme example of pressures that were also at work on other good men after the Two Acts became law in December 1795. As such it provides a useful model against which to

---

[3] 'Lines, written at Bridgewater, in Somersetshire, on the 27th of July 1797; during a long excursion, in quest of a peaceful retreat', in Thelwall, *Poems*, 129–30.

[4] Thelwall, *Poems*, pp. xxxvii, xxxviii.

compare the withdrawal of Coleridge, Wordsworth, and their contemporaries from active political life between 1795 and 1798. This appears most clearly from their coincidence at Stowey in July 1797.

'The men proscribed for loving human kind': A retrospect from retirement

> Is the Patriot come yet? Are Wordsworth and his sister gone yet? I was looking out for John Thelwall all the way from Bridgewater, and had I met him, I think it would have moved almost me to tears.
>
> (Marrs, i. 117)

July 1797 was a busy month at Nether Stowey. Coleridge had brought Wordsworth and Dorothy over from Racedown at the beginning of the month; they found Alfoxden to let, signed the lease on 7 July, and probably moved in nine days later on 16 July (Reed, p. 199). Meanwhile Charles Lamb had paid a brief visit for a week, 7 to 14 July, and when he left 'the Patriot' John Thelwall was expected at any moment. He arrived at Stowey on 17 July on a walking tour that had taken him out of London to Salisbury, then north over Salisbury Plain to Fonthill, Bath, and Bristol.[5] Next morning before breakfast he walked with Sara Coleridge to meet Wordsworth, Dorothy, and Coleridge at Alfoxden, and stayed ten days in their company,

> Conciliated, that, some there are—some few,
> Still warm and generous, by the changeling world
> Not yet debauch'd, nor to the yoke of fear
> Bending the abject neck: but who, erect
> In conscious principle, still dare to love
> The man proscrib'd for loving human kind.[6]

Thomas Poole's cousin Charlotte was less conciliatory. On 23 July she wrote in her journal, 'We are shocked to hear that Mr. Thelwall has spent some time at Stowey this week with Mr. Coleridge, and consequently with Tom Poole. . . . To what are we coming?'[7] Her 'shock' at Thelwall's presence explains

---

[5] Thelwall published an account of his tour in the *Monthly Magazine* between Aug. 1799 and April 1800; unfortunately, it breaks off just before his arrival at Stowey.
[6] Thelwall, *Poems*, 139.
[7] M. Sandford, *Thomas Poole and his Friends* (2 vols; London, 1888), i. 235.

Coleridge's anxiety to dissuade him from returning to live at Stowey permanently, for fear of compromising his friend Poole: 'Very great odium T. Poole incurred by bringing *me* here', he told Thelwall, 'when Wordsworth came & he likewise by T. Poole's agency settled here—You cannot conceive the tumult, calumnies, & apparatus of threatened persecutions which this event has occasioned round about us' (*CL* i. 343).

Coleridge had been corresponding regularly with Thelwall since April 1796, when he wrote comparing their political activities at Bristol and London and enclosed a copy of his recently published *Poems* (*CL* i. 205). Their mutual awareness dates from the previous year and possibly as early as Autumn 1794 when Thelwall may have read *The Fall of Robespierre*. In July 1797, though, Thelwall's political career had been 'concluded' by violent opposition whereas Coleridge seems to have anticipated continuing activity and involvement. The well-known anecdote from Coleridge's *Table Talk* underlines the difference between them: 'John Thelwall had something very good about him', Coleridge recalled; 'We were once sitting in a beautiful recess in the Quantocks, when I said to him, "Citizen John, this is a fine place to talk treason in!"—"Nay! Citizen Samuel," replied he, "it is rather a place to make a man forget that there is any necessity for treason!"'[8] It would be fascinating to eavesdrop on the rest of their conversation, but two things at least are evident from this brief recollection. While admitting that much-needed reforms were at this moment equated with 'treason', Thelwall was glad to be distanced from London and politics. Coleridge, on the other hand, was in a teaseful mood for conspiracy. He could afford to be: Coleridge had never faced organized violence as Thelwall had recently done in East Anglia, nor had he been prosecuted for high treason. Although Coleridge certainly experienced the contrary motives to political involvement or retirement after 1795, repression left him unscathed except, perhaps, for his financial loss on the *Watchman*.

This was one obvious reason why Coleridge's support for reform and opposition to the war should have survived intact, until the French invasion of Switzerland on 13–14 February 1798 encouraged him to take stock of his allegiance in 'France, an

---

[8] S. T. Coleridge, *Table Talk*, ed. T. Ashe (London, 1884), 103.

Ode'. One month before he wrote that poem, William Frend had presided over a dinner at the Crown and Anchor Tavern in London, where the company present resolved 'That this meeting will have nothing to do with politicks'.[9] At that same moment in January 1798, however, Coleridge had still been vehement in his opposition to British warmongering, and *'peppered'* his sermons with politics while preaching as a candidate for the unitarian ministry at Shrewsbury. William Hazlitt was in the congregation, and recalled what Coleridge had said in *My First Acquaintance with Poets*:

> The sermon was upon peace and war; upon church and state—not their alliance, but their separation—on the spirit of the world and the spirit of Christianity, not as the same, but as opposed to one another. He talked of those who had 'inscribed the cross of Christ on banners dripping with human gore.' He made a poetical and pastoral excursion,—and to shew the fatal effects of war, drew a striking contrast between the simple shepherd boy, driving his team afield, or sitting under the hawthorn, piping to his flock, 'as though he should never be old,' and the same poor country-lad, crimped, kidnapped, brought into town, made drunk at an alehouse, turned into a wretched drummer-boy, with his hair sticking on end with powder and pomatum, a long cue at his back, and tricked out in the loathsome finery of the profession of blood. (Howe, xvii. 108)

The 'poor country-lad' turned 'wretched drummer-boy' is an avatar of Coleridge's self of early 1794, when he had spent four months as a 'horse-soldier'. The substance of his sermon as recollected by Hazlitt does not suggest any marked change in Coleridge's position since his lectures of 1795, and was probably similar to the political sermons he preached 'great part extempore' when on his *Watchman* tour in January 1796 (*CL* i. 176). Despite Coleridge's claim to have 'snapped [his] squeaking baby-trumpet of sedition' in October 1796 (*CL* i. 240), to be 'out of heart with the French' in December 1796 (*CL* i. 268), and 'wearied with politics, even to soreness', 23 July 1797 (*CL* i. 338), his opposition up to February 1798 is markedly consistent. One should therefore be wary of any generalized pattern of retreat from politics into retirement. Although Coleridge was

---

[9] CUL Add. MSS 7887/55. The dinner was on 12 Jan. 1798 and among the company were William Maxwell, Felix Vaughan, Horne Tooke, Josiah Wedgwood, and Jonathan Raine.

living at Stowey from January 1797 and no doubt sometimes disillusioned by current events, his political interests had not disappeared overnight. The same was true for Wordsworth at Racedown after September 1795.

'The country [at Racedown] is delightful,' Dorothy wrote in an undated letter, 'we have charming walks, a good garden, a pleasant house', and she added that her 'brother handles the spade with great dexterity' (*E Y*, p. 163). Her description makes their life together comparable to the retreat anticipated by Thelwall in his 'Lines Written at Bridgewater', 'suspending oft the arm | And half-driven spade', though Wordsworth seems to have been more concerned to get on with the digging than Thelwall. In *The Prelude*, Book Eleven, Wordsworth looks back to spring 1796 as a moment when he had been 'dead | To deeper hope' (xi. 24–5), but the letters written by Wordsworth and Dorothy during their residence at Racedown are extraordinarily cheerful: 'I have lately been living upon air and the essence of carrots cabbages turnips and other esculent vegetables,' Wordsworth told Francis Wrangham on 25 February 1797, 'not excluding parsely the produce of my garden—' (*E Y*, p. 178). He was 'ardent in the composition' of *The Borderers* at this time (*E Y*, p. 172), and had been toying with his imitation of Juvenal's eighth satire since November 1795 and probably earlier (*E Y*, pp. 157–8).

Although Wordsworth's stay at Racedown was the period of his post-Godwinian 'despair', contemporary evidence shows him to have been in buoyant spirits and writing poetry. He had moved away from metropolitan politics and Godwin's intellectual friends, but kept in close touch with contemporary publications and political affairs. Joseph Gill, the caretaker at Racedown, scribbled an 'Almanack for the Year 1797' in the back of his diary which reads as a reminder of war and civil discontent,

> Subjects wicked were
> Savage Murders threatening—
> Sad Tumults forbear
> Swords War and fighting[10]

—and as a grim antiphonal voice to Wordsworth's Juvenalian satire:

[10] BUL, Pinney Papers, Account Book 1685. The 'Almanack' is in Gill's hand-writing.

Alas twas other cause than lack of years
That moistened Dunkirk's sand with blood and tears . . .

(*EY*, p. 173)[11]

Ironically, too, Wordsworth's years at Racedown are the first
moment when the extent of his reading and political contacts can
be established with certainty. In December 1795 Cottle sent him
Southey's 'Joan of Arc', and Basil Montagu had forwarded the
second edition of *Political Justice* by 21 March 1796 (*EY*, pp.
163, 170). Four days later Azariah Pinney wrote from Bristol
offering him copies of 'Coleridge's Watchman',[12] and by May
Wordsworth had read Coleridge's *Poems* and particularly
admired 'Religious Musings' (*CL* i. 215–16). Just under a year
later, on 20 March 1797, James Losh sent Wordsworth a large
package of books and pamphlets from Bath. Among these were

Monthly Magazines from Feby. to December 1796 inclusive—
Conciones ad Populum—Protest against certain Bills—by Coleridge.
Burke's Two letters to a Member of Parliament and letter to the Duke of
Portland. Estlin's Evidences of Christianity. Coleridge's ode to the new
year. Erskine's view of the causes and consequences of the present War.
(*LD* ii; *EY*, p. 186n.)

These pamphlets most likely belonged to Losh himself, for he
noted that he had read them all in his diary during the previous
year. The following month he dispatched 'another large parcel of
pamphlets' to Racedown, but did not list the contents in his diary.
To judge by his previous reading of pamphlets not included in his
first parcel, it might have comprised a pamphlet by Thomas
Beddoes, Helen Williams's *Letters from France*, copies of the
Watchman, and John Thelwall's *Rights of Nature*, all of which
Losh had recently read at Bath. Wordsworth's reading of
Coleridge's work during 1796–7 goes some way to explaining
similarities in their ideas that appear in passages of *The Borderers*
and in his 'Lines Left upon a Seat in a Yew-tree'. Losh's parcels
show that Wordsworth remained interested in contemporary
pamphlets and controversy, and perhaps indicate that he had
done so consistently ever since he read Burke, Paine, and other

[11] *EY*, p. 173n., points out that under '"tears" is written, possibly in Wrangham's
hand, "Dutch Mistresses"'.
[12] BUL, Pinney Papers, Letter Book 13.

'master pamphlets of the day' while staying with Nicholson in London in 1791. While at Racedown he also kept in touch with his London friends Mathews, Wrangham, and Montagu, and returned there briefly in June 1796 when he also met Godwin.

James Losh's diary records that he sent four letters to Wordsworth during 1796, and presumably Wordsworth was writing to him too.[13] This is significant, because Losh was also regularly in correspondence with his friends John Tweddell and Felix Vaughan, and he was visited at Bath by George Dyer on 9 and 10 September 1796 (LD i). Through Losh, then, Wordsworth retained a link with the group of good men from Cambridge that he had joined at William Frend's house back in February 1795, and whose political careers up to that moment had so closely resembled his own. But in more recent months, and particularly since Wordsworth's departure from London in August 1795, there had been significant differences between them. Although Wordsworth treats this as a period of personal crisis in *The Prelude*, Books Ten and Eleven, it seems to have been less painful for him than the contemporary experiences of Losh, Tweddell, and Vaughan.

Losh had moved from London to Bath sometime between 20 November 1795, when Godwin met him at tea (GD vii), and 28 February 1796 when Losh's diary reveals him writing to John Tweddell from Bath (LD i). The immediate cause for the move was the collapse of his health, probably due to tuberculosis, but he also attributed this breakdown to the strain of his political activities in London. On 31 December 1798 he wrote in the back of his diary:

Tho' I retain my opinions of the value of Liberty in general, and of the corruptions of our own government in particular, I am resolved to withdraw for ever from Politics, never to interfere farther than by calm discussion, and when that cannot be had I am determined to be silent—nothing I trust shall ever induce me to take any active part with any *party* whatever—Temperate argument shall be the only means I will ever use to promote those great truths which I consider as essential to human happiness—Every species of war I consider as unlawful to a *Christian man*, and all bitterness of contention, even in words, shou'd be abstained from by a sincere follower of the humble Jesus. (LD iii)

---

[13] Losh notes that he wrote to Wordsworth on 5 July, 20 Aug., 7 Oct., 18 Nov.

Losh's recourse to 'argument' as the means 'to promote those great truths' recalls Wordsworth's position in 1794–5, and their mutual response to *Political Justice* and friendship with Godwin himself at that time. But Losh did not in fact 'withdraw for ever from Politics', and supported parliamentary reform until the end of his life. In 1831, for instance, he wrote about his petitioning efforts as a member of the Friends of the People nearly forty years before: 'Sound information is now more generally diffused than it was in 1793, and the necessity of reform is more striking, and more deeply impressed upon the minds of a majority of the people.'[14] In 1796 and immediately afterwards, though, Losh believed that 'by wholly changing [his] mode of life, and by steady perseverance in temperance and retirement, [he had] supported, and perhaps rather amended, a broken constitution'—thereby repairing the damage caused by his political exertions and disappointments (LD iv).[15] On 23 September 1800 he noted in his diary that for the sake of his health, 'no temptation ought to induce [him] to engage *actively* in political disputes'. His ideal existence at this moment corresponded to that of Wordsworth, Coleridge, and Thelwall between 1795 and 1798: 'a country life, with a farm or a good garden (as may best suit me), is nearly, if not quite, essential to my comfort . . . at the same time, society is necessary to me, and therefore the neighbourhood of a large town is preferable to any other situation' (LD v).

Like Wordsworth and Coleridge, and despite his worries about his health, Losh's retirement from '*active*' political life was not the complete withdrawal from politics that some of his comments suggest. Late in January 1797 Losh published his own translation of Benjamin Constant's *Observations on the Strength of the Present Government of France, and Upon the necessity of Rallying Round it*, a copy of which survives in Bath Public Library and confirms Losh's unaltered commitment to reform. 'The men who wish to be considered as peculiarly the friends of government in this country', he writes in a footnote, 'think that every man who denies the absolute perfection of our Constitution, must be a plotter of anarchy and confusion, and every republican, a plunderer and an assassin.—Their great leader has even asserted,

---

[14] James Losh, *Observations on Parliamentary Reform* (London, 1831), 8.
[15] Noted in the back of the fourth volume of Losh's diary, after brief epitaphs of his friends John Tweddell, Felix Vaughan, and Charles Ward—all of whom died in 1799.

that, in some cases, opinions may be prosecuted with advantage.'[16] Losh may have had the Two Acts in mind when he wrote this but he was probably also thinking of the 1794 treason trials, which Thelwall described as Pitt's attempt to establish a 'system of massacre for opinion' (*Tribune*, i. 254). Felix Vaughan had acted for the defence during those trials, and had been a very close friend of Losh's throughout the early 1790s when both were active in political and legal circles in London. However, Vaughan's experiences since then would certainly have exacerbated Losh's fears about his own health, and the baleful influence of politics.

Felix Vaughan had left Jesus College, Cambridge, in 1790. During the summer he witnessed the *Fédération* at Paris, just at the time Wordsworth and Jones were walking to the Alps, and his subsequent tour to Orléans and Blois anticipated Wordsworth's residence there just over a year later. In 1799 Losh remembered that Vaughan had been a 'Tookite' (LD iv), which implies that he had joined the SCI; his membership is recorded in the Society's minutes for 15 June 1792, when Vaughan joined Tooke, John Frost, Thomas Cooper, Thomas Walker, William Maxwell, Thomas Holcroft, and his friend Losh in donating a guinea each to a benefit fund for Paine.[17] A manuscript note in the Treasury Solicitor's files dated 30 April 1792 also has Vaughan listed as a member of the third division of the London Corresponding Society.[18] This was the division of founder member Thomas Hardy, and it met at The Bell Tavern in Exeter Street just off The Strand. Vaughan was, therefore, an active member of the Corresponding Society three months after it had been founded and on 3 May 1792 he was present at a meeting of the central committee of delegates (Thale, p. 11). Thereafter his most important contribution to the society was legal advice. On 25 September 1793, for example, a government spy reported that a 'Petition to his Majesty [had been] declared treasonable by Mr. Vaughan—to draw up another' (Thale, p. 83). Following Vaughan's successful defence of Daniel Isaac Eaton who had been prosecuted for

---

[16] Benjamin Constant, *Observations on the Strength of the Present Government of France, and Upon the necessity of Rallying Round it*, trans. James Losh (Bath, 1797), 29.

[17] TS 11 962 3508. Minute Book of SCI. Losh's contribution is endorsed '13 July', a month late.

[18] TS 11 966 3510 B. Miscellaneous papers.

seditious libel in *Hog's Wash*, the society ordered silver medals to be struck and presented to Eaton's counsel and to the foreman of the jury (Thale, p. 117). His connection with the Corresponding Society seems to have lasted until August 1797, when the accounts indicate that he returned twenty guineas he had received 'as part of his fees' for the defence of John Gale Jones at Warwick in March 1796 (Thale, pp. 394, 405).

By 1797 Vaughan's career as a barrister looked bright. Losh commented that 'it ought to be said, to the credit of the country, that in spite of political prejudice he was rising fast to eminence at the Bar', but added ruefully that Vaughan had fallen 'a victim to . . . doing so' (LD iv). Felix Vaughan died in April 1799 worn out, Losh believed, by 'his desire of distinguishing himself in his profession' though he did add that Vaughan 'had a feeble constitution' like himself (LD iv). Their mutual friend, the lawyer Charles Ward, died within days of Vaughan and on 25 July 1799 another close friend, John Tweddell, died at Athens although Losh did not hear of this until three months later on 22 October. '*I* am now the only one of ye three remaining', he wrote at the back of the fourth volume of his diary: 'Politics I have wholly abandoned, and from the Law I seek for nothing but a very moderate increase to my income—A distinguished situation, in either one or the other line, wou'd now be as irksome, and even disgusting, to me, as it wou'd formerly have been the subject of joy and exultation' (LD iv). Ten years after the fall of the Bastille, Losh's sense of soured potential in the loss of his friends stands as a personal epitaph for their shared hopes and aspirations during the revolutionary decade. More than Vaughan and Ward, perhaps, the fate of John Tweddell corresponds to Wordsworth's 'lost man' of 'Lines Left upon a Seat in a Yew-tree'.

'Where is Tweddel?' Wordsworth asked Losh on 11 March 1798 (*EY*, p. 213). His immediate purpose was to find out as much as possible from him about Germany, having just 'come to a resolution' to go there with Dorothy and Coleridge. But his question has another, less happy implication. John Tweddell had been one of the most promising scholars of his generation at Cambridge, but his life after leaving the university proved a disappointment. Henry Gunning remembered that Tweddell had 'carried off every prize for which he could be a candidate', including one for his speech at Trinity chapel on 4 November

1790 in which he welcomed the French Revolution, and he graduated BA in 1790 coming second to Francis Wrangham in the 'Classical Medals' (Gunning, ii. 79–80). In 1792 Tweddell was elected a fellow of Trinity College. He took his MA the following year, and in 1794 he moved to London and was frequently in Godwin's company throughout the year. Since 1792 he had been associated with the Friends of the People, and his name appears among those who signed the society's original *Declaration* on 11 April 1792.[19] He told Isabel Gunning that he supported Charles Grey, that he was 'acquainted with almost all the leading men in opposition', and thought it 'not improbable' that he might be offered a seat in parliament.[20] Godwin mentions in his diary that he had met Tweddell with James Mackintosh at the House of Commons on 30 December 1794 and they coincided again at Frend's house and in Wordsworth's company the following February. But after that meeting Tweddell seems to have dropped out of Godwin's circle of friends and, a month after Wordsworth left London, he took the boat for Hamburg on 24 September 1795. It seems likely that the immediate cause of his departure was his disappointed love for Isabel Gunning, though the circumstances of this remain vague. Tweddell continued to live in exile on the Continent, travelling from country to country, and when Wordsworth wrote to Losh in March 1798 he was apparently at Odessa in Russia (*E Y*, p. 213 n.).

Although Tweddell does not seem to have been as actively involved in reformist politics as Losh and Vaughan, his letters to Losh published in *The Remains of John Tweddell* reveal a similar revulsion from political life that borders upon misanthropy. 'I know of nothing that I am fit for that I can command', he told Losh on 20 June 1797, writing from St Petersburg:

—as for pursuing any profession, that is now too late. All the disgust which I once had is multiplied (and you may conceive this) an hundred fold. If the career you allude to, be a political one, I do not know that it is open to me—and even if it were, what am I to do? come in for a borough and be an M.P.? I will confess to you this was once among my ambitious projects—But it is no more so.[21]

---

[19] *Declaration Agreed to on the 11th of April 1792, by the Society Entitled the Friends of the People* (London, 1792).
[20] Paston, 'Tweddell', p. 328.
[21] Tweddell, *Remains*, p. 162.

5. Silhouette of John Tweddell, 'one who own'd|No common soul'.
Frontispiece to *The Remains of John Tweddell* (1815).

A little later in the same letter his 'disgust' appears even more extreme. 'So few things in this world are worth the pains,' Tweddell writes, 'I am so little alive to what the world is so greedily running after, that if it were not to remove the futile objection of passing my youth without any ostensible pursuit, I could be more happy to remain in a corner unnoticed, than to take any active part in the busy scenes of this silly world.'[22] Precisely what caused Tweddell's bitterness is uncertain. More than any of his contemporaries, though, his early promise and subsequent disdain for 'the world' appear as a model for Wordsworth's 'lost man', 'one who own'd | No common soul':

> In youth, by genius nurs'd,
> And big with lofty views, he to the world
> Went forth, pure in his heart, against the taint
> Of dissolute tongues, 'gainst jealousy, and hate,
> And scorn, against all enemies prepared,
> All but neglect: and so, his spirit damped
> At once, with rash disdain he turned away,
> And with the food of pride sustained his soul
> In solitude.
>
> (ll. 13–21)

Wordsworth was certainly acquainted with Tweddell before he left for the Continent, and probably heard of his travels and disgruntled scorn for his once 'ambitious projects' from Losh during 1796–7. Their Cambridge background, their presence at Frend's house in February 1795 and almost simultaneous departure from London in August–September, may have suggested Tweddell as Wordsworth's barren *alter ego* in his 'Lines'. Tweddell's disappointed prospects of marriage and a career in law or politics correspond to the 'neglect' which prompted the solitary's 'rash' rejection of 'the world' and his proud, unfruitful isolation. This ironic parallel between Tweddell and Wordsworth is underlined by a further strange coincidence. Tweddell's confession of misanthropy, 20 June 1797, was written at the moment of Coleridge's stay with Wordsworth and Dorothy at Racedown, and just before their removal to Alfoxden. As Wordsworth and Coleridge were entering the months of their happiest commitment to writing, Tweddell stood at the opposite pole of

[22] Tweddell, *Remains*, p. 163.

embittered failure, a living embodiment of all the 'strange reverses' that had succeeded his speech in Trinity chapel seven years before. For Wordsworth and Coleridge at Alfoxden and Stowey, the strangest reversal of all was the presence of a government spy sent to investigate their suspicious activities in the 'beautiful recesses' of the Quantocks: '"a place"', as John Thelwall said, '"to make a man forget that there is any necessity for treason!"'

Spy Nozy and the French invasion plot

Rouse, British Spirits, rouse! now is the time for Exertion! —The Enemy is insulting your Coasts; and is, perhaps, encouraged in that daring Insolence, by the presumptuous hopes that there are Englishmen so debased as to be ready to lend an assisting Hand towards enslaving their Country . . .

(*Felix Farley's Bristol Journal*, 4 Mar. 1797)

On 8 and 11 August 1797, Dr Daniel Lysons of Bath sent two letters of information to the Duke of Portland at the Home Office. The second only of these letters has survived:

Bath   11th: Aug: 1797

My Lord Duke,
    On the 8th. inst. I took the liberty to acquaint your Grace with a very suspicious business concerning an emigrant family, who have contrived to get possession of a Mansion House at Alfoxton, late belonging to the Revd. Mr. St. Albyn, under Quantock Hills—I am since informed, that the master of the House has no wife with him, but only a woman who passes for his Sister—The man has Camp Stools, which he & his visitors carry with them when they go about the country upon their nocturnal or diurnal expeditions, & have also a Portfolio in which they enter their observations, which they have been heard to say were almost finished —They have been heard to say they should be rewarded for them, & were very attentive to the River near them—probably the River coming within a mile or two of Alfoxton from Bridgewater—These people may *possibly* be under Agents to some principal at Bristol—
    Having got these additional anecdotes which were dropt by the person mentioned in my last I think it necessary to acquaint your Grace with them, & have the honour to be &c

D. Lysons

Duke of Portland[23]

The source of Lysons's 'anecdotes' was one Charles Mogg, a former servant at Alfoxden. He had told the story of the 'emigrant

family' to Lysons's cook in Bath, from whom it was evidently
passed on to Lysons himself. With hindsight, it is easy to detect
the innocent activities misrepresented here: the walks in the
grounds of Alfoxden and the surrounding countryside, the reading of *The Borderers* 'under the Trees' in the park on 23 July with
Wordsworth, 'a woman who passes for his Sister', Coleridge,
Sara, Poole, and John Thelwall sitting on 'Camp Stools'. More
interesting, though, is the absence of any reference to Thelwall's
presence in Lysons's letters of information, and his readiness to
identify Wordsworth and Dorothy as a French 'emigrant family'
and therefore likely 'under Agents' to a spymaster in Bristol.
Equally odd, in the circumstances, is the prompt response of the
Home Office in sending an experienced government spy, James
Walsh, across the country to check Lysons's story. *En route*, he
interviewed Charles Mogg at Hungerford, and he elaborated
Lysons's account in detail. Walsh immediately wrote back to his
master at the Home Office, John King, who was one of Portland's
under secretaries:

Bear Inn   Hungerford Berks
11 Augt. 1797.

Sir

    Charles Mogg says that he was at Alfoxton last Saturday was a Week,
that he there met Thomas Jones who lives in the Farm House
at Alfoxton, who informd Mogg that some French people had got
possession of the Mansion House and that they were washing and
Mending their Cloaths all Sunday, that He Jones would not continue
there as he did not like It. That Christopher Trickie and his Wife who live
at the Dog pound at Alfoxton, told Mogg that the French people had
taken the plan of their House, and that They had also taken the plan of
all the places round that part of the Country, that a Brook runs in the

---

[23] HO 42/41. Domestic Correspondence George III, June–Dec. 1797. The original
account of the Spy Nozy incident appeared in Chapter ten of *Biographia*, but the full
circumstances of the business were not clarified until 1934 in A. J. Eaglestone's essay
'Wordsworth, Coleridge, and the Spy' in E. Blunden and E. L. Griggs (eds) *Coleridge:
Studies by Several Hands* (London, 1934), 73–87 [cited hereafter as Eaglestone].
Eaglestone reproduced the correspondence between Spy Nozy and his master in
London, and provided a commentary. Subsequent accounts draw on his work: Mary
Moorman follows Coleridge in regarding the episode as 'amusing and absurd'
(Moorman, pp. 329–32), whereas E. P. Thompson treats the matter seriously in
'Disenchantment or Default?'. The account here is based on my own transcription of
the MS letters, now in the PRO; for the identity of Spy Nozy and his activities as an
informer in the 1790s see my article 'Who was Spy Nozy?', *TWC* xv (Spring 1984),
46–50.

front of Trickie's House and the French people inquired of Trickie wether the Brook was Navigable to the Sea, and upon being informd by Trickie that It was not, they were afterward seen examining the Brook quite down to the Sea. That Mrs. Trickie confirmd every thing her Husband had said. Mogg spoke to several other persons inhabitants of that Neighbourhood, who all told him, They thought these French people very suspicious persons, and that They were doing no good there. And that was the general opinion of that part of the Country. The French people kept no Servant, but they were Visited by a number of persons, and were frequently out upon the heights most part of the night.

Mogg says that Alfoxton lays about Twelve miles below Bridgewater and within Two Miles of the Sea. Mogg says that he never spoke to Doctor Lysons, but that a Woman who is Cook to the Doctor had lived fellow Servant with Mogg at Alfoxton, and that in his way from thence home, he called upon her at the Doctors House in Bath last Monday, when talking about Alfoxton, He mentioned These circumstances to Her.

As Mr. Mogg is by no means the most intelligent Man in the World, I thought It my Duty to send You the whole of his Storry as he related It.

I shall wait here Your further Orders and am

Sir
Your most obedient
Humble Servt.
J. Walsh.[24]

Mogg might not have been 'the most intelligent Man in the World', but he was convinced that the 'suspicious persons' at Alfoxden were 'French people'. A. J. Eaglestone observed that 'rustics are always prone to put down people of outlandish habits as foreigners; and the French were the foreigners most in men's minds then'.[25] Britain had certainly been preoccupied with France ever since 1789, but credulous 'rustics' is not a satisfactory explanation for the 'general opinion' at Stowey and Alfoxden. Why were Wordsworth and Dorothy not mistaken for 'French people' or emigrants when they moved to Racedown in 1795? The root of all the suspicion was evidently the enquiry as to 'wether the Brook was Navigable to the Sea', and subsequent sightings of 'the French people . . . examining the Brook quite down to the Sea'. Coleridge later explained in *Biographia* that he had been *'making studies'* for his projected poem 'The Brook' (*BL* i. 196), but his interest evidently worried local inhabitants—and the Home Office too. As soon as John King received Walsh's letter from Hungerford, he replied with further instructions:

> Whitehall
> Aug: 12th: 1797.
>
> Sir,
>   I have considered the contents of your letter to me from the Bear Inn, Hungerford of yesterday's date—you will immediately proceed to Alfoxton or it's neighbourhood yourself, taking care on your arrival so to conduct yourself as to give no cause of suspicion to the Inhabitants of the Mansion house there—you will narrowly watch their proceedings, & observe how they coincide with Mogg's account, & that contained in the within letter from Mr. Lysons to the Duke of Portland—If you are in want of further information or assistance, you will call on Sr: P: Hales Bart. of Brymore, near Bridgewater, & upon shewing him this letter you will I am confident receive it—You will give me a precise account of all the circumstances you observe with your sentiments thereon; you will of course ascertain if you can the names of the persons, & will add their descriptions—& above all you will be careful not to give them any cause of alarm, that if necessary they may be found on the spot—Should they however move you must follow their track, & give me notice thereof, & of the place to which they have betaken themselves—I herewith transmit you a bank note for £20.
>
> J. King[26]

Walsh seems to have been prepared to dismiss Mogg as an ignorant servant but King took his story more seriously, an index of his interest being the twenty pounds enclosed with his instructions. King's overriding concern was that the 'Inhabitants of the Mansion house' should be given 'no cause of suspicion' that they were being watched. Walsh's principal task was to clarify the suspects' identity, their circumstances, names, and descriptions. Above all, King stressed that they were not to be alarmed 'that if necessary they may be found on the spot'. For John King, as for the local residents at Alfoxden, the main cause for concern was whether or not 'the Inhabitants of the Mansion house there' were French. As it turns out, they had genuine reasons to be worried.

Five months earlier, in February 1797, the country had

[26] HO 42/41.

been alarmed by the French landing 1,200 soldiers on the Pembrokeshire coast near Fishguard. In the early stages of the war with France invasion had been considered unlikely, but Buonaparte's recent successes in his Italian campaign inevitably appeared threatening. As a contemporary pamphlet put it: 'The menace of a French Invasion, which formerly afforded a subject for ridicule, cannot now be treated in so light a manner'.[27] In February 1797 the unthinkable happened, and the French landing was no less alarming because of the small numbers involved, the swiftness of their surrender, and the discovery that they were mostly convicts. In retrospect it is easy to dismiss this abortive attempt as a hastily planned enterprise that was doomed from the start. At the time, though, its effect on public opinion was considerable. It demonstrated the country's vulnerability and confirmed that the French were actively considering 'the grand attempt'.[28] Public anger and consternation was the result, and it contributed to the confusions at Stowey in July 1797. Most disturbing of all was the discovery that the coast of Somerset had been the original location for the landing if all had gone according to plan.

The French ships had first been sighted off the north coast of Devon near Ilfracombe, some 40 miles west of Stowey. Here 'they had scuttled several merchantmen, and [had attempted] to destroy the shipping in the harbour'.[29] The commander of the Surrey Dragoons, then barracked in Barnstaple, reported the incident to Lord Clifton:

This Coast & Neighbourhood have been greatly alarmed by the Appearance of three French Frigates & a Lugger off the Island of Lundi, & Ilfracomb: & the Detatchment under my Command have been called upon by the regulating off: of the Impress Service & the Inhabitants of Ilfracomb to march to their Protection. We were there all Day yesterday,

---

[27] Havilland Le Mesurier, *Thoughts on a French Invasion* (Edinburgh, 1798), 3.

[28] Among the HO papers in the PRO, Kew, is a 'Memorandum of the Coastes and Bays of Great Britain and Ireland, and their general Defence. Jan. 1797'. This official note contains no reference to the defence of the Welsh coast, and comfortably assumed that 'The Coasts of the Bristol Channel St. Georges Channel . . . demand such peculiar and great arrangements to attack them, that they probably do not enter into the contemplation of an Enemy'. Events in the following month were to disturb this complacency. HO 42/40, Domestic Correspondence George III, Jan.–May 1797.

[29] Lt.-Col. Orchard, Commander of the North Devon Volunteers, to the Duke of Portland, 23 Feb. 1797. Repr. in *Bristol Gazette and Public Advertiser* (2 Mar. 1979).

6. The French Invasion near Fishguard, February 1797. From a volume containing a pamphlet describing the invasion, James Baker, *A Brief Narrative of the French Invasion near Fishguard Bay* (Worcester, 1797).

& have at present Videttes out all along the Coast, where any Landing Places offer. The enemy have disappeared for the present. Their Force indeed was too small for even a pilfering Invasion; nor had I the smallest Idea of their attempting to land: Their Appearance however has greatly agitated the Minds of all Ranks; & brought forth the Volunteer Companies from all the Neighbourhood. They shew a very loyal & truely British Spirit.[30]

The alarming news would have travelled swiftly up the coast, where it doubtless 'agitated the Minds' of Charles Mogg, Christopher Trickie, and Thomas Jones at Alfoxden, and Daniel Lysons at Bath as well. The ships quickly left Ilfracombe, and were next sighted off the coast near Fishguard on the evening of Wednesday, 22 February. Here the soldiers disembarked under the command of an American veteran, Colonel William Tate. Within two days the invasion attempt collapsed, confronted by the local militia led by Lord Cawdor who sent an account of the whole incident to the Duke of Portland on Friday 24 February:

Fishguard, Friday, Feb. 24

My Lord, In consequence of having received information, on Wednesday night at eleven o'clock, that three large ships of war and a lugger had anchored in a small roadsted upon the coast, in the neighbourhood of this town, I proceeded immediately, with a detachment of the Cardigan militia and all the provincial force I could collect, to the place. I soon gained positive intelligence they had disembarked about 1200 men, but no cannon. Upon the night's setting in, a French officer, whom I found the second in command, came in with a letter, a copy of which I have the honour to inclose to your Grace, together with my answer: in consequence of which they determined to surrender themselves prisoners of war, and accordingly laid down their arms this day at two o'clock. I cannot at this moment inform your Grace of the exact number of prisoners, but I believe it to be their whole force. It is my intention to march them this night to Haverfordwest, where I shall make the best distribution in my power. The frigates, corvette, and lugger got under weigh yesterday evening, and were this morning entirely out of sight. The fatigue we have experienced will, I trust, excuse me to your Grace for not giving a more particular detail: but my anxiety to do justice to the officers and men I had the honour to command, will induce me to attend your Grace, with as little delay as possible, to state their merits, and at the same time to give you every information in my power upon this

[30] HO 42/40.

subject. The spirit of loyalty which has pervaded all ranks throughout this country, is infinitely beyond what I can express.

I am, &c.   CAWDOR.[31]

The French prisoners were dispersed to Fishguard and Haverfordwest, and on 26 February Portland wrote to Lord Milford, Lieutenant of Pembrokeshire, of 'His Majesty's . . . judged expedient that the principal Officers who commanded this Expedition should be forthwith sent up to Town under a proper escort'.[32] On the same day Lord Cawdor wrote again to Portland, telling him of the ill-health of the prisoners and the problems in finding suitable quarters for them; he added that he intended to travel to London with the 'first and second in command of the French forces', and that he had 'endeavoured to secure all Papers that may tend to furnish information'.[33] These papers included a full copy of Tate's orders, and they were evidently scrutinized by the Home Office. The text of Tate's *Instructions* was published in 1798 and its authenticity was officially endorsed—by John King.[34]

Tate had received his orders from Lazare Hoche, one of the most able and experienced French generals who had already attempted a landing in Ireland in 1796. The *Instructions* reveal that Wales was in fact an alternative to Tate's highest priority, which had been to attack Bristol:

should Col. Tate, on arriving opposite the mouth of the Severn, learn that the river is little or not at all defended, and that the wind and tide allow him to sail up, he will endeavour to execute a *coup de main* on Bristol, which is the second city in England for riches and commerce; the destruction of Bristol is of the very last importance, and every possible effort should be made to accomplish it.[35]

Tate evidently followed these instructions by sailing up the coast as far as Ilfracombe, before changing course for the coast of Wales. Hoche's expectations sound quite unreasonable given the

---

[31] *Dodsley's Annual Register for the Year 1797* (London, 1800), 'Appendix to the Chronicle', pp. 72–3.
[32] HO 43/8. Domestic Entry Book, Aug. 1796–Mar. 1797.
[33] HO 42/40.
[34] *Authentic Copies of the Instructions Given by General Hoche to Colonel Tate Previous to His Landing on the Coast of South Wales, in the Beginning of 1797* (London, 1798), 13 [cited hereafter as *Instructions*].
[35] *Instructions*, pp. 7–8.

size of the detachment under Tate's command, and a gross misjudgement of the readiness of the British defences. Nevertheless the *Instructions* continue with details as to how the '*coup de main* on Bristol' was to be effected:

For this purpose, it will be proper to reconnoitre the mouth of the Severn, in the day time, and to sail up the Avon at night fall, within five miles of the town, where the landing should be made, on the right bank, in the greatest silence, and the troops being supplied with combustible matter, Col. Tate is to advance rapidly in the dark, on that side of Bristol which may be to windward, and immediately to set fire to that quarter. If the enterprize be conducted with dexterity, it cannot fail to produce the total ruin of the town, the port, the docks, and the vessels, and to strike terror and amazement into the very heart of the capital of England.[36]

Having attacked Bristol, they were to re-embark for Cardiff, and then 'proceed towards Chester and Liverpool'. There were three main objectives to Tate's campaign, apart from terrorizing the whole country by spreading 'panic as generally as possible'.[37] It was hoped that the attack on sea ports would 'embarrass the commerce of the enemy', and that discontented Englishmen would join Tate and 'raise an insurrection'—as John Oswald had hoped back in 1792 when he proposed an attack on London. Finally, and perhaps more realistically, Tate's activities were 'to prepare and facilitate the way for a descent, by distracting the attention of the English government'.[38]

The *Monthly Magazine* reported Tate's exploits in March 1797, and dismissed his 'most extraordinary' landing in Wales as a misguided attempt 'to create an alarm on the British coast and to rid the French Republic of a number of desperate persons'.[39] Tate did, however, succeed in alarming 'the British coast', and the invasion scare resulted in a financial crisis in London (Lefebvre, ii. 193–4). At Bristol, John Pinney wrote to his London banker mentioning 'that 2000 French are landed at St. Davids & not knowing what they may effect I wish you would send me down a certificate of the Stock I have'.[40] The government took the matter

[36] *Instructions*, p. 8.
[37] *Instructions*, p. 12.
[38] *Instructions*, p. 9.
[39] *Monthly Magazine*, iii (March 1797), 231.
[40] BUL, Pinney Papers, Letter Book 12. Letter dated 2 Mar. 1797.

equally seriously, and summoned Tate to London for interrogation; the purpose of publishing his *Instructions* in 1798 was most likely to excite anti-French feeling, and to encourage public vigilance. When the initial panic receded a little, Portland and John King may well have recalled a dubious incident at Fishguard reported five months before Tate's landing in September 1796. On 12 September Portland wrote to Lord Milford that he had

received information, that a very suspicious Person has lately been frequently seen in the neighbourhood of Fishguard, in the County of Pembroke, making observations of the Country; and that he has a particular Box or Chest, which he never opens, in the presence of any body—It is, therefore, very much to be wished, that Your Lordship should immediately recommend it to the Magistrates in that neighbourhood to use their utmost vigilance, in tracing out the Person in question; and, should he be found taking observations on the Coast, or in any other way acting suspiciously, that he should be minutely examined as well as the contents of his Box.[41]

Was this an artist or poet *'making studies'* for some future work?—or a French spy getting to know the lie of the land? The 'suspicious Person' with 'a particular Box' precisely anticipates Lysons's information of the man with 'Camp Stools' and 'a Portfolio' at Alfoxden in August 1797. In September 1796 Portland had left the matter to the local magistrates. After February 1797 an identical report of 'observations' being taken along the coast of the Bristol Channel demanded swift and thorough investigation. Tate's orders had revealed French intentions to land in that area and to attack Bristol, and John King had read those instructions closely. Lysons's story of the 'emigrant family' who were 'very attentive to the River near them' could not be put down to rumour and hearsay in a Somerset village, and James Walsh was immediately sent down to Hungerford to interview Charles Mogg, and then on to Stowey.

Inner emigrants

James Walsh's presence at Stowey in August 1797 was the result of ministerial expectations of a second French invasion attempt on the Somerset coast, following the recent adventures near

[41] HO 43/8.

Fishguard and the information received from Colonel Tate. The
'Spy Nozy' incident, which with hindsight appears so humor-
ously mistaken, was dependent on a complex sequence of contemporary events and—at the time—was a serious concern for
the Home Office. In this perspective, it helps to establish the
position of Wordsworth and Coleridge at Alfoxden and Stowey
up to their departure for Germany a year later in August 1798.

Walsh arrived at the Globe Inn, Stowey, on 15 August 1797
and swiftly got on to the scent. 'I had not been many minutes in
this House before I had an opportunity of entering upon my
Business', he wrote to John King,

By a Mr. Woodhouse asking the Landlord, If he had seen any of those
Rascalls from Alfoxton. To which the Landlord reply'd, He had seen
Two of them Yesterday. Upon which Woodhouse asked the Landlord, if
Thelwall was gone. I then asked if they meant the famous Thelwall. They
said yes. That he had been down some time, and that there were a Nest of
them at Alfoxton House who were protected by a Mr. Poole a Tanner of
this Town, and that he supposed Thelwall was there (Alfoxton House)
at this time. I told Woodhouse, that I had heard somebody say at
Bridgwater that They were French people at the Manor House. The
Landlord & Woodhouse answer'd No. No. They are not French, But
they are people that will do as much harm, as All the French can do . . .
I think this will turn out no French Affair but a mischiefuous gang of
disaffected Englishmen. I have just procured the Name of the person
who took the House. His name is *Wordsworth* a Name I think known to
Mr. Ford.[42]

It was the mention of '*Thelwall*' that gave Walsh his lead to the
identification of 'those Rascalls from Alfoxton' as 'a mischiefuous gang of disaffected Englishmen', rather than French
spies. James Walsh and Thelwall knew each other well, and
Walsh had consistently provided the government with information on Thelwall's activities ever since 1792. In November of that
year he had helped to close the Society for Free Debate, at which
Thelwall regularly spoke, by employing an *agent provocateur* to
cause a disturbance which was then used as a pretext for banning
further meetings. In response, Thelwall resolved to 'assert and
vindicate' the right to political discussion, and circulated a poster
offering twenty guineas reward for a room in which debates could

[42] HO 42/41.

be held. No room was forthcoming, and there the matter rested until 'revived by himself' when he started his political lectures in November 1793.[43]

James Walsh was therefore responsible, if only indirectly, for Thelwall's emergence as political lecturer and leader of the popular reform movement. Between November 1793 and May 1794 Walsh regularly attended and reported Thelwall's lectures. Not surprisingly, Thelwall knew his face and at the Corresponding Society's meeting at Chalk Farm, 14 April 1794, he recognized Walsh and made fun of him. Another spy, John Groves, reported what happened:

By 3 oClock I am sure there were upwards of 2000 persons—I saw Mr. Walsh come in . . . Thelwal accosted Walsh with a 'How do you do Sir,—I hope your late Irish Journey agreed with you—I suppose you will give a very good Account to morrow of our proceedings to day, & let Government know all about it?['] . . .

In short [Walsh] was badgered about by half dozens & dozens till he was obliged to retreat—at last he came in again—Some were for shoving him out—others for hissing & hooting him, but [Thomas] Hardy & Thelwal desired he might be let alone as their Meeting was legal peaceable & Constitutional & would shake his employers with terror—[44]

This amusing encounter reveals that Thelwall and Walsh knew all about each other's activities. But Thelwall's triumph on 14 April was short-lived for just one month later Walsh had his revenge: as Mrs Thelwall recalled, he was present at Thelwall's arrest on 13 May 1794. The Corresponding Society's Committee of Correspondence had just concluded a meeting in Thelwall's house at 2 Beaufort Buildings:

The members of the committee, &c., went on before Thelwall, leaving him for a few minutes, to inform his family of his intended absence. He then left the house; but, before he got out of the Buildings, he was met, near his door, by a man of the name of Walsh, said to have been an itinerant spy, and five or six other persons.

'Mr. Thelwall, I believe,' said this man, offering to shake him by the hand.

---

[43] For Walsh, Thelwall, and the Society for Free Debate, see *Thelwall Life*, pp. 96–9.
[44] Thale, p. 136.

'The same,' returned Thelwall. Upon which two of the king's messengers, the Secretary to Mr. Dundas, and one of the Bow-street runners, came up.

'Then, sir,' said one of them, tapping him on the shoulder, 'you are my prisoner.'[45]

In December 1794 Walsh was listed among the witnesses scheduled to appear at Thelwall's trial, although it is not clear whether he was called to the witness box.[46]

From 1792 up to August 1797 James Walsh dogged Thelwall's career as lecturer and reformist, but when he arrived at the Globe Inn, Nether Stowey, he was two weeks too late. 'The famous Thelwall' was indeed 'gone', and had been since 27 July when he travelled to Bristol and on into South Wales. As Thelwall's comment to Coleridge suggests—'"Nay! Citizen Samuel . . . it is rather a place to make a man forget that there is any necessity for treason!"'—his visit to Stowey was the end of his years of political activity. Thelwall and his old stooge James Walsh parted there for the last time, but the 'nest' of 'disaffected Englishmen' remained and occupied Walsh's attention for one more day. Having established that the suspects were not French, his final report of 16 August mistakes the 'Rascalls from Alfoxton' for 'a Sett of Violent Democrats', potential leaders of a rebellion that might assist the French should they land in the area. 'The house was taken for a Person of the name of Wordsworth,' Walsh had discovered,

who came to It from a Village near Honiton in Devonshire, about five Weeks since. The Rent of the House is secured to the Landlord by a Mr. Thomas Poole of this Town. Mr. Poole is a Tanner and a Man of some property. He is a most Violent Member of the Corresponding Society and a strenuous supporter of Its friends, He has with him at this time a Mr Coldridge and his Wife both of whom he has supported since Christmas last. This Coldridge came last from Bristol and is reckoned a Man of superior Ability. He is frequently publishing, and I am told is soon to produce a new work. He has a Press in the House and I am inform'd He prints as well as publishes his own productions.

Mr. Poole with his disposition, is the more dangerous from his having established in this Town, what He stiles *The Poor Mans Club*, and placing himself at the head of It, By the Title of the *Poor Mans Friend*. I

---

[45] *Thelwall Life*, pp. 157–8.
[46] The list of witnesses survives in TS 11 954 3498.

am told that there are 150 poor Men belonging to this Club, and that Mr. Poole has the intire command of every one of them. When Mr. Thelwall was here, he was continually with Mr. Poole.

By the directions on a letter that was going to the Post yesterday, It appears that Thelwall is now at Bristol.

I last Night saw Thomas Jones who lives at Alfoxton House. He exactly confirms Mogg of Hungerford, with this addition that the Sunday after Wordsworth came, he Jones was desired to wait at Table, that there were 14 persons at Dinner. Poole & Coldridge were there, and there was a little Stout Man with dark cropt Hair and wore a White Hat and Glasses (Thelwall) who after Dinner got up and talked so loud and was in such a Passion that Jones was frightened and did not like to go near them since. That Wordsworth has lately been to his former House and brought back with him a Woman Servant, that Jones has seen this Woman who is very Chatty, and that she told him that Her Master was a Phylosopher. That the Night before last Two Men came to Alfoxton House, and that the Woman Servant yesterday Morning told Jones that one of the Gentlemen was a Great Counsellor from London, and the other a Gentleman from Bristol.[47]

Walsh's letters to John King are garbled and mistaken, but they raise some interesting points about Wordsworth's and Coleridge's radical careers over the previous five years. Walsh had evidently never heard of 'Coldridge', which perhaps indicates that the Home Office was ignorant of his political activities at Bristol too. From Walsh's earlier report of 15 August, though, it seems that '*Wordsworth*' had come to the attention of the Bow Street magistrate Richard Ford although it is not (for the moment) clear how this happened. Possibly Wordsworth's letters from Annette had been opened, as coming from an enemy country; Walsh's interest in 'a letter that was going to the Post' for Thelwall once again exposes the insecurity of the postal system under Pitt's administration. Perhaps an informer had noted Wordsworth's presence in London in 1795, and the suspicious company he was keeping. A third possibility is that Wordsworth's brother Richard was known to Ford in a legal connection, and that William had escaped investigation altogether.

On one reading Walsh's reports are ludicrous, laughable. But his misjudgement is also ironic, and becomes potentially tragic

[47] HO 42/41.

with the recollection that similar misinformation supplied by Walsh and his colleagues had come close to costing that 'little Stout Man with dark cropt Hair' his life, back in 1794. Walsh's letter highlights the predicament of all good men during years of increasing repression, when 'our very looks are decyphered into disaffection', as Coleridge said in *Conciones*: 'This beautiful fabric of Love the system of Spies and Informers has shaken to the very foundation. There have been multiplied among us "Men who carry tales to shed blood!"' (*Lects. 1795*, p. 60). By summer 1797 popular alarm was such that wholly innocent activities could be misrepresented as 'violent', to the extent that Poole's benefit club for the poor appeared to Walsh as a likely disguise for a private army preparing to help the French. By mistaking Wordsworth and Dorothy as French *emigrés* and then, with Coleridge, Thelwall, and Poole, as 'Violent Democrats', Walsh clarifies their true identity as inner emigrants withdrawn upon their own resources in a country no longer tolerant of their opinions. The dinner at Alfoxden, when Thelwall's audience had dwindled to thirteen friends plus the perennial informer Thomas Jones, was a feast of defiance and a wake for their own 'revolutionary youth'. The moment provides a context for their removal to Germany in 1798, which effectively concludes the radical years, and it finds a memorial in two poems written shortly before their departure: 'Fears in Solitude' and 'Tintern Abbey'. Each poem recapitulates Coleridge's and Wordsworth's respective experiences in the period covered by this study, and suggests the contrasting implications of political failure for their subsequent careers.

Epilogue

Daring to Hope

Fear, rage, solitude

Coleridge wrote 'France, an Ode', 'Frost at Midnight', and 'Fears in Solitude' between February and April 1798. All three poems were published together by Joseph Johnson in a quarto pamphlet later that year; as a group, they register a number of disturbing currents in Coleridge's political, personal, and creative life even in this most fruitfully productive springtime. In 'France, an Ode' Coleridge recapitulates his allegiance to 'Liberty', formerly as the end of revolution in France and—after French aggression in Switzerland—presently in a communion of 'intensest love' with the omnipresent God of 'earth, sea, and air'. By contrast, 'Frost at Midnight' is wholly personal in reference, wishfully interceding between Coleridge's recollected childhood 'In the great city, pent mid cloisters dim' and little Hartley's future joy amid 'far other scenes' of nature's true grandeur. In returning to Coleridge's schooltime and earlier days at Ottery, 'Frost at Midnight' does not admit the more immediate and disturbing experiences of intervening years which are the subject of 'France, an Ode'. The two poems, written perhaps within days of each other in February 1798, segregate the public and political claims of the one from the meditative and subjective world of the other. 'Fears in Solitude' brings both into a discomfiting juxtaposition that is at once an accurate register of Coleridge's self in spring 1798, and which also has important consequences for his later development.

Coleridge's hymn to the serenity of nature and the comfort of family and friends in 'Fears in Solitude' is qualified by his unregenerate awareness of political failure and isolation. The poem does not resolve this tension which is focused upon Coleridge's solitary self, an inner emigrant at a last station of retreat,

> A GREEN and silent spot amid the hills!
> A small and silent dell![1]

---

[1] Quotations from 'Fears in Solitude', 'France, an Ode', and 'Frost at Midnight' will be from the texts in *Fears in Solitude, Written in 1798, During the Alarm of an Invasion. To which are added France, an Ode; and Frost at Midnight* (London, 1798). Coleridge arranged for Johnson to publish this pamphlet while in London, late Aug.–Sept. 1798, *en route* for Germany. See *CL* i. 417–18, and Tyson, pp. 173–4.

Coleridge's solitude is not contingent upon 'silent dell' and enfolding hills, but is primarily the result of his own fearful 'bodings' during the 'Alarm of an Invasion' which isolate him from the warmongering 'countrymen' to whom his poem is addressed. In this respect he resembles Wordsworth's recollected self on first visiting Tintern Abbey in summer 1793,

> more like a man
> Flying from something that he dreads, than one
> Who sought the thing he loved
>
> (ll. 71–3)

—both are isolated and alienated in their own country, their 'Mother Isle', because of contemporary political circumstances. Wordsworth had 'dreaded' the consequences of Britain entering the French war in February 1793; Coleridge's 'fears' derive from the immediate counter-threat of a French invasion of Britain five years later.

The initiating movement of 'Fears in Solitude' celebrates the beauty of the Quantock Hills and 'spirit-healing' landscape. This tranquil contemplative verse is punctured, however, with the realization that for 'such a man' as Coleridge responsive feeling 'perforce' also breeds a 'weight' of responsibility for his fellows, and especially so at the present crisis of

> Invasion, and the thunder and the shout,
> And all the crash of onset; fear and rage
> And undetermined conflict—even now,
> Ev'n now, perchance, and in his native Isle:
> Carnage and screams beneath this blessed sun!
> We have offended, O my countrymen!
> We have offended very grievously,
> And have been tyrannous.

Imminent invasion now appears as a consequence of British 'offence' and 'tyranny' in provoking revolutionary violence during the Terror, a last redefinition of Price's millenarian *Nunc dimittis* in the carnage of 'chastising Providence'. Coleridge goes on from this to elaborate a national blasphemy in three areas of contemporary life that had preoccupied him since his years at Cambridge. His first target is British imperialism and concomitant slavery 'borne to distant tribes' like a 'pestilence', which he had condemned in his Greek 'Ode' of 1792 and subsequent *Lecture on the Slave Trade*. Secondly, he cites 'the scheme of perjury' embracing government and established church in the necessity for subscription:

> O blasphemous! the book of life is made
> A superstitious instrument, on which
> We gabble o'er the oaths we mean to break,
> For all must swear—all, and in every place,
> College and wharf, council and justice-court,
> All, all must swear . . .

Priestley, Frend, Dyer, Robinson, 'the great and good Dr. Jebb' would all have agreed. But Coleridge's strident reassertion of the dissenters' argument for toleration also betrays a personal frustration in failure to achieve even a moderate reform of an obstinately 'superstitious' establishment. Finally Coleridge denounces popular support for the war, 'this whole people . . . clamorous | For war and bloodshed', and then concludes his catalogue of offence with a resounding prophecy that

>   evil days
> Are coming on us, O my countrymen!
> And what if all-avenging Providence,
> Strong and retributive, should make us know
> The meaning of our words, force us to feel
> The desolation and the agony
> Of our fierce doings?

The breakdown of progress finds its cause in human 'vice and wretchedness', 'folly and rank wickedness', a point that Coleridge had argued consistently since 1795 while asserting the efficacy of true '*Religion*' as a means to amelioration. But his acknowledgement of 'Providence' in 'Fears in Solitude' offers no reassurance for assuming an 'all-avenging' and 'chastising' aspect. Throughout the poem Coleridge's awareness of a radical collapse of hope in France and Britain finds no compensating alternative that might resemble Wordsworth's great statements of belief in 'Tintern Abbey' or, indeed, his own conclusion to 'France, an Ode'. At first sight tranquil and golden, the 'spirit-healing' landscape of 'Fears in Solitude' puts forth its own emblems of 'undetermined conflict':

May my fears,
My filial fears, be vain! and may the vaunts
And menace of the vengeful enemy
Pass like the gust, that roar'd and died away
In the distant tree, which heard, and only heard
In this low dell bow'd not the delicate grass.
But now the gentle dew-fall sends abroad
The fruitlike perfume of the golden furze:
The light has left the summit of the hill,
Tho' still a sunny gleam lies beautiful
On the long-ivied beacon.

The possibility of disturbance is admitted even as the gust of wind
is banished from Coleridge's 'dell'. The 'sunny gleam' may gild
the 'long-ivied beacon' but in doing so illuminates its former
function as a signal-light to warn of attack, once more reminding
of present fears. Although superficially attractive, hill and dell
offer no assurance of guardianship or rest, and it is for this reason
that Coleridge attempts a last redeeming discovery in the sudden
expanse of scenery viewed from the hilltop. Once again, though,
the possibility is subverted—this time by the analogy of
landscape and a 'society' already acknowledged as degenerate:

Homeward I wind my way; and lo! recall'd
From bodings, that have well nigh wearied me,
I find myself upon the brow, and pause
Startled! And after lonely sojourning
In such a quiet and surrounded scene,
This burst of prospect, here the shadowy main,
Dim-tinted, there the mighty majesty
Of that huge amphitheatre of rich
And elmy fields, seems like society,
Conversing with the mind, and giving it
A livelier impulse, and a dance of thought . . .

That startling 'burst of prospect' initially appears as an invigor-
ating release, a vital participation after his wearying lonely
sojourn. But there is a second movement here too, in which
Coleridge's 'bodings' of 'the vaunts | And menace of the vengeful
enemy' are reflected in the ominous 'shadowy main | Dim-tinted'
and the 'huge amphitheatre' of scenery recognized as an image of
'society'. Coleridge wishfully offers society as a community of
'converse' and 'a dance of thought'; more certainly, that society
was the original condition for his own retreat to the 'small and

silent dell' and his meditation on present evil and coming retribution. The 'burst of prospect' viewed from the summit initiates a
contrary process of contraction and withdrawal, and the whole
poem comes to an uneasy rest at 'beloved STOWEY' with
Coleridge proferring a grace for the healthful ministry of nature
and solitude:

> I behold
> Thy church-tower, and (methinks) the four huge elms
> Clust'ring, which mark the mansion of my friend;
> And close behind them, hidden from my view,
> Is my own lowly cottage, where my babe
> And my babe's mother dwell in peace! With light
> And quicken'd footsteps thitherward I tend,
> Remembering thee, O green and silent dell!
> And grateful, that by nature's quietness
> And solitary musings all my heart
> Is soften'd, and made worthy to indulge
> Love, and the thoughts that yearn for human kind.

The conclusion of 'Fears in Solitude' is at odds with all that has
gone before, for the poem actually relates an experience by which
his heart had been 'wearied', not 'soften'd': 'Nature's quietness |
And solitary musings' had wakened thoughts of 'strife' and
human anguish, rather than yielding a 'spirit-healing' tranquillity. Coleridge's indulgence is self-deception, but it arises from a
need to believe in the beneficent influence of nature to moral good
that the poem has significantly failed to answer. Three months
after Coleridge wrote 'Fears in Solitude', Wordsworth was to
make a similar but more tentative claim in 'Tintern Abbey' for the
workings of nature and memory to 'acts | Of kindness and of
love'. In comparison with Wordsworth's poem, 'Fears in Solitude' suggests Coleridge's inability to discover an assuaging
consolation in providence, nature, or society. The prospect
offered no ground for optimism beyond assuming the burden of
guilt and admitting the justice of punishment—'We have
offended, O my countrymen!'—and this forms Coleridge's true
position of last resort in spring 1798.

From his early days at Jesus College Coleridge's political,
philosophic, and religious beliefs had been involved as a progressive and mutually sustaining whole. 'Fears in Solitude' marks a
disabling inversion of this ideal, effectively throwing him 'out of

the pale of love' which was the foundation of his self-image and imaginative life hitherto. When coupled with opium illness and marital unhappiness, Coleridge's self-implication in the collapse of revolutionary idealism can be seen to have issued in the paralysed creativity of the years immediately following. It finds a report in the anguished self-inquisition of the 'Letter to Sara Hutchinson' and 'Dejection: An Ode', and was the most obvious reason for Coleridge's disguise and distortion of his radical self in subsequent letters, articles, and in *Biographia*. Here, too, is the immediate cause of Coleridge's need for *The Recluse*, the earliest announcements of which date from the month before Coleridge wrote 'Fears in Solitude'. Not only would *The Recluse* sustain the redemptive momentum of the early years of Revolution; by projecting Wordsworth as its author Coleridge effectively sublimated his own culpability for revolutionary failure to date. 'Tintern Abbey' is Wordsworth's answer to the Coleridge of 'Fears in Solitude'; it is also the closest that he ever came to fulfilling Coleridge's idea of *The Recluse* in September 1799 as

a poem, in blank verse, addressed to those, who, in consequence of the complete failure of the French Revolution, have thrown up all hopes of the amelioration of mankind, and are sinking into an almost epicurean selfishness, disguising the same under the soft titles of domestic attachment and contempt for visionary *philosophes*. (*C L* i. 527)

The politics of 'Tintern Abbey'

The composition of 'Tintern Abbey' in July 1798 focuses more gradual changes in Wordsworth during that summer. The poem is Wordsworth's most impressive celebration of those moments when 'We see into the life of things', but it was also his last expression of belief in the One Life itself. 'Tintern Abbey' is a coda to the months of mutual influence and creativity Wordsworth had shared with Dorothy and Coleridge since mid-1797, when most of the *Lyrical Ballads* were written. But Wordsworth's concern with the restorative power of memory in 'Tintern Abbey' also foreshadows the poetry he would write at Goslar the following winter, which would form the germ of *The Prelude*.

The transitional movement of 'Tintern Abbey' appears in a reticent acknowledgement of uncertainty that serves to qualify

Wordsworth's repeated claims to faith. It emerges most obviously in the conditional mood of many lines, for example in the following:

> such, perhaps,
> As may have had no trivial influence
>
> (ll. 32–3)

and:

> Nor less, I trust,
> To them I may have owed another gift
>
> (ll. 36–7)

and, later on:

> other gifts
> Have followed, for such loss, I would believe
> Abundant recompence.
>
> (ll. 87–9)

Throughout 'Tintern Abbey' Wordsworth's thanks for the 'other gifts' of nature and memory appear in a context of personal loss, 'changed, no doubt, from what [he] was' (l. 67), and an awareness of quotidian 'solitude, or fear, or pain, or grief' (l. 144) that had informed Coleridge's 'Fears in Solitude'. While 'Tintern Abbey' is a hymn to the One Life in nature 'and in the mind of man', it also articulates a sombre elegiac voice in 'The still, sad music of humanity' and 'all | The dreary intercourse of daily life' (ll. 92, 132). That joyless mean of existence is the shadow that falls between Wordsworth's intimated doubt—'If this | Be but a vain belief' (ll. 50–1)—and his countering affirmation, 'How oft, in spirit, have I turned to thee | O sylvan Wye' (ll. 56–7). Similarly, his claim that

> Nature never did betray
> The heart that loved her
>
> (ll. 123–4)

—is modified by its implied recollection of other and earlier betrayals, even in the prayer of 'chearful faith' with which the poem concludes.

Wordsworth's poetry of 'chearful faith' in 'Tintern Abbey' is complicated by, and derives its power from, a lasting awareness of insecurity that issues in the poem's characteristic idiom of assertion and simultaneous reservation. One immediate reason for this was, perhaps, Wordsworth's incipient doubt about the adequacy of One Life to his own spiritual experience—even as he gave that vision of a living universe its fullest and most beautiful expression. But more fundamentally, and in a longer perspective, 'Tintern Abbey' represents a moment of transition that quietly re-enacts the more violent oscillations of his political and philosophic opinions in earlier years. This intersection of a meditative philosophic poem with the revolutionary experience of the decade is the key to understanding 'Tintern Abbey' as Wordsworth's reply to 'Fears in Solitude' and, beyond that, its identity with *The Recluse*.

Wordsworth's and Dorothy's walking tour from Bristol up the Wye valley and back took four days, from 10 to 13 July 1798. Before setting off they both visited James Losh at Bath on 8 July, Losh noting in his diary 'Miss Wordsworth and Wordsworth . . . at Dinner Do. Tea & Supper' (LD iii). On the following day Losh continues, 'The Wordsworth's all night and at Breakfast. Walk with them', which suggests that he may have accompanied his guests towards Bristol, from where on 10 July the Wordsworths continued together over the Severn to Chepstow and the Wye, then on to Tintern. What did Wordsworth and Losh talk about on those two days at Bath? The conversation must have turned on the forthcoming *Lyrical Ballads* and projected trip to Germany; a little earlier in the year Losh had noted 'were there any place to go to emigration would be a prudent thing for literary men and the friends of freedom' (LD iii). But if this much is a reasonable conjecture, they doubtless also touched on political affairs, mutual acquaintances, and shared experiences following their coincidence at Paris six years before in autumn 1792. As Wordsworth parted from Losh in July 1798 it seems highly likely that politics, poetry, his recent past and immediate future would have been much on his mind. On the evening of 10 July, perhaps, he arrived at Tintern and then or shortly afterwards began to compose his poem (Reed, pp. 33, 243).

The opening lines of 'Tintern Abbey' anchor the whole upon Wordsworth's earlier visit to the Wye 'five years' previously. At that particular moment Wordsworth's belief had been

That if France prospered good men would not long
Pay fruitless worship to humanity

(P. x. 222–3)

—a hope that he had recently vindicated against the death of
Louis and the September Massacres in *A Letter to the Bishop of
Llandaff*. Days before he walked up the Wye to Tintern, though,
Wordsworth had watched the British fleet arming in the Solent
for war with France—a sight that gave him additional cause for
doubt. He described the scene in his fragmentary poem 'At the Isle
of Wight', and some curious echoes of this poem are heard at the
beginning of 'Tintern Abbey':

> How sweet to walk along the woody steep
> When all the summer seas are charmed to sleep;
> While on the distant sands the tide retires
> Its last faint murmur on the ear expires;
> The setting sun [   ] his growing round   5
> On the low promontory—purple bound
> For many a league a line of gold extends,
> Now lessened half his glancing disc de[scends]
> The watry sands athwart the ? [   ]
> Flush [   ] sudden [   ] not [   ] 10
> While anchored vessels scattered far [   ]
> Darken with shadowy hulks [   ]
> O'er earth o'er air and ocean [   ]
> Tranquillity extends her [   ]
> But hark from yon proud fleet in peal profound
> Thunders the sunset cannon; at the sound   16
> The star of life appears to set in blood,
> And ocean shudders in offended mood,
> Deepening with moral gloom his angry flood.

(*PW* i. 307–8)

The first four lines of this fragment seem to be recollected, five
years later, in the 'steep and lofty cliffs' of 'Tintern Abbey'; in the
'sweet inland murmur' of the River Wye and, at the end of the
poem, once again in 'these steep woods and lofty cliffs'. But in
recalling the fragment of 1793 these verbal echoes also identify
changes in Wordsworth himself. In the earlier poem the tranquillity of evening is shattered by the cannon, the 'gold' and
'purple' sunset is transformed in Wordsworth's eyes to a sky of

'blood', and his 'Evening Voluntary' concludes as a war requiem for France. In 'Tintern Abbey', of course, there is no violent dislocation of feeling, but the landscape and natural scenery are comparably stylized and subordinate to the poet's mood. Wordsworth's quirky footnote—'The river is not affected by the tides a few miles above Tintern'—establishes the distance of the open sea and, by implication, the disturbance of his former self as well.

Although it is not superficially apparent, Wordsworth's reposeful landscape in the first paragraph of 'Tintern Abbey' reminds of the misgivings and betrayal he had endured five years before, and is valued precisely because of that memory of former unease. His isolation then enhances present joy in Dorothy's companionship, his 'dear, dear Friend'. It also defines the antiphonal relation of 'Tintern Abbey' to 'Fears in Solitude' by which Wordsworth answers Coleridge's dejection with a subdued reminder of a comparable experience in his own past, asserting visionary insight and

> that blessed mood,
> In which the burthen of the mystery,
> In which the heavy and the weary weight
> Of all this unintelligible world
> Is lighten'd
>
> (ll. 38–42)

—against his own awareness of revolutionary failure, and Coleridge's despair:

> —O my God!
> It is indeed a melancholy thing,
> And weighs upon the heart, that he must think
> What uproar and what strife may now be stirring
> This way or that way o'er these silent hills . . .

While Wordsworth's recollection of 1793 differentiates his present self in 1798, it also lends urgency to the admitted possibility that his beliefs now may ultimately turn out to be 'vain' as his former confidence in France had proved. That tremor of anxiety is amplified elsewhere in 'Tintern Abbey', where the poem touches deeper memories and associations in the subtitled date, 'July 13, 1798'.[2] This was very likely the day on which Wordsworth completed his poem on returning to Bristol. It was also the eighth anniversary of the day Wordsworth first set foot in France in 1790, along with Robert Jones whom he was intending to visit in North Wales when he walked past Tintern in 1793. The date therefore had a personal significance for Wordsworth that served to connect Tintern and France; moreover, the day was also celebrated in the revolutionary calendar as the eve before Bastille day, the anniversary of the Revolution itself.

Wordsworth had witnessed the ceremony of *Fédération* on 14 July twice. In 1790 he was an interested visitor, and told Dorothy that 'the whole nation was mad with joy, in consequence of the revolution' (*E Y*, p. 36). Two years later he had joined the *Fête* at Blois as a patriot himself, and would have heard Grégoire—'a man of philosophy and humanity'—declare that 'The present augurs well for the future. Soon we shall witness the liberation of all humankind. Everything confirms that the coming revolution . . . will inaugurate the federation of all mankind!' The subtitle of 'Tintern Abbey' inevitably recalls Wordsworth's own experience of revolution at these two moments in 1790 and 1792. It also invokes the millenarian optimism of those early years in Grégoire's prophecy, but defers 'the coming revolution' once again until tomorrow: a 14 July perpetually postponed. No longer identified with revolutionary action or progress, human regeneration has become the prerogative of the individual mind in communion with nature and, introspectively, with itself. It was precisely this reconciliation of revolutionary idealism with subjective experience that Coleridge was unable to sustain after spring 1798, and which defines Wordsworth's identity as poet of *The Prelude* over the next seven years.

In 'Tintern Abbey', as later in *The Prelude*, the fructifying treason of memory 'augurs well' for times to come, enabling Wordsworth to confront human suffering and vicissitude with a redeeming continuity:

[2] For a brief discussion of revolutionary associations of 13 July, among them the death of Marat, see J. R. Watson 'A Note on the Date in the Title of *Tintern Abbey*', *TW C* x (Autumn 1979), 379–80. See also K. R. Johnston, 'The Politics of *Tintern Abbey*', *TW C* xiv (Winter 1983), 6–14, and R. A. Brinkley, 'Vagrant and Hermit: Milton and the Politics of *Tintern Abbey*', *TW C* xvi (Summer 1985), 126–33.

> While here I stand, not only with the sense
> Of present pleasure, but with pleasing thoughts
> That in this moment there is life and food
> For future years . . .

(ll. 63–6)

The lines immediately following are the imaginative axis of the whole poem: 'And so I dare to hope,' Wordsworth writes,

> Though changed, no doubt, from what I was, when first
> I came among these hills . . .

His recognition of future possibility and simultaneous acknowledgement of erosion, of change, draw upon the past to construe hope in despite of loss. Unlike Coleridge in 'France, an Ode' or 'Fears in Solitude', Wordsworth's 'dare to hope' embraced the crisis of a generation left without 'light | To guide or chear', turning the experience of defeat to 'food | For future years'. By reflecting wider anxieties within the horizons of personal experience at this moment in mid-1798, Wordsworth had already fulfilled Coleridge's 1799 idea of *The Recluse* as a poem of philosophic restitution for the collapse of the Revolution in France and the associated demise of reform at home. The whole fabric of 'Tintern Abbey'—language, mood, philosophic bias—is grounded in Wordsworth's radical years. It expresses the redemptive wish that he had shared with Coleridge and other friends of liberty, in his pleased recognition of nature as

> The guide, the guardian of [his] heart, and soul
> Of all [his] moral being

(ll. 111–12)

—and it gives thanks for Dorothy's healing presence since Racedown days in maintaining this 'saving intercourse' with nature and his true self. 'Tintern Abbey' does all of these things, but in the context of a lasting vulnerability—'And so I dare to hope' —that was the common legacy of revolution to Wordsworth, Coleridge, and their contemporaries. Wordsworth's consciousness of human weakness and fallibility,

> The still, sad music of humanity,
> Not harsh nor grating, though of ample power
> To chasten and subdue

—was the hardest lesson of revolution, but for Wordsworth it proved most fruitful. More than the aspiration he felt with his generation,

> —a time when Europe was rejoiced,
> France standing on the top of golden hours,
> And human nature seeming born again

—it was failure that made Wordsworth a poet.

Appendix

Wordsworth and Daniel Isaac Eaton's *Philanthropist*

On 8 June 1794 Wordsworth wrote to William Mathews suggesting that a suitable title for their projected political journal might be '"*The Philanthropist a monthly Miscellany*"' (*EY*, p. 125), but by the following November they had apparently abandoned the scheme as impractical (*EY*, p. 134). However, shortly after Wordsworth's meeting with Godwin, Frend, Dyer, and the others on 27 February 1795, Daniel Isaac Eaton began publishing a weekly periodical entitled the *Philanthropist*. The first number appeared on 16 March 1795, and publication continued through forty-two issues until 18 January 1796. The coincidence of Wordsworth's arrival in London and the first appearance of Eaton's *Philanthropist* is curious, and perhaps indicates that Wordsworth was involved in production of the journal until he left London during the summer.

Besides elaborating his own idea of a journal in his letters to Mathews of 1794, Wordsworth twice expresses a wish for 'employment . . . in . . . a newspaper' (*EY*, pp. 136, 138). Furthermore, the company Wordsworth joined on 27 February 1795 provides a likely group of contributors and editors for the *Philanthropist* as published. All were liberal intellectuals who supported reform and an end to the war, and at least six—Godwin, Holcroft, Losh, Wordsworth, Frend, and Dyer—had expressed their opinions in journals, pamphlets, and petitions. Eaton was a well-known radical publisher and bookseller, prosecuted and acquitted in 1793 for publishing *The Rights of Man* and in 1794 for seditous libel in *Hog's Wash* when he was successfully defended in court by Felix Vaughan. Eaton's *Philanthropist* was a 'miscellany' of political and philosophic essays, contemporary comment, extracts from other publications, and original poetry. Contributors remained anonymous, adopting a pen-name or initials presumably to avoid prosecution. Nevertheless, it is possible to conjecture authorship from the contents alone. On 27 July 1795 an extract from Robinson's *Political Catechism* appeared, which might indicate Frend's or Dyer's presence among the editors.[1] On 14 December 1795 the *Philanthropist* contained 'An Essay

---

[1] *Philanthropist* (27 July 1795), 1–5.

On the Influence of Some Human Institutions on Human Happiness' which opens with a Godwinian claim that the 'law of necessity must be submitted to', and goes on to consider the 'melancholy state of the lower orders of society' as a consequence of 'imperfections of the present organization of society'. The essay subsequently considers depreciation in 'the value of the spinner's labour', and concludes by identifying the expense of government as a principal cause of 'the wretchedness of the lower orders in all countries'.[2] The concern for the poor was of course common to many pamphlets of the period, but the mention of 'spinner's labour' might recall Frend's appendix to *Peace and Union*, 'The Effect of War on the Poor', while the author's initial under the essay—'W' —could stand for William.

These examples are, admittedly, conjectural and Wordsworth's involvement is even more difficult to identify. But at least two contributions may suggest his presence. On 31 August 1795, just after Wordsworth's departure for Bristol, the *Philanthropist* published a poem entitled 'Lines, Addressed to the EDITOR of the PHILANTHROPIST', the sixth stanza of which has a bearing upon Wordsworth's 'Salisbury Plain':

> But, Ah! such scenes delight the men alone,
> Who void of love to man, and fond of war,
> Made dupes by Princes to support the throne,
> That rules by rapine and continual jar,
>   For what can War but endless War still breed,
>   Till truth and right from Violence be freed.[3]

The obvious link to Wordsworth is in his closing stanzas of 'A Night on Salisbury Plain',

> Say, rulers of the nations, from the sword
> Can ought but murder, pain, and tears proceed?
> Oh! what can war but endless war still breed?

> (Gill, p. 37; ll. 507–9)

—and both poems share a common source in Milton's sonnet 'On the Lord General Fairfax at the Siege of Colchester':

> For what can war, but endless war still breed,
> Till truth, and right from violence be freed . . .

> (ll. 10–11)

The debt to Milton is not evidence for Wordsworth's authorship of the *Philanthropist* 'Lines', but it does suggest possibilities for his involvement. 'A Night on Salisbury Plain' was known to Wordsworth's London friends; on 20 November 1795, for example, he told Wrangham that he

---

[2] *Philanthropist* (14 Dec. 1795), 1–8.
[3] *Philanthropist* (31 Aug. 1795), 5.

recollected 'reading the first draught of it to [him] in London' (*E Y*, p. 159). The *Philanthropist* 'Lines' are signed 'Clericus', which could be a disguise for Rev. Wrangham, who was also collaborating with Wordsworth on their imitation of Juvenal during 1795. At the very least, then, the *Philanthropist* poem and Wordsworth's 'Salisbury Plain' indicate current popularity of Milton's republican poetry among reformists; it may reflect a familiarity with Wordsworth's manuscript poem, read sometime during his stay in London before August 1795, and therefore a direct link to Wordsworth himself. Finally, 'Lines Addressed to the EDITOR of the PHILANTHROPIST' might be Wrangham's work, possibly with Wordsworth as an unacknowledged collaborator.

Further evidence of Wordsworth's writing in the *Philanthropist* is difficult to identify, not just due to the anonymity of contributions but because much of the material reflects opinions common to a wide range of reformist periodicals and pamphlets, which Wordsworth also shared. Consequently, a comparison of verbal and stylistic features in the *Philanthropist* and in Wordsworth's contemporary writing might offer a more fruitful approach than analysis of contents. On this basis, Wordsworth could have written the editorial article in the third issue of the *Philanthropist* which appeared on 30 March 1795.

This editorial opens by declaring 'the intention of the Philanthropist'

to have proceeded in a regular discussion of *those subjects*, which involve in their consideration the rights, and happiness, of man, and not to have engaged the attention of the public with the political concerns of the day, till he had *enforced*, and inculcated some truths of a very pressing, and important nature. (Italics added)[4]

The similarities to Wordsworth's letter to Mathews of 8 June 1794 are striking: 'There is a further duty incumbent upon every enlightened friend of mankind; he should let slip no opportunity of explaining and *enforcing those general principles* of the social order which are applicable to all times and to all places' (*E Y*, p. 124, italics added). Besides the verbal and stylistic similarities, Wordsworth's concern to enforce 'general principles' and 'truth' in his letter is identical to the editorial purpose of the *Philanthropist*. The article continues with a summary of the present crisis—'look which way we please on the political horizon, all is darkness, wretchedness, and horror'—and an account of the distress caused by war:

How many honest, and flourishing families in the course of the last two years have been plunged into the most dreadful abyss of bankruptcy, want, and penury! How many unfriended wretches have been turned loose on the mercy of mankind, (that bleak, and unfeeling mercy, as

4 *Philanthropist* (30 Mar. 1795), 1.

expressed by a most excellent English Poet,) and have been driven through necessity, and to support exhausted, and famishing life, either to a violation of the laws of their country, by which they have been brought to a most ignominious termination of their lives, or have been obliged to enlist into that most wicked, yet at the same time, much to be pitied, profession, where they cease to be the friends of the human race, but where they become its destroyers, its murderers, and its plunderers. But are these the worst calamities our Nation has experienced! How many thousands of our brave countrymen have been most inhumanly., and unfeelingly sacrificed! What tears have their disconsolate wives, and infant children, now deprived of their best friend, if not of the only friend they had, shed for their premature, and unhappy fates![5]

Once again, the editorial has much in common with Frend's appendix to *Peace and Union* and Cooper's *Reply to Mr. Burke's Invective*, but it may also have a connection with Wordsworth as well. The reference to 'unfriended wretches' recalls Wordsworth's 'unfriended individual' in his letter of 24 December 1794 (*E Y*, p. 137), and 'turned loose on the mercy of mankind' might be compared with Wordsworth's Female Vagrant in 'Adventures on Salisbury Plain' who ' "lived upon the mercy of the fields" ' (*Gill*, p. 145, l. 541). Furthermore, the pressure of 'necessity' in driving the 'unfriended wretch' from hunger to crime or enlistment anticipates Wordsworth's concerns when he revised 'Salisbury Plain' late in 1795, and the painful circumstances of Robert in 'The Ruined Cottage' two years later.

These echoes and similarities between Wordsworth's writing and the *Philanthropist* editorial only present material for conjecturing Wordsworth's involvement in the journal. On the other hand, the editorial also offers significant evidence of the contemporary intellectual background to Wordsworth's poetry in 1795, specifically to the sailor's story in 'Adventures on Salisbury Plain'. Until firm evidence as to the contributors to the *Philanthropist* emerges, it is unlikely that a definite connection with Wordsworth can be established. In the absence of such evidence, it is nevertheless safe to say that the group Wordsworth joined at Frend's house represents a likely cross-section of editors and contributors to Eaton's journal, if only because those present were the intellectual core of the metropolitan reform movement and known writers as well. If one looks elsewhere for likely contributors, Thelwall, Wrangham, Mathews, Vaughan, come to mind, but the number of possibilities seems limited. On balance, it seems likely that, while in London Wordsworth was moving in circles connected with Eaton's *Philanthropist*, he may well have contributed himself in some capacity, but at present there is no substantial evidence to confirm this.

[5] *Philanthropist* (30 Mar. 1795), 3–4.

Bibliography

1. Manuscripts cited

Individual MSS are listed under the library and collection in which they are deposited.

Bibliothèque Municipale de Blois, France
Procès Verbaux des Sociétés Populaires.

Bodleian Library, Oxford
Abinger-Shelley papers:
   b. 227/2(b): Godwin's draft letter to Paine, 1791.
   b. 229/2: Miscellaneous notes by Godwin, including a reference to Wordsworth.
   c. 531: Godwin, autobiographical fragment relating to events of 1794–5.
   c. 537: Godwin's reflections on his life, 10 Oct. 1824.
   c. 604/3: Godwin's biographical notes on Coleridge to 1799.
   e. 196–227: The Diary of William Godwin.
Lovelace–Byron papers:
   71: Volume of letters entitled 'Frend. from 1815', containing correspondence of William Frend to Lady Byron, 1831–8.

Manuscript English Letters:
  c. 22: Letters of Robert Southey.

Bristol University Library
Pinney papers:
  Account Book 1685: The Diary of Joseph Gill.
  Domestic Box R/3: Papers of Basil Montagu.
  Letter Book 12: A letter of John Pinney to his London banker, 2 Mar.
  1797.
  Letter Book 13: Letters of Azariah Pinney to Wordsworth, 1795–6.

Cambridge University Library
Additional Manuscripts:
  7886/263, 264: Letters of Felix Vaughan to William Frend, 1790.
  7887/55:   Dinner at the Crown and Anchor, 12 January 1798.

Dove Cottage Library
D C M S A/Montagu 8/26: 'Basil Montagu's Narrative of the Birth and
  Upbringing of his son.'

Public Record Office
Home Office Papers:
  HO 42/40: Correspondence relating to Fishguard invasion of
    February 1797.
  HO 42/41: Correspondence between Daniel Lysons, John King, and
    James Walsh: the 'Spy Nozy' incident.
  HO 43/8: Correspondence relating to Fishguard invasion, 1797.
Treasury Solicitor's papers:
  TS 11 952 3496 (2): Miscellaneous papers including subscription
    arrears due to SCI.
  TS 11 952 3496 (3): Miscellaneous papers relating to LCS, includ-
    ing a copy of Godwin's *Cursory Strictures* bought at Kearsley's
    bookshop.
  TS 11 954 3498: Miscellaneous papers, including a list of witnesses
    called at Thelwall's trial, Dec. 1794.
  TS 11 960 3506 (1): List of SCI members headed 'Penny Post';
    Notebook of subscribers to SCI.
  TS 11 961 3507: Minutes of SCI, Volume One.
  TS 11 962 3508: Minutes of SCI, Volume Two.
  TS 11 966 3510 B: Miscellaneous papers relating to LCS.

Tullie House Library, Carlisle
B/320 1–5: The Diary of James Losh, 1796–1802.

2. Literary sources

Chaucer, Geoffrey, *Complete Works*, ed. F. N. Robinson (2nd edn; Oxford, 1974).

Coleridge, Samuel Taylor, *Collected Coleridge* (Bollingen Series 75; Princeton, NJ): i. *Lectures 1795 on Politics and Religion*, ed. L. Patton and P. Mann (1971); ii. *The Watchman*, ed. L. Patton (1970); . iii. *Essays on his Times*, ed. D. V. Erdman (3 vols, 1978); iv. *The Friend*, ed. B. Rooke (2 vols, 1969); vii. *Biographia Literaria*, ed. J. Engell and W. Jackson Bate (2 vols; 1983).

—— *Collected Letters*, ed. E. L. Griggs (6 vols; Oxford, 1956–71).

—— *Complete Poetical Works*, ed. E. H. Coleridge (2 vols; Oxford, 1912).

—— *Fears in Solitude, Written in 1798, During the Alarm of an Invasion. To which are added France, an Ode; and Frost at Midnight* (London, 1798).

—— *Poems*, ed. J. Beer (London, 1973).

—— 'Reflections on Entering into Active Life', *Monthly Magazine*, ii (July–Dec. 1796).

—— *Table Talk*, ed. T. Ashe (London, 1884).

De Quincey, Thomas, *Collected Writings*, ed. D. Masson (14 vols; Edinburgh, 1889–90).

Dyer, George, *Poems* (London, 1792).

Fawcett, Joseph, *The Art of War: A Poem* (London, 1795).

Godwin, William, *Caleb Williams*, ed. D. McCracken (Oxford, 1970).

Hazlitt, William, *Complete Works*, ed. P. P. Howe (21 vols; London, 1930–4).

Lamb, Charles and Mary, *Works*, ed. E. V. Lucas (7 vols; London and New York, 1903–5).

—— Charles and Mary Anne, *Letters*, ed. E. J. Marrs (3 vols; Ithaca, NY, 1975–8).

Langhorne, John, *The Country Justice: A Poem* (London, 1774).

Milton, John, *Complete Shorter Poems*, ed. J. Carey (Longmans Annotated English Poets Series; London, 1968).

—— *Paradise Lost*, ed. A. Fowler (Longmans Annotated English Poets Series; London, 1968).

Shakespeare, William, *Complete Works*, ed. P. Alexander (London and Glasgow, 1951).

Southey, Robert, *Joan of Arc* (Bristol, 1796).

—— *Life and Correspondence*, ed. C. C. Southey (6 vols; London, 1849–50).

—— *New Letters of Robert Southey*, ed. K. Curry (2 vols; New York and London, 1965).

—— *Poems* (Bristol, 1797).

—— *Poetical Works* (10 vols; London, 1837–8).

Southey, Robert, *Selections from the Letters of Robert Southey*, ed. J. W. Warter (4 vols; London, 1856).

—— *Wat Tyler* (London, 1817).

Spenser, Edmund, *Poetical Works*, ed. J. C. Smith and E. de Selincourt (Oxford, 1970).

Thelwall, John, *Ode to Science. Recited at the Anniversary Meeting of the Philomathian Society, June 20, 1791, By Brother Thelwall* (London, 1791).

—— *Poems Written in Close Confinement in the Tower and Newgate, under a Charge of High Treason* (London, 1795).

—— *Poems, Chiefly Written in Retirement* (2nd edn; Hereford, 1801).

Wordsworth, Dorothy, *Journals*, ed. E. de Selincourt (2 vols; London, 1952).

Wordsworth, William, *The Borderers*, ed. R. Osborn (Cornell Wordsworth Series; Ithaca, NY, 1982).

—— *Letters of William and Dorothy Wordsworth*, ed. E. de Selincourt, 2nd edn, *The Early Years, 1787–1805*, rev. C. L. Shaver (Oxford, 1967).

—— *Lyrical Ballads, 1798 and 1800*, ed. R. L. Brett and A. R. Jones (London, 1963).

—— *Poetical Works*, ed. E. de Selincourt and H. Darbishire (5 vols; Oxford, 1940–9).

—— *The Prelude, 1799, 1805, 1850*, ed. J. Wordsworth, M. H. Abrams, and S. Gill (New York, 1979).

—— *Prose Works*, ed. A. B. Grosart (3 vols; London, 1876).

—— *Prose Works*, ed. W. J. B. Owen and J. W. Smyser (3 vols; Oxford, 1974).

—— *'The Ruined Cottage' and 'The Pedlar'*, ed. J. Butler (Cornell Wordsworth Series; Ithaca, NY, 1979).

—— *The Salisbury Plain Poems*, ed. S. Gill (Cornell Wordsworth Series; Ithaca, NY, 1975).

—— *William Wordsworth*, ed. S. Gill (Oxford Authors Series; Oxford, 1984).

Wrangham, Francis, *Poems* (London, 1795).

3. Literary criticism and scholarship

Abrams, M. H., 'English Romanticism: The Spirit of the Age' in N. Frye (ed.), *Romanticism Reconsidered* (New York, 1963).

Adams, M. Ray, 'Joseph Fawcett and Wordsworth's Solitary', *PMLA* xlviii (June 1933).

—— *Studies in the Literary Backgrounds of English Radicalism* (Lancaster, Pa., 1947).

Altick, R., *The English Common Reader* (Chicago and London, 1957).

Beatty, A., 'Joseph Fawcett: *The Art of War*. Its Relation to the Early Development of William Wordsworth', *University of Wisconsin Studies*, ii (1918).

Beer, J., 'The Revolutionary Youth of Wordsworth and Coleridge: Another View', *Critical Quarterly*, xix (1977).

—— *Wordsworth and the Human Heart* (London, 1978).

Bennett, B. T., *British War Poetry in the Age of Romanticism, 1793–1815* (New York and London, 1976).

'Bliss was it in that Dawn: The Matter of Coleridge's Revolutionary Youth', *Times Literary Supplement* (6 Aug. 1971).

Brinkley, Robert A., 'Vagrant and Hermit: Milton and the Politics of *Tintern Abbey*', *The Wordsworth Circle* xvi (Summer 1985).

Brinton, C., *Political Ideas of the English Romanticists* (Oxford, 1926).

Chard, L., *Dissenting Republican: Wordsworth's Early Life and Thought in Their Political Context* (The Hague, 1972).

Cornwell, J., *Coleridge, Poet and Revolutionary, 1771–1804* (London, 1973).

Curtis, J., *Wordsworth's Experiments with Tradition: The Lyric Poems of 1802 with Texts of the Poems Based on Early Manuscripts* (Ithaca and London, 1971).

Darlington, B., 'Two Early Texts: *A Night Piece* and *The Discharged Soldier*' in J. Wordsworth (ed.), *Bicentenary Wordsworth Studies* (Ithaca and London, 1970).

Dean, L. W., 'Coleridge and the Sources of Pantisocracy: Godwin, the Bible, Hartley', *Boston University Studies in English*, v (1961).

Eaglestone, A. J., 'Wordsworth, Coleridge, and the Spy' in E. Blunden and E. L. Griggs (eds), *Coleridge: Studies by Several Hands* (London, 1934).

Ellis, A. M., *Rebels and Conservatives* (Bloomington and London, 1967).

Erdman, D., 'Wordsworth as Heartsworth; or, was Regicide the Prophetic Ground of Those Moral Questions?', in D. Reiman, M. Jaye, and B. T. Bennett (eds), *The Evidence of the Imagination: Studies of Interactions between Life and Art in English Romantic Literature* (New York, 1978).

Everest, K., *Coleridge's Secret Ministry* (Hassocks, Sussex, 1979).

Fink, Z. S., 'Wordsworth and the English Republican Tradition', *Journal of English and Germanic Philology*, xlvii (1948).

Fruman, N., 'Coleridge's Rejection of Nature and the Natural Man', *Coleridge's Imagination* (Cambridge, 1985).

Gibbs, W. E., 'An Unpublished Letter from John Thelwall to S. T. Coleridge', *Modern Language Review*, xxv (1930).

Gill, Stephen, 'The Original Salisbury Plain: Introduction and Text' in J. Wordsworth (ed.), *Bicentenary Wordsworth Studies* (Ithaca and London, 1970).

Gill, Stephen, 'Wordsworth's Breeches Pocket: Attitudes to the Didactic Poet', *Essays in Criticism*, xix (1969).
—— 'Wordsworth's Poetry of Protest, 1795–97, *Studies in Romanticism*, xi (1972).
Gillcrist, T. J., 'Spenser and Reason in the Conclusion of *Salisbury Plain*', *English Language Notes*, vii (1969–70).
Gravil, R., Newlyn, L., and Roe, N. (eds), *Coleridge's Imagination: Essays in Memory of Peter Laver* (Cambridge, 1985).
Griggs, E. L., 'Coleridge's Army Experience', *English*, ix (1953).
—— 'Robert Southey's Estimate of Samuel Taylor Coleridge: A Study in Human Relations', *Huntingdon Library Quarterly*, ix (1945).
Grob, A., 'Wordsworth and Godwin: A Reassessment', *Studies in Romanticism*, vi (1967).
Harris, R. W., *Romanticism and the Social Order, 1780–1830* (London, 1969).
Hartman, G., 'Wordsworth's *Descriptive Sketches* and the Growth of a Poet's Mind', *P M L A* lxxvi (1961).
—— *Wordsworth's Poetry, 1787–1814* (New Haven and London, 1964).
Hayden, D. E., *After Conflict, Quiet: A Study of Wordsworth's Poetry in Relation to his Life and Letters* (New York, 1951).
Hoadley, F. T., 'The Controversy over Southey's *Wat Tyler*', *Studies in Philology*, xxxviii (1941).
Hooker, E. N., 'Wordsworth's *Letter to the Bishop of Llandaff*', *Studies in Philology*, xxviii (1931).
Jacobus, M., *Tradition and Experiment in Wordsworth's Lyrical Ballads, 1798* (Oxford, 1976).
Johnston, K. R., 'The Politics of *Tintern Abbey*', *The Wordsworth Circle*, xiv (Winter 1983).
—— *Wordsworth and 'The Recluse'* (New Haven and London, 1984).
Jones, H. M., *Revolution and Romanticism* (London, 1974).
Kitson, P., 'Coleridge's *The Plot Discovered*: A New Date', *Notes & Queries* (Mar. 1984).
Lindenberger, H., *On Wordsworth's 'Prelude'* (Princeton, 1963).
Logan, E., 'Coleridge's Scheme of Pantisocracy and American Travel Accounts', *P M L A* xlv (1930).
MacGillivray, J. R., 'The Pantisocracy Scheme and Its Immediate Background', *Studies in English by Members of the University of Toronto* (Toronto, 1931).
Meyer, G. W., 'Wordsworth and the Spy Hunt', *American Scholar*, xx (1950–1).
—— *Wordsworth's Formative Years* (Ann Arbor, 1943).
Newlyn, L., *Coleridge, Wordsworth, and the Language of Allusion* (Oxford, 1986).

Pollin, B. R., and Burke, R., 'John Thelwall's Marginalia in a Copy of Coleridge's *Biographia Literaria*', *Bulletin of the New York Public Library*, lxxiv (1970).

Reed, M. L., *Wordsworth: The Chronology of the Early Years, 1770–1799* (Cambridge, Mass., 1967).

Roberts, C. W., 'The Influence of Godwin on Wordsworth's *Letter to the Bishop of Llandaff*', *Studies in Philology*, xxix (1932).

—— 'Wordsworth, *The Philanthropist*, and *Political Justice*', *Studies in Philology*, xxxi (1934).

Roe, Nicholas, 'Citizen Wordsworth', *The Wordsworth Circle*, xiv (Winter 1983).

—— 'Radical George: Dyer in the 1790s', *Charles Lamb Bulletin*, NS xlix (Jan. 1985).

—— 'Robespierre's Despotism and a Word coined by Coleridge', *Notes & Queries* (Aug. 1981).

—— 'Who Was Spy Nozy?', *The Wordsworth Circle*, xv (Spring 1984).

—— 'Wordsworth, Samuel Nicholson, and the Society for Constitutional Information', *The Wordsworth Circle*, xiii (Autumn 1982).

—— 'Wordsworth's Account of Beaupuy's Death', *Notes & Queries* (Sept. 1985).

Schneider, B. R., *Wordsworth's Cambridge Education* (Cambridge, 1957).

Sheats, P., *The Making of Wordsworth's Poetry, 1785–1798* (Cambridge, Mass., 1973).

Tilney, C., 'An Unpublished Southey Fragment', *National Library of Wales Journal*, ix (1955).

Todd, F. M., *Politics and the Poet: A Study of Wordsworth* (London, 1957).

Watson, G., 'The Revolutionary Youth of Wordsworth and Coleridge', *Critical Quarterly*, xviii (1976).

Watson, J. R. (ed.), *An Infinite Complexity: Essays in Romanticism* (Edinburgh, 1983).

—— 'A Note on the Date in the Title of *Tintern Abbey*', *The Wordsworth Circle*, x (Autumn 1979).

Welsford, E., *'Salisbury Plain': A Study in the Development of Wordsworth's Mind and Art* (Oxford, 1966).

Whalley, G., 'Coleridge and Southey in Bristol, 1795', *Review of English Studies*, NS i (1950).

—— 'The Bristol Library Borrowings of Southey and Coleridge, 1793–8', *The Library*, 5s, iv (1949).

Willey, B., *The Eighteenth Century Background* (London, 1940).

Winegarten, R., *Writers and Revolution: The Fatal Lure of Action* (New York, 1974).

Woodring, Carl, *Politics in English Romantic Poetry* (Cambridge, Mass., 1970).

Woodring, Carl, *Politics in the Poetry of Coleridge* (Wisconsin, 1961).

Woof, R., 'Wordsworth and Coleridge: Some Early Matters' in J. Wordsworth (ed.), *Bicentenary Wordsworth Studies* (Ithaca and London, 1970).

Wordsworth, Jonathan (ed.), *Bicentenary Wordsworth Studies* (Ithaca and London, 1970).

—— *The Borders of Vision* (Oxford, 1982).

—— *The Music of Humanity* (London, 1969).

—— 'Startling the Earthworms', *Times Literary Supplement* (3 Dec. 1976).

Wuscher, H. J., *Liberty, Equality and Fraternity in Wordsworth, 1791–1800* (Uppsala, 1980).

4. History, politics, religion, philosophy

A. PRIMARY SOURCES

i. Cambridge, dissent, political pamphlets to 1789

An Address to the Public from the Society for Constitutional Information (London, 1780).

A Second Address to the Public from the Society for Constitutional Information (London, 1780).

Day, Thomas, *Two Speeches of Thomas Day, Esq., at the General Meetings of the Counties of Cambridge and Essex, held March 25, and April 25, 1780* (London, 1780).

Dyer, George, *A History of the University and Colleges of Cambridge* (2 vols; London, 1814).

—— *An Inquiry into the Nature of Subscription* (2nd edn; London, 1792).

—— *The Privileges of the University of Cambridge* (2 vols; London, 1824).

Fawcett, Joseph, *Sermons Delivered at the Sunday-evening Lecture for the Winter Season at the Old Jewry* (2 vols; London, 1795).

Frend, William, *An Address to the Inhabitants of Cambridge Exhorting them to Turn from the False Worship of Three Persons to the Worship of the One true God* (St Ives, 1788).

—— *Appendix to Thoughts on Subscription* (St Ives, 1789).

—— *Thoughts on Subscription to Religious Tests, in a Letter to Rev. H. W. Coulthurst* (St Ives, 1788).

Gunning, Henry, *Reminiscences of the University, Town and County of Cambridge, from the Year 1780* (2 vols; London, 1854).

Jebb, John, *Works*, ed. J. Disney (3 vols; London, 1787).

Lindsey, Theophilus, *An Historical View of the State of the Unitarian Doctrine and Worship* (London, 1783).

Price, Richard, *Observations on the Importance of the American Revolution* (London, 1785).

—— *Observations on the Nature of Civil Liberty, the Principles of Government, and the Justice and Policy of the War with America* (London, 1776).

Priestley, Joseph, *A General View of the Arguments for the Unity of God* (2nd edn; Birmingham, 1785).

—— *A Letter to the Right Honourable William Pitt, On the Subjects of Toleration and Church Establishments* (London, 1787).

—— *An Essay on the First Principles of Government; and on the Nature of Political, Civil, and Religious Liberty* (London, 1768).

Robinson, Robert, *A Political Catechism* (London, 1784).

—— *Arcana, or the Principles of the Late Petitioners to Parliament* (Cambridge, 1774).

Tyrwhitt, Robert, *Two Discourses on the Creation of All Things by Jesus Christ* (2nd edn, Cambridge, 1787).

ii. Burke, Paine, and France

Authentic Copies of the Instructions Given by General Hoche to Colonel Tate Previous to His Landing on the Coast of South Wales, in the Beginning of 1797 (London, 1798).

Barlow, Joel, *Advice to the Privileged Orders in the Several States of Europe, Part I* (London, 1792).

—— *Advice to the Privileged Orders, Part II* (London, 1795).

—— *The Conspiracy of Kings* (2nd edn; London, 1792).

Bowles, John, *The Real Grounds of the Present War with France* (London, 1793).

Brissot, J. P., *New Travels in the United States of America*, trans. Joel Barlow (London, 1792).

Burke, Edmund, *Reflections on the Revolution in France, and on the Proceedings in Certain Societies in London Relative to that Event*, ed. C. C. O'Brien (Harmondsworth, 1968).

—— *Substance of the Speech of the Right Honourable Edmund Burke in the Debate on the Army Estimates* (London, 1790).

Constant, Benjamin, *Observations on the Strength of the Present Government of France, and Upon the Necessity of Rallying Round it*, trans. James Losh (Bath, 1797).

Erskine, Thomas, *A View of the Causes and Consequences of the Present War with France* (London, 1797).

Grégoire, Henri, *Discours sur la Fédération du 14 Juillet 1792* (Orléans, 1792).

Le Mesurier, H., *Thoughts on a French Invasion* (Edinburgh, 1798).

Mackintosh, James, *Vindiciae Gallicae: A Defence of the French*

Revolution and its English Admirers against the Accusations of the Rt. Hon. Edmund Burke (London, 1791).

Miles, William, *The Conduct of France towards Great Britain Examined* (London, 1793).

Paine, Thomas, *Reasons for Wishing to Preserve the Life of Louis Capet, As Delivered to the National Convention* (London, 1793).

—— *The Rights of Man*, ed. H. Collins (Harmondsworth, 1969).

Price, Richard, *A Discourse on the Love of our Country, Nov. 4, 1789, at the Meeting-House in the Old Jewry, to the Society for Commemorating the Revolution in Great Britain, with an Appendix* (2nd edn; London, 1789).

Priestley, Joseph, *Letters to the Right Honourable Edmund Burke, Occasioned by his Reflections on the Revolution in France* (Birmingham, 1791).

The Fishguard Invasion by the French in 1797: Some Passages Taken from the Diary of the Late Reverend Rowlands, Sometime Vicar of Llanfiangelpenybont (London, 1892).

Watson, Richard, *A Sermon Preached Before the Stewards of the Westminster Dispensary, with an Appendix* (2nd edn; London, 1793).

Williams, Helen Maria, *Letters Written in France, in the Summer 1790* (London 1790).

—— *Letters from France* (2nd edn; London, 1796).

Wollstonecraft, Mary, *A Vindication of the Rights of Men, a Letter to the Rt. Hon. Edmund Burke; Occasioned by his Reflections on the Revolution in France* (London, 1790).

Young, Arthur, *Travels, During the Years 1787, 1788, and 1789, in the Kingdom of France* (London, 1790).

iii. Protest; reform; philosophical works

Address of the Bristol Constitutional Society for a Parliamentary Reform, to the People of Great Britain (Bristol, 1794).

Beddoes, Thomas, *Essay on the Public Merits of Mr. Pitt* (London, 1796).

Cobbett, William, *A Complete Collection of State Trials . . . from the Earliest Period to the Present Time* (33 vols; London, 1809–28).

—— *The Parliamentary History of England. From the Norman Conquest, in 1066, to the Year, 1803* (36 vols; London, 1806–20).

Cooper, Thomas, *A Reply to Mr. Burke's Invective Against Mr. Cooper, and Mr. Watt* (Manchester, 1792).

Declaration Agreed to on the 11th of April 1792, by the Society Entitled the Friends of the People (London, 1792).

Dyer, George, *A Dissertation on the Theory and Practice of Benevolence* (London, 1795).

—— *Four Letters on the English Constitution* (London, 1812).

—— *The Complaints of the Poor People of England* (2nd edn; London, 1793).

Eaton, Daniel Isaac, *Hog's Wash, or a Salmagundy for Swine* (London, 1793).

Fox, Charles James, *A Letter from the Right Honourable Charles James Fox to the Worthy and Independent Electors of the City and Liberty of Westminster* (London, 1793).

Free Thoughts on the Offices of Mayor, Aldermen, and Common Council of the City of Bristol (Bristol, 1792).

Frend, William, *An Account of the Proceedings in the University of Cambridge against William Frend, M.A.* (Cambridge, 1793).

—— *A Sequel to the Account of the Proceedings in the University of Cambridge* (London, 1795).

—— *Peace and Union, Recommended to the Associated Bodies of Republicans and Anti-Republicans* (St Ives, 1793).

—— *Scarsity of Bread. A Plan for Reducing the High Price of this Article in a Letter to William Devaynes, Esq.* (2nd edn; London, 1795).

Gerrald, Joseph, *A Convention the Only Means of Saving us from Ruin* (London, 1793).

—— *The Address of the British Convention Assembled at Edinburgh, November 19, 1793, to the People of Great Britain* (London, 1793).

Godwin, William, *Considerations on Lord Grenville's and Mr. Pitt's Bills, Concerning Treasonable and Seditious Practices, and Unlawful Assemblies, By a Lover of Order* (London, 1796).

—— *Cursory Strictures on the Charge Delivered by Lord Chief Justice Eyre to the Grand Jury, October 2, 1794* (London, 1794).

—— *Political Justice* (2 vols; London, 1793).

—— *Thoughts Occasioned by the Perusal of Dr. Parr's Spital Sermon* (London, 1801).

—— *Uncollected Writings, 1785–1822* (Gainesville, Florida, 1968).

Holcroft, Thomas, *A Narrative of Facts Relating to a Prosecution for High Treason* (London, 1795).

Jones, John Gale, *Sketch of a Speech Delivered at the Westminster Forum on the 9th, 16th, 23rd, and 30th December 1794* (London, 1795).

Lee, Richard, *Account of the Proceedings of a Meeting of the London Corresponding Society, Monday, October 26, 1795* (London, 1795).

—— *The Voice of the People* (London, 1795).

The London Corresponding Society's Addresses and Regulations (London, 1792).

Losh, James, *Observations on Parliamentary Reform* (London, 1831).

Paley, William, *The Principles of Moral and Political Philosophy* (London, 1795).
—— *Reasons for Contentment Addressed to the Labouring Part of the British Public* (London, 1793).
Priestley, Joseph (ed.), *Hartley's Theory of the Human Mind on the Principle of the Association of Ideas; with Essays Relating to the Subject of it* (London, 1775).
Smith, Adam, *An Enquiry into the Causes of the Wealth of Nations* (2 vols; London, 1776).
Thale, M. (ed.), *Selections from the Papers of the London Corresponding Society, 1792–1799* (Cambridge, 1983).
Thelwall, John, *An Appeal to Popular Opinion Against Kidnapping and Murder in a Narrative of the Late Atrocious Proceedings, at Yarmouth* (2nd edn; London, 1796).
—— *Peaceful Discussion, and not Tumultuary Violence the Means of Redressing National Grievances* (London, 1795).
—— *Political Lectures* (4th edn; London, 1795).
—— *The Rights of Nature, Against the Usurpations of Establishments* (3rd edn; London, 1796).
—— *The Speech of John Thelwall at the Second Meeting of the London Corresponding Society, November 12, 1795* (London, 1795).
—— *The Tribune* (3 vols; London, 1795–6).
The Trial of John Frost for Seditious Words (London, 1794).
The Trial of the Rev. Thomas Fyshe Palmer (Edinburgh, 1794).
Thompson, George, *Slavery and Famine, Punishments for Sedition, with some Preliminary Remarks by George Dyer* (London, 1794).

B. SECONDARY SOURCES

i. Historical studies

Alger, J. G., *Englishmen in the French Revolution* (London, 1889).
—— *Paris in 1789–1794* (London, 1902).
Aulard, F. A., *La Société des Jacobins* (6 vols; Paris, 1889–97).
Beik, P. (trans. and ed.), *The Documentary History of Western Civilisation: The French Revolution* (London, 1971).
Bimbenet, Eugene, *Histoire de la Ville d'Orléans* (5 vols; Orléans, 1884–8).
Birley, R., *The English Jacobins, 1789–1802* (London, 1924).
Briggs, A., *The Age of Improvement* (London, 1959).
British Public Characters of 1798 (London, 1798).
Brown, P. A., *The French Revolution in English History* (London, 1918).
Collins, H., 'The London Corresponding Society' in J. Saville (ed.), *Democracy and the Labour Movement* (London, 1954).

Cookson, J. E., *The Friends of Peace: Anti-War Liberalism in England, 1793–1815* (Cambridge, 1982).

Ditchfield, G. M., 'The Parliamentary Struggle over the Repeal of the Test and Corporation Acts, 1787–1790', *English Historical Review*, lxxxix (1974).

Fieldhouse, D. K., *The Colonial Empires: A Comparative Survey from the Eighteenth Century* (London, 1966).

Goldstein, L., *Ruins and Empire* (Pittsburg, 1977).

Goodwin, A., *The Friends of Liberty: The English Democratic Reform Movement in the Age of the French Revolution* (London, 1979).

Hampson, N., *The French Revolution: A Concise History* (London, 1975).

Horn, P., *The Last Invasion of Britain: Fishguard, 1797* (Fishguard, 1980).

Lefebvre, G., *The French Revolution*, i. *From its Origins to 1793*, trans. E. M. Evanson (London and New York, 1962); ii. *From 1793 to 1799*, trans. J. S. Hall and J. Friguglietti (London and New York, 1964).

—— *Études Orléanaises* (2 vols; Paris, 1962–3).

Mémoires de la Société des Sciences et des Lettres De la Ville de Blois, 1834–5 (Blois, 1836).

Murphy, M. J., *Cambridge Newspapers and Opinion, 1780–1850* (Cambridge and New York, 1977).

Palmer, R. R., *The World of the French Revolution* (London, 1971).

Rogers, C. B., *The Spirit of Revolution in 1789* (Princeton, 1949).

Thomis, M., and Holt, P., *Threats of Revolution in Britain, 1789–1848* (London, 1977).

Thompson, E. P., 'Disenchantment or Default? A Lay Sermon' in C. C. O'Brien and W. D. Vanech (eds), *Power and Consciousness* (London and New York, 1969).

—— *The Making of the English Working Class* (Harmondsworth, 1968).

Thompson, J. M., *Leaders of the French Revolution* (Oxford, 1962).

Walzer, M., *Regicide and Revolution: Speeches at the Trial of Louis XVI*, trans. M. Rothstein (Cambridge, 1974).

Wright, D. G., *Revolution and Terror in France, 1789–1795* (London, 1974).

5. Newspapers and periodicals

Anti-Jacobin; or, Weekly Examiner (2 vols; London, 1799).

Ascherson, N. (ed.), *The French Revolution: Extracts from 'The Times', 1789–1794* (London, 1975).

Blackwood's Magazine.

Bristol Gazette and Public Advertiser.
Cambridge Intelligencer.
Dodsley's Annual Register.
Felix Farley's Bristol Journal.
Gentleman's Magazine.
Réimpression de l'Ancien Moniteur depuis la Réunion des États-Généraux jusqu'au Consulat (Mai 1789–Novembre 1799) (31 vols; Paris, 1840–7).
Monthly Magazine.
Monthly Review.
Morning Chronicle.
Philanthropist.

6. Biographical works

i. Coleridge, Southey, Wordsworth

Carnall, G., *Robert Southey and his Age: The Development of a Conservative Mind* (Oxford, 1960).

Cottle, J., *Reminiscences of Samuel Taylor Coleridge and Robert Southey* (2nd edn; London, 1848).

Evans, B., and Pinney, H., 'Racedown and the Wordsworths', *Review of English Studies*, viii (1932).

Gillman, J., *The Life of Samuel Taylor Coleridge* (London, 1838).

Haller, W., *The Early Life of Robert Southey, 1774–1803* (New York, 1817).

Harper, G. M., *William Wordsworth: His Life, Works and Influence* (London, 1916).

—— 'Wordsworth at Blois' in *John Morley and Other Essays* (Princeton and London, 1920).

Landon, C., 'Wordsworth's Racedown Period: Some Uncertainties Resolved', *Bulletin of the New York Public Library*, lxviii (1964).

Lawrence, B., *Coleridge and Wordsworth in Somerset* (Newton Abbot, 1970).

Legouis, E., *The Early Life of William Wordsworth, 1770–1798*, trans. J. W. Matthews (London, 1897).

MacGillivray, J. R., 'Wordsworth and J. P. Brissot', *Times Literary Supplement* (29 Jan. 1931).

Moorman, M., *William Wordsworth, A Biography: The Early Years, 1770–1803* (Oxford, 1957).

Muirhead, J. P., 'A Day with Wordsworth', *Blackwood's Magazine*, ccxxi (June 1927).

Nesbitt, G. L., *Wordsworth: The Biographical Background of his Poetry* (New York, 1970).

Wordsworth, Christopher, *Memoirs of William Wordsworth* (2 vols; London, 1851).

ii. Other biographical sources, letters, diaries

Belsham, T., *Memoirs of the Late Reverend Theophilus Lindsey* (London, 1812).

Binns, John, *Recollections of the Life of John Binns* (Philadelphia, 1854).

Browning, O. (ed.), *The Despatches of Earl Gower* (Cambridge, 1885).

Burke, Edmund, *Correspondence*, ed. T. W. Copeland *et al.* (10 vols; Cambridge and Chicago, 1958–78).

Bussière, G., and Legouis, E., *Le Général Michel Beaupuy* (Paris and Perigueux, 1891).

Cestre, C., *John Thelwall: A Pioneer of Democracy in England* (London, 1906).

Corry, J., *The Life of Joseph Priestley* (Birmingham, 1804).

Courtney, W., *Young Charles Lamb, 1775–1802* (London, 1982).

De Morgan, S., *Threescore Years and Ten* (London, 1895).

Disney, J., *Memoirs of Thomas Brand Hollis, Esq.* (London, 1808).

Dyer, George, *Memoirs of the Life and Writings of Robert Robinson* (London, 1796).

Erdman, David, 'The Life of John Oswald' (unpublished typescript).

—— 'The Man who was not Napoleon', *The Wordsworth Circle*, xii (Winter 1981).

Farington, Joseph, *The Diary of Joseph Farington*, ed. K. Garlick, A. Macintyre, and K. Cave (16 vols publ.; New Haven and London, 1978–84).

'George Dyer', *Emmanuel College Magazine*, xv (1905).

Gibson, W., *Grégoire and the French Revolution* (London, 1932).

Godwin, William, *Memoirs of the Author of 'A Vindication of the Rights of Women'* (London, 1798).

Hardy, Thomas, *Memoirs of Thomas Hardy* (London, 1832).

Hilbish, F. M. A., *Charlotte Smith* (Philadelphia, 1941).

Hughes, G., *With Freedom Fired: The Story of Robert Robinson, Cambridge Non-Conformist* (London, 1955).

Knight, F., *The Strange Case of Thomas Walker* (London, 1957).

—— *University Rebel: The Life of William Frend, 1757–1841* (London, 1971).

le Grice, C. V., 'College Reminiscences of Mr. Coleridge', *Gentleman's Magazine*, NS ii (1834).

Litchfield, R. B., *Tom Wedgwood: The First Photographer* (London, 1903).

Locke, D., *A Fantasy of Reason: The Life and Thought of William Godwin* (London, 1980).

Losh, James, *The Diaries and Correspondence, 1881–33*, ed. E. Hughes (2 vols; Durham and London, 1962–3).

Marshall, P., *William Godwin* (New Haven and London, 1984).

McLachlan, H. (ed.), *The Letters of Theophilus Lindsey* (Manchester, 1920).

Muirhead, J. P., *The Life of James Watt* (London, 1858).

Necheles, R. *The Abbé Grégoire, 1787–1831* (Westport, Conn., 1971).

Norton, C. E. (ed.), *Reminiscences by Thomas Carlyle* (2 vols; London, 1887).

Paston, G., 'The Romance of John Tweddell' in *Little Memoirs of the Eighteenth Century* (London, 1901).

Paul, C. K., *William Godwin; His Friends and Contemporaries* (2 vols; London, 1876).

Payne, E. A., 'The Baptist Connections of George Dyer', *Baptist Quarterly* x (1940–1).

Place, Francis, *Autobiography*, ed. M. Thale (Cambridge, 1972).

Raven, J., 'George Dyer of Emmanuel', *Emmanuel College Magazine*, vii (1895).

Robinson, E., 'An English Jacobin: James Watt, Junior, 1769–1848', *Cambridge Historical Journal*, xi (1953–5).

Rutt, J. T., *The Life and Correspondence of Joseph Priestley* (2 vols; London, 1832).

Sadleir, M., *Archdeacon Francis Wrangham, 1769–1842* (Oxford, 1937).

Sandford, M., *Thomas Poole and his Friends* (2 vols; London, 1888).

Stephens, A., *Memoirs of John Horne Tooke* (2 vols; London, 1813).

The Life of John Thelwall by his Widow (London, 1837).

The Venerable Francis Wrangham, M.A., F.R.S., A Memoir (1832).

Tomalin, C., *The Life and Death of Mary Wollstonecroft* (London, 1974).

Tweddell, John, *The Remains of John Tweddell*, ed. Robert Tweddell (London, 1815).

Tyson, G. P., *Joseph Johnson: A Liberal Publisher* (Iowa, 1979).

iii. More general biographical sources

Dictionary of National Biography

Dictionnaire de biographie française

Grattan, T., *Beaten Paths; and Those who Trod Them* (2 vols; London, 1862).

Hutton, S., *Bristol and its Famous Associations* (Bristol and London, 1907).

Lonsdale, H., *The Worthies of Cumberland* (6 vols; London, 1867–75).

Meteyard, E., *A Group of Englishmen* (London, 1871).

Venn, J., *Alumni Cantabrigiensis, Part II, 1752–1900* (6 vols; Cambridge, 1940–54).

Welford, R., *Men of Mark 'Twixt Tyne and Tweed* (3 vols; London, 1895).

Index

alarm, British *see* panic, British
Alfoxden House *see* Wordsworth, at Alfoxden
Allen, Robert 110
Amis des noirs 43
Anti-Jacobin; or, Weekly Examiner 138–40
    'Friend of Humanity and the Knife-Grinder' 138–9
Association for the Preservation of Liberty and Property 98, 164

Barbauld, Anna Letitia 44
Barlow, Joel 82–3
Bassigny Regiment 50, 53, 55, 59 n.
Beaufort Buildings 117, 146, 148, 172, 175, 234, 259
Beaumont, Sir George, and Lady Margaret 3–4, 5, 12
Beaupuy, Michel 7, 41–2, 66–7, 137, 195
    at Blois 50–1, 55–60
Beddoes, Thomas 240
Bedford, Duke of 153
Bedford, Horace 115, 206
benevolence 112–13, 115, 123, 211, *see also* Coleridge, and Pantisocracy; Coleridge, and Godwin
Berkeley, George 216
Binns, John 9
    and Godwin 116, 152
    and LCS 152, 169–70, 175
    and Philomathean Society 169–70
Birmingham riots (1791) 91, 96, *see also* panic; Priestley, Joseph
Biron, Duke 51
Blois 45, 46, 48–51, 53–4, 56, 58–9
Bonney, John Augustus 28
Botany Bay 9, 125, 128, 164, 177–8, 213, *see also* repression
Braxfield, Robert MacQueen, Lord 14, 178, 182, *see also* repression
Brissot, Jacques Pierre 43, 45, 53, 166
Bristol, projected French attack on 255–7, *see also* Fishguard, French invasion of
Bristol Library 115

British Convention 8, 81–3, 178, 182, *see also* Revolution, British
Brunswick Manifesto 43
Burke, Edmund 40, 48, 58, 89, 93, 102, 126
    Reflections on the Revolution in France 13, 17, 20, 23, 27, 30–1, 33, 91, 107
Burney, Dr Charles 137–41
Butler, James 131

Calvert, Raisley 186–7, 190
Cambridge Constitutional Society 30, 89–90, 93, *see also* Robinson, Robert
Cambridge Intelligencer 90, 108, *see also* Flower, Benjamin
Cambridge University 9, 14–16, 17–22
    and dissent 19, 85–88, 98–9
    and London radicals 18–19, 85–6, 90, 93
Carlyle, Thomas ix, 40–1
Carra 40
Cartwright, Major John 29, 89, 93, 192
Cawdor, Lord 254–5, *see also* Fishguard, French invasion of
Charles I 144
Chaucer, Geoffrey 118
    Canterbury Tales 57
    'Pardoner's Tale' 143
coastal defences, British 252 n.
Coleridge, George 84–5
Coleridge, Hartley 263
Coleridge, Samuel Taylor
    and Beaupuy 62
    and Berkeley 216
    and Birmingham riots 96, 101
    at Bristol 4, 14, 87, 145, 147–52, 154–6
    at Bristol Guildhall 150–1, 154–5
    and *Cambridge Intelligencer* 90, 108–9
    certainty, anxiety for 113
    creativity 3, 4, 26, 268
    disillusion 238–9, *see also* failure and isolation
    and dissent 84, 112, 265